A Competitive Book of

FOOD SCIENCE and TECHNOLOGY/AGRICULTURE

For

JRF, SRF, NET, ARS, PH.D, BHU, CFTRI, NIFTEM AND OTHER EXAMINATIONS

GAJENDRA KUMAR RANA

2024

JAIN BROTHERS (New Delhi)
16/873, East Park Road, Near Dr. N. C. Joshi Hospital,
Karol Bagh, New Delhi -110 005
Phones : 011- 23618426, 45097398
E-mail : jain_bros@hotmail.com
Website : www.thejainbrothers.com

Published by :

Shri Sunil Kumar Jain
for
Jain Brothers (New Delhi)
16/873, East Park Road, Karol Bagh,
New Delhi-110 005
Phones : 011-23618426, 45097398

Available at:

1. **Pusa Agricultural Book Service**
Shishir Hostel, IARI, PUSA
New Delhi, Ph.: 011-25841048
2. **Jain Book Mart**
9/3125, Gurudwara Gali No. 4,
Dharampura, Gandhi Nagar,
Delhi-31, Mobile: 91-8470890439
E-mail: jainbookmart@gmail.com

Branch Office at :

1. **M/s SUNIL BOOK SERVICE**
Fatima Nagar, Opp. Andhra Bank,
KAZIPET-506004 (A.P.)
Ph. : 0870-2459617, Mob. : 9390115435
E-mail : kpkulshrestha@yahoo.com
2. **M/s JAIN BROTHERS**
Vidya Vihar, Pilani (Rajasthan)
Phone : 01596-242144

First Edition : 2017
Second Edition : May, 2018
Third Revised Edition : June, 2019
Fourth Revised Edition : July, 2020
Fifth Revised Edition : Oct, 2024

Price : ₹ 325.00

ISBN : 978-81-8360-239-6

Laser Typesetting by :

CINOGRAPHICS
E–41, New Multan Nagar,
New Delhi – 110 056

प्रो. प्रमोद कुमार मिश्रा
कुलपति
Prof. Pramod Kumar Mishra
Vice Chancellor

जवाहरलाल नेहरू कृषि विश्वविद्यालय
कृषि नगर, अधारताल, जबलपुर ४८२००४ (म.प्र.)
Jawaharlal Nehru Krishi Vishwa Vidyalaya
Krishi Nagar, Adhartal, Jabalpur 482 004 (M.P.)
Ph.: 0761-2681706 (O), Fax. 0761-2681389
E-mail: mishravcjnkvv@gmail.com

No.: VC/TC/.......
Dated: 18th January, 2023

FOREWORD

Education and competition are two universal ingredients of all human cultures. The will and wish to face the competition germinates from the early hood. As much as the achievement is important in life, more important than that are the means used to achieve the end, therefore, while keeping high goals in life, the means to achieve them should also be good,

It gives me immense pleasure that back to back an updated version. the fifth edition of "A Competitive book of Food Science and Technology/Agriculture" covering relevant syllabus for JRF, SRF, NET, ARS, Ph.D., BHU, CFIRI, NIFTEM., and other Examinations" authored by Mr. G.K. Rana, Food Scientist. It is very important for students preparing for competitive examinations to study subjects thoroughly and have a deep understanding of the syllabus.

The author put up lot of efforts and gathered extensive material from the available literature on the subject to present the details of the specific pattern of the particular preparation. This book covers all the major topics of Food Science & Technology and that will surely help students for preparing various examinations.

This book has specificity of the contents that will make it incredibly relevant and helpful in the intended context, It is anticipated that through this book the aspirants will be able to achieve their goals.

18/01/23

(P.K. Mishra)

Preface to Revised and Enlarged Fifth Edition

Planning and execution phases are important to frame a unique book to fulfill the requirements of aspirants. My book "A Competitive book of Food Science and Technology/Agricultures for JRF, SRF, NET, ARS, Ph.D, BHU, CFTRI, NIFTEM and other examinations" is produced to briefly summarise the topic, this book's main goal is to help readers learn about/get ready for exams because a lot of books must be read quickly, which is tough job.

The author welcomes the valuable suggestions from the end of entire education community and aspirants for further improvement who are holding and reading the same book.

(Dr. GAJENDRA KUMAR RANA)

Preface to the First Edition

This book is for the students of food science and technology. During my student life I wish to study by my own notes or books, but it is not possible for every student, some of the students are still suffering financially or morally. I have frequently been asked for suggestions and help in the matter of study that how do I prepare?

My book "*Competitive book of Food Science and Technology/Agriculture for JRF, SRF, NET, ARS, Ph.D, BHU, CFTRI, NIFTEM and other examinations*" is produced to summarise the subject as I had found it difficult to learn the subject when I joined the college. The principal purpose of this book is to serve an easy way to learn/prepare for examinations as it is difficult to read many books in short available time.

This book will be particularly useful for juniors, seniors, undergraduates, Post graduates and Ph.D Scholars, Food scientists and technologist, plant physiologists, food microbiologists, biochemists, agricultural engineers, nutritionists, food engineers, food packagers, molecular biologists and many others.

Gajendra Rana

Date: 15/01/2017

Dedicated to

My Pitaji, Mataji and Rana Family

and the Mankind......

Contents

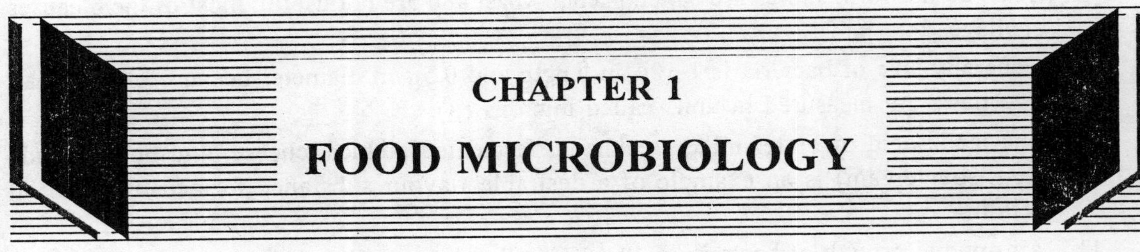

CHAPTER 1

FOOD MICROBIOLOGY

Food Microbiology is the study of the micro-organism that inhibit, create or contaminate food. Viruses differ from bacteria in that they require a vector (i.e. virus contaminated food or hands) to enter the body and cause disease.

- Bacteria are single celled microorganisms found in nearly all environments
- Viruses are extremely small parasites and they require living cells of human or animals and bacteria for growth.
- Molds are typical form of fungus and comprises of 25% of earth biomass and grow in food with a fuzzy or cotton appearance making food unfit.
- Yeast refers to fungi which are not filamentous but are unicellular and ovoid or spheroid and which reproduce by budding or fission.
- **Mycotoxins:** toxins produced by mould or fungi.
- **Aflatoxins:** Produced by fungi or molds aspergillus or aspergillum parasiticus.

  Aflatoxins in all food article has a limit of 30mg/kg.

  Process of warming food that has been frozen so that food can be eaten or prepared to be served is THAWING three safe ways of

  (1) Refrigerator thawing (2) Cold water thawing (3) Microwave thawing
- Never keep food in danger zone in thawing between 40°F – 145°F.
- Bacteria can grow rapidly in these temperature.

1. Mould α-amylase is used in the baking industry, due to its instability.
2. *Saccharomyces ellipsoideus* (yeast) pure culture is added as starter in wine making, and It is also called 'Must' SO_2 is added at 50-70 ppm to check the action of wild yeast and bacteria.
3. Acquiring a smooth flavour and aroma wine takes about 6-12 month.
4. *Acetobactor, Lactobacillus* and *Leuconostoc* are the organisms responsible for spoilage of wine.
5. Moulds can grow over a wide range of pH is 2.0-8.5.
6. Alcohol is result of semi fermentation while Acetic acid is result of complete fermentation.
7. Alcoholic fermentation is anaerobic.

8. Yeast do not form spores are called pseudo-yeast and are not useful, most of them causes spoilage.
9. Generally size of bacteria is 1-10μ in length and 0.5μ in diameter because of the small size these are measured in units called microns (μ).
10. The lactic acid of butter milk, sreekhand, fermented pickles, cheese, and butter (made from sour cream) is an example of a desirable flavour substance formed by bacterial action.
11. An optimal growth of bacteria at 20-45°C called mesophilic.
12. Facultative bacteria are capable of growing with or without free oxygen.
13. Temperature between enzymes action good is 0-60°C and optimum temperature is 37°C and they are inactivated at 80°C.
14. Proteolyte organisms are involved in protein degradation.
15. Moulds and a few gram (–) negative bacteria digest fat.
16. PAB (Propionic Acid Bacteria) is used in the production of swis cheese.
17. Most popular soft drink in market 'cola' is an extract obtained from tree cola (*Cola acuminata*).
18. Soft drinks: - 1. Carbonated- *a*) Artificial flavor *b*) Natural fruit juice
    2. Fruit flavoured (still) 3. Sparkling (soda water)
19. HFCS stand for High Fructose Corn Syrup is sweetner made from corn syrup.
20. Acids (citric acid, tartaric acid, phosphoric acid, lactic acid and malic acid) are used to taste and enhance flavour and mild preservation of beverages.
21. **Vermouth** is a fortified wine prepared by the addition of spice mixture or their exhausts at various stages during fermentation (Joe 1975). First produced in Italy.
22. Up to 14% alcohol wines are called table wines while more than it is called dessert wines.
23. Water used in brewing should be hard whether soft salts should be added at desired level.
24. In manufacture of beer steeping of ground malt in hot water vessels is called the *mash tun*.
25. Alcohol content of beers varies from 2.5-7% by volume.
26. In India alcohol percentage in beers is 4-5% with the calorific value of about 30 kcal/100 ml.
27. *Rhizopus sonti* is used in production of sonti which is beer of rice in India.
28. Sucrose percentage in fresh coconut juice is about 12.3-17.4%.
29. Kattha (Catechu) is tannin rich material derived from the heartwood of the same tree and the chemical catechin (antioxidant), arecoline (stimulant) are present in this.
30. **Sensitivity of organisms to irradiation**
    - o 10^{3-4} - 10^{7} rads – microorganisms are killed
    - o 10^{3} - 10^{6} rads – insect are killed
    - o 10^{3} - 10^{4} rads – sprouting of potato, onion, carrot etc. are inhibited
    - o 10^{2} - 10^{3} rads – dose is lethal for human

31. Types of spoilage in canned foods are flat sour, toxic spoilage, hydrogen swells and metallic salts.
32. Preservatives are "chemical agents which serve to retard, hinder or mask undesirable change in food" by Jacob.
33. Benzoic acids, esters of p-hydroxy-benzoic acid, o-chlorobenzoic acid or salicylic acid are organic preservatives.
34. Sulphur dioxide is only permitted preservative generally used in the form of sulphites, are inorganic preservatives.
35. Sodium benzoate, sulphites and sorbic acid are permitted preservatives used in fruits and vegetables in India.
36. Spoilage in pickles may be due to low salt content of brine, incomplete curing, and high pH, under processing or use of poor closure.
37. Removal of water from a product while it is frozen by sublimation is called freeze drying.
38. The drying in shade is superior with respect to colour and appearance and texture as compared to cabinet drying.
39. Ionic (radiation) sterilization is also called as cold sterilization.
40. Enzymes do not get inactivated and pulses sprout after irradiation and irradiated fruits go through the natural ripening and maturing.
41. *Clostridium botulinum* appears to be the most radiation resistant organism.
42. Physical hurdles, Physico-chemical hurdles, microbially derived hurdles and miscellaneous hurdles are potential hurdles for use in preservation of foods.
43. Lakes typically uses include: coated tablets, cake and doughnuts mixes, hard candies and chewing gums and cosmetics.

    Lake colors are basically made by combining dyes with salts to get insoluble compounds. Lakes are oil dispersive (not oil soluble) and can be mixed with oils, fats and sugars.
44. Annatto is a yellow carotenoid preparation obtained from the seed of the *Bixa orellena* (lipstic tree).
45. Metallic colour like the compounds of metals like copper, lead, zinc and coltar colours like picric acid, metanil yellow are banned from usage.
46. Aglycone kermesic acid is extracted from kermes insects and used as food colourant.
47. Alkanet is pigment extracted with alcohol from the roots of *Alkanna tinctoria* Tansch.
48. Biliproteins from algae is divided into two main groups red phycoerythrins and the blue phycocyanins.
49. Canthaxanthin from the pink mushroom *Cantharellas cinnabarina* and red palm oil with lycopene and lutein are food colour.
50. Congo Red, Melachite Green, Orange G, Sudan III and lead chromate are harmful hence prohibited to be used in food preparation.
51. The pink dye Rhodamine B, Orange RN II and Blue VRS are carcinogenic and causes pathological lesions of vital organs like kidney, spleen and liver.

52. Metanil yellow causes degeneration of reproductive organs, sterility, stomach trouble and cancer.
53. Citric acid and its derivatives, phosphates and salts of Ethylene Diamine Tetra Acetic Acid (EDTA) are the most popular chelating agents used in foods.
54. *Tears of wine:* - Appearance of droplet just above the level of wine around the inner side of the wine glass. This phenomenon was first correctly explained by physicist "James Thomson in 1885". It is a result of the flow of liquid caused by surface tension gradients. It is due to the fact that alcohol has a lower surface tension than water.
55. Specific gravity indicates the amount of air incorporated in the product viz. Whipped cream, egg white foam and cake batter.
56. *By Arrhenius:* -(*i*) Acids are those substances, which yield hydrogen ion (H+, proton) on ionization in an aqueous solution. (*ii*) Bases are substances, which yield hydroxyl ion (OH) on ionization in an aqueous solution.
57. *Causes/causal agents for food poisoning*: -
    1. Microbes viz bacteria, viruses or parasites.
    2. Natural chemicals (toxins) in food products.
    3. Manufactured/ synthesized chemical is food products.
    4. Improper food handing storage and poor hygiene and physical hazards.
    5. Inadequate cooking procedures.
    6. Social causes.
    7. Economic causes.
    8. Cultural causes.
    9. Demographic causes.
    10. Water.
58. *Cryptosporidium spp.* and *Giardia lamblia* are the parasitic pathogens most commonly encountered in water borne illness.
59. Macrobiotic diets aim to avoid the "toxins" that come from eating dairy products, meats, and oily foods. A macrobiotic diet consists largely of whole grains, cereals, and cooked vegetables. The plan originated from Japan and came to the US in 1960. (George Ohsawa).
60. This concept was popularized by Michio Kushi and developed in to the lifestyle as it is known today.
61. Microbial food spoilage may be due to bacteria, yeast and mold.
62. Bacterial Soft rot in vegetables is mainly caused by *Erwinia caotovora.*
63. Sprouted barley is used in the manufacture of beer.
64. Cider is produced using sugar, yeast, and crushed fermented apples.
65. Dye reduction test is carried out to determine the extent of bacterial contamination and growth in milk.
66. Presence of coli form bacteria in water implies that water has been contaminated by Sewage.
67. **Lagering** a form of beer maturation occurs after the completion of fermentation.
68. Botulin is mycotoxin (neurotoxin) produced by *clostridium botulinum* fungus causing botulism disease.

69. Lactic acid producing yeast. *Saccharomyces cerevisiae* (Baker yeast).
70. *Saccharomyces cerevisiae* (Bakers yeast) is engineered yeast species used to produce lactic acid, by the heterologous expression of LDH genes, creating novel metabolic pathways for lactic acid production (Dequin and Barre, 1994; Porro et al., 1995). It is a safe non pathogenic organism.
71. Mold as found on bread, fruits, damp paper or other surfaces are actually composed of millions of microscopic cells joined together to form chains. The chains usually have numerous branches, called hypae.
72. Mould can thrive in conditions too adverse for bacteria or yeasts.
73. *Propionates* in bread making are added to inhibit mold growth.
74. Bread mold is *Rhizopus stolonifer.*
75. Ropiness in bread is caused by *Bacillus lichenformis.*
76. Red colour in the crumb of the dark bread has been caused by *Geotrichum auranticum.*
77. Molds are most common causes of spoilage of fruits and vegetables.
78. Canned food shows flat sour spoilage type of spoilage.
79. Flat sour spoilage of canned foods is due to *Bacillus*.
80. Maltose-glucoamylase are used to make beer.
81. Cellulose is being breakdown in form of glucose by insulin.
82. Bactariostatic agent Euganol is present in clove.
83. Aflatoxin is produced by fungus, *Aspergillus sp.*
84. Yoghurt contains *Lactobasillus* probiotic.
85. Yoghurt contains useful bacteria for guts.
86. Freezing is good because at low (temp.) no pathogens can grow easily.
87. Most bacteria are effective at 4.5- 5.5 pH range.
88. Barely malt is also used to make beer.
89. Illness caused by food is called food borne illness.
90. Decaying of vegetables due to soft root bacteria is about 36%.
91. Decaying of vegetables due to *penicillium* is about 30%.
92. The substances or various preservation factors, inhibiting the microbial growth till death is called *hurdle*.
93. Naturally produced peptides that inhibit other microorganisms, similar in effect to antibiotics are referred as *bacteriocins*.
94. *Eugenol* oil which is bacteriostatic in nature is obtained from cloves.
95. Nitrous oxide represses some fungi.
96. UV light has germicidal effect at the wave length between 210 to 290 nm.
97. Bacteria shows maximum resistance against the heat during late lag phase.
98. *Cinnamic acid* acts as bacteriostatic.

99. Slime production in juices is due to *Leuconostoc mesenteroides*
100. Inactivation of enzymes during blanching is done to prevent browning reaction.
101. *Sourkraut* is the fermented cabbage.
102. Primary aim of blanching of fruit is to destroy the enzymes.
103. Downy mildew is due to *Phytapthora.*
104. Watery soft rot is due to *Sclerotiana sclerotium.*
105. Yeasts and molds are most likely to be responsible for the spoilage in jam and jellies.
106. Softness of pickles is due to *Penicillium.*
107. Red spot on the surface of meat is caused due to *Pseudomonas syncyanea.*
108. Putrefcation is caused by *Clostridium.*
109. Green rot in egg is due to *Pseudomonas flurenscens.*
110. *Clostridium* may survive *pasteurization* of milk and cheese making process and produce LBD (Late Blowing Defect).
111. *Trimethylamine* (TMA) a simplest tertiary amine is the main cause of the fishy odour in fish (or pungent) and other aquatic animals.
112. Canned meat is generally spoiled by *Clostridium*
113. Pasteurization of milk is done at 62.8 °C for 30 min to eliminate *Coxiella burnetti.*
114. *Coxiella burnetti* is responsible for Q fever.
115. Heating of cream at low temperature is called *Vacreation* and it is also called pasteurization of cream.
116. Sweet curdling in milk is caused by *bacillus cereus* and *bacillus subtilis*
117. Ropiness of milk which is observed throughout milk is caused by *Enterobacter aerogens*
118. Maltiness in butter is due to *Streptococcus lactis.*
119. Fishiness in milk is caused by *Aeromonas hydrophila.*
120. Rusty spot in cheese is due to *Lactobacillus plantarum.*
121. Blue milk is caused by *Pseudomanas cyanogens*
122. *Goitrogens* are present in cabbage which can cause goiter.
123. Benzoic Acid is most effective to yeast
124. Toddy (alcoholic beverages) from coconut is prepared by fermentation and contains 4-6% alcohol
125. Yogurt is produced by fermentation involving *lactic acid* bacteria.
126. *Trichinella spiralis* is commonly associated with fecal contamination.
127. *Staphylococcus aureus* cannot tolerate oxygen.
128. Bacterial growth curve is divided into four phases viz. lag, log, stationary and death phase.
129. Bacteria are classified according to their shape of cells.
130. Cocci are spherical, *bacilli* are elongated cylindrical, *spirilla* and *vibrio* are in spiral forms.

131. Bacterial spores are more resistant to most processing conditions than yeast and mold spores.

132. Bacteria (few exceptions) cannot grow in acidic medium while yeast and mold can survive.

133. According to their oxygen requirement, bacterias are of two types *aerobic* and *anaerobic*.

134. Yeasts are unicellular plants widely distributed in nature. Yeasts are oval-shaped and slightly larger than bacteria.

135. Yeast grows well in slightly acidic medium in presence of water and sugar.

136. Molds are multicellular, filamentous fungi having cottony appearance on food.

137. Optimum temperature for growth of bacteria, yeasts and moulds ranges between 16-38°C.

138. Microorganisms that can grow at low temperature storage are known as *psychrophiles*.

139. Micro-organisms that grow well at refrigeration temperature but better at room temperature are *psychrophiles*.

140. Microorganisms that can grow at high temperature storage are known as *thermophiles*.

141. Microorganisms that can grow at 30-40°C are known as *mesophiles*.

142. Bacterial spoilage can cause food infection or intoxication.

143. *Pediococcus botulinum* can produce toxin which causes botulism.

144. Thermal death time curve is used to explain the relationship between number of microorganisms and heat treatment time at a particular temperature.

145. Microorganisms can be destroyed or inactivated by heat or cold treatment.

146. Heat treatment used for microbial destruction involves *pasteurization* and *sterilization*.

147. Cold treatments of food to check microbial growth are *chilling*, *freezing* and *refrigeration*

148. Bacterias that can transmit food borne infections in humans are *Pediococcus, Salmonella, Shigella, Vibrio, Streptococcus, Bacillus* and *Campylobacter.*

149. Microorganisms in food can also be controlled by drying treatment by reducing moisture content.

150. *Water activity* is generally the amount of water available for microorganisms.

151. Most bacteria require water activity in range of 0.90-1.00 a_w.

152. Some yeasts and molds can grow at water activity as low as 0.65 a_w.

153. Presence of sugar and salts also inhibits the growth of microorganisms.

154. *Smoke* can also be used for preservation of food products.

155. Chemical preservative used to inhibit the growth of microorganisms are: sodium benzoate, sorbic acid, propionates, formate and sulphur dioxide.

156. Microorganisms can be inactivated by irradiation techniques such as x-rays, microwaves, UV rays and ionizing radiation.

157. Irradiation is also known as cold sterilization as it can sterilize the food without raising its temperature.

158. Microorganisms are usful in food fermentation processes such as alcohol production, beer making, cheese making, yoghurt manufacture, amino acid production, bread production etc.

159. Baker's yeast is used for bread fermentation.
160. Intermediate moisture food (IMF) generally has water activity in range of 0.60-0.80 a_w and moisture content of 15-50%.
161. *Lactobacillus bulgaricus* and *Streptococcus thermophilus* are used as culture in yoghurt manufacture.
162. *Bacillus species* generally causes spoilage in UHT milk.
163. Kefir can be prepared using culture of *Acetobacter*, *Lactobacillus and Lactococcus.*
164. Sufu, tempeh and Tao-si are fermented products of soybean.
165. With respect to gram staining, bacteria are divided into two groups: gram negative and gram positive.
166. Food infection is generally caused by *Salmonella, Bacillus cereus* and *E. coll.*
167. *Asepsis* means preventing the entry of microorganisms.
168. Coagulation of proteins and inactivation of their metabolic enzymes by the application of heat leads to the destruction of microorganisms present in foods.
169. Fruit and tomato products should be heated at 100°C for 30 minutes so that the spore forming bacteria which are sensitive to high acidity may be completely killed.
170. Aseptic canning is a technique in which food is sterilized outside the can and then aseptically placed in previously sterilized cans which are subsequently sealed in an aseptic environment.
171. Decomposition of carbohydrates by microorganisms or enzymes is called '*fermentation*'
172. *Fermentation* is the process of conversion of simpler molecules into complex one using microorganisms under specific conditions.
173. *Sauerkraut* is a mixture of salt and shredded cabbage and the amount of salt is critical to assuring food safety and should not be adjusted.
174. *Sauerkraut* is fermented (by lactic acid bacteria) product of cabbage for 3-6 weeks.
175. Vegetable juices are mostly spoiled by bacteria.
176. Bioprocess technology is the study of use of biological organisms and biological materials such as enzymes for food processing and preservation.
177. Bioprocesses helps in industrial production of enzymes, amino acids, antibiotics, yeast, SCP and organic acids etc.
178. Beer, wine, ethanol, yoghurt and cheese are examples of fermented products made using microorganisms.
179. Lactic acid bacteria is widely used in preparation of fermented dairy products.
180. Single cell proteins (SCP) term was coined by C.L. Wilson. Single cell proteins can be prepared using bacteria, actinomycetes, molds and higher fungi and yeasts,
181. Yeasts used for SCP production are *Candida spp.*, *Debaryomyces spp.*, *Hansenula sp.* and *Kluveryomyces spp.* etc.
182. Algae used for the SCP production are *Chlorella and Spirulina.*
183. Bacteria used for the SCP production are *Acinetobacter, Cellulomonas, Methylococcus, Methylomonas* and *Pseudomonas* etc.

184. Molds used for the SCP production are *Agaricus, Aspergillus, Morchella* and *Trichoderma* etc.
185. Production of baker's yeast is multistage, aerobic and fed batch process.
176. *S. cerevisiae* and *S. carlsbergensis* are generally used as brewing yeasts.
187. Dried yeast can be grown on molasses, wood sugar, whey, ethanol and hydrocarbons.
188. Invertase and Lactase enzyme can be extracted from yeast commercially.
189. *Corynebacterium glutamicum* is generally used for commercial production of glutamic acid and lysine.
190. Examples of antibiotics include penicillin, streptomycin, neomycin, cephalosporin and erythromycin etc.
191. Penicillin can be produced by *Penicillium chrysogenum* and *Penicillium notatum*. Alexander Fleming discovered *Penicillin* antibiotic.
192. Alexander Fleming, Florey and Chain received noble prize for discovery of *penicillin* (1928)
193. Downstream·processing involves separation, concentration, filtration, purification and drying of final products of fermentation.
194. Downstream processing is the most expensive unit operation in bioprocesses.
195. Nucleosides and nucleotides can also be produced microbially.
196. Organic acid produced by microbial fermentation includes citric acid, lactic acid, gluconic acid etc.
197. Citric acid can be produced using surface and submerged fermentation processes.
198. *Aspergillus niger* is generally used for microbial production of citric acid.
199. Bacteria which is used to absorb ethylene from storage chamber is *mycobacterium*.
200. Commercial polysaccharide produced from microbial processes includes *xanthan gum*, *dextrans* and *pullulans* etc.
201. *Pullulan* is a fungal polysaccharide produced by *Aureobasidium pullulans*.
202. *Xanthan gum* is a bacterial polysaccharide produced by *Xanthomonas campestris*.
203. *Dextrans* are bacterial polysaccharide produced by *Leuconostoc mesenteroides, L. dextranicum and L. citrovorum.*
204. Pigments like *carotenes* and *lycopenes* can also be produced by microbial processes.
205. Microencapsulation of enzyme can be used to extend the shelf life of enzymes.
206. Microorganisms can also be used for waste treatment.
207. Fermenters design plays a crucial role in the yield of final product.
208. Recently bioprocesses are used to produce *bioactive compounds* that can be utilized as *nutraceuticals*.
209. Conversion of laboratory level process to plant level process is known as scale up.
210. Computer applications can be used in fermentation industries for data logging, data analysis, process modeling and process control.
211. Isolation of solid fermentation products can be done using filtration, centrifugation, coagulation and flocculation.

212. Primary separation of fermented products involves liquid extraction, dissociation extraction, sorption processing and precipitation
213. Purification of fermented products involves fractional liquid-liquid extraction, chromatography, crystallization and drying.
214. Immobilization of microbial cells can be done by carrier binding, cross-linking and entrapping methods.
215. Fermentation plant design includes pumps and piping, heat exchanger, instrumentation and control and foam control.
216. Anything that we eat and is beneficial for our body is called as food.
217. The undesirable change in a food that makes it unsafe for human consumption is referred as food spoilage.
218. Food preservation involves increasing shelf life of food and ensuring safety for human consumption.
219. *Pasteurization* is a high temperature treatment.
220. Normally bacteria stops division at 5 degree celcius.
221. Common food poisoning microbes are *Clostridium* and *Salmonella.*
222. Botulism is caused by *Clostridium botulinum.*
223. Botulinal toxin is produced by *Clostridium botulinum* a gram positive anaerobic bacteria.
224. Botulism prevention involves proper heat sterilization before the canning.
225. *Clostridium perfingens* poisoning is associated with meat products.
226. *Clostridium perfingens* poison is an enterotoxin produced during sporulation.
227. *Salmonellosis* involves an enterotoxin and cytotoxin.
228. The major carrier of salmonellosis is meat and eggs.
229. *Saccharomyces cerevisiae* is used in production of Scotch whisky.
230. *Leuconostoc species* is used in idli fermentation.
231. *Glycerol, glycols* and *sorbitols* are used as humectants in food industry
232. Aflatoxin, citrinin and ochrotoxin are mycotoxins.
233. Hops (flowers of hop plant) contribute characteristic aroma and bitter flavor to beer.
234. Vodka, whiskies, rum and tequila are distilled alcoholic beverages.
235. Mold modified foods include soy sauce, miso, sufu, tempeh and ang kak etc.
236. Industrial alcohol can be produced from molasses as well as wheat starch.
237. Castor oil is used as antifoaming agent in industrial production of alcohol.
238. Most resistant spores of *Clostridium botulinum* have strain of $D_{121.1}$ of 0.89 min.
239. Sorbic acid is used on cheese and canned foods to control mold.
240. Lactic acid bacteria are used in cheese making and fermented dairy products.
241. Pascal is unit of pressure.
242. *Staphylococcus aureus* and *Clostridium botulinum* micro-organisms cause food borne intoxication.

IMPORTANT POINTS

- Sorbic acid is used on cheese and canned foods to control mold.
- Chlorine compound is used as germicidal.
- Sodium benzoate used in soft drinks and acidic foods as preservatives.
- Ethylene oxide and ethyle formate used to control microorganisms on spices, nuts and dried fruits.
- Best pH for microbial growth is 6.6-7:5.
- Best pH for molds growth is 4.0.
- Microorganisms are ubiquitous in distribution
- Microbes can obtain their O_2 from the food material (in which they are growing) by the chemical process called as reduction.
- Sexual spores of molds called *Perfect* and classified as either *Oomycetes* or *Zygomycetes* and asexual spores called as *Imperfecti*.
- As per septation if non-seperate then called *Ascomycetes* or *Basidiomycetes*.
- *Oomycetes* (sexual spores/perfect) are not common in food.
- Yeast manufactures bread, beer, wine, vinegar and surface ripened cheese.
- Yeast spoils fruit juices, syrups, molasses, honey, jellies, meats, wine, beer etc.
- Sugar is the best food for yeasts.
- Psychrophil bacteria grow best at 15-20 °C.
- Mesoophil bacteria grow best at 32-37 °C.
- Thermophile bacteria grow best at 50-65 °C.
- Thermophile bacteria does not produces poison during spoilage of food.
- In syrup/brine movement of water from the cells into the concentrated (> 80%) syrup or brine called osmosis
- *Plasmosis* equalises conecentration inside and outside of the cell and also called as partial dehydration of cell.
- Yeast and molds grows on high sugar/salt products that is why they are more tolerant than bacteria in sugar/salt.
- Due to presence of formaldehyde (in fish) with addition of smoke (temperature) it kills microorganisms in fish and meat *e.g.* roasted fish and meat.
- Molds do not contain Chlorophylls.
- Molds can grow easily on sugar/acidic matter *e.g. Aspergillus*, *Penicillium*, *Rhizopus* and *Helminthosporium* etc.
- Full growth of bacteria takes place in 7 phases viz. 1 – 7/ A – H. Phase–3, Logarithmic phase (C - D) where it is most rapid and constant.

Food poisoning microbes are:

(1) *Clostridium botulinum* – minimum pH 4.7 – 5.0.

(2) *Clostridium perfringens*.

(3) *Staphylococcus aures*.

(4) *Bacillus cereus*.

(5) *Aspergillus spp*.

- Raw eggs/milk may be carrier of salmonella that's why both of them must be used after boiling upto 80°C for 10 minutes.
- Milk borne organisms causing food poisoning are *Brucella, Mycobacteria, Beta Hemolytic, Streptococci* and *Campylobacter.*
- Ackee a fruit of *sapindaceae* (soapberry) family poisoning is due to *hyloglycin toxins* amino in unriped fruit. Ackee fruits are cultivated in Nigeria.
- Amines are organic compounds that contain one or more nitrogen atoms and are often actually dependent on nitrogen atoms.
- Pressor amines are alkaline substances that raises the blood pressure. These are found naturally occuring in certain foods.
- Dopamine is present in broad beans 5-hydroxy-tryptamine or serotanin is found in banana and octapamine in citrus fruits. Tyramine is found chiefly in foods in which bacterial decomposition occur and formed by the action of bacteria on tyrosine.
- Biogenic amines are a group of low molecular nitrogenous organic compounds mainly performed from amino acids in foods through microbial decarboxylate catalyzed reaction.
- BAs exist in various kinds of food especially seafood and its derived product, cheese, wine and beers, which are rich in substrates (free amino acids).
- Excessive amounts of BAs in food could be harmful for human health.

  BAs are commonly used as indicators of the safety and quality for foods. Most toxic BA, histamine (HIS) poisoning is characterized by symptoms of tachycardia and palpitations (FAO/WHO, 2012).
- Other BAs such as cadaverine, tyramine, tryptamine and putrescine can also enhance the toxicity of HIS.
- Aged cheese is the source of pressor amines.
- *Aminita muscaria* contains alkaloid muscarin and *Aminita phalloides* contains hepatotoxic factors are poisonous to human health.

  Poisons in natural spices and flavours:

  (1) Mustard (brown) – *Allylisothiocynate*

  (2) *Capsicum annum* – Capsicum

  (3) Nutmeg and Mare (*Myristica fragrans*) – Myristicin

  (4) Tonka beans, Lavendar, Yellow sweet clover – Coumarin

  (5) Japanese wild ginger (*Sassafras mieroanthum*) – Safrol

  (6) Worm wood (In France, now banned) – Thujone
- **Cyanogenic glycosides** are bioactive plant products derived from amino acids. HCN in lima bean (*phaseolus lunatus*), Cassava (Manishot esulenta) Linamarin a cyanogenic glycosides in Sorghum, linseed. Developed most common cyanogenic glycoside in fruits kernel is *amygdalin.*
- Tumour and Cancer causing is species of fern (*Pteridium aquilinum*) and causes tumour in intestine of mouse (Large size). It is known as eagle fern.
- **Toxic compounds in food and water:**

  (1) *Selenium* – in Great Plains of the USA.

(2) *Fluorine* – in Andhra Pradesh (India) in workers of the Public Health Department – 1951 and it must be < 10 ppm.

(3) Since 1945 nitrates and nitrites @ 64-140 ppm of nitrate nitrogen in well waters is recognised as hazardous to healthy babies.

(4) Oxalates – in 1960 oxalic acid in rhubarb leaves reported and causes poison.

Probiotics:- Probiotics are live bacteria and yeasts that are good for human health. The term has been applied to consumable products that produce a number of clinical benefits. Some important probiotic products are yogurt, kefir, sauerkraut, tempeh, kimchi, miso, kombucha, pickles, and butter milk.

Prebiotics: These are not microorganisms but they are substrates for the indigenous probiotic type bacteria that reside in the colon and enhance the production of valuable vitamins.

Non dairy fermented food products:

(1) Fish sauces are popular products in South East Asia and also known as ngapi (Burma), nuoc-man (Combodia and Vietnam), nam-pla (Laos and Thailand), Ketjap-ikan (Indonesia) with the ratio of 3:1 fish and salt respectively.

(2) Fish pastes (common in South Asia).

(3) Soy sauce from fermented parts of boiled soybeans, roasted grains, brine and *Aspergillus oryzae* or *Aspergillus sojae molds.*

(4) Breads by *Saccharomyces cerevisiae, Saccharomyces uvarum.*

(5) Idli by *Lactobacillus meseteroides.*

(6) Sauekraut is a fermented product of fresh cabbage by *Leuconostoc mesenteroides, L. fallax* and *Lactobacillus plantarum.*

(7) Olivea : Same as Sauekraut

(8) Pickles : Sauekraut and other types from mango, carrot cauliflower and lime etc.

(9) *Wines* – from peaches, pears, grapes, (Pressed juice for wine making called Must).

(10) *Cider* – from Apple and pulp called cheese.

(11) *Champagne* – A sparkling wine made by a secondary fermentation of wine is produced by adding sugar, citric acid, and a Champagne yeast starter to bottles of a previously prepared selected table wine.

(12) *Palm wine/Nigerian palm wine* – by palm sap, sweet and dirty brown in colour, with 10-12% sugar (sucrose).

(13) *Sake* – by rice in japan 12-15% alcohol and hydrolysis is carried out by *Aspergillus oryzae* to yield the koji.

(14) *Kombucha* – home prepared tea that is produced by fermentation of sweetened black tea with a mixed culture of bacteria and yeasts, mainly consumed in China, Russia and Germany. Most predominant organism involved in fermentation is *Acetobacter xylinum.*

Miscellneous/other food products:

(1) Coffee beans-seed of the cofee plant.

(2) Cocoa beans-dried and fully fermented fatty seed of *theobroma cacao.*

(3) *Soy sauce/Shoyu* – in two stage manner first stage koji (mixture of beans and wheat flour is inoculated with *aspergillus oryzae* and *aspergillus sojae*

(4) *Tempeh*– Fermented soy product by *Rhizophus stobnifer*.

(5) *Miso* – Fermented soy product by *Rhizophus stobnifer* in Japan

(6) Ogi– the staple fermented cereal pudding of Nigeria.

(7) *Ontjom* (oncom) – fermented food from Java and Indonesia.

(8) Brewing is completed in two steps (methods) – (1) Infusion (2) Decoction.

(9) Beer is brewed from cereal grains commonly from malted barley,

(10) Wines are prepared by grapes viz. *Vitis vinifera, Vitis laburseca, Vitis rotundifolia.*

(11) Other than grape, plum and peer etc. also used to make wine.

(12) Sulphur dioxide at 50-70 ppm is added to check the growth of wild yeast and bacteria.

(13) Methylglyoxal (CH_3COCH_2OH), Acetaledehyde (CH_3CHO) and pyruvic acid are the secondary products of wine making or alcohol production.

(14) The clear wine (after fermentation) is ready for maturation and amelioration; it takes about 6 months for the wine to mellow down and to use raw and harsh flavour.

(15) Traditionally maturing is done in Oak wood barrels which are tilted periodically.

(16) Packaging and marketing are done after the maturing or ageing of wines.

(17) *Cider* – it is a fermented product of apple, for cider making apples varieties must have rich tannin content.

(18) Hydraulic press or pneumatic press can be utilized for expressing the crushed apples for juice.

(19) For clarification or control of polyphenol oxidase enzyme there is no chemical preservative is recommended.

(20) The distillation of fruits wines results – Brandy.

(21) Scotch/malt whiskey is made by malted barley.

(22) US whiskey and bourbons are made by maize and rye.

(23) Straight rye whiskey is made by rye and it is minimum 51% rye and it contains 15% alcohol.

(24) Irish whiskey is also prepared by malt barley.

(25) Indian whiskey is also prepared by barley, maize or both.

(26) Distilled/rectified grain of malted barley, rye or maize (and flavoured by juniper berries) is Gin.

(27) Vinegar is French word and it means vin (wine) + egre (sour) (Literal meaning of vinegar – sour wine)

(28) Fruit juice by which real vinegar is prepared by fermentation.

(29) Market vinegar is synthetically prepared vinegar by the dilution of glacial acetic acid to a legal standard of 4%.

(30) **Types of vinegar:**

(1) Cider vinegar (2) Wine vinegar

(3) Spirit vinegar (4) Malt vinegar

(5) Rice vinegar (6) Coconut vinegar

(7) Other vinegars.

- Alcohol in wines is 9-16% and in fruit brandy 12%.
- Nisin, subtilin and pimaricin (antifungal) are antibiotics.

Thermal Death Point of some microorganisms/casual organisms:

S.No.	Microorganisms/casual organisms	Temperature in °C	Time (minutes)
1.	*Salmonella typhosa*	60	4.3
2.	*Staphylococcus aurens*	60	18.8
3.	*Eschiria coli*	57.3	20-30
4.	*Streptococcus thermophillus*	70-77	15

(*Source* : Kalia M and Sood S. 2008)

- The time required to destroy all microorganisms at constant temperature is known as *thermal death time*.
- Saur kraut is a defect of sauer kraut.
- *Acetobactor spp.* causes sourness in beans.
- *Pseudomonas synxantha* causes yellow colour during spoilage of milk.
- Nisin (an antibiotic) is produced by *Streptococcus lactis* and is narrow spectrum.
- Tintometer is used for measurement of coloured food.
- FSSAI is responsible for protecting and promoting public health through the regulation and supervision of food safety in India.
- Food safety and standards act 2006 is a consolidating statue related to food safety and regulation in India
- FSSAI (Food Safety and Standard Authority of India) established on 5th August 2011. It consists of a chairperson and 22 members. It is located in 5 regions in the country.
- Consumer protection act. – 1986.
- Prevention of Food Adulteration Act in 1954
- Kefir belongs to the class of acid and alcohol fermentation of milk. It contains Lactoccus, Leuconostoc, Lactobaccilus , Accetobacter and yeasts.
- Kefir belongs to the class of acid and alcohol fermentation of milk.
- Trimethylamine is responsible for fishy flavour and Linolenic acid is also responsible for fishy flavour.
- Canned meat blackening is due to *Clostridium nigrificans.*
- **Colour of Meat:**
  - (a) Red spot on the surface of meat is due to *Serratia marcescens*
  - (b) Blue colour - *Pseudomonos syncyanea*
  - (c) Black colour - *Cladosporium*
  - (d) *Penicillium expansum.*
- **Colour of Eggs:**
  - (a) Green rots in egg - *Proteus melanovogenes.*
  - (b) Black spot - *Proteus melanovogenes.*
  - (c) Pink spot - *Sporotrichum species.*

- **Colour of Milk:**
  - (a) Yellow - *Pseudomonas synxantha*
  - (b) Brown - *Pseudomonas putrefaciens*
  - (c) Blue - *Pseudomonas synoyonea*
  - (d) Red - *Brevibacterium erythrogenes.*
  - (e) Green - *Pseudomonas flurescens*
- **Rice:** Uncooked rice can be contaminated with spores *bacillus cereus* and cause food poisoning. Cooked rice if left standing at room temperature, spores grow into bacteria that thrive and multiply in the warm, hot environment and cause food poisoning.

  A desire to consume raw rice is a psychological disorder pica which is linked to serious health issues.
- *Citrinin* and *patulin* are toxins produced by *pencillium spp.*
- Citrinin is found in many foods including bread sausage, fruits and juices etc.
- *Citrin* is a protein and active mainly in liver, kidney and heart. Within the cells of these organs, citrin is involved in transporting molecules into and out of mitochondria.
- Bacteriocins are proteinaceous or peptides toxin produced by bacteria to inhibit the growth of bacterial stains. Bacteriocins have the ability to inhibit protein synthesis in bacteria, along with acidification of food at the early 18-20 hours during fermentation.
- Bacteriocins are potential alternatives to traditional antibiotics. Bacteriocins can be produced in situ by probiotics and can be bioenginered.

CHAPTER 2
FOOD CHEMISTRY

Food chemistry is the study of chemical processes and interaction of all biological and non-biological components of food

1. Cereals contain α and β type amylase where α-amylase is endoenzyme and β-amylase is exoenzyme. Germination increases the level of α-amylase many times and does not increase the level of β-amylase.
2. Methionine and tryptophan are sulphur containing amino acids which are deficient in quality.
3. Raffinose, Stachyose and Verbicose are known for the flatulence production.
4. Protein concentrates contain minimum 70% protein.
5. *Elaeis guineensis* (oil palm) is the world's most important source of oil.
6. Olive (*Olea europaea*) is also used as oil source.
7. Oil % in coconut is about 60-65%.
8. Copra is obtained from drying of layer of white meat on the inside the coconut.
9. Riboflavin, thiamine and nicotinic acid are available in groundnut.
10. Groundnut oil contains 80% unsaturated fatty acid.
11. Protein isolates must contain about 85-90% proteins.
12. Ratio of saturated to polysaturated fatty acids should be 1:1 (FAO/WHO).
13. About 80% of the oil is produced by expeller's method.
14. Most commonly employed solvent in solvent extraction method is Hexane.
15. Hydrogenated fat has good keeping quality and are prepared from refined deodorized oils.
16. Hydrogenation takes place in presence of catalysts prepared from nickel, platinum or palladium.
17. Fat in homogenised milk is more readily digested by infants than ordinary milk.
18. Water content in fresh fruits is about 70-96% carbohydrates 2-27% and fibre 0.2-3.1% where in banana 27% and watermelon 3% carbohydrates are presents.
19. Polysaccharides viz. Cellulose and hemicelluloses are not digested in the human body.
20. Leafy vegetables contain 2.7-4.4% protein.
21. Allyl sulphide present in onion and garlic is chemically amino acid.
22. After cooking green vegetables turn olive brown in presence of pheophytin acid and with the combination of salt it turns bright green.

23. Pectic substance presents as protopectin in immature vegetables.
24. Calcium in spinach combines with oxalic acid to form calcium oxalate which is not absorbed by the human body.
25. Cellulose has no nutritional significance in body but its role as roughage is important in maintaining good health.
26. Formic, succinic, citric, acetic, malic, fumaric, tartaric and benzoic acids are organic acids present in fruits and vegetables.
27. Papain is used as a stabiliser in beer and other beverages and as a meat tenderiser.
28. The natural flavours of vegetables are due to mixtures of aldehydes, alcohol, ketones, organic acids and sulphur compounds.
29. Amino acid s-methyl l-cysteine sulphoxide is also present in raw cabbage and appears to be a precursor of cooked cabbage flavour.
30. Curcubitacins and oxygenated tetracyclic triterpenes which may occur in both the free form and as glycosides in cucumbers may impart bitterness.
31. Solanine and chaconine are responsible for greening of potato.
32. During cooking potatoes fibre becomes soften. Starch gets gelatinised and protein gets cogulated.
33. Sodium bicarbonate added to the cooking water disintegrates the hemicellulose and cellulose and produces a soft texture in a short cooking period.
34. $CaCl_2$ is used to prevent softening of canned tomatoes.
35. Green vegetables should be cooked for a very short time less than 7 minutes to retain the colour.
36. During cooking chlorophyll is converted to pheophytin while to retain green colour acid or alkali are added.
37. Colour of chlorophyll is enhanced in the presence of copper and weak acid.
38. The presence of ascorbic acid with copper or iron accelerates the oxidation and undesirable colour changes of Anthocyanin compounds.
39. The anthocyanins are changed to unattractive blue or gray colour due tap waters alkali in nature.
40. Dimethyl sulphide is a key volatile compound produced when cabbage is boiled.
36. Acid and prolonged cooking heat can turn chlorophyll to pheophytin which has olive green colour. Bases turn chlorophyll to chlorophyllin which a brighter green.
41. Pungency in onions is an acid derived from (+)-s-(prop-l-cyl)-L-cysteine sulphoxide.
42. Maleic Hydrazide treated onions at the rate of 2000ppm inhibited rooting, sprouting, rotting and prolonged the storage life upto 150 days.
43. Compared to most fruits and vegetables, mushrooms have greater *tryptophan content.*
44. Mushroom contains a disaccharide of glucose called trehalose.
45. 1g spirulina contains carotenoids equivalent to 1kg vegetable and yellow fruits.
46. Food security and malnutrition can be addressed by Sprulina as dietary supplement for long term space members and it requires less land and water than livestock to produce

protein and energy. Dried sprrulina contains 5% water 24% carbohydrates, 8% fat and about 60% protein

47. ω,-3 fatty acids are present in plum, papaya and guava.
48. Custard apple (seethaphal) is a rich source of iron.
49. Foods containing anthocyanins should not be preserved by potassium metabisulphide *e.g.* grape squash or crush.
50. Bitterness in citrus fruits is due to limoninoids (triterpenes) and flavanone glycosides (flavonoids).
51. Pectic substances are methylated polymer of galacturonic acid present in the primary cell wall and middle lamella.
52. Amylase, lipase, pectic enzymes, Invertase, chlorophyllase and peroxidase enzymes are increased during ripening.
53. Softness of ripen fruit is result of hydrolysis of hemicellulose.
54. Commercially used chemical for fruit ripening is ethaphon (2-chloro ethyl phosphonic acid).
55. Optimum pH for the activity of the enzyme polyphenolase is between 5 and 7.
56. Refrigeration causes damage of peels of banana but edible part is not affected by it.
57. Indoles found in citrus fruits and gooseberry bind carcinogens and protect against cancer.
58. Salad means "salted herbs".
59. Calcium, iron and antioxidant value of Jaggery is higher than sugar and honey.
60. Fructose is most soluble and it is most different to crystallize.
61. Fructose, maltose and galactose caramelises at 110°C, 180°C and 170°C respectively,
62. D-glucose is dextrose while D- fructose is hexose.
63. Isomalt is derived from beet sugar due to less hygroscopic nature its shelf life is better.
64. Molasses contains NMT 25% water and NMT 5% mineral ash.
65. Maple syrup is evaporated sap of the sugar NMT 35% water.
66. Honey contains 17.2% water, 82.5 carbohydrates, fructose 38%, glucose 31%, maltose 7% and sucrose 2%.
67. Jaggery contains 65-85% sucrose, 10-15% invert sugar and 2.5 % ash.
68. Caramel sugar can be prepared from soybean, tapioca or sago.
69. Brittle candy that solidifies before it has a chance to crystallise.
70. High fructose corn syrup (HFCS) in an acceptable substitute for sucrose.
71. Sugar alcohols (xylitol, sorbitol, manito, matitol, lactito, isomalt) known as polyols are white crystalline, slightly hygroscopic, water soluble powder.
72. Polyols are generally stable to heat and do not take part in Millard type browning reaction due to the absence of reduced aldehyde group.
73. Aspartame made by combining two amino acids aspartic acid and phenylalanine, and adding methyl alcohol to form a methyl ester.

74. Saccharin is sodium ortho benzene sulphonamide or the calcium salt.
75. According to Preservation of Food Adultration Act (PFA) 1954, not more than 100 ppm of saccharine may be used.
76. Neohesperidin dihydrochalcone is natural non calorie sweetener isolated form citrus peels and seeds. It is approved as sweetener-959) since 1994 in European Union.
77. Glycyrrhizin is obtained from the roots of European leguminous plant **Glycrrhiza glabra** (licorice) and it is a non calorie natural sweetener.
78. Steiva (*Stevia rebaudiana*) contains an intensive sweetening agent called *steviosido* extracted from leaves. It does not show browning during cooking and is non-fermenting. It is 50 to 30 times sweeter than sugar.
79. Stevioside is stable at high temperature and over a pH range from 3-9.
80. Fish is an excellent source of eicosapentaenoic acid (EPA) from which the body can make a hormone like compound called a prostagladin. This particular prostagladin reduces the blood clotting rate and thus the likelihood of a clot blocking the coronary arteries.
81. Margarine is made from one or more optional fat ingredients churned with cultured pasteurized skim milk whey.
82. Soybean oil has both ω-6 and ω-3 polyunsaturated fatty acids with good amount of vitamin E.
83. Rice bran oil contains a high amount of unsaponifiable components such as tocotrienols and oryzanol.
84. Sesame oil contains ω,-3 and ω,-6 fatty acids as well as lecithin.
85. Canola oil is rape seed oil and the name is derived from Canadian and oil. It is also rich in ω,-3 and ω,-6 polyunsaturated fatty acids.
86. Palm oil is produced from the fruit of the *Elaeis guineensis* palm.
87. Flesh pericarp of the palm consists 75% olein (liquid) and 25% stearin (solid).
88. Egg yolk, whole egg, gelatin, pectin, starch paste, casein, albumin and fine powders such as paprika or mustard are used as Emulsifier/stabiliser.
89. Pyrolysis is the thermal breakdown of oil.
90. Formation of free fatty acids when heat and steam break a fatty acid molecule away from the glycerol molecule in a process called "hydrolysis".
91. Oleoresin is a concentrated, viscous, resinous extract obtained by solvent (alcohol) extraction of the plant material.
92. Essential oil thymol is present in ajwain (Trachyspermum ammi).
93. 2-butyl propeny disulphide, 1-(1-methyl-thiopropy)-1-propenyl disulphide and 2-butyl (3-methyl thioallyl) is present in volatile oil asafoetida.
94. Caraway seeds kala jeera contain *D-carvone* and *D-limonere* the flavouring substance.
95. Cineol, retpinyl acetate, pinece, sabinene and porenol are present in cardamom.
96. 96. The pungency of chili extracts are expressed in terms of "*scoville value*" scale method developed by Scoville in 1912.

97. *Capsaicin* kills pancreatic cancerous cell and prevents prostate cancer.
98. Cinnamon contains Eugenol, cineole and cinnamaldehyde.
99. Methyl hydroxy calcone polymer present in cinnamon is flavonoids which act as antioxidant.
100. Eugeniol the phenolic compound is present in clove oil.
101. Geraniol is the active principle present in coriander's essential oil.
102. Thalides present in coriander seeds, cumin seeds contains pthalides both increase the level of anticancer protective enzymes.
103. During crushing Allin (inactive form) which is converted by allinase enzyme to allicin (active form) in garlic and it breakdowns in allyldisulphide.
104. Methyl (2-propenyl) trisulphide is present in garlic which has antiplatelet activity besides this garlic possesses hypoglyceimic property.
105. Gingerol and shagaol the volatile oil present in ginger and Ginger can kill ovarian cancer.
106. Dithiolthiones sulphur containing compounds protects against the toxic effect of Aflatoxin present in mustard seeds.
107. Onion can lower blood cholesterol and lipid levels and is also useful in preventing heart disease.
108. Capasicin, piperidene and sinapic acid are present in pepper.
109. Colour of saffron is due to pigment crocin, picrocrocin, β-carotene and glycosides.
110. Star anise (*Ilficium verum*) medium sized evergreen tree has high antioxidant value.
111. Cynadine-3-glucoside is the pigment responsible for red colour in tamarind.

     Red tamarind extract can be used as colours agent (red tamarind ratha puli) a mutant tamarind variety abundant in Tamil Nadu.
112. Tartaric acid and potassium bitartrate are present in tamarind pulp.
113. Turmeric may be a potential weapon, against Alzheimers; an old age disease.
114. Curcumin,demethoxy curcumin and bisdemthoxy curcumin are three main curcuminoids present in turmeric.
115. Curcumin or diferuloyl methane is major curcuninoid.
116. Vanilla (*Vanilla planifolia*) contains active principle is "vanillin".
117. The principle compounds of the peppermint oil are menthol, menthyl acetate, menthyl isovalerate and menthone.
118. Coriander leaves/herbs are called cilantro.
119. Curry leaves have antihyperlipidemic effect and have low glucaemic effect.
120. Dr. Ann Wigmore is pioneer in knowing the importance of wheat grass known as "green blood".
121. Alfalfa is a good laxative and natural diuretic.
122. MSG is extracted from Japanese seaweed; it contains 12% sodium while common salt contains 40% sodium.

123. Ajinomoto (Japan) is the bestselling brand name of MSG.

124. In rasmalai saffron is added to colour and flavor.

125. In roasting of coffee the flavour is largely due to 2-thifuron and its methyl and ethyl esters.

126. The key phytocompounds of chicory are hydroxy coumarins, flavonoids, inulin and sesquiterpene lactones.

127. Inulin is a prebiotic non digestible food material that selectively stimulates the growth of health promoting bacteria (lacto bacilli and bafidobacteria).

128. Tea is declared as national drink (India) in 2013.

129. In green tea production weathering and fermentation are completely omitted.

130. Oolong tea is partially fermented.

131. Roasting of cocoa bean is done at 210°F (98 °C) for 10-15 minutes.

(To make 1 kg of chocolate, about 300-600 beans are roasted and then cracked and deshelled by winnower to get known as chocolate liquor. Nibs are ground, using various methods, into a thick paste.

132. Dutch processed cocoa (pH 6.8-7.5) is less bitter and is emulsified more easily with milk than the natural processed (pH 5.2-6.0) one.

133. Fat in cocoa according to BIS specifications: 1.) Normal 20% 2.) Medium 10-20%, 3.) Low 10%

134. Fruit punch contains 25% of total fruit juice and 65% of sugar.

135. Blending of equal parts of milk and an emulsion of protein from groundnut is called Miltone. *Miltone:-* A new product has been developed by CFTRI, Mysuru. It is a milk-based beverage and contains in equal proportion of milk and protein emulsion from groundnut. It can be substituted for ordinary milk and has 3.5% proteins, 2% fat and 5% sugar.

136. Egg nog, mixing of eggs (whole) or egg yolks to milk. Egg nogs made with a variety of ingredients, like juice, hard drinks, coffee.

137. Sprouted cereals and pulses, flour rich in alpha-amylase enzyme called ARF's (Amylase rich food) ARF, help to increase the energy density.

138. A chemical bond is the physical process responsible for the attractive interaction between atoms and molecules, which confer stability to diatomic and polyatomic chemical compound.

139. Ionic bonds are a type of chemical bond that involves a metal and non-metal ion through electrostatic attraction (opposite charges).

140. Avocado has a fat content of about 28%.

141. Anthocyanins react with metal iron and release acids which further erode the can making holes in them called pinholes.

142. Jackfruit has the distinct flavour due to 13 ester, 9 alcohol, 5 aldehydes, 5 acids and traces of 2-acetyl-1-pyrroline.

143. Pectic substance occurs in the three forms at different stages in the cycle of the fruit.

144. Propectin (insoluble parent molecule) present in unripe stage.
145. Pectin/pectinic acid (intermediate compound) present in ripe fruits.
146. Pectic acid present in over ripe fruits.
147. Pears, guava, apples, banana, litchi etc. exhibit a pinkish brown discolouration when cut caused by leuocoanthocyanins.
148. Hesperidin found in peels of orange while naringin found in peels of grapefruit.
149. Besides polyphenol, Tyrosine, chlorogenic acid, catechins, mono and dihydroxy phenol compounds are also oxidised to yield the brown pigments.
150. To check the enzymatic browning of fruits blanching is done at 100°C for 2-10 minutes.
151. Lowering of pH upto 4 has a significant affect on reduction of enzymatic browning.
152. Antioxidants viz. sulphur-di-oxide, Sulphites and bisulphites are used to inhibit browning.
153. Ascorbic acid browning is due to reaction between ascorbic acid (de hydro ascorbic acid) and amino acids.
154. Climacteric fruits have the ability to continue to ripen when they are harvested.
155. Protopectin is chemically menthylated very long polymer of galacturonic acid.
156. Bitterness in fruits is mainly due to presence of limoninoids and flavonoids.
157. Limoninoids also called triterpenes.
158. Flavanone glycoside and naringin are flavonoids.
159. Anthoxanthins are divided into four types.
160. Flavones (rutionol):- 1) Flavonols (kaempferol) 2) Flavonones (naringin)
3) Flavonols: - *a*) Catechins (gallocatechins) and *b*) Leucoanthoxyanins (leucocyanidins).
161. In cabbage, the compound s- methyl-l- cysteine sulphoxide is present in raw state, which is supposed to be the precursor of the cooked cabbage flavour.
162. "Pheophytin a" is a pale greenish gray compound while "pheophytin b" is olive green in colour.
163. 163. Iron + anthocyanins – *cause black discolouration.*
164. Iron + red cabbage – *cause blue discolouration.*
165. Betacyanins: - Impart the distinct colour of beets within this group are betanidin and betanin.
166. Saturated fat: - Double (-C=C-) bonds can react with hydrogen to from single bonds; they are called saturated because the second bond is broken up and each half of the bond is attached to (saturated) with a hydrogen atom.
167. Saturate fat are solid at room temperature and tend to be derived from animal sources *e.g.* Butter.
168. All fats and oils have unique flavours and odours *e.g.*, Olive oil for salad dressing (for flavour) and lard for pastry (due to its blandness).
169. Fats containing saturated fatty acids from C_4 to C_8 are liquid at room temperature but these containing C_{10} or higher saturated fatty acids are solid.

170. Optical activity of fatty substances is usually recorded in terms of angular rotation through 200 mm.

171. The Redwood viscometer is conveniently used for obtaining the relative viscosities of oils, and the time of efflux of a definite volume (usually 50 ml) is determined at the required temperature.

172. Tintometers/colorimeter – The removal of acidity (neutralisation).The removal of coloured matter (bleaching). The removal of taste and smell (deodorisation).

173. Refining of oil involves the following steps:- 1) Sedimentation, 2) Filtration, 3) Centrifugation, 4) Neutralisation, 5) Bleaching and 6) Deodorisation.

174. A process by which a part or in some cases nearly all the unsaturated acids in an oil are caused to combine with hydrogen under the influence of a catalyst called as *Hydrogenation* or hardening. $(C_{17}H_{33}CO.C)_3\ C_3H_5 + CH_2 = (C_{17}H_{35}CO.C)_3\ C_3H_5$

175. The commercial process of hydrogenation is based on the scientific search of the French chemist "Paul Sabatier".

176. Addition of antioxidants retards the rancidity (spoilage) of fats.

177. Storing fats in coloured glass also retard the rancidity of fats.

178. Temperature at which a fat gives off smoke from the surface of the fat is termed as Smoking point.

178. Acid value is a measure of the free acidity, and is defined as the number of milligrams of potassium hydroxide required to neutralise the free fatty acids in 1g of the fat or oil.

179. *Iodine value:* - The iodine value is defined as the percentage of iodine absorbed by an oil fat or wax.

180. The saponification value may be defined as the numbers of milligrams of potassium hydroxide which are required to saponify completely 1g of the substance.

181. All unsaponifiable substances which are insoluble in water but soluble in light petroleum spirits.

182. A first-grade oil of olive is known as 'Virgin' or sublime oil.

183. Olive oil mainly consists of (Oleic acid upto 70%) (linoleic acid upto 15%) and palmitic acid upto 0.3-3.5%) stearic acid-1·5%

184. Weight of 100 fruits of sunflower is 40-60 gram.

185. Rapeseed oils (*Brassica campestris*) trade name is Colza oil.

186. *Saponify*: turning of fat or (spacing) oil into soap by reaction mix alkali.

187. Iced tea a form of cold tea was introduced in 1904 world's fair in St. Louis. Concept of tea in bag was patented by Robert Lawson in 1903. Commercially tea bags were appeared in 1904 around the world by Thomas Sullivan.

188. Tea provides 70% of our daily fluoride intake.

189. Fluoride is needed to support bone mineralization and protect teeth against dental caries.

190. Vit-B1, vit-B2, vit-B6, vit-B12, Folate, Carotene, Niacin and Pantothenate are the vitamins found in tea.

191. RNI = Reference nutrient intake.
192. EAR = Estimated average requirements.
193. Thiamine is needed to release energy from carbohydrates.
194. White tea is made by youngest leaves or leaf buds.
195. Herbal teas contain no true tea leaves, herbal and "medicinal" teas are created from the flowers, berries, peels, seeds, leaves and roots of many different plants.
196. Green teas come from countries in the far East such as China and Japan.
197. Black teas mostly come from plantation in Africa, India, Srilanka and Indonesia.
198. An alkaloid substance found in teas is Theine.
199. A hybrid of *Arabica Maragogype* called the elephant bean because of its large size originated from the Maragogype country in the Bahia state of Brazil (Maragogype).
200. A slimy layer (parenchyma) is membrane or seed skin (spermodern) is referred to in the coffee trade as the "silver skin".
202. Roasting of coffee is carried out at 287.7 °C temperature.
203. 2-thiofuron and its methyl and ethyl ester derivatives are responsible for flavour in coffee.
204. The coffee oils called coffee essence, coffee oil or caffeol.
205. Coffee made from fine powdered and coarse ground coffee in the ratio of 90:10 gives a perfect blend.
206. Potassium caffeine chlorogenate (in bean chiefly) is stimulant in coffee.
207. Turkish coffee is served hot from a special coffee pot called "cezve".
208. Americana coffee, extract a shot of espresso and fill the rest of the 6-8-ounce cup with hot water.
209. According to the Indian Standards Institution, 20% cocoa fat can be used in beverages.
210. Theobromine and caffeine in cocoa are 1.1-3.2 and 9-55 (mg/150ml of beverage) respectively.
211. Soups are of about 3 kinds: - clear soups, thick soups, and cream soup.
212. Human blood contains 0.9% salt (sodium chloride).
213. The essential oil (2.5 to 5% in the dried fruits) is dominated by thymol (35 to 60% furthermore), α-pinene, p-cymene, limonene eugenol γ-terpinene have been found.
214. Colorless plastids are Leucoplasts.
215. Legumes are deficient in *Methionine* and rich in *Lysine*
216. Fishy flavour is due to - Linolenic acids
217. Vitamin B_1 is not an antioxidant.
218. Most stable oil is Rice bran oil.
219. Dough is sticky due to more amount of water, high amylase activity and less salt
220. β-*carotene* form of carotene contains oxygen.

221. Vinyl Chloride, a potential migrant from PVC is responsible for a cardinal irritation.
222. Natural antioxidant present in oil is Vitamin E.
223. Deficiency of Folic acid causes B_{12} pernicious anemia and digestive problems.
224. Human intestinal flora cannot digest cellulose and hemicellulose.
225. *Hesperidin antioxidant* is present in Citrus family
226. Generally red, blue and green colour in fruits and vegetables is due to anthocyanin pigment.
227. Protein % in Fish is 18.
228. Enzymatic browning of fruits and vegetables is due to polyphenoloxydase enzyme.
229. Conversion of glycogen to glucose in liver by insulin or glucazon.
230. Protein biosynthesis by ribosome requires magnesium.
231. Sulphur is presented primarily in the cell protein in the term of cysteine and methionine.
232. During cell division the Amino acids characters are transmitted in the form of nucleic acid.
233. The principle functions of the cell wall include- protection, mechanical support and maintenance.
234. Each ribosome consists of two unequal subunits composed of RNA and proteins.
235. Tannins are Mucopolysaccharides.
236. Primary structure of protein is due to peptide bonds.
237. Secondary structure of protein is α-helix, β-pleated.
238. Protein can be denaturated by heat.
239. The protein present in milk is casein.
240. Albumins are neutral proteins (pH 6.75).
241. Milk casein is a *glycoprotein.*
242. Beans are found to be deficient in methionine amino acid.
243. Pentose sugars are widespread in nature and can be either D-ribose as in ribonucleic acid (RNA) or 2-deoxyribose as in DNA.
244. A rebose sugar is a pentose sugar but pentose sugar is not necessarily a ribose sugar.
245. Proteins are generally divided into three groups: simple, conjugated and derived proteins.
246. Cereals are deficient in *lysine* and rich in *methionine*.
247. Lipids are present to the extent of 1-2% in wheat and rice and 3% in maize.
248. Wheat germ contains lipids 6-11% and bran 3-5% and endosperm 0.8-1.5%.
249. Sweetest sugar in fruit is *fructose*.
250. Sliced potatoes are kept in saline water to prevent enzymic browning.
251. *Papain* is a proteolytic enzyme available in papaya fruit.
252. Gibberelin hormones extend the shelf life of fruits.
253. In cola soft drinks the common colourant is tannins.

254. Red colour in water melon is due to *lycopene.*
255. Acidity decreases in fruits as the ripening increases.
256. After slicing the fruits, the slices are kept in sodium chloride to lower the water activity of fruits.
257. Gelatin is used as the clarifying agent of fruit juice.
258. Algin is a *polysaccharide* from cell walls of brown algae. Algin is used to lower cholesterol.
259. Many coenzymes are Vitamins.
260. To digest cellulose a fungus produces an exoenzyme.
261. Two sugars are differing only in configuration around one specific carbon atom are called *Epimers.*
262. Ergotism is called as the Anthony's fire due to burning sensation of gangrene of limbs.
263. With the oxidation of aldehydic carbon of glucose, compound formed is gluconic acid.
264. Vitamin C is the example of sugar acids.
265. LDL is lipo-proteins, the major portion of cholesterol.
266. In disaccharides two monosaccharides are joined together by *Glycosidic bond.*
267. Honey contains levulose and fructose sugar.
268. α-amylase is liquefying enzyme.
269. Hemicelluloses are polymer of xylose.
270. Disaccharides produced after hydrolysis of cellulose are cellubiose.
271. Simplest form of carbohydrate is monosaccharides.
272. The product of heating of sugar above its melting point in acidic condition is *caramel.*
273. Saponifiable lipid is complex in nature.
274. A small amount of starch, that is not digested in small intestine is called *resistant starch.*
275. Waxes come under complex category of lipids.
276. Number of carbon atom in stearic acid is 18.
277. Linolenic acid is polyunsaturated fatty acid.
278. Butter scotch aroma can be obtained by heating glucose with Glutamine at 180°C.
279. Trans form of oleic acid is *elaidic acid.*
280. Arachidonic acid contains 20 carbon atoms ($C_{20}H_{32}O_2$).
281. Chemical method for moisture analysis is Karl fisher titration.
282. Amount of fatty acids which is insoluble in water is called *Hehner value.*
283. Temperature at which fatty acid rises in a cylinder is recorded as *Slip point.*
284. Nelson Somogy's method is for the estimation of sugar.
285. In Napin Clark method 2- 4 *dinitrophenyl hydrazine* chemical is being used
286. The intensity of colour during the anisidine value of fat/ oil is 350 nm.

287. Amphoteric nature present in *proteins.*
288. Amphoteric compound is a molecule or ion that can react both as an acid and as a base.
289. Many of the oils and fats undergo a change in flavour before the onset of the rancidity which is known as *Reversion.*
290. Peroxide value is the measure of *Rancidity.*
291. Benedict's test is used to identify reducing sugar in a sample.
292. Biurett test is done for the qualitative analysis of protein.
293. Iodine test is exclusively for detection of the presence of Polysaccharides.
294. During Benedict's test sugar gets oxidized and Cu^{+3} gets reduced.
295. Ninhydrin test is used for amino acids and proteins.
296. Imino group of hydroxyl proline is responsible for giving yellow colour with ninhydrin.
297. Soxhlet method is based on the principle of *Solvent extraction.*
298. Digestion, Distillation and Titration are the basic steps of *Kjeldahl's method.*
299. In gas chromatography the area under a graph show the concentration of the substance present in the sample.
300. In partition chromatography mobile and stationary phase is liquid.
301. In ion exchange chromatography the interaction between solute and stationary phase are primarily *electrostatic.*
302. PAGE (Polyacrylamide Gel Electrophoresis) is type of chromatographic technique
303. In isoelectric focusing the gradient increases from low pH at anode.
304. Most effective preservative of canned food is tylosin. Tylosin is effective against gram positive bacteria. It inhibits protein synthesis by combining with SOS ribosomal subunit zinc, potassium, and calcium.
305. Carbohydrate content in potato is 22%.
306. Richest source of riboflavin is *bael.*
307. Richest source of iron is dry *karonda.*
308. Methionine is the precursor of ethylene.
309. "Elephants foot yam" is rich sources of Vitamin A and B_6.
310. The limiting amino acid in green vegetables is methionine.
311. Spinach is rich in Vitamin A.
312. Chillies are rich source of Vitamin A and C.
313. Red colour of carrot is due to *carotene.*
314. Yellow coloured vegetables are rich source of Vitamin A.
315. Enzyme responsible for converting pectin into pectic acid is Pectic Methyl Esterase (PME).
316. Enzyme responsible for converting protopectin into pectin is proto-pectinase.
317. Toughening effect on canned bean is due to Ca.
318. Vitamins which is not found in fruits and vegetables is Vitamin B_{12}.

319. Polyhydroxy butyrate polymer is biodegredable plastic.

320. Bitterness in peach is due to *prunasin acid* and best maturity index for Grape is TSS (Total Soluble Solid).

321. Carbohydrates occur in plants, animals and microorganisms in various form and levels.

322. Glucose is the main sugar in animals.

323. Glycogen is the storage polysaccharide in animals.

324. Carbohydrates are classified into three main groups *monosaccharides, oligosaccharides* and *polysaccharides*.

325. Glucose, fructose, galactose, xylose and ribose are included in *monosaccharides*.

326. Sucrose, lactose, maltose, raffmose, stachyose and verbascose are included in *oligosaccharides*.

327. Cellulose is the most abundant polysaccharide in biological system.

328. Starch, glycogen, cellulose, hemicelluloses, lignin, pectin, modified starches, carboxy methyl cellulose, chitin and arabinoxylahs are included in *polysaccharides*.

329. Some of these polysaccharides act as dietary fibre.

330. Dietary fibres are of two types: soluble fibre and insoluble fibre.

331. Soluble fibres include pectin and gums.

332. Insoluble fibre includes cellulose, hemicelluloses and lignin.

333. Main characteristics of carbohydrates are mutarotation, caramelization, and crystallization.

334. Mutarotation is change in optical rotation that occurs by caramelizaiton when the corresponding sterocenters interconvert cyclic sugars show mutarotation. Caramelization is also known as non enzymatic browning. Glucose, maltose, fructose and galactose all shows mutarotation. Mutarotation was discovered by French chemist Augustin-Pierre Dubrunfaut in 1844.

335. Caramel formation occurs when sugars are subjected to heat in absence of water or heated in concentrated solution.

336. Caramelization of sucrose needs heating to a temperature of about 200°C.

337. Crystallization is an important property of sugars which enables it to form crystals.

338. Proteins are made up of about twenty different amino acids. Protein metabolism is key physiological process in all forms of life.

339. Amino acids in protein are joined together with peptide bonds.

340. Amino acids are grouped into polar and non-polar amino acids based on their polarity.

341. Wheat proteins such as gliadins and glutenins contain low levels of polar side chains or amino acids.

342. Protein occurs in products from animal as well as plant origin.

343. Animal products are utilized as protein source in non-vegetarian diets.

344. Legume products are utilized as protein source in vegetarian diets.

345. Out of twenty amino acids, only nine amino acids are essential, which means these should be included in diets.

346. Those proteins which yield only amino acids on hydrolysis are known as simple proteins such as albumin, globulin, glutelins, prolamins, scleroprotein, histones and protamines.
347. Conjugated proteins are those containing an amino acid combined with a non protein material such as lipid, nucleic acid or carbohydrate.
348. Examples of conjugated proteins are phosphoproteins, lipoproteins, nucleoproteins, glycoproteins and chromoproteins.
349. Derived proteins are obtained by chemical or enzymatic methods.
350. Examples of derived proteins include proteoses, peptones and peptides.
351. Sources of proteins are meat, milk, eggs, pulses, beans and nuts etc.
352. Protein molecules exhibit four structural forms: primary, secondary, tertiary and quaternary.
353. Denaturation refers to changes in molecular structures of proteins.
354. Proteins are also involved in non-enzymatic browning *i.e. millard reaction.*
355. Functional properties of proteins include emulsifying, foaming, water absorption, binding and texture improvement.
356. Lipids are substances mostly made up of esters of fatty acids and glycerol.
357. Fatty acids are generally classified into 3 groups: short chain, medium chain and long chain.
358. Fatty acids are of two types on the basis of presence of multiple bonds *i.e.* saturated and unsaturated.
359. Saturated fatty acids are those having single bonds between C-C.
360. Unsaturated fatty acids are those having double or triple bonds between C-C.
361. Examples of saturated fatty acids are butyric, caproic, caprylic, capric, lauric, myristic, palmitic, stearic, arachidic and valeric etc.
362. Examples of unsaturated fatty acids are myristoleic, palmitoleic, oleic, linoleic, linolenic, arachidonic, EPA and DHA etc.
363. Hydrogenation of fats consists of addition of hydrogen at double bonds of unsaturated acyl groups.
364. Hydrogenation process is important as it converts oil into plastic fats for production of margarine.
365. Oxidative rancidity of fats refers to oxidation of fat which results in deterioration in flavour of fat.
366. Hydrolytic rancidity of fats refers to hydrolytic changes in fat resulting from enzyme activity.
367. Water is an essential constituent of food found in two forms: free and bound water.
368. Fruits are good source of carbohydrates, sugars, vitamins and water, but deficient in proteins.
369. Fruits contain many pigments such as anthocyanin, lycopene and carotene etc.
370. Fresh cut fruits and vegetables undergo enzymatic browning involving enzyme polyphenol oxidase.

371. Addition of sodium chloride or sugar to cut fruit prevent browning.

372. In immature fruits, pectin is present while ripened fruits contain pectic acid.

373. The principal organic acids present in fruits are malic, citric, oxalic, benzoic and tartaric acid.

374. The white portion of the skin of citrus foods is called *pith.*

375. Blanching is the process of heat treatment to inactivate the natural enzymes of vegetables.

376. The most heat resistant enzymes and indicators of adequacy of blanching are catalase and peroxidase.

377. The types of protein present in cereals are albumins, globulins, prolamines (gliadins) and glutelins.

378. The gliadins and glutelins are known as gluten proteins.

379. The gluten has unique elasticity and flow properties which are used for baking bread and other products.

380. Cereals contain 6-12% protein, they are generally deficient in lysine.

381. About 95% of minerals are the phosphates and sulphates of potassium, magnesium and calcium.

382. Phytates present in cereals decrease the absorption of iron.

383. Cereals are poor source of calcium and iron particularly rice is a very poor source of these two elements.

384. Ragi is a rich source of calcium and iron. Millets (ragi, bajra, jowar) are rich in minerals and fibre.

385. Parboiling which includes soaking in water and steaming of paddy results in seeping of vitamins present in outer layer into the grain.

386. Cereals do not contain either vitamin A or C except maize which contains small amount of carotenes.

387. Certain grains contain many enzymes and of these the amylases, proteases, lipases and oxido-reductases are of importance.

388. Rice bran contains 12-15% protein, 14-20% oil if the paddy is raw and 18-25% if parboiled and is a rich source of B-group vitamins.

389. Water soluble B vitamins and other water soluble nutrients diffuse into the endosperm during parboiling and hence the loss of nutrients is less in parboiled rice even after polishing the presence of vitamin E is particularly noted in parboiled rice.

390. Collagen fibres shrink or shorten at a temperature of 600°C but higher temperatures or boiling cause transformation to water soluble gelatin.

391. The acid content of fruits decreases with ripening.

392. Avocados are particularly rich in proteins and fat.

393. Lactulose is a non-absorbable sugar used in the treatment of constipation and hepatic encephalopathy.

394. Acid value is a measure of the free acidity, and is defined as the number of milligrams of potassium hydroxide required to neutralise the free fatty acids in 1g of the fat or oil.

IMPORTANT POINTS

- *Fructose* (lavulose/fruit sugar) is a highly soluble sugar that does not readily crystallize.
- It is much sweeter than cane sugar and is found in honey, ripe fruits and some vegetables.
- It is also a product of the hydrolysis of sucrose.
- Fructose known as levorotatory due to *Left light polarization.* It possess a ketone (CO) group and called Ketohexose.
- **Carbohydrate is mainly of three types:**

(a) Monosaccharides (2C) *e.g.* $C_6H_{12}O_6$

(b) Disaccharides (2-10C) *e.g.* $C_{12}H_{22}O_{11}$

(c) Polysaccharides (>10C) *e.g.* $(C_6H_{10}O_5)$

Classification of carbohydrates on the basis of carbon atom:

1. ***Monosaccharides*** ($C_6H_{12}O_6$) contains 2 carbons–

(a) Glucose (dextrose) or corn sugar (b) Galactose (c) Mannose (d) Triose (e) Tetrose (f) Pentose (g) Hexose (h) Fructose (fruit sugar)

2. ***Oligosaccharides*** contains 2-10 carbon–

(a) Disaccharides – *e.g.* maltose, lactose, cellobiose and stachyose

(b) Trisaccharides – *e.g.* Aldoses, ketoses

(c) Tetrasaccharides – *e.g.* Lychnose, maltotetraose, nystose and sesamose

(d) Penta saccharides – *e.g.* Verbascose

3. ***Polysaccharides*** contains > 10 carbon–

(a) Storage polysaccharides – amylase, amylopectine

(b) Glycogen (in animal cell)

(c) Structural polysaccharides–

(i) Cellulose (ii) Hemicelulose (iii) Pectin (calcium pectate)

- Starch, glycogen and cellulose are homopolysaccharides.
- Fibre, blood sugar, muscles and gum are heteropolysaccharides.

- **Digestion of raw material by some enzymes**

(a) Starch – amylase – Glucose

(b) Sucrose – sucrase – Glucose + Fructose

(c) Maltase – maltase – Glucose + glucose

(d) Lactose – lactase – Glucose + galactose

Classification of protein:

(A) ***On the basis of structure (yields only amino acids)***

(1) *Simple proteins*:

(a) Albumins – in blood, egg (water soluble)

(b) Globulins – in blood, potato, ground nut (water insoluble)

(c) Glutelins – in wheat (insoluble in all neutral solvent)

(d) Prolamins – in gliadin (wheat), Zein (maize) soluble in alcohol @ 70-80 %

(e) Fibrous protein – *e.g.* Collagen, elastin, keratin (in hair, skin etc.)

(f) Histanes – blood protein (Soluble in water)

(g) Pritanubs – *e.g.* Salmon sperm (salmine) (Soluble in water)

(2) *Conjugated proteins (united to some other molecule)*:

(a) Nucleoproteins - group of nucleic acid (RNA and DNA)

(b) Glycoprotein – combined with carbohydrates *e.g.* Mucin

(c) Phosphoproteins – Phosphorus available *e.g.* Caseinogens(milk), ovovitelin (egg yolk)

(d) Haemoglobons – combined with haem *e.g.* Blood

(e) Lactoproteins – A protein normally present in milk.

(3) *Derived proteins*:

(i) Primary protein derivatives

(a) Proteins – *e.g.* Casein (curdled milk), fibrin (coagulated fibrinogen)

(b) Meta proteins – molecules are altered to form protein soluble in weak acid and alkali.

(c) Coagulated proteins – insoluble- precipitation by heat/alchohol *e.g.* Egg proteins (albumins)

(ii) Secondary protein derivatives

(a) Proteose – Soluble in water, not cogulated by heat

(b) Peptone – Soluble in water, not cogulated by heat

(c) Peptides – Containing 2 or more amino acids

e.g. 2 amino acids called a Dipeptide

3 amino acids called as Tripeptide

Many amino acids called as Polypeptide

(B) ***On the basis of nutrients value***

(1) *Incomplete proteins* : Neither maintain life nor support growth *e.g.* Most vegetable proteins except soy protein, maize and animal protein gelatin.

(2) *Complete proteins* : Maintain life and support growth *e.g.* All animal protein except gelatin, glycinin (soy), gluten (wheat), glutelin (maize)

(3) *Partial complete/incomplete proteins* : Maintain life but fail to support normal growth *e.g.* Gliadin (wheat), hardein (barley) and prolamin (rye)

- Proteins are precursors of enzymes, Antibodies, hormones and vitamins.
- Degradation of fat to free fatty acid and glycerol is *lipolysis.*
- Losses during blanching are related to length of time the product is submerged in the heating or cooling medium.
- In 70% of flour recovery the loss of potassium, magnesium and calcium are decreased by 74, 84 and 50% respectively.
- Minerals are slight sensitive to heat during processing but susceptible to leaching into the processing or cooking water *e.g.* During canning.

Colour Responsible Agents (Pigments)

- Green – Chlorophyllus
- Yellow/Orange – Carotenoids
- White – Flavonoids
- Red/Voilate – Anthocyanins
- Pink/Red colour of muscles – Myoglobin
- Slow heating of milk causes browning a little due to reaction of Sugar (lactose) with amino acid.

  For avoiding of browning in some fruits and vegetables
- Physical method to regulate enzymatic browning include thermal treatment, prevention of oxygen irradiation. Heat treatment such as blanching, can easily inhibit the enzymatic activity because enzyme, which are composed of proteins are denaturated.

  Example: Use of low temperature and addition of sodium chloride or sugar to the cut fruit prevent browning.
- Sulphur dioxide (SO_2) controls enzymatic browning in fruits and vegetables.
  1. BHA, BHT and NGDA are antioxidants.
  2. The best known and most widespread red pigment is Bixin (*Bixa orellana*) plant, *Cocens cniti* female insects extract, Grape skin extract and Caramel also used as red pigment/colour.
  3. Stabilizers – improves and stabilize the texture of foods inhibits crystallization *e.g.* sugar and ice.
  4. ETDA (Ethylene diamine tetra acetic acid), polyphosphates, citric acid are used as sequestrants.

Foods are classified on the basis of acidity

(a) Low acid food –pH > 5.0 *e.g.* Peas, maize and asparagus etc.

(b) Medium acid food –pH 5.0 – 4. *e.g.* Meat, soups, sauses and sphaghetti etc.

(c) Acid food –pH 4.5-3.7 *e.g.* Tomato, pears, fig and pineapples etc.

(d) High acid food –pH < 3.7 *e.g.* Pickles, berries, citrus, grape and dahi (yoghurt) etc.

- Meat fats are rich sources of saturated fatty acids.
- Glycogen and glucose are carbohydrates present in meat.

- Protein is Greek word and it meant proteios means primary and discovered by **Bergilius (name of scientist)** Proteins are made up of about twenty different amino acids. Protein metabolism is key physiological process in all forms of life.
- Simple protein contains only amino acid while conjugated protein contains amino acids and non amino acid *viz.* Lipid, sugar, metal etc.

S.No.	*Structural protein*	*Named*
1.	Muscle protein	Collagen
2.	Silk protein	Fibrolin
3.	Hair and wool protein	Keratin
4.	Insect wing protein	Elastin
5.	Soybean protein	Glycinin
6.	Wheat protein	Gluten
7.	Rice protein	Oryzein
8.	Maize protein	Zein
9.	Regulatory protein	Enzyme
10.	Transport protein	Myoglobin, Haemoglobin

(*Source* : Kalia M and Sood S. 2008)

- Enzyme is greek word and discovered by Eduard Buchner (1897) while named by W. Kuhne in the year 1877 and these are catalyst in nature.
- Defect of beer is Sarcina sickness due to *Pediococcus cerevisae*.
- If enzyme reacting with water termed as *hydrolytic* while reacting with oxygen is called *oxidizing*.
- Vitamin introduced/discovered by Funk during 1911 and it acts as catalyst and are about 13 in number.

S.No.	*Vitamin*	*Called also as*	*Sources*	*Deficiency Symptoms*
1.	A	Retinol	Ripe, mango, papaya, carrot	Xeropthailmia
2.	B_1	Thiamin	Fish (Trout), Pork, Sunflower seed, bread, green peas.	Beriberi
3.	B_2	Riboflavin	Cheese, almonds, beef, boiled eggs, mushrooms, spinach.	Nose and lips, skin cracking
4.	B_3	Niacin/Nicotanamide	Fish, peanuts, green peas	Whiteness of hair.
5.	B_5	Pantathonic acid	Mushrooms, banana, avocados, eggs.	Whiteness of hair
6.	B_6	Pyridoxine	Sunflower seed, pistachio seed, fish, banana.	Mouth corner, skin cracking
7.	B_7	Biotin	Barley, brewer's yeast, fish	Paralysis, body pain, hair fall
8.	B_9	Folic acid	Beans, lentil, spinach, lettuce, asparagus, orange, broccoli	Anaemia, digestive problem

9.	B_{12}	Cynocobalmin	Shelfish, beef (liver), all bran skim milk	Pernicious anaemia
10.	C	Ascorbic acid	Pepper, guava, kiwifruit, cirtus, tomatoes, peas.	Scurvy, collagen
11.	D	Calciferol	Cod liver oil, Salmon, raw, milk, caviar, eggs, mushrooms	Rickets (children) Austiomletia (young/adult)
12.	E	Tocopherol	Leafy vegetables, nuts, sun-flower seed, avocado, broccoli, kiwi fruit	Sterility
13.	K	Filoquinon	Green leafy vegetables, Salad, Chilli powder, asparagus, soy-bean, olive oil.	Non coagulation of blood

(*Source* : Kalia M and Sood S. 2008)

- Sugar percentages in following—
  (1) Cereal – 70-75% (2) Sugar – 100% (3) Jaggery – 95%.
- Flatulence sugar high in soybean and low in greengram.
- 1 molecule of palmitic acid releases 131 ATP.
- Removal of amino acid is called Deamination.
- Transamination means exchange/transfer of amino acid with keto (acceptor) and amino acid (donor).
- End product of proteins is Urea.
- Every protein contains about 13-19% nitrogen.
- Availability of protein in pulses is found by multiplication of determined nitrogen content to 6.25 while in cereals it is 5.25/5.80.
- Auxitocin, insulin and pesifricin hormones are protein in nature.

Protein % in important food materials:

S.No.	*Particulars*	*Protein %*	*Category*
1.	Amaranthus (pseudo cereal)	15	Incomplete protein
2.	Cereals	7-12	–do–
3.	Pulses	20-28	–do–
4.	Oilseeds	16-22	–do–
5.	Milk	3-4	Complete protein
6.	Fish/meat	18-20	–do–
7.	Egg	12-14	–do–

(*Source* : Kalia M and Sood S. 2008)

Acids as per availability of carbon atoms:

S.No.	*Carbon atoms*	*Name*	*Formula*
1.	1C	Formic acid	HCOOH
2.	2C	Acetic ácid	CH_3COOH
3.	3C	Propunic acid	NH_2 CH_3CH_2COOH
4.	4C	Butyric acid	$CH_3(CH_2)_2COOH$
5.	5C	Pentathoni acid	$CH_3(CH_2)_3COOH$

(*Source* : Kalia M and Sood S. 2008)

- Double charged molecules are called Jeuter ions viz. + and – (positive and negative).
- Acidic and alkali behaviour/nature of protein/amino acid called amphoteric nature.
- Glycine (α amino acid) neither D nor L configuration presents.
- **Aromatic amino acids are:**
- 1. Tryptophene
  2. Tyrosine β parahydroxy α amino propionic acid
  3. Histidine 4 – imidizole α amino propionic acid
  4. Phenylalini – β phenyl α amino propionic acid
- Molecular weight is the major thing in soap making more molecular weight means more soap production.
- When oil is boiled many times it produces furfural derivatives.
- Linolic, orchidonic and linolinic acids are essential fatty acid which are not synthesized by human body.
- Essential amino acids are 10 for child (8 + 1 argenin + 1 histedine) and 8 for adults.
- In blood Fe (haemo) and protein (globin) are present.

Types of fat:

1. Simple : oils and fats
2. Compound : (*a*) Phospholipids (*b*) Sphingolipids (*c*) Glycolipids (*d*) Sulpholipids
3. ´Waxes.
4. Derived lipids.
5. Lipase promotes breakdown of fat.
6. Enzymatic reaction is faster $10^8 – 10^{11}$ times than non enzymatic reactions.
7. Milard reaction occurs at the rate of low temperetature.
8. Caramelization reaction depends upon type of sugar and is achieved at high temperature at 110 °C or more.

9. MSG (monosodium glutamate) used as intensifier in China and Japan ($C_5H_8NO_4Na$) sodium 2 amino pentanediate.
10. Ceretonin reduces tension/mental stress while smoking increases tension due to check the supply of O_2 to brain.
11. Biochemistry is a Greek word Bio means life Logos means study, Father of agricultural biochemistry – Justus von Lebig.
12. Queen of beverage is Tea (*Cammelia spp.*) family Theaceae/Camaliaceae, origin China important weed of Tea *Imperata cylindrical* (Thatch grass).

- Reducing sugar – sugar capable of reducing the Cu^{2+}, Ag^+ and Ferricynide are called reducing sugar.
- MSG acts as colour retention/stabilizing agent @ 5.0 mg/kg of final product
- Polyphenol oxidase plays central role in processing of black tea.
- Standard free energy change for glucose is 2840 kJ/mol
- Reynolds number is a dimensionless number
- At sea level atmospheric pressure equals to 101.325 kPa
- Liquids with high surface tension values also have high latent heat values
- The thermal conductivity of ice is more than water
- Iodine solution is used to test the presence of starch in the milk.
- The pioneer of UHT (Ultra High Temperature or Ultra Heat Treatment) milk processing was Dr. Harold Burton

  By heating milk above 135°C (275°F) for 2 to 5 seconds.
  - A treatment in which product is heated to a temperature of 135°C to 150°C in continuous flow in a heat exchanger for a sufficient length of time to achieve commercial sterility with an acceptable amount of change in product.
  - UHT milk packaged in a sterile container if not opened has a typical unrefrigerated shelf life of six to nine months.
  - UHT process can cause Maillard browning and change the taste and smell of dairy products.
  - Ultra pasteurization or super pasteurization involves heating milk at temperature above those used for pasteurizatation. Yet below those used for UHT processing. It prevent thermal alteration of sensory properties and extend the shelf life. This milk is processed at 125-138°C for 2-4 seconds.
- Milk is pre-heated before UHT treatment to avoid fouling
- Sterlization refers to complete elimination of all micro-organisms
- Milk plasma is also called skim milk
- Caesin content of milk represent about 80% of milk proteins
- Lactic acid bacteria produce Lactic acid from Lactose

- Milk is an emulsion of fat in water
- Freezing point of milk is – 0.55 °C
- HTST (High Temperature Short Time) pasturization involves heating of milk to 71.5°C for 15 seconds. It is also called continuous process or plate pasturization process.
- Sterilization of milk, heating milk to temperature 115°C for 15 minutes or 145°C for 3 seconds and ensure preservation period of 15 days from date of manufacturing.
- Sterilized Milk show absence of albumin by negative turbidity test.
- **Potato starch and Corn starch:** The gelling and pasting property of starch depends on its amylose content. The greater the percentage of amylose lesser the percentage of amylopectin greater will be its gelling property. On the other hand greater the percentage of amylopectin and lesser the percentage of amylose greater will be its pasting property.

  Potato contain 20-22% amylose and 78% amyloprotein where as corn contains high 55% amylose and in some cases 70-75% and 45% amylopectin. Potato contains greater amount of amylopectin and lesser amylose and forms a paste like mass with water so potato starch is called pasting type. Corn contains greater amount of amylose and lesser amount of amylopectin and it forms a jelly like mass with water so corn starch is called gelling type.

  Corn starch has been found to be suitable in producing polylactide biodegradable polymers of various grades by fermentation process.
- **Difference between starch and cellulose**

  They are both polysaccharide but they differ in respect that starch is composed by α-D(+) glucose units but cellulose is composed of β-D(+) glucose units. *Anabolism catabolism* short notes.
- **Anabolic pathways (Anabolism)** are involved in the biosynthesis reactions involving the formation of complex molecules from simple precursors and endergonic in nature. Building glucose from carbodioxide is example.
- **Catabolic pathways (catabolism)** are involved in the oxidative breakdown of complex molecules to simpler ones with a concomitant release of energy and exergonic in nature. Energy bonds stored is complex molecules such as glucose and fats is released in catabolic pathways.

CHAPTER 3

FOOD ENGINEERING

Food Engineering is a specialized sub field in Agricultural Engineering and is focused on the application of Engineering to the production and distribution of food.

1. Freezing is also used as means of preservation.
2. Viscometer is used for evaluating the flow characteristics of fluid.
3. The density of one substance in relation to the density of another material (*e.g.* water) is known as specific gravity, S.G. of milk is 1.032 at 15.5°C.
4. *Types of baking ovens:* -
   1) Internally and externally fired ovens.
   2) Side- flue and similar ovens.
   3) Steam-pipe ovens or steam-tube ovens.
   4) Hot air ovens.
   5) Peelend drawplate ovens.
   6) Vienna ovens, Vienna bread
   7) Adapting an ordinary oven for baking
   8) Travelling ovens
5. *Irradiation:* 1) *Low dose*- for insect infestation and sprout inhibition.
   2) *Medium dose*- reduction of microbial load.
   3) *High dose*- treatment to attain sterilization.
6. In Radiation absorption the Gray (Gy, SI Unit) is used as a unit of the radiation quantity absorbed dose which measures the energy deposited by ionizing radiation in a unit mass of matter being irradiated.
7. Gauges used in the base steel for containers are generally in the range of 0.125 mm to 0.3 mm.
8. Slow/sharp freezing is done at (–) 4°C to (–) 29°C for 3-72 hours.
9. Quick freezing is done at (–) 32°C to (–) 40°C.
10. Dehydro freezing – drying the food to about 50% of its volume or weight.
11. Bananas suffer from chilling injury at temperature lower than 12°C. The suitable temperatures are 13±1°C for storage.
12. Lyophilisation is a dehydration process typically used to preserve a perishable material or make the material more convenient for transport.

13. Freeze-drying-technically known as lyophilisation, lyophilisation or cryodesiccation.
14. *Sautéing*: -Cooking in just enough oil to cover the base of the pan is sautéing (conduction).
15. Simmering is the process when foods are cooked in water at a temperature below the boiling point (82-99°C) on low flame. The pan is covered at all times with a well fitted lid. This retains the steam formed within as well.
16. *Braising*:- fry (food) lightly and stew it slowly in a closed container.
17. Radioactive foods are those that have become accidentally contaminated by radioactive substances from weapons testing or nuclear reactor accidents. This type of contamination is totally unrelated to irradiated food which has been processed for preservation and other purposes.
18. Irradiated foods are those that have been deliberately processed with certain types of radiation energy to bring about some desirable properties (for example, to inhibit sprouting or to destroy food-poisoning bacteria).
19. Food treated by irradiation or traditional pasteurization must be handled, packaged, and stored following good manufacturing practices (GMPs).
20. Under hypobaric storage, when gas is in equilibrium with its surroundings, the diffusivity increase by ten folds and concentration gradient decreases to one-tenth.
21. Kneading discs are employed along the screw to decrease mechanical energy.
22. 1 Ton of refrigeration is the capacity of unit to change the temperature by 1°C in 24 hr. 1 ton = 3.516 kW
23. Heat required for 1°C temperature change of any matter with volume is 1 kg (Specific heat).
24. Microwaves are reflected by glass.
25. There are three types of deformation recognized in rheology viz. Elastic, viscous and plastic.
26. Dehydrated vegetable powder spoilage is due to Non-Enzymatic browning.
27. A nanometer is equal to 10^{-9} m
28. Process that prevents the loss of flavouring compounds is freezing.
29. The angle of repose is the angle formed by an inclined plane and the horizontal when a body is put on it and is about to slide downward and it is 23-28 in wheat.
30. 10 °C will be in °F – (50) °F.
31. Orange juice is concentrated by *Evaporation.*
32. Leaf products from plant are dryed by belt dryers.
33. Microorganisms are also used in preservation of food products.
34. Refrigerator and mixer grinder are the motor driven appliances.
35. Dry grinding of whole spices is achieved by grinding jar operated at a speed of more than 17,000 rpm.
36. *Fat bloom* is delayed by sorbitan acetate.

    Fat bloom is caused by changes in fat crystals in chocolates.

    Sugar bloom is due to crystals formed by the action of moisture on the sugar.
37. Mango will have chilling injury if stored at 55 °F (12·8°C)

38. Yeast serves as leavening agent in bread production by formation of gases through heat treatment.
39. First canning was done by- Nicholas Appert.
40. All enzymes are inactivated by temperature above 80°C.
41. Sterilization of foods in hermetically sealed containers by irradiation is called *Radappertizing*.
42. Supercritical fluid extraction process is based on diffusion.
43. Heating of foods for preserving is known as *processing*.
44. Extrusion cooking is a HTST process.
45. Longer exhausting of can at 79 °C gives better results than a short one at above 87 °C.
46. In modern food processing, nutrients losses are seldom in excess of 25%.
47. The freezing point of milk is always lower than water.
48. The generic term that include heating by both microwave and radio frequency energy is called *dielectric heating*.
49. The transfer of heat by electromagnetic waves is done by radiation.
50. Direct electrical heating of foods is accomplished by Ohmic heating.
51. Air blast freezers typically are operated at temperatures of – 30 to – 45 °C.
52. Pressurized packed foods are called *aerosols*.
53. The lethal rate is reciprocal of thermal death time.
54. Aseptic canning is based on high temperature and more time.
55. Storage of food under reduced pressure is called hypobaric storage.
56. Major source of antifreeze protein is fish.
57. Air blasts freezers typically are operated with force of air velocities of 10- 15 m/s.
58. Minimal heat treatment of market milk at 62.8 °C is for 30 min.
59. In slow freezing Crystal size is big.
60. For the low acid foods 3 min. is usually taken as the minimum processing goal.
61. In canned fruit, major function of syrup is conduction of heat.
62. Freeze crack is seen when foods are frozen to Cryogenic freezing.
63. Thermophiles are destroyed in the processing of sugar by a combination of heat and H_2O_2.
64. The boiling of water will lead to disinfection of water.
65. Most effective preservative of canned foods is *tylosin* $C_{46}H_{77}NO_{15}$.
66. Phenomena play an important role in preservation of jam and jellies is *gelatinization*.
67. Effectiveness is opposing factor in screening operations.
68. Hydrophilic solids are unfloatable.
69. Rate of filtration is maximum at early stage.

70. The vacuum filters are limited to maximum filtering pressure of one bar.
71. Use of filter aid is to increase the filtering efficiency.
72. Rotary drum filters are used for filtration of large quantities of free filtering material.
73. The separation of solids from suspension in liquid by gravity alone is called as *Sedimentation*.
74. Turbines are very effective impellers over a wide range of viscosities.
75. Axial flow, high speed impeller is nothing but a propeller.
76. Baffles are used to improve the rate of mixing and to minimize vortex formation.
77. The equipment in sedimentation process is being carried out is called thickeners.
78. Fluid consists of gases and that area subset of the phases of matter and include liquids, gases, plasmas and to some critical plastic solid.
79. The viscosity of hydrogen increases with temperatures.
80. Density is parameter of compressible fluids is sensitive to temperature and pressure.
81. Tomato ketchup is good example of non Newtonian fluid and pseudoplastic.
82. 1 atmospheric pressure is equal to 1.03 kgf / cm^2.
83. Manometer is a simple device for measuring pressure differences.
84. At critical moisture content constant rate period ends and falling rate period starts.
85. Tray dryer is commonly used for wet filter cakes and wet lumply solids.
86. Drying by direct contact with a heated surface is called *conduction*.
87. Drying by heated air is called as *convection*.
88. Heat flow mechanism through solids is called *conduction*.
89. SI unit of thermal conductivity is W / Km.
90. Materials of very low thermal conductivity values are called *heat insulators*.
92. Radappertisation is sterilization of food by high dose of irradiation for destruction of all microorganisms.
93. Air blasts freezers typically are operated with force air velocities of 10 – 15 m/s.
94. Minimal heat treatment of market milk at 62.8 °C is for 30 minutes
95. Standardized milk should contain a minimum of 4.5% fat and 8.5% SNF.
96. Toned milk should contain a minimum of 3.0% fat and 8.5% SNF.
97. Double toned milk should contain a minimum of 1.5% fat and 9.0% SNF.
98. Glycol is being used in immersion freezing.
99. pH, moisture and oxidation-reduction potential are the intrinsic factors for the microbial growth.
100. Thermophiles are destroyed in the processing of sugar by a combination of heat and - H_2O_2.
101. Ammonia refrigerant is commonly used in cold storage in our country.
102. Father of modern refrigeration is James Harrison (1851).

103. Hydro cooling is a rapid precooling method.
104. In cucumber, chilling injury symptoms are occurred at < 7°C.
105. Loss of weight represents loss of water is the operating principle behind oven drying for determining moisture content of foods.
106. Industrial processing method is most effective for making dried potato flakes in drum drying.
107. Pasteurization involves heating foods at high temperatures for short periods of time in order to reduce the risk of food poisoning.
108. Appertization or canning was the first attempt for preservation of food via heat processing.
109. Pasteurization of milk generally destroys most of the pathogenic bacteria.
110. Equilibrium moisture content is the moisture content remaining in the dry material when drying rate drops to 0 at specified conditions.
111. Molecular diffusion is the transfer of the mass caused by random movement of molecules.
112. Important application of mass transfer to food system includes moisture transfer, diffusion in porous foods, diffusion of solutes and diffusion of aroma compounds.
113. Extraction, distillation, gas absorption, crystallization and food packaging are associated with mass transfer in foods.
114. Electrical conductivity of foods generally exhibits a linear increase with temperature.
115. Flash 18 is related to thermal processing of canned foods.
116. D_{250} value is number of minutes at 250°F to accomplish 1 log cycle reduction.
117. The difference in equilibrium moisture content between adsorption and desorption curves is called hysteresis.
118. Hysteresis is generally observed in hygroscopic products.
119. Water activity is the ratio of vapor pressure of water in food and vapor pressure of pure water.
120. At equilibrium condition, the water activity of the food is equal to relative humidity.
121. The process of water gain is termed adsorption and that of water loss is termed desorption.
122. The amount of water absorbed generally decreases with increase in temperature.
123. Dilatometry was one of the earlier methods used to find glass transition temperature by measuring change in volumetric thermal expansion coefficient.
124. Glass transition temperature can be determined by using dilatometry, dynamic thermal mechanical analysis (DMTA) and differential scanning calorimetry.
125. Porosity is defined as the ratio of empty space volume of food materials to total volume.
126. Shrinkage is defined as the relative volume change to the original volume.
127. Pick's law is often used to describe a moisture diffusion process.
128. The first step in sizing a spray drier is the determination of the droplet size.
129. In freeze drying, the product is frozen and the frozen water is removed by sublimation under vacuum.

130. Industrial freeze driers are of two types: tray freeze drier and tunnel freeze drier.
131. Membrane processing of foods includes reverse osmosis, nano filtration, ultra filtration and microfiltration.
132. Membrane fouling restricts the large scale use of membrane technology in food industry.
133. Membrane processing is generally used in beverage industry.
134. Physical type evaporators include short tube evaporator, long tube vertical rising film evaporator, long tube vertical falling film evaporator, forced circulation evaporator, scraped surface thin film evaporator, plate evaporator and thin film spinning cone evaporator.
135. The energy input into an MVR (Mechanical Vapour Recompression) evaporator is altered by fan speed.
136. Freezing times are basic design criteria for freezing substances.
137. Planck's equation can be used for determination of freezing time.
138. Freezing systems are of two types: direct contact and indirect contact.
139. Types of heat exchangers are: tubular heat exchanger, triple tube heat exchanger, plate heat exchanger and scraped surface heat exchangers.
140. Flow of granular solid is affected by gravitational force, friction, cohesion and adhesion.
141. Friction factor represents the ratio of pressure drop to the viscous energy.
142. Polymorphism is the existence of number of alternative crystal structures and can be studied by dilatometry, temperature controlled X rays diffraction, NMR and DSC techniques.
143. The best way of preserving pure fruit juice is by freezing.
144. The 1000 grain weight is a good indicator of the grain size, which can vary relative to growing conditions and maturity.
145. The bulk density of cereal grains is determined by measuring the weight of a grain sample of known volume.
146. Parboiling is a hydrothermal treatment followed by drying before milling for the production of milled parboiled grain.
147. Hardness is related to the degree of adhesion between the starch granules and surrounding protein.
148. Microoganisms are most dominant cause of food deterioration and can be eliminated by heat treatment.

IMPORTANT POINTS

- Freezing was given by Clarence Bridseye in the year 1930.
- An extruder is thermodynamic unit and it is of two types one is Single screw extruder and another is Twin screw extruder.
- The flow of extruder is of three types — (1) Drag flow (2) Pressure flow (3) Leakage flow.
- Meat and fish products are ideally stored in modified atmosphere viz. Hypobaric storage.

- Blanchers are mainly of two types first one is Steam blanchers second one is Hot water blancher.
- **Pasteurization** — @ 63-65 °C for 30 minutes LTLT.
  @ 72 °C for 15 seconds HTST
  @ 85-90 °C for 1-4 seconds flash heating (UHT)
- **Parboiling of paddy**—
  (a) Steeping of paddy in hot water at the rate of 54.4-65.6°C for 9-12 hrs.
  (b) Steaming at the rate of 110-118.3°C for 8-12 hrs.
  (c) Drying till 11-13% moisture level.
- **Homogenization of milk:** Process of forcing milk through a homogenizer to prevent creaming or the rising of fat to top of container.
- **Clean-In-Place :** CIP cleaning, also referred to as Clean-In-Place cleaning, is a procedure of cleaning interior product contact surfaces such as process pipes, vessels and equipment, without disassembly. Typical food and beverage applications cleaned using an automated CIP system are product transfer lines, processing tanks, homogenizers, mixers, blenders and fillers.
- **Cleaning-Out-of-Place (COP)** is a method used when parts cannot be cleaned-in-place and must be disassembled from the process. Typical process parts cleaned-out-of-place in parts washers and cabinet washers include hoses, clamps, fittings, scale buckets and other disassembled process components.
- **'Best before' date:** This is a system of marking food products with a specific date before which the food will retain its original quality or 'shelf life'. The system is generally applied to low risk foods, some of which have long shelf-lives, such as canned goods, drinks, biscuits and other dry products.
- **Freeze drying:** Is also known as lyophillization is a low temperature dehydration process that involves, freezing the product and lowering pressure and removing the ice by sublimation.
- **Accelerated freeze drying:** This is a process of food dehydration for certain foods such as peas, prawns and coffee. The process involves placing prepared pieces of quick-frozen food under vacuum and gently heating.
- **Deep freeze:** This is the process of storing a range of foods at –18°C and below at which the growth of many micro-organisms is virtually reduced and the shelf life greatly increased.

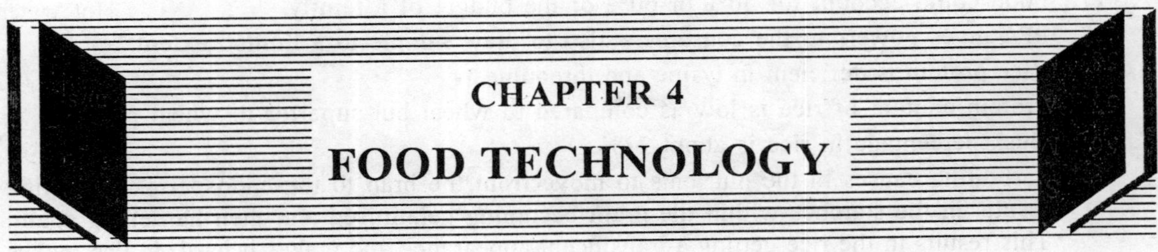

1. **Food Science:** It has been defined by 'Margaret (1968)' as the application of the physical, biological and behavioural science to the processing and marketing of foods.
2. **Food Technology:** It can be defined as the science dealing with the knowledge of doing things efficiently and effectively.

or

3. Food Technology deals with engineering and other scientific and technical problems involved in transforming edible raw materials and other ingredients into safe, nutritious and appetizing food products (Desrosier, 1977).
4. **Solubility:** the amount of solute that can be dissolved in given amount of solvent at a given temperature is expressed as solubility.
5. Sodium chloride or calcium chloride depresses temperature of water. 29 parts of salt to 71 parts of ice (Saturated salt solution) gives a freezing mixture with a temperature of – 21°C and used as medium for making homemade ice cream.
6. A food additive is a substance or a mixture of substance, other than a basic food stuff, which is present in a food as a result of any aspect of production, processing, storage, packing or flavours.
7. Sodium benzoate is used in soft drinks and acidic foods.
8. Butylated hydroxyl anisole (BHA), butylated hydroxyl tolune (BHT), propyl gallate, nordihydro guiaretic acid (NDGA), tocopherols and ascorbic acid are important antioxidants.
9. Benzyle peroxide is an oxidizing agent which is used in bleaching of flour to retaining yellow colour.
10. Presently there are about more than 1200 different flavouring agents available.
11. Flavour enhancer or potentiators are compounds which do not have flavour but intensify the flavour of other compounds present in foods *e.g.* MSG, 5-nucleotides.
12. Annatto, caramel, carotene and saffron are the best examples of natural food colour.
13. Inorganic materials such as iron oxide is used to give redness and titanium dioxide to intensify whiteness.
14. In India 12 natural pigments and 11 synthetic dyes are permitted to be added in foods.
15. Four natural sources of pigments: 1. Betalains provide red to yellow colour, 2. Chlorophyl gives green, 3. Anthocyanin infuses purple, 4. Carotenoids provide yellow to orange.
16. Rice is a processed food while wheat, maize, apple, plantain, yam etc. are primary foods.

17. Food could account for 50% or 60% of the budget of a family.
18. PFA gives powers to the consumers also to draw sample to a limited extent.
19. Rice protein is deficient in lysine and threonine.
20. Protein content of rice is low as compared to wheat but superior to wheat protein.
21. Husk percentage in rice is about 21%.
22. Parboiling causes in the nutrients to move from the bran to the endosperm. Parboiling results in the starches within the grain becoming gelatinised and then hardening again. This results in the rice getting a translucent appearance and makes it hard. It also makes the cooked rice firmer and less sticky resulting in grains being distinct and separate. Parboiled rice has proven to have better food value.
23. CFTRI method of parboiling needs 3-4 hrs at 65-70°C (water).
24. Rice bran contains 15% oil and it is rich source of òleic and linoleic acids (unsaturated fatty acid).
25. Hard wheat has more gluten than soft wheat.
26. For wheat popcorn expansion volume is the most critical quality factor.
27. Popping occurs at about 177°C (2.5 tonnes/cm^2) stream pressure inside the kernel.
28. Sorghum protein is superior to wheat protein in biological value and digestibility.
29. Phytin is a major factor for the poor digestibility of grain in millets (pearl millet).
30. Ragi malt is malted finger millet; or flavor. It is healthy and delicious drink.
31. Ragi malt is malted finger millet or flavour. It is healthy and delicious drive.
32. Dhokla is popular in North India while dosa, idli, uthappam are popular in south India.
33. Flint corn, dent corn, sweet corn, popcorn, flour corn and waxy corn are principal varieties of maize.
34. Generally canned corn is sweet corn.
35. At pouring syrup or brine, temperature should be 79- 82°C and 0.32cm to 0.47cm is left head space in the can.
36. Generally heat exhausts method is used in the case of cans.
37. Processing in canning refers heating or cooling of canned foods to inactivate bacteria.
38. After processing containers are cooled quickly to prevent over cooking.
39. 1-2 ppm chlorine is used as sterilizer in cool water.
40. Add an equal quantity of sugar by weight in sour fruits and ¾ in sweeter varieties.
41. In citrus juice sulphur dioxide is added at 200- 300ppm (sugar upto 35- 50%).
42. 13.61-18.14 kg at 10°C CO_2 added in carbonization.
43. RTS (Ready to serve) formulated by Ahmed (1996).
44. Concentration by freezing was first applied to fruit juices by Gore (1914). It doesn't loose volatile flavours and aroma.
45. Concentration in vacuum evaporators destroys volatile flavouring materials.
46. Sodium benzoate is a preservative added in ketchup to increase storage life.
47. Pickling is preservation of fruits and vegetables in common salt or in vinegar.
48. Physical methods of preservation includes by removal of heat (by cold), by addition of heat (thermal processing), by removal of water (evaporation or dehydration) and by irradiation

while chemical methods includes by addition of acids, by salting/brining by addition of sugar and heating by addition of chemical preservatives and by fermentation.

49. Potassium metabisulphite or sodium benzoates are used as preservatives in squashes.
50. Orange contains vitamin B_1.
51. *Coffea arabica* is indigenous to Ethiopia and introduced to India through Arabia.
52. Roasting of coffee resulting increase of formic and acetic acid while chlogenic and other acids like citric and malic acids are destroyed.
53. Roasting also results the pH of coffee brew comes down.
54. Bitterness of coffee beverage is due to tannins viz polyphenolic substance.
55. Pouring boiling water on the coffee powder is permissible.
56. The plant part chicory is used as substitute for coffee is root.
57. Commercially mainly 3 forms of tea are there black tea, green tea and oolong/red tea.
58. Polyphenols present in tea leaves are *catechins* and *glallocatechins*.
59. Enzymes involved in fermentation of tea are polyphenol oxidase.
60. Cocoa powder is highly prized as nutritious beverage.
61. Nibs are cotyledons of the cocoa.
62. Cocoa contains cocoa butter/fat is about 50-55%.
63. Cocoa is the natural source of *theobromine* and contain about 2-3% by weight.
64. Active ingredient in Asafoetida (hing) is alkyl dysulphides (imported from Iran and Afghanistan).
65. Thymol presents in Bishops seeds (ajowan, omum).
66. Caper (kobra, mullukatari) contains rutic acid and saponin.
67. Carvone (Terpenoids) presents in caraway seeds (shiajeera, seemai, shembu), which is smaller than jeera.
68. Cineol, borneol and camphor are present in cardamom (choti elaichi, yelakki).
69. Percentage of capsaicin in chillies is about 2%.
70. Cinnamon bark (dalchini, lavang patti) contains *cinnamaldehyde*.
71. Cinnamon leaves (tejpat, talisupatri) contains Eugenol active ingredient.
72. Coriander leaf, seed and entire plant contains decylaldehyde.
73. Cumin (white jeera) contains cinnamaldehyde while kalunji (black jeera) contains carvone and limonene.
74. Betel leaf contains chavicol.
75. CIMAP stands for Central Institute of Medicinal and Aromatic plants at Lucknow founded in 1959.
76. Kokam/Kokum (*Garcinia cambogia*) Fruit Extract Enhances keeping quality of fresh fish, garlic and that of pork.
77. Sugarcane contains 12-15% sugar (sucrose, glucose and fructose).
78. pH of cane juice is acidic viz 5.0-5.4.
79. Thiamine, riboflavin, niacin, pantothemic acid, biotin and vitamin D are present in cane.
80. Sugar is mainly of three types' Raw sugar, Refined sugar and White sugar.
81. Glucose and fructose crystallize more slowly than sucrose due to invert sugar.
82. Temperature of caramillization is 118-120°C.
83. Rhodamine B and Metanil yellow are permitted food colours.

84. Moisture in mysore pak, shone papadi is less than 3%, pedha, barfi, jalebi contains 10-20% while rasogolla and shrikhand have more than 20%.
85. Chikki contains about 10-12% protein which help to fight malnutrition and shelf life of it, is about 8-12 weeks.
86. Fructose in high fructose syrup is about 42% and it is twice sweetening power than glucose.
87. Maple syrup is obtained by evaporating the sap of the maple tree (*Acer saccharum*).
88. Honey contains 38% fructose and 31% glucose.
89. For biscuits and cakes wheat flour with low protein content is desirable while for breads, flours should have high protein content.
90. Na_2CO_3 is chemical formula of baking soda.
91. Sodium chloride, pen sulphates, potassium bromate, phosphates, lime water and organic acids (lactic and succinic acids) are bread improver.
92. Science of formation and deformation of dough is called rheology.
    Rhelogoical properties of dough, and gluten during mixing are affected greatly by flour composition and ingredients (water, salt, yeast, fat and emulsions and low or high protein content) processing parameters are (mixing time, energy, temperature).
    - Kneading involves stretching and folding the dough in a rhythmical manner that develops the gluten in dough and relaxes excess gases.
    - Omission of salt in dough leads to a significant reduction in dough and bread quality and also sensory attributes of bread, where the bread is described as sour/acidic and yeasty flavor. Sodium chloride have strengthening or tightening effect on the gluten during mixing salt must be added in early stage of dough mixing to give maximum dissolution time and accelerate gluten formation, tighten the dough and increase the mixing time.
93. Extrusion meters measures the amount of force requires to extrude the dough.
94. Batter is a homogenous mixture of ingredients with liquid to make a mass that is of a soft plastic character.
95. Hearth is the heated baking surface of the flour of an oven.
96. Plasticity is property where material does not regain its original form even after force removal while in elasticity shape/form is regained after removal of force.
97. Troughs are large containers for holding large masses of raising dough.
98. Baking process involves all three types of heat transfer viz conduction, convection and radiation.
99. Flour, eggs and milk are ingredients that provide structure to cake while sugar, shortening and baking powder make it tender.
100. A cookie contains less amount of liquid as compared to cake and more amount of fat, egg and leavening agents.
101. Microwaves penetrate food to a depth of 2.5-7.5 cm.
102. Cooking is the process of subjecting foods to the action of heat.
103. **Results of cooking:** - 1. Improves the taste and food quality 2. Destruction of microorganisms 3. Improves digestibility 4. Increases variety 5. Increases consumption of food 6. Increases availability of nutrients 7. Increases antioxidant value 8. Concentrates nutrients 9. Pesticide residue minimization.

104. About 70-80% of pesticides residues are removed by cold water washing.

105. The green leafy vegetables must be washed with 2 percent salt water in a large bowl.

Dough is a viscoelastic material which behave as both liquid and solid. It exhibit a viscous fluid likes when force is applied to it by emission (fluid lives and an elastic solid likes).

106. **Terms under cutting:-**

i) Cut - To divide into pieces or to shape with knife

ii) Chop - To cut into specified shape

ii) Mince - To chop very fine

iv) Dice - To cut into small uniform cubes

v) Slice - To cut into uniform slices.

vi) Grate - To cut finely with a grater.

107. Marinating is soaking a food in a marinade to add flavour to tenderize it or both.

108. There is less chance for burning and scorching or overcooking in waterless cooking.

109. Water molecules vibrate in food 2450 million times a second in microwave cooking.

110. In wheat most of the B vitamins in the grain are present in the scutellum.

111. Crude fibre and soluble carbohydrates are the two carbohydrates present in cereals.

112. Cereals contain potassium, magnesium and calcium about 95% out of all minerals.

113. Parboiled rice contains B vitamin more than raw polished rice.

114. The tip of each kernel is covered by stiff hairs called the brush.

115. Disodium phosphate enables the starch to gelatinise faster and increases alkalinity.

116. ARF (Amylase Rich Food) is rich in enzyme alpha-amylase.

117. Wheat contains glutamic acid and mono sodium glutamate is its familiar compound.

118. Release of glucose in blood by carbohydrates is called *glycemic index*.

119. **Insulin Index:** represents how much the food ingested elevates the concentration of insulin in the blood during the 2 hour period after the food is ingested.

120. Rice proteins are rich in glutamic acid (precursor for glutamine) and *arginine*.

121. Stickiness in fresh rice is due to alpha amylase while it is inactivated during storage and cooked grains get separated easily.

121a. Glycemic index of pulses is low while for cereals it is high (due to fibre) and lowers blood sugar.

122. Anthocyanins and carotenoids pigments are present in coloured rice.

123. Parboiling involves steeping, steaming and drying steps.

124. Acetyl 1-1pyrroline aromatic compound which is responsible for aroma in rice.

125. *Pandanus latifolius* leaves contain 2-acetyl 1-1 pyrrole which may be added to non aromatic rice varieties which smells like basmati.

126. Protein percentage in rye is about 12% while in cereals its range is 6-12%.
127. Paste is result of wet milling while flour/grit is result of dry milling.
128. Iron, thiamine, riboflavin and niacin are rich in bajra.
129. As quinoa (*chenopodium quinoa*) for edible seeds has quantity of lysine, cysteine and methionine amino acids.
130. FAO declared quinoa (*Chenopodium quinoa*) as food in the year 2013.
131. Absence of amylase in the starch does not form a opaque gel while it is possible in case of amylopectin.
132. Cooled and stored starch becoming less soluble like in its original state is called retro gradation.
133. Hard and brittle chapattis on storage are *e.g.* of above.
134. Changes due to dry heat in granules of starch are known as dextrinisation.
135. Pita bread is an Arabian food.
136. Pita bread, bhatura, idli, dosa, appam, kali, bread, biscuit and dhokla are fermented foods.
137. Cake, cooked rice and chapattis are unfermented food.

$$\text{Swelling number: } \frac{\text{Volume of cooked rice}}{\text{Volume of uncooked rice}}$$

138. The sugar escapes digestion due to lack of α-galactosidase activity and digested by micro flora of the lower intestinal tract resulting in the production of large amount of carbon dioxide, hydrogen and small amount of methane.
139. Red gram is deficient in tryptophan.
140. 8 parts cereals and 1 part of pulses gives a protein quality equivalent to animal protein.
141. Germinated legumes contain some extent of vitamin C
142. Flatulence is generated by swallowed air, digestion and high fibre foods
143. Flatulence is produced by oligosaccharides.
144. Human intestinal mucosa does not contain α-galactosidase, which help to cleave the α-(1-6) galactose linkage.
145. β-N- oxalyl-L- α, β diamine propionic acid the neurotoxin responsible for lathyrism present in lathyrus.
146. Hard water contains chlorides and sulphates of calcium and magnesium salts and take long time to get cooked.
147. Sodium bicarbonate softens the cellulose and hastens cooking.
148. Phytates, tannins and saponins are antinutrients present in pulses.
149. Galactomannan polysaccharide reduces plasma cholesterol in hyper cholesterolemic men which is present in cluster bean.
150. Black gram contains α-linolenic acids which lowers cholestrol.

151. Nuts reduce total and LDL (bad) cholestrol without affecting the levels of HDL (good) cholesterol.

152. Nuts are good source of Si, K, Fe, Mn, Cu, Mg, P and Zn.

153. Phytochemicals in nuts include ellagic acid, flavonoids, phenolic compounds, luetolin (a major antioxidant) and tocotrienols.

154. The major proteins of groundnut are arachin and aonarachin-II.

155. Resveratrol is a naturally occurring antioxidant present in the pink skin of conarachin.

156. Tofu contains 7.8% proteins.

157. Textural vegetables protein (TVP).

158. The fermenting agent using to make Temph is *Rhizopus oligoporus*.

159. *Bacillus subtilis* is inoculated to make Natto.

160. *Aspergillus oryzae* helps in making of soya sauce.

161. Soya sauce is an excellent preserving agent in pickles and preserved foods due to presence of salt and minerals.

162. Soya flour in breads improves water binding capacity as well as colour.

163. Cooking soybean in their pods in boiling salted water is Edamame. It is Japans favourite and used as appetiser.

164. Antioxidant melatonin is presents in walnut.

165. Soybeans are rich in isoflavones like genistein and diadzein which protect against cancer, heart disease and osteoporosis.

166. Seasmol is present in sesame which has superior oxidative stability.

167. Regular consumption of Aflatoxin is linked to liver cancer.

168. Various cutting styles
- Julienne (Matchstick) - cut to 3 × 2.5 mm thin strips. (carrots, julienne, celery or potatoes)
- Brunoise - 2 mm dice. (carrot, celery and turnips)
- Jardinere - Long and thick baton 2 × 2 × 15 mm.
- Spiral - long thin spiral strips.
- Macedoine (large dice) - 5 mm dice.

169. In foam mat drying liquid food is converted to a stable foam through the addition of a stabilizer to the liquid. The foam is rapidly dried in air.

170. Cutting makes the food smaller in size which increases the surface area. This results in greater loss of nutrients from food.

171. Food is coated with dry ingredients like flour bread crumbs or powders called Dredging.

172. The food is first coated (dredged) with a layer of flour. Then it is dipped in egg mixture, which binds the flow layer to the food and gives a smooth feel is called Breading.

173. Marination is the process of dipping foods in a paste called marinade made from flavouring agents, curd, oil, ginger-garlic-onion paste, spices and salt so that these infuse into the food.

174. The basic formula of carbohydrates is $C_nH_2O_n$
175. Sucrose C_nH_2O (n-1) (have one less oxygen).
176. Amino acids are compounds containing carbon, hydrogen, nitrogen, and sometimes sulphur.
177. Cholesterol is a sterol compound made by animals and is used to make certain steroid hormones in the body. It is not found in plants.
178. A homogenous mixture, there by the solute molecules (dissolved substances) are dispersed uniformly throughout the solvent molecules (medium) is solution.
179. Solubility is the amount of solute that can dissolve in a given amount of solvent at given temperature.
180. Vapour pressure is the pressure exerted by the vapour molecules above the liquid in a state of equilibrium.
181. Boiling point is the temperature at which the vapour pressure of the liquid equals the pressure surrounding the liquid.
182. The temperature at which the liquid changes state from liquid to a solid is freezing point (water 0°C/32°F). (Milk 0.53°C).
183. The property of a fluid that resists the force tending to cause the fluid to flow is termed as viscosity.
184. *Newtonian foods*: -These are homogeneous mixture which exhibits no change in viscosity on application of shear. *e.g.*: - water, fruit juice, oil, milk, honey.
185. *Non- Newtonian foods*: - These are heterogeneous mixture which exhibit changes in viscosity with increase in shear *e.g.*: - Tomato paste, mayonnaise, margarine, apple sauce, corn starch suspensions.
186. Cereals whole grains are rich in Vitamin B complex.
187. Parboiling retains the vitamin E in grain.
188. Germ oils are rich in Vitamin E.
189. Wheat proteins are rich in glutamic acid (present in the form of glutamine, an amide) and low in tryptophan.
190. Normal process takes 2-3 days while (CFTRI) hot soaking process takes 3-4 hrs in rice parboiling.
191. Change in colour, odour changes, unpleasant to smell are main disadvantages of parboiling.
192. Whole wheat flour, Refined flour (Maida), Semolina (suji) wheat bran, Amylase rich food (ARF), macaroni products, Bulgur wheat, peeled whole wheat and wheat malt extracts are wheat product (result of milling).
193. Muesli is a mixture of corn flakes, Wheat flakes, Oats and dry fruits are popular food of America and Europe.
194. Rice hull/husk, Rice bran, Rice bran oil, Rice pollard, broken grains, Aromatic rice, puffed rice/parched rice and flaked rice are milled rice products.

195. Tortillas (pronounced tortiya) is a traditional Mexican thin flat bread (resembling the Indian chapatti) made from finely ground wheat flour or corn flour from Mexico, also called Nachos and the prepared dough is called Masa.
196. Nixtamal is the treated corn that is used to make Masa.
197. In bread making propionate inhibits mould growth.
198. Reduction in trypsin inhibits and Phytins are result of fermentation/germination.
199. By increasing fecal extraction of total bile acids dried beans lowers serum lipids.
200. In pulse the undigested carbohydrates like raffinose cause flatulence as they initially escape digestion due to absence of α- galactocidase activity and are later digested by micro flora in lower intestinal tract causing production of carbon dioxide, hydrogen and methane.
201. Pulses contain low fat which is mostly of the unsaturated kind.
202. Pulses have energy – 340 kcal/100g.
203. Germination of pulses reduces tannin up to 25–50%.
204. It decreases about 50-60% of Phytates. Increases riboflavin and niacin content by 70%.
205. Soaking of pulses looses of magnesium and calcium.
206. Raw soybeans contain lipoxidase which oxidises Vitamins A and carotene in food resulting in reduced plasma vitamin A and carotene.
207. The safe limit for cyanide is between 10-20 mg/100 gm. of pulses, normally present within this range in most pulses except lima beans and linseed.
208. Saponins that cause toxic effects are sapotoxins.
209. Tannins are higher in legumes with black and red seed coat rather than those with white seed coat.
210. Heat treatment to the tune of autoclaving at 120°C for 15-30 minutes is capable of inactivating all trypsin inhibiters.
211. Lathyrus dal (Khesari dal) was banned in 1961.
212. Three low toxic varieties of the Khesari dal are mahateora, ratan and prateek.
213. Soy flour packages should clearly state that it has been heat treated.
214. The very large percentage of the population consumes 1150-5750 mg/day which is termed as "hygienic safety range" of sodium intake given by renowned Swedish hypertension expert "Dr. Bjorn Folkow".
215. Salt is sodium chloride by weight it is 40% sodium and 60% chloride.
216. Sodium is an essential nutrient, a mineral that the body cannot manufacture (synthesize) itself.
217. Chloride preserves acid base balance in the body.
218. pH range of high acid food is below 3.7.
219. Sodium benzoate is effective in pH range of 2.5-4.0.
220. Sugar is class I preservative.

221. Eugenol oil in cloves have antimicrobial effect.
222. MSG is used as Flavour Enhancer.
223. Primary aim of blanching fruits is to inactivate the enzyme.
224. Sodium bicarbonate is preferred to retain green colour during blanching.
225. Temperature range of UHT sterilization is 135-150 °C
226. Espresso coffee drink is an Italian traditional drink.
227. Addition of lost nutrients due to processing is called *restoration.*
228. Frozen storage temperature is – 18°C.
229. Highest TSS is in jam.
230. Peeling is essential during ginger processing.
231. Cold sterilization preserves the most of the nutrients.
232. Horticulture produce must be kept in wooden box for transportation.
233. Aeration during storage of grains will give hot spot.
234. Lye peeling solution contains 2% H_2SO_4.
235. Lentil is easily dehusked.
236. Flavouring compound in Onion is Allyl propyl disulphide.
237. Flavouring compound in garlic is Allyl disulphide (Allicin).
238. Tofu is prepared from soybean.
239. Beany flavour in soy products is due to Lypoxinase and isoflavons.
240. Generally most of oilseeds which are legumes contain 40% oil and 20% proteins.
241. Irradiation of foods is done by gamma rays.
242. Dhurrin degrades to form HCN, found 40-50 DAS in sorghum leaves.
243. Starch content of corn 67-70%.
244. Husk content of rice 33%.
245. Kimchi is the Korean dish.
246. Noodles are originated in China.
247. Lowest digestibility of the protein in Maize.
248. Botanical name of the Rice is *Oryza sativa.*
249. Iodine solution is used to test the presence of starch in the milk.
250. Wheat is deficient in Lysine.
251. Father of Canning is Nicolas Appert and he was a confectioner (1749-1841)
252. Rice contains Vitamin A Precurssor Golden Rice.
253. Mango is climateric fruit.
254. Hurdle technology is the best for food preservation.
255. The spread ratio of biscuit and cookies is measured by diameter divided by thickness in mm (AACC, 2000).

256. EDTA is the most common chelating agent used in foods.
257. Old flour is also called Aged flour.
258. Aged flour is often called unbleached flour is aged and bleached by oxygen in the air.
259. In blanching chemical for color retention is sodium bicarbonate.
260. Linseed contains 40-42% oil out of which 50-60% is Linolinic acid.
261. Color agents used in foods are of two types: *natural and synthetic colors*.
262. Chelating agents are not antioxidants as they only serve as scavengers of metals which catalyze oxidation.
263. Wheat milling is done for separation of endosperm bran and germ.
264. Milling type which uses **compressive** and **shearing** forces is **roller mill.**
265. Optimum jelly must contain 0.5-1% acid, 65 brix TSS, 3.2 pH and 0.5-1.0% Pectin.
266. Effective way of processing food is low temp with vacuum (vacuum cooling)
267. Freeze drying consist of two phenomena- 1. Transfer of water vapour from ice surface through, the dried layer, 2. Heat transfer from the exterior to the ice surface.
268. Fumigant used in grain storage is ethylene bromide and aluminium phosphate.
269. In jelly salt is not used.
280. A Jelly is a semi solid.
270. Saffron is obtained from flowers.
271. Kernel weight of good rice is 30-40 mg.
272. Separation of the component of a mixture of 2 or more liquids by differences in their vapor pressure is known as *distillation.*
273. The method commonly employed in the extraction of essential oils from herb and leaf material is *steam distillation.*
274. Liquid preparation consist mainly of essentials oils and resins are *fixative*.
275. Dipsol used for drying chilies is an oil based emulsion (CFTRI method).
276. The main determinant of price of dried chilies is *pungency.*
277. For good quality dried chilies the pods should be partially withered and ripe.
278. The optimum temperature for drying chilies is 55°C.
279. The important constituents of colour and capsaicin are concentrated in pericarp and seeds.
281. A perfect jelly should be transparent.
282. Weeping of Jelly is due to excess acid.
283. Inadequate homogenization for ice-cream mix may result is a texture defect called - *Buttery*
284. TSS is determined by Hand refractometer.
285. Marmalade is made by fruit orange.
286. During storage of marmalade to prevent the browning we should use – Potassium metabisulphite (for colourless fruits).
287. TSS of freshly prepared syrup should be maintained for preservation is 65%.
288. Candy is a product of Fresh fruits.

289. Intermediate moisture food should contain moisture- 30% to 50%.
290. Synthetic drinks should provide energy about 48 kcal.
291. TSS of ready to serve beverages should contain at least 10% juice.
292. Nectar should contains at least fruit juice about 20%. (Nectar are a type of non carbonated soft drink made by muddling the fresh fruits).
293. For making cordial suitable fruit is lime.
294. Squash should contain TSS of about 40-50%.
295. Flame peeling is used only in Garlics.
296. Yellow Fruits are not rich source of Vitamin-B complex.
297. Perishable Fruits have higher percentage of moisture.
298. Wax coating increases the shelf life of the Fruits.
299. Coating of wax on fruits act as a barrier.
300. Harvesting indices plays an important role to maintain the quality of fruits and vegetables.
301. Pre harvest treatment reduces sprouting tuber crops during storage.
302. Post harvest losses of fruits and vegetables in India is about- 30%.
303. The main object of Post Harvest Technology is to reduce the losses.
304. Fruits and Vegetables are classified as body building as well as energy foods.
305. Post Harvest quality and shelflife of fruits and vegetables are controlled by post harvest factor.
306. Peel and pulp colour of citrus fruits and Tomatoes is indicator of maturity Indices.
307. Cultural operation of fruits and vegetables are known as preharvest fact.
308. Pruning increases the fruit size.
309. Vegetables are rich sources of minerals.
310. Fruits are rich sources of vitamins.
311. Adolphus Williamson Green – co-founder of the National Biscuit Company (1898) (the birth of the packaged food industry)
312. Mostly harvesting should be done during morning time.
313. Blanching inactivates polyphenol oxydase enzyme to check the enzymatic browing.
314. During maturity TSS of Grapes should be near about 14-16° Brix.
315. Specific grevity should be maintained during harvesting time of mangoes is 1.
316. Post harvest quality and shelf life of fruits can be controlled by packing.
317. Irrigation should be stopped three weeks before harvesting in tuber crops.
318. Pectin is measured by jell meter.
319. Sodium benzoate is used for preparation of tomato kechup.
320. Canning and bottling is the permanent method of preservation of fruits and vegetables.
321. Edible banana fruit is seedless because of Vegetative parthenocarpy.

322. Wax coating treatments enhances the shelf life of fruits because it blocks respiration.
323. Mango fruit is also referred as 'Bathroom fruit"
324. Lemon fruit is not suitable for jam making.
325. Karonda (Dry) is a rich source of iron.
326. Edible banana is triploid.
327. Refractrometer is used to determine T.S.S. (total soluble solids).
328. Vegetables are canned in brine.
329. Fruits are blanched before canning at 80°C.
330. The edible part of pomegrante is aril.
331. Papaya is rich in Vitamin A.
332. An ideal fruit for making jelly should be rich in pectin and acid.
333. In India, Mango has the highest production in fruits.
334. Agriculture and Processed Products Development Authority (APEDA) came in existence as Act. in 1985 and effective from 1986.
335. Fruit thinning growth regulator is IAA.
336. Ethephon acts as an aid for mechanical harvesting.
337. $KMnO_4$ is ethylene absorbent.
338. Chemical formula of potassium metabisulphite is is $K_2S_2O_7$.
339. Granulation can be reduced by spraying of Urea.
340. Meristem of the plant is considered free from viruses.
341. Tomato puree should have 9% TSS.
342. For many fruits the tartness and flavours are determined by sugar to acid ratio.
343. In controlled atmospheric storage O_2 is used.
344. TSS of Tomato ketchup should not be less than 25%.
345. Strength of brine is being measured by salometer.
346. Potato stored at above 10 °C is preferred for chip making.
347. Pectin content should be optimum for better gel formation in jelly.
348. Chilling injury is most common in banana.
349. Pectin helps in gel formation in jelly.
350. According to FPC specifications a tomato paste must contain 25% TSS.
351. Export variety of mango is Alphanso.
352. In modified atmosphere the potassium permangnate is being used as Ethylene absorber.
353. Hot brine of 1 to 3 % concentration is used for covering of the vegetables.
354. Lye peeling of fruits and vegetables is done in aqueous solution of NaOH 1–2% strength.
355. Polyolefin can be used for increasing the shelf life of citrus fruits.
356. pH range of high acid foods is below 3.7.

357. Canned foods should be stored in the Dry food store..
358. Polystyrene is used for acidic foods.
359. Picowaved is the term used to label foods treated with low level ionizing radiation.
360. Benzoates can be used for the preservation of jam.
361. Potassium benzoate has low acute toxicity upon oral and dermal exposure.
362. Antibiotics like nisin, niacin, pediocins are used in vegetables, fish meat and dairy processing as biopreservatives.
363. Glycol is being used in immersion freezing.
364. Tomato puree should have 9% TSS.
365. Middle lamella of the cell wall is rich in calcium pectate
366. TSS of the fruit syrup is 65%.
367. Avocado fruit is having the highest amount of fat.
368. Catalase accelerates the ripening of climacteric Apple.
369. Preservative used in squash is SO_2.
370. TSS of fruit squash is 40%.
371. Salt acts as preservative in mango pickle.
372. Carbonated beverages are very popular among the large population because of its Thirst quenching nature.
373. Sugar present in jelly should be - 60%-65%
374. In fruit candy, the mode of preservation is osmosis.
375. Golden shreds marmalade is bitter in taste.
376. Maximum solubility of sugar at 20 °C is equal to 67.5%.
377. Prolong fruits are coated by Carboxymethyl cellulose (CMC).
378. Cellars are underground rooms, for the storage of fruits and vegetables.
379. Trehalose sugars are found to be effective coating agent for fruits.
380. Astringency in fruits are found due to the presence of tannins.
381. For the preparation of 6° brix syrup amount of water required to make 100g syrup is 94 g.
382. Moisture content of dehydrated onion should not exceed 8%.
383. pH, Pectin content and sugar content should be optimum for better gel formation in jelly.
384. Barbados cherry is richest source of the vitamin C.
385. Wine made from Barbados cherries in Hawaii was found to retain 60% of the ascorbic acid.
386. Phosphoric acid is used in non fruit beverages.
387. Red colour in chilli is due to *cryptoxanthin.*
388. For the preparation of jam inversion should be not more than 14%.
389. Ethylene increases the rate of *respiration*.

390. The sparkling clear sweetened fruit juice is *cordial.*
391. Yellow orange color in Saffron is due to *crocetin.*
392. A jam should have not less than 68% TSS.
393. Fruit drinks have TSS of 10%.
394. For canning of fruits the syrup strength is of 50 – 60 °Brix.
395. Benzoic acid is more effective against pH 2.5 – 4.0.
396. Propionic acid has found to be much effective to prevent ropiness in bread.
397. Antimicrobial activity of sodium chloride is related to its ability to decrease the water activity
398. In aseptic packaging, preservatives used to sterilize the packaging material is Hydrogen peroxide
399. Phosphoric acid is found in carbonated non alcoholic beverages.
400. Oxidative property of hydrogen peroxide makes it the effective preservative.
401. Tocopherol antioxidants function as an electron donor, metal chelator and oxygen scavenger.
402. Nisin is used as an antimicrobial agent.
403. Natamycin is also called pirmaricin.
404. Sucrose esters are emulsifier and antimicrobial agent.
405. Allicin is Allyl sulphide.
406. Monelin protein is manifold sweeter than sucrose.
407. Calcium stearate is used as an anticaking agent.
408. Sorbitol compound is the polyhydric alcohol.
409. Lecithin is used as emulsifier.
410. Carboxmethyl cellulose is used as stabilizer.
411. Calcium chloride can be used as Firming agent.
412. Sugars, Salt and spices are class-I preservatives.
413. Alginates are used as emulsifiers.
414. Vanilla can be preserved by using alcohol.
415. Sugar more than 70% acts as preservative.
416. Vinegar is used as preservatives in ketchup.
417. Baking powder is used in baking as leavening agent.
418. Sodium metabisulphite acts as dough softener.
419. At 17% of moisture wheat is soaked to give its optimum milling properties.
420. Corn gluten is rich in the corn protein known as zein.
421. Starch granules are present in Protein matrix.
422. Gliadin and glutenin protein fractions constitutes of gluten.
423. Gasohol is a mixture of 90% gasoline and 10% ethanol.

424. Rice is used in the preparation of the sake (Japanese wine)
425. Gluten which is formed in dough is sticky, tough and rubbery and elastic.
426. Water used in biscuits helps in formation of gluten, in maintenance of particular temperature during mixing and facilitates activities of enzyme and yeast in dough.
427. For yellow layer cakes all the improvement effected by bleaching is in the Gluten and Starch.
428. Percentage of dry gluten of wheat is related to the percentage of protein.
429. Food products under batter system include cakes.
430. .Bleaching of soft flour results in drop in flour pH value.
431. The most effective hydrogen bond forming components in wheat flour in addition to water is Pentosans.
432. Pasta product is prepared from durum wheat.
433. Terpenoids, flavonoids and sulphur compounds etc. used as flavoring compound.
434. Samolina is obtained from durum wheat.
435. Whole wheat flour is also known as graham flour.
436. Single screw extruders consist of 3 sections.
437. Lactic acid percentage by weight maximum in sweet dahi should be - 0.70%
438. Crème filling is important for snack cake.
439. GSM can be used as the anti stalling agent in bread.
440. Percent of salt increases, the rate of acid production becomes lower.
441. Sodium metabisulphite breaks the gluten bond and makes dough soft.
442. Middle lamella of the cell wall is rich in calcium pectate.
443. Avocado's have the highest amount of fat.
444. According to FPO specifications, a tomato paste must contain 25% TSS.
445. Catalase is heat resistance enzyme.
446. Sodium benzoate is added to tomato sauce to extend the shelf life.
447. Potato contains 2% proteins and 0.3% fat.
448. Preservative used in squash is SO_2.
449. TSS of fruit squash is 40%.
450. Sliced potatoes are kept in saline water to prevent enzymic browning.
451. Papain is a proteolytic enzyme.
452. Gibberelin hormones extend the shelflife of fruits.
453. Salt acts as preservatives in mango pickle.
454. In cola soft drinks the common colourant is tannins.
455. Slime production in juices is due to *leuconostoc mesenteroides*.
456. NIR (Near Infrared spectroscopy) can be used as non-destructive method of determining crude fat.
457. Inactivation of enzymes during blanching is done to prevent Browning reaction.

458. Carbon dioxide in carbonated beverages acts as preservative, sparkling agent and enhancement of flavour.
459. Red colour in water melon is due to lycopene.
460. Tetra Pak is a multinational food packaging company of Swedish origin.
461. Golden shreds marmalades are bitter in taste.
462. Maximum solubility of sugar at 20 °C is equal to 67.5% .
463. Chip sona - I is variety of potato which is used to make chips.
464. UV light has germicidal effect at the wave length between 210 to 290 nm.
465. Polyolefin can be used for increasing the shelflife of citrus fruits.
466. Storage of food under reduced pressure is called hypobaric storage.
467. Canned foods should be stored in the dry food store.
468. PVA stands for polyvenyl alcohol.
469. Most resistant spores of *Clostridium botulinum* have strain of $D_{121.1}$ of 0.89 min.
470. Major source of antifreeze protein is fish.
471. Polystyrene is used for acidic foods.
472. Picowaved is the term used to label foods treated with low level ionizing radiation.
473. Gelatinization plays an important role in preservation of jam and jellies.
474. Sonication is the method of preservation of food by ultrasound.
475. Mango variety having strong flavour is langra.
476. Pineapple variety suitable for canning is Kew.
477. Apple and Banana are climacteric type of fruit.
478. Pineapple, litchi and grape are non-climacteric type of fruit.
479. Most suitable packaging material for cut flowers is Cardboard boxes.
480. Emission of Ethylene during transportation of cut flowers causes a disorder which called as sleepiness.
481. First commodity for which grading and marketing rules were framed is grape.
482. Cauliflower curds can be stored for a month at 0°C with 85-90% RH.
483. For curing, sweet potatoes are kept for 10 days at 80°C and 30% RH.
484. Tomato fruits for canning are harvested at red ripe stage.
485. World Processing Tomato Council (WPTC) is in France (created in 1998)
486. Maleic Hydrazide (MH) is used for controlling sprouting of onions in storage.
487. Melons for distant marketing are picked at green mature stage.
488. For distant marketing, tomato fruits are harvested at mature green stage.
489. For Low Sugar content, potato tubers are stored at 10 °C.
490. For long-term storage, potato should be stored at 15-20 °C.
491. For longer storage of cucumber fruits, the temperature should be 20 °C.
492. Potato is the staple vegetable in Indian diet.
493. Cluster bean (Guar) is used for extraction of gum.

494. Vegetables are subjected to drying after blanching.
495. According to FPO, the maximum limit of SO_2 allowed in squashes and cordials is 350 ppm.
496. The toxicity of SO_2 increases at High temperature.
497. Concentration of SO_2 in concentrated juice is 1500 ppm.
498. SO_2 content in pure KMS is 57.7%.
499. The term 'climacteric' was first used by Kidd and West (1927).
500. O_2 requirement for apple storage in controlled atmosphere (CA) is 3%.
501. Storage temperature for asparagus is 0-5°C.
502. Storage temperature for banana is 15-16°C.
503. Vacuum cooling is most suitable for leafy vegetables.
504. Vegetable which is not blanched before drying is onion.
505. Moisture content in dried vegetable is 3%.
506. Best maturity indices of orange are Brix: acid ratio.
507. The term "three quarterful or full three quarter" is used to denote fruit maturity in Banana crop.
508. Storage of fruits and vegetables, where the gas composition is changed from that of normal atmosphere and a precise control is maintained over the atmospheric composition during storage period is known as *Controlled Atmospheric* (CA) *Storage*.
509. During controlled atmospheric storage composition of CO_2 and O_2 set of gases is controlled.
510. At 4.5 pH fruits and vegetables are divided into acidic and non-acidic for thermal processing.
511. In precooling, water is mostly removed by conduction.
512. Albinism is an important physiological disorder of strawberry.
513. Calliper grade is the maturity measurement for banana.
514. Formation of absicission layer is maturity index of Melons.
515. Oil content is the maturity index for avocado.
516. As fruits mature, the specific gravity will increase.
517. 'Solidity' is the maturity index for leafy vegetables.
518. Leaf change is important maturity index for bulbous vegetables.
519. Mango fruits can be best stored at a temperature of 8°C.
520. Bitterness in peach is due to Prunasin acid.
521. Grape is non-climacteric fruit.
522. Guava fruit is botanically known as berry.
523. Mostly dry fruit are rich in fats.
524. Red colour of tomato is due to lycopene.
525. In onions pink colour is due to *quercitin.*
526. Hen and Chicken disorder is associated with grapes.

527. The membrane lipid hypothesis is given by Raison and Lyons.
528. The point at which the dried products just become lumpy is known as critical point.
529. A Point which have 5% Low RH than the Critical Point is Danger Point.
530. Lye peeling is done at a temperature of 93°C.
531. Cauliflower is associated with 'browning' disorder.
532. Degreening is not applicable in guava.
533. Under normal conditions orchid flowers can be stored upto 2 weeks at 5-7°C.
534. The primary reason for blanching is to inactive the enzymes.
535. A food with a pH of 3.5 is considered to be high acid.
536. Ether is a solvent used for testing fat content.
537. Olive oil is rich in omega 3 fatty acids.
538. Gas chromatography analytical methods can be used to distinguish flavoured compounds.
539. Wet ashing is a quick test for sugar content during the early stages of the brewing process for beer.
540. Enzyme activity causes sliced apples to turn brown.
541. Chlorophyll does not have antimicrobial activity.
542. Gluten is derived from wheat.
543. Food preservation is the science which deals with the methods of prevention of decay or spoilage of food, thus allowing it to be stored in a fit condition for future use.
544. Sulphur dioxide is widely used in the preservation of juice, pulp, nectar, squash, crush, cordial and other products.
545. Potassium metabisulphite (KMS) is commonly used as a stable source of sulphur dioxide.
546. The maximum amount of sulphur dioxide allowed in fruit juice is 700 ppm, in squash, crush and cordial 350 ppm and in RTS and nectar 100 ppm.
547. Carbonation is the process of dissolving sufficient carbon dioxide in water or beverage so that the product when served gives off the gas as fine bubbles and has a characteristic taste.
548. Syrups containing 66 per cent or more of sugar do not ferment, thus sugar acts as a preservative by osmosis and not as a true poison for microorganisms.
549. Fruit syrup, jam, jelly, marmalade, preserve, candy, crystallized fruits and glazed fruits are preserved by sugar.
550. Salt at a concentration of 15 to 25 per cent is sufficient to preserve most products.
551. Peas and whole kernel corn undergo fluidized bed freezing.
552. Dehydro freezing is a process where freezing is preceded by partial dehydration.
553. *Lager* is bottom fermented and *ale* is top fermented beer.
554. Caffeine is present in coffee, tea and chocolates,
555. Brewer's yeast is *Saccharomyces cerevisiae.*
556. Sauerkraut is fermented product of cabbage.
557. Mustard seeds and mustard oil contains toxic factor *erucic acid.*
558. Vinegar contains 4% acetic acid.

559. The fruit content in jam should not be less than 40%.
560. To allow even distribution of fruit peel and slices in marmalade and not float to the surface, they are soaked in sugar solution.
561. Marmalade should contain NLT 45% fruit from which it is made.
562. Fruit chutney should contain minimum 40% of fruit in the final product.
563. The tomato paste should have NLT 25% total soluble solids.
564. The tomato puree should have NLT 9% total soluble solids.
565. The brown pigment formed in the maillard reaction is melanoidin.
566. For jelly, fruits with high pectin and high acid are preferred.
567. Papain is the enzyme extracted from papaya, ficin from figs.
568. The process of bringing the fruit and vegetable to room temperature after cold storage is called thawing.
569. Minimally processed foods involve processing operations such as peeling, shredding, cutting etc.
570. The cereal crops that are grown for their edible fruit are generally called grain, but botanically referred to as caryopsis.
571. The cereal seed consists of two major components, the endosperm and embryo or germ.
572. The endosperm encompasses the bulk of the seed and is the energy source of stored food.
573. A semi permeable layer under the pericarp, which is called testa, surrounds the embryo and is derived from the inner ovary wall.
574. Wheat is a single-seeded fruit, 4 to 10-mm long, consisting of a germ and endosperm enclosed by an epidermis and a seed coat
575. The endosperm cells are packed with starch granules, which lie embedded in a matrix that is largely protein.
576. The corn seed is a single fruit called the kernel. It includes an embryo, endosperm, aleurone, and pericarp.
577. 80% of dry matter of cereals is carbohydrate.
578. The fibre constituents are cellulose, hemicellulose and pentosans, out of which starch is the most important carbohydrate in all cereals.
579. All the cereals, whole wheat, ragi and bajra contain high amount of fibre.
580. Rice contains less amount of protein compared to other cereals.
581. Within the endosperm (Rice) the concentration of protein increases from the center to the periphery.
582. Freshly harvested paddy normally has a moisture content of 18-25%.
583. For long storage, the grain should be dried to 13% moisture or less.
584. One fourth by the weight of paddy consists of husk, which makes up the largest milling by product of rice.

(**NLT** : Not less than ; **NMT** : Not more than)

585. Rice husk has high ash content, about 20%, the major portion of which (over 90%) consists of silica.

586. Fully burnt white ash of husk contains 95% silica and can be used for manufacturing sodium silicate, silica gel and insulating bricks etc.

587. Wheat types may be classified as hard or soft wheat and strong or weak.

588. The botanical name of corn is *Zea mays* and used as food and feed.

589. Corn-germ contains about 21 per cent proteins and 32 per cent fat and since the germ constitutes about 13 per cent of the grain, it is an important source of proteins and fat.

590. Barley is used to a small extent as a food in the form of pot barley or pearl barley or barley flour and mostly used for preparation of malt.

591. The oat, grain consists of husk, aleurone layer, germ and endosperm.

592. The important oat products of commerce are rolled oats and oat flakes. Oats free from the husk are called groats.

593. Apart from maize and sorghum, the major millet crops of India are Pearl millet called bajra and finger millet known as ragi.

594. Minor millets are grown and they are: the common millet or proso millet, foxtail millet and kodo millet.

595. Barley malt is used in brewing and in the preparation of malt extract for pharmaceutical purposes and in the preparation of, malted milk powder.

596. Ready-to-serve breakfast cereal foods include flaked breakfast cereals, puffed break-fast cereals, shredded and granular breakfast cereals and puffing by extrusion.

597. The total dietary fibre content of oat in consideration with the hemicellulose content of oat hull is between 30 and 50%.

598. Collagen fibres shrink or shorten at a temperature of 600°C but higher temperatures or boiling cause transformation to water soluble gelatin.

599. The smallest unit of collagen molecular structure is tropo collagen.

600. The unsaturated glycerides in oil can be converted to more saturated glycerides by the addition of hydrogen through the process known as hydrogenation.

601. Smoking temperature is defined as the lowest temperature at which visible fumes consisting of volatile gaseous products of decomposition are evolved.

602. Mannitol is used in sugar free chewing gum and xylitol is used in pastries, jam and Ice cream.

603. Alitame is a dipeptide based amide. It is 2000 times sweeter than sucrose.

604. Aspartame is made by combining two amino acids — aspartic acid and phenylalanine. It is 200 times sweeter than sucrose.

605. Saccharin is "sodium orthobenzene sulphonamide" or its calcium salt and is 300 times sweeter than sucrose.

606. Food additives are the substances other than basic food ingredient used for processing, preservation and storage of food products.

607. Food additives are generally used to solve product specific problems.

608. Fortification and enrichment are also related to food additives.
609. Antioxidants are the substances added to fats and fat containing foods (such as snacks) to retard oxidation and prolong keeping time.
610. BHA, BHT, PG and TBHQ are used as antioxidants in food products.
611. ADI (Acceptable Daily Intake) value for BHA is upto 0.5mg/kg body weight and for BHT is 0.3 mg/kg body weight.
612. Ascorbic acid and tocopherols are naturally occurring antioxidants.
613. Antioxidants prevent lipid oxidation by interrupting free radical chain mechanism.
614. Antioxidants prevent browning in cut fruits and vegetables.
615. Chelating agents are also known as sequestrants.
616. Chelating agents are the compounds that form complexes with metal ions and thus prevent oxidative rancidity and discoloration reactions.
617. Examples of chelating agents include Sorbic acid, poly carboxylic acid, polyphosphates and EDTA.
618. Ethylene gas causes fruits to ripen.
619. Drying is removal of free water by means of sun drying or any conventional method.
620. Sun drying will not allow fruit products to dry below 15-20% moisture level.
621. In foam mat drying (The best method) glycerol-mono stearate, egg albumin, ground nut protein isolate, guar, guava and carboxymethyl cellulose are used as foaming agents.
622. The optimum amount of the foaming agent to be used is 0.3-1.5%. The strips could be dried crisp in 30-45 minute to a moisture content of 1.5-2.0%.
623. Absolute fresh (an hour from the field to the can) fruits and vegetables are needed.
624. Heat peeling needs to exposing fruits or vegetables to 105°C for 10-60 seconds.
625. Caustic soda (Sodium hydroxide) or lye solution is used at 1-2% strength for lye peeling for 30 sec. to 2 min.
626. Due to reaction with NaOH or citric acid aluminium-equipments should be avoided for cooking, steel are best for use.
627. Leaves of plants or vegetables are low in carbohydrates and energy but they are good source of β-carotene, calcium, riboflavin, folic acid, ascorbic acid, iron and vitamin K.
628. Chlorophyll *a* is intense blue green in colour and chlorophyll-*b* is dull yellow green in colour in ratio of 3a:1b.
629. Chlorophyll *a* present in florets and *b* in stalks of broccoli.
630. Anthocyanidins are Anthocyanin without sugar in their structure. They are pelargonidin (red), cyaniding (reddish blue) and delphinidin (blue).
631. Betacynins and betaxanthins are together known as *betalains*.
632. Anthoxanthins give colour to cauliflower, onions and spinach or other leafy vegetables (colourless or white to yellow colour).
633. Gamma rays are the principle irradiation used in food irradiation (Wavelength < 2Å).
634. 1 Rad = 10 μJ energy absorbed by 1g. material.
635. Ionization are measured in rads/kilorads/megarads n, n_0 exp $(-D/D_0)$ where n = number of live organisms, n_0 = initial number of organisms, D = dose radiation received (rads) and D_0 = d constant depending on the type of organisms, and environmental factors.

IMPORTANT POINTS

- *Restoration* – Addition of selected nutrient to a food to restore nutrient lost through processing.
- *Fortification* – To add that nutrient which are not available normally/existing in foods. *e.g.* Addition of Vit. D to milk.
- *Enrichment* – Addition of nutrient in precooked/raw food materials. *e.g.* Flour.
- *Synthetic food* – Made from non food source *e.g.* Cold drinks, soft drinks, fruit juice etc.
- *Imitation* –to look like and replace a food that has a standard but they do not meet the standard requirements.
- *Hermetic closure*– Hermetic means a container that is sealed completely against the ingress of gases and vapours.
- A small amount of lemon juice, vinegar, citric acid or other harmless acid is added to the brine in which the vegetables are canned so that after sterilization the pH will be below 4.5 called Lemon juice methods.
- Tomato juice is often preserved by heating to about 120 °C in continuous flash sterilizer, cooling continuously and canning hot.
- Antiseptics (Sugar, salt and vinegar) may be used as permanent preservatives – sugar @ 75%, salt (more effective than sugar) @ 15%, Acetic acid (more effective than salt) @ 2%.
- Effectiveness as preservative = Sugar < salt < acetic acid.
- Benzoic acid and sulphurous acid @ 0.2% used as preservative.
- 1.5-2.0% of salt acts as preservative for vegetable and green beans including maize (whole kernel).
- Sourness of acid reduced and sweeteness of sugar increased by addition of NaCl (Table salt).

Salt percentage:

	Ground meats	– 2-4%
	Bacon	– 2.25%
	Hams	– 5.0%
	Corned meat	– 6.0%

- 3 Kg. of salt is added in 1000 lit. of milk in cheese making and finally 1/3 of added salt remains in cheese.
- *Salt does* : 1. Flavour (enhancement) 2. Whey removal 3. Hardening 4. Sprinking the curd 5. Retarding lactic acid fermentation 6. Inhibiting undesirable fermentation 7. Producing desirable texture are the role of salt in cheese making.
- Wild or objectionable fermentation in bread making is checked by salt.
- Salt (brine) used as secondary heat transfer media in ice manufacturing and in cooling air in meat coolers and other cold storage practices.

HIGH SOLID HIGH ACID FOOD

Solid Food materials are Viscoelastic in Nature

- **Jam :** Pulp 45% + Sugar 55%, TSS/Soluble solids 68.5 Brix. Acid 0.5-0.6%, invert sugar minimum 40%, pH – 3.
- **Jelly :** Pulp not less than 45% + Sugar 55%, TSS/Soluble solids 65 Brix, Pectin 0.5-1.0% Acid 0.5-1.0%, invert sugar minimum 40%, pH – 3.2.

- **Marmalade :** Suspended slices of fruit or peel. - made from the juice and peel of citrus family with sugar and water.
  Fruit butter : 5 : 2 (Fruit : sugar), soluble solid not less than 43%.
  Preserves : 45 parts fruit, 55 parts sugar 68% solid achieved by contenuous cooking.
- Solid food materials are viscoelastic in nature.
- **Candied fruits :** gradually concentrating fruits in syrup by repeated boiling until the fruit is heavily impregnated with sugar, this process being followed by drying to overcome stickness. Commonly used fruit- dates, cherries, and pineapple.
- **Glaze :** Glaze fruits are prepared by coating candied fruit with concentrated solution of sugar etc.
- **Fruit confectioneries :** Candies in which fruits are used.

Classes of Preservatives

S.No.	*Class-I*	*Class-II*
1.	Common salt(NaCl)	Benzoic acid and Sodium benzoate
2.	Sugar	Methyl and Propyl P-pydroxybenzoates(Parabens)
3.	Dextrose	Sorbets
4.	Glucose(Syrup)	Propionate
5.	Wood smoke	Sulphites(Sulphur dioxide)
6.	Spices	Nitrite
7.	Vinegar/acetic acid	Nitrates
8.	Honey	

(*Source* : Kalia M and Sood S. 2008)

- Sodium benzoate in ice is used for refrigeration of fresh fish.
- pH of Sodium benzoate for best activity is 2.5-4.0.
- Parabens are much better than Benzoic acid. (Parabens are a class of preservative used in cosmetic and pharmaceutical products.)
- Parabens are more active at pH 7.0.
- Sorbates can not be used in yeast raised baked goods but may be used in leavened product.
- Propionates generally used in bakery products at 0.2%.
- 50-100 ppm solution of sulphur dioxide or sulphites may be used to clean holding tanks or may be added prior to fermentation in wine making.
- In curing of meat and fish Nitrites are used.
- DEPC (Diethylpyrocarbonate) is used as preservative in wine and some fruits at the rate of 0.02% or maximum 5ppm would remain after 24 hours after botling.
- DEPC (Diethylpyrocarbonate) break downs to ethyl alcohol, carbon dioxide and water with in 48 hours.
- Hydrogen peroxide (H_2O_2) has germicidal properties at 0.1% and lower is effective as preservatives.

- Hydrogen peroxide (H_2O_2) can also kill the anaerobic spore forming bacteria.
- Surface sterilization may be done with Hydrogen peroxide (H_2O_2) to kill bacteria.
- Chlorine is most effective at low pH values.
- CO_2 is used as preservative in carbonated juice.
- Germicidal ice is prepared by benzoic acid+ice.
- Dried ripe banana is known as "Banana fig".
- Sugar predominant in (1) Hard dried dates – Sucrose (2) Soft dried dates – invert sugar.
- Dates are picked at dung stage.
- Kishmish Khanas room (dark) where ripe bunches of grapes are hunged till berries acquire a greenish or light amber tint.
- Sundried grapes are Monucca/Raisin (Haitha).
- Ripe jack fruits are sliced and the seeds removed are called Bulbs which can be dried in the form of sheets/slabs the method is developed and patented by CFTRI.
- Evaporation and dehydration are quite similar but in evaporation only temperature is controlled and natural draft is depended. In dehydration the heated air is circulated by blowers. The temperature, humidity and velocity of air may be controlled and varied as per the objected stuff and stages.
- Air velocity about 2.5-5.0 meter/sec. In cabinet dryer for about 10-20 hrs. In case of fruits and vegetables.
- Freeze Drying involves three steps:
  (1) First frozen on trays in the lower chambers.
  (2) Frozen materials dried in the upper chamber under high vaccum.
  (3) The material dries directly by sublimation of ice without passing through the intermediate liquid stages.
- Heat treatment at 54-65°C for drying.
- Durofume process of fumigation for in stored foods is developed by CFTRI Mysore.
- For packaging of highly hygroscopic food stuff like fruit juice powder accelerated freeze dried products (*e.g.* Meat minces etc.) brown casing paper '60 gauge' and aluminium foil '0.04 mm', polythene '150 gauge' pouch with a 2 ply corrugated liner waxed carton can extend shelf life about 1 year under field conditions.
- Oxygen supply when unlimited used for cell growth and when limited used for alcohol production.
- Preservation by radiation was first carried out by Masachasetts Institute of Technology (MIT) in the year 1943.
- Some side effects of radiation of foods are serious off flavours, vitamin destruction and quality defects.

- Refrigeration and freezing are two types of cold preservation in refrigeration at home level tempreture must be about 4-7°C and commercially it may slightly lower (Storage for a day only).
- At –18°C or below the freezing is done (Storage for month or year).
- Temperature of chill storage is –1 to –4°C.
- Relative humidity for most of the food is 80-95%.
- Relative humidity for dry and granular food is 50%.
- At –20°C with in 30 minitus the process is called quick fast freezing.
- Most heat resistant microorganism is bacteria.
- Bacterial cells are least resistant during the logarithmic growth phase.
- Bacterial cells are most resistant during the late phase and maximum at stationary phase.
- Moist heat is more effective as compared to dry heat *e.g.* Autoclaving.
- With the 3-15% Caustic soda for 30 second - 2 minutes lye peeling is done, NaOH may also used as lye solution.
- Boiling then cooling then canning is called Blanching.
- Syrup is used for preservation of fruits while Brine is used for preservation of vegetables.
- Syrup/brine should be added at 79-82°C temperature.
- Space left inside the can during filling may be 3.2-4.7mm.
- A simple syruper consists of about 227 liter capacity and made up of stainless steel/ aluminium.
- Exhausting prevents discolouration of food (canned) product because oxidation is prevented.
- Exclusion of air helps in better retention of Vitamins (specially'C'), overfilling is avoided with the help of exhausting and also under filling.
- In water exhaust box cans are placed in such a manner that the level of water is 1.3-2.5cm and time 5-25 minutes at the rate of temperature 82-87°C (at centre temperature should be 79°C).
- Jars are placed in high vacuum machine.
- Increase in altitude decreases boiling point of water.
- Increase in altitude increases pressure and temperature of processing.
- 1-1.5% HCl added in water and sprayed on apple to remove the residual spray material from the apple.
- Blanching of apple – the fruits are immersed in boiling 3% brine for 3-4 minutes.
- Firm ripe that are just developing colour mangoes are choosen for blanching, 2% brine solution used prevents enzymatic browning.
- 1-2% lye solution for 20-30 second looses the skin of grapes.
- 1.6 Kg/100 liter (salt:water) is necessary for brine solution in case of soaked okra making.

- Blanching time and temperature for mushrooms is 7 minutes at 100°C.
- 8 Kg salt and 12 Kg sugar per 500 litres of water may be used for brine solution, for peas it may be 12 Kg salt and 20 Kg sugar respectively.
- Cabbage is cut-out in size of 2.5cm thick and blanched for 5-6 minutes, in blanching tartaric or citric acid solution of 1.0% strength and cooled in 2.0% prevents discolouration.
- Pumpkin pieces are steamed in retorts at 115°C for 20 minutes or until softened and cans are sealed hot, Process conducted at 120°C for 75-90 minutes.
- For canning purpose the specific gravity of potato must be 1.075, 5-15% lye solution and temperature near to boiling point.
- 2.5 cm or less diameter, 2.5-3.0 cm may be also used blanching at 2-4 minutes in water at 88-100°C temperature for carrots.
- Carrot may be peeled by lye solution of 5-10% NaOH.
- Wheat milling results 12% bran, 3% germ, 85% endosperm.
- Bread is made up by hard wheat.
- Biscuit, cookies, pastries, soft dough cakes are made up by soft wheat.
- Durum wheat is used in macroni, spaghetti and noodle preparation.
- Protease enzyme gives strechability (gluten) for the bread making in relation to acquire volume and form structure.
- pH of water is used in bread making must be 4.5-6.0 and hardness 50-100 ppm of $CaCO_3$ is best.
- Albumin (egg white) improves the foaming ability of dough and yolk acts as better emulsifying power in dough, incorporation of both improves binding action, leavening effects, colour, texture, flavour and nutritional value.
- At the rate of 1.25-2.5% salt must be added in dough.
- Baking soda used as leavening agent in bread making at 1-7%.
- Intermediate proofing means roasting of the rounded dough.
- Final proofing at 35°C and 80-85% RH.
- For Baking at 200-230°C temperature with the RH 80-85% for 15-40 minutes are required.
- Sugar in plants is the product of photosynthesis.
- Juice is 70-80% of sugarcane.
- Sugarcane residue called bagasse contains 25% juice.
- Clarification of sugarcane juice by heat and lime called Defacation process and it raises temperature to 95°C or above.
- Makhan is indigenous butter and ghee is clarified butter.
- Green tea is not fermented product but is semi fermented product or oolong and graded as — (1) Gunpowder (2) Imperial (3) Broken oolong.

- Caffeine is about 3 mg/100ml. in coffee.
- Mucilage binds the pulp with the stone of coffee.
- When yeast fermentation starts to subside, lactic acid fermentation begins then beans are dried called raw beans of coffee.
- Roasting gives typical taste and is the only real cooking that coffee needs.
- Tea- *Camellia robusta*
- Coffee – *Coffee robusta/arabica*
- Cocoa – *Theobroma cöcoa*
- Temperature of roasting at which flavour developes in coffee is 150-250°C (205°C).
- Final dried'beans contain about 10-15% moisture.
- Percolation and infusion are other methods by which coffee may be fermented.
- Cocoa contains about 0.04% caffeine and 1.04% theobromine.
- In curing of cocoa the moisture must be reduced at 8-13%.
- The bean of cocoa after cracking termed as Nibs.
- Original starch converted in alcohol about 75%.

Moisture % in fruits/vegetables:

S.No.	*Particular (Fruits/Vegetables)*	*Moisture %*
1.	Perishable	> 70
2.	Semiperishable	20-70
3.	Nonperishable	12-14

(*Source* : Kalia M and Sood S. 2008)

- **Intermediate moisture** fruits/food are Honey, Tubers, Khajur (Dates) with the moisture percentages 40-50%.
- Blanching is hydrothermal treatment of fruits and vegetables to retain colour, quality and decay of spoilage.
- **Types of peeling :** (1) *Hand peeling e.g.* Papaya, potato. (2) *Abrasion peeling*- hot water treatment *e.g.* Ber, peach, potato etc. (3) *Lye peeling* – NaOH at the rate of 1-2% solution and deep fruits and vegetables in solution for 30 seconds then white layer and seed may be separated *e.g.* Tomato, orange, lime etc. (4) *Flame peeling* – with very thin layer of peels fruits and vegetables are treated *e.g.* Garlic, Onion to intense heat to char the peel and facilitate its rapid removal.
- Strength of brine is measured by Salometer while Refractometer is used for syrup.
- 1:1(NaCl: Sugar) inhibits enzymatic browing in canning.
- Freezing (frozen) at the rate of (–) 18°C extends shelf life of vegetables for 8-10 months and for fruits 10-12 months.

- **Freezing types :-**
  1. Sharp/slow freezing—at 15 to 29°C for 3-72 hrs by simple blower/ fans ice crystals forms, room temperature—23 to 29°C *e.g.* Meat, butter.
  2. Quick freezing—at –40°C for 30 minutes in small ice crystal *e.g.* Sugar coating, candy, pieces of fruits and vegetables etc.
  3. Refrigeration—(A) Cryogenic freezing—at –60°C temperature (liquid N_2 and solid CO_2) *e.g.* Mushroom slices, tomatoes and whole strawberry etc.

     (B) Dehydrofreezing—partial dehydration about 50% moisture dehydrated.

     (C) Freeze drying—at –18°C for 24 hrs. *e.g.* Paste and pulp.
- Frozen product are deficient in vit. C or it causes loss of vit. C.
- House of glycogen is liver.
- Translation is the last step of protein formation.
- Coconut water contains 94.5% water and also contains vit. B, C and E.
- Movement of solvent in solution till equilibrium is termed as Osmosis.
- Respiration quotient can be find out by volume released by CO_2 divided by volume absorbed by O_2.
- Respiration quotient of carbohydrates, fat and protein is 1.0, 0.7 and 0.8-0.9 respectively and in case of protein it is 0.8 for amide group and 0.9 for ammonia group.
- Ethylene ($CH_2{=}CH_2$) discovered in the year 1934 by Gane Richard and it is synthesized by methionine.
- The effect of ethylene ($CH_2{=}CH_2$) inhibited by CO_2 and Ag^+ at the rate of 5-10% (or up to 5-10%).
- Oilseed requirement for average person is 38g/capita/day.
- Linoleic acid is 56-60%, 64% and 78% respectively in soybean, sunflower and safflower.
- Sweetest variety of jowar contains 16-23% Brix sugar.
- Potato contains carbohydrate 70-75% and water about 20-25%.
- Iodine no. of soybean is 140 and linessed is 180.
- Pulses are deficient in methionine and rich in lysine while cereals are deficient in lysine.
- Winterization of rice bran oil is due to removal of saturated glycosides.
- Oil % in rice bran is 16%.
- Waxy rice contains a high proportion of Amylopectine.
- TSS of cane sugar must be 20-24 Brix.
- For 10 kg. of grapes 1.5 g. of KMS needed.
- Juice, RTS, Nector pasteurized at about 85 °C for 25-30 minutes.
- 30-50% sugar must in case of Jam if it is < 30% the crystallization takes place.
- Synthetic drinks have water 88%, carbohydrate 12% and energy 48Kcal.

- Fruits must be washed with HCl at the rate 1:20 with water for the insecticidal effect removal.
- Clarification is the removal of suspended material from the juice.
- Permissible limit of KMS is 350-450 ppm.
- After pasteurization juice may be kept at –18 °C for 3-4 days.
- Intermediate moisture fruits eg. Honey and khajur(dates) contains 17-18% sugar.
- Food allergy given by Walzer 1927.
- The formula of KMS is $K_2S_2O_5$.
- In canning washing of fruits by chlorine @ 25-50 ppm.
- Initial temperature of dehydration is 43°C then 60-66°C (vegetables) and then 66-71°C (fruits).
- Off flavour in fruits and vegetables is due to peroxidise and discolouration due to Polyphenol oxidase enzyme.
- Juice or liquid fruit products are preserved by addition of sodium benzoates.
- **Hurdle technology :** combination treatment are applied because it is expected that the use of combined preservative factors will have greater effectiveness at inactivating microorganisms than those of any single factor.
- **Hurdle technology:** aims to improve the total quality of foods by application of an intelligent mix of hurdles. Over the years the insight into the hurdle effect has been broadened and the application of hurdle technology was extended (Leistner and Gorris, 1994).

SODIUM RELATED TERMS ON FOOD PACKAGES

- **Sodium free** - Less than 1mg of sodium per serving.
- **Very low sodium** - 35 mg or less per serving.
- **Reduced (or less) sodium** - At least 25% less sodium per serving than the usual sodium level.
- **Light (for sodium-reduced products)** – If food is low calories and "low fat" and sodium is reduced by at least 50% per serving.
- **Light in sodium** - If sodium is reduced by at least 50% per serving.
- **Instantized Milk Powder developed by** – D. D. Peebles (US). This development open field for other dehydratable products.
- **Process optimization** is the discipline of adjusting a process so as to optimize (best or most effective use) some specified set of parameters without violating some constraints like equipment optimization operating procedures and control optimization.

  1kW = 1000N-m/s

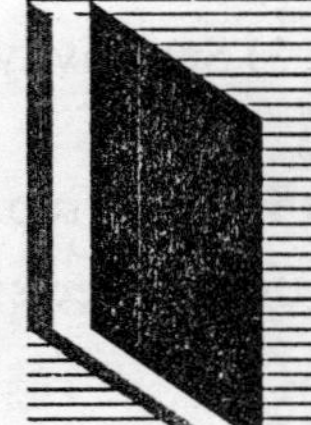

CHAPTER 5

FOOD QUALITY

Term food quality is sum of all properties and attributes of a food item that are acceptable to the customer. It includes: Appearance, Texture, Flavour, Nutritional content and Ethical and sustainable production.

1. Out of 11,500 standards of BIS there are 1,200 are related to agriculture and 700 related to food.
2. The term quality is a composite of the characteristics that differentiate the end uses of a product, and of their significance in determining the acceptability of the product by buyers.
3. Central Food Advisory Board established in 1937.
4. Food adulteration committee setup in 1943.
5. Department of Food and Agriculture started in 1956.
6. Food and Agriculture Organisation (FAO) 1945. Head office at Rome
7. Codex Alimentarius Commission was setup in 1962.
8. The International Commission for Uniform Methods of Sugar Analysis Ltd. (ICUMSA) is a world-wide body which brings together the activities of the National Committees for Sugar Analysis in more than twenty member countries.
9. Defence Ministry prepares specification known as Army Crops Specifications for their purchases of food grains and pulses.
10. AGMARK (1937) stands for *Agricultural produce (Grading and Marketing) Act.*
11. Regional Agmark Laboratories are established at 21 centres and are under technical control of the Central Agmark Laboratory Nagpur.
12. The Food Department of Government of India's specifications are known as Fair Average Quality (FAQ) specifications.
13. The Consumers Protection Act enacted in 1986.
14. The Central Consumers Protection Act came in 1987.
15. According to BIS cocoa used for beverage should contain 20%, 10-20% and 10% cocoa fat, medium fat cocoa and low fat cocoa respectively.
16. Quality of fish can be ascertained by the brightness of the eyes of fish.
17. The flavour of food has three components –odour, taste and a composite of sensations known as mouth feel.
18. Tasting of coffee or tea or fruit juice is done by slurping.
19. The test time generally 10 to 12 a.m. in the morning.

20. **Sensory tests are grouped in to four types:-** 1) Difference test 2) Rating test 3) Sensitivity test 4) Descriptive test

21. Brix or Balling hydrometer gives directly the percentage of sugar by weight in the syrup.

22. Rheology is defined as the science of deformation and flow of matter. It has three aspects; elasticity, viscous flow and plastic flow.

    Percent sag is measured in Jelly like substance

$$\text{Percent sag} = \frac{\text{Depth in container} - \text{Depth in plate}}{\text{Depth in container}} \times 100$$

23. Instrument used for liquids and semisolids.

    a. Bakers jelmeter pectin in fruit juice – pectin in fruit juice.

    b. Stormer viscometer – viscosity of non-newtonian liquids.

    c. Brook field synchrolectric viscometer – fluid viscosity

    d. Bostwick consistometer – consistency in tomato ketchup and sauces

    e. Efflux tube viscometer – puree (fluid)

    f. Adams consistometer- puree, sauce, fruit pulps

    g. Penetrometer-tenderness of foods

    h. Brabender farinograph- plasticity of dough

    i. Instrument used for solids.

    j. Magness:- Taylor pressure tester (compression) – Firmness and ripeness of fruits and vegetables.

    k. Succulometer (compression):- maturity of corn, storage quality of apple

    l. Fibrometer:- cutting principle (green beans)

    m. Shortometer :- breaking strength of pastry, cookies and crackers.

    n. Crystal texturometer (cutting)

    o. Voldokevich bite tenderometer (cutting and shearing)

    p. Grinding and extensibility

    q. Kramer- shear press: meat tenderness.

    r. Tensile strength (find out the tensile strength of chapatti)

    s. Compressometer: Device used to determine the strain or deformation of a specimen.

    t. Warner- Bratzler shear force machine (measure the tenderness of meat)

    u. Shear press (fruits and vegetables)

    v. Universal testing machine

24. If milk is watered the solids are present in lower concentration and the specific gravity will be closer to water than for pure milk.

25. Preservatives in milk are prohibited by law.

26. Laddu, toor dal and turmeric are commomnly adulterated by Metanil yellow.
27. The adulterant testing kit has been developed by the Centre for Consumer Education Research and Training, Chennai.
28. All the non permitted colours are mutagenic and potential carcinogens (most of these).
29. Elements which are toxic in small doses are cadmium, arsenic, antimony and cobalt.
30. Industrial Toxicology Research Centre Lucknow; found that silver foil used for sweets and in pan masala contain carcinogenic nickel, lead, chromium and cadmium.
31. Silver foil with the purity 99.9% can be used in edible form.
32. Australian vetch (*Vicia sativa*) contains the toxic amino acid p-cyanoalamine.
33. FSSAI works under Ministry of Health and family Welfare, GOI.
34. Food Safety and Standard Act 2006 has become operational in the entire country from 05/08/2011.
35. Quality management system certification as per -IS/ISO 9001.
36. Environmental management system certification as per -IS/ISO 14001.
37. Occupational Health and Safety Management System certification as per -IS 18001.
38. Service quality management system certification as per-IS 15700.
39. HACCP certification for food safety as per-IS/ISO 15000.
40. Food safety management system certification as per -IS/ISO 22000.
41. The Directorate of Marketing and Inspection of Central Government has 21 labs and 50 sub-offices spread all over the country.
42. CCFS- Central Committee for Food Standards came in 1947.
43. Central Food Laboratories (CFL) is situated at Kolkata.
44. Food Research and Standardization Laboratories at Ghaziabad.
45. Public Health Laboratories is situated at Pune.
46. As a nongovernmental organisation ISO has no legal authority to enforce their implementation.
47. The Codex Secretariat is located in Rome and is financed by the FAO and WHO, there are 165 member countries.
48. Codex India is the National Codex Contact Point (NCCP) for India located at DG Health services Ministry of Health and Family Welfare, New Delhi.
49. 3SB = four basic taste sensations that humans comprehend are sweat, salty, sour and bitter.
50. Grain size of sugar classified below: - as per crystal

    Large (L) = used in Punjab, Haryana, North India

    Medium (M) = Maharashtra, Madhya Pradesh, (Central India)

    Small (S) = Southern India.
51. Colours = criterion for sugar grading is the colour of the grain which has been denoted by numbers 31, 30, and 29 meaning whites, whiter and white respectively.

52. Sugar is graded in 9 types viz:-

    1. L31, L30, L29 2. M31, M30, M29 3. S31, S30, S29

53. Regular sugar found in every homes sugar bowl.
54. *Sugars are:* - *i*) Regular, *ii*) Fruit sugar, *iii*) Bakers special, *iv*) Superfine, *v*) Confectioners, *vi*) Coarse sugar and *vii*) Sanding sugar.
55. *Brown sugars*: - Turbinado sugar, Muscovado or Barbados Sugar, Free flowing brown, Demerara sugar.
56. Liquid sugars – Invert sugar.
57. Invert resembles honey in composition but not in flavour and is produced commercially by acidic or enzymatic hydrolysis:, and are less prone to crystallization.
58. Milk of lime [(CaO + H_2O-Ca $(OH)_2$)] is used for classification of sugar.
59. The Brix of juice at mud stage in sugar making (from cane juice) is 13-14° Brix.
60. *Steps involved in sugar making are as follows*:- 1) Harvesting, 2) Extraction clarification, 3) Evaporation, 4) Boiling, 5) Centrifugation, 6) Drying and grading and 7) Storage.
61. In the sugar factory, the bagasse fuel is renewable and the gases it produces essentially CO_2 are more than used up by the new growing cane. Add to that the factory used to slow grade heat (a system called co- generation) and one can seed that a well run cane sugar estate is environment friendly.
62. Reducing power of sugar meant basis for reducing sugar tests. The free aldehyde or ketone group will reduce alkaline solutions of metallic salts to oxides or free metal. Hence called reducing and non-reducing sugars.
63. Caramelisation temperature for following sugars is as follows: - fructose, sucrose, galactose and maltose, 110°C, 170°C, and 180°C respectively.
64. Types of honey: - Comb honey, cut comb, liquid comb, Liquid honey, naturally crystallised honey, whipped (or creamed) honey.
65. Sugar products: - honey, corn syrup, Jaggery (Gur) or dried sugar cane juice, molasses, maple syrup.
66. Honey products: - Dried honey, flavoured/fruited honey, Honey stix, Infused honey, Kosher honey, and Organic honey.
67. Kosher foods are those that conform to the Jewish dietary regulations of Kashrut (dietary law), primarily derived from Leviticus and Deuteronomy.
68. Poly hydric alcohols, also known as polyols.
69. The FDA considers both glycerine and sorbitol GRAS.
70. Objective analysis of liquids is measured / done by following instruments:

    1. *Stormer viscometer*:-The time taken to make 100 revolutions helps to measure the consistency.
    2. *Brook fied synchro electric viscometer*: - The resistance offered by the spindle to the sample is the measuring index.

3. *Bostwick consistometer*: - Length of flow of substance is propositional to consistency.
4. *Efflux- tube viscometer*: - Time taken for the substance to pass through is measured.
5. *Adams consistometer*:- The extent of flow is measured.
6. *Penetrometer*: - The tenderness is measured.
7. *Bloom gelometer*: - The number of shots required indicates the products tenderness.
8. *Brabender farinograph*: - Used for testing plasticity of wheat dough for baked products.
9. Percent sag (To determine tenderness)

   P.S. = {(depth in container – depth in flat plate)/ depth in container} × 100

   or (a–b/a) × 100

   a = depth in container b = depth in flat plate

   Bakers jellmeter – pectin in fruit juice.

71. **Instruments for determining properties in solids**
    1. Magness-Taylor pressure test: - The spring contracts and measured the compression force required to press the good.
    2. *Succulometer*: -To measure the volume of extracted liquid.
    3. *Tenderometer*- Measures the shearing as well as compression force.
    4. *Fibrometer*: - An instrument that cuts the food in to piece.
    5. *Shortometer*- Tenderness.
    6. *Crystal texturometer*: - A series of rods that pierce the sample.
    7. *Voldokevich bite tenderometer*: - Cutting and shearing.
    8. *Kramer shear press*: - to determine the shearing force and action.
    9. *Compressimeter*: - it measures the compressibility and not shearing strength.
    10. *Shear press*: - Textural characteristics.
    11. *Bratzler shear* :- Measures the tenderness of meat.
    12. *Universal testing machine*: - It measures seven aspects of texture-cohesiveness, hardness, springiness, gumminess, chewiness and fracturability.
72. The government for the first time passed a central act in 1954 called the Preservation of Food Adulteration Act (PFA). The law came into force from 1 June 1955.
73. There are 4 central food laboratories in India (as per PFA-1954)

    1. Central food laboratory Kolkata 2. Central food laboratory Mysore

    3. Central food laboratory Pune 4. Central food laboratory Ghaziabad
74. By section '3' GOI (ECA) Essential Commodity Act 1955, promulgated the Fruits Products Order (FPO) cold storage order in 1980.
75. The infant milk substitutes, Freeding, Bottles and infant food Act (1992) specifies that all these substitutes should have labels with the statement "Mothers' milk is best for young baby" in capital letters.

76. The food commodities which come under the act (AGMARK) are cereals (and products), legumes (and products), eggs, butter, ghee, oils and oil seeds categorized as below: - (central AGMARK lab-Nagpur):- 1. Special, 2. Good, 3.Fair and 4. Ordinary

77. Directorate of Marketing and Inspection (DMI) under ministry of Agriculture and farmers welfare, was set up in 1935 (GOI) at Faridabad (HR) (HQ)branch head office (BHO) at Nagpur and 11 Regional offices at

1. Delhi	2. Mumbai	3. Chennai	4. Kolkata
5. Hyderabad	6. Chandigarh	7. Jaipur	8. Lucknow
9. Bhopal	10. Kochi	11. Guwahati.	

78. Principles of food presentation is "What you can – Eat, What you can't- can"

79. Protection against microbial decomposition
    a) Asepsis
    b) Removal of micro organisms
    c) Stopping the growth and activity of micro organisms
    d) Destruction of micro organisms

80. Protection against self decomposition of food
    a) Inactivating or destroying food enzymes.
    b) Delaying chemical reactions

81. Protections against insect, rodent and animal infest.

82. Protection against losses by mechanical causes.

83. Nitrites and sulphites can both cause asthma, nausea, vomiting and headaches in some people.

84. The new breed of protective compounds is small proteins. They are called Bacteriocins (yogurt contains Bacteriocins); Also called Class I preservative (includes salt and sugar too).

85. Based on Appert methods (father of canning) of food preservation, the packaging of food in sealed airtight tin-plated wrought iron cans was first patented by an English man Peter Durand, in 1810.

86. Following spoilage can be possible in cans
    1. Flat sour 2. Botulism 3. Hydrogen bulge 4. Metallic reactions and spoilage

87. In curing the application of pellets of salt, 'corns are often called corning'.

88. The curing of fish is sometimes called kippering.

89. Drying is a method of food preservation that works by removing water, which is required for decay and the growth of microorganisms.

90. The antioxidants in ghee can be added at the rate of 0.05%

91. Addition of Seasame oil in ghee as adulterant can be identified by boundiness test.

92. As per FPO specifications, the drained weight of canned fruits should not be less than 55%.

93. Extraction of aromatic compound into fat is called soxhlet extraction.
94. ISO 14000 deals with environment management.
95. As per FSSAI, maximum amount of moisture in wheat is 12 %.
96. Duo trio test in sensory evaluation is difference test.
97. Standard screen openings are rectangular in shape.
98. F value is used to measure efficiency of canned foods.
99. ISO 9000:2000 represents audit documentation.
100. Food safety act was passed in year 2006 abroad and 2008 in India.
101. ISO Series 9000 series released in 1987.
102. In HACCP 'P' refers point.
103. Adulteration of vanaspati oil in ghee is tested by boudin test.
104. Codex Alimentarius comes under Non mandatory regulation.
105. Codex Allimenterius is combinely regulated by FAO and WHO.
106. When two identical samples and one unidentical sample are taken for evaluation it is duo trio test.
107. For the good quality of food colour, sensory and texture are necessary.
108. Toughness of food may observed by mouth and finger.
109. Scoring/Numbering in food evaluation is termed as hedonic test.
110. Hedonic evaluation is also known as sensory evaluations.
111. Body which deals with agricultural produce export etc. is APEDA.
112. WHO (World Health Organization) deals with various health issues.
113. PFA comes in the year 1954 and substituted by FSSAI 2006
114. As per the FPO regulations amount of preservatives added to canned fruit must not exceed the permitted limit.
115. Agricultural produce (Grading and Marketing) Act (1937) is also called Agmark Act.
116. he FPO (Food Products Order) came in the year 1955.
117. At 37°C food poisoning bacteria will multiply most rapidly.
118. Alum is used for the sedimentation of impurities present in water.
119. Major adulterants in milk are: Urea, formalin, caustic soda, benzoic acid, salicylic acid, hydrogen peroxide, sugars and melamine.
120. Defence Food Research Laboratory (DFRL) established on 28th Dec. 1961 under DRDO (Defence Research and Development Organization) Ministry of Defence (GoI) is located at Mysore (Karnataka) to cater the needs of Indian Army for logistical support in the area of food supplies and varied food challenges of Indian Army and paramilitary forces.
121. To compare the treatments against a pre- determined control is Dunnet test.
122. Experience to pleasurable or unpleasurable is hedonic rating test.
123. The percentage of adulterated food sold in various parts of India is about 30-35%.

IMPORTANT POINTS

	Colours in Plant/Firm	Indication/use as symbol
1.	Red	Fire equipments, Danger, Stop
2.	Green	Safety, First Aid
3.	White	Traffic lanes
4.	Yellow	Good visibility
5.	Black and yellow strip	Caution

- Syrup and brine rooms should be separate from rest of factory.
- Pest remedies, cleaning compounds etc. must have separate chamber/room.
- Height of tanks, hopper, buckets, elevators etc. must be minimum 15 cm. and covered.
- **Chemicals for cleaning–**

(a) *Strong alkalise e.g.* Sodiun hydroxide (NaOH) or Caustic soda and Lye, Sodium metasilicate.

(b) *Weak alkalise e.g.* Trisodium phosphate (TSP).

Standards for quality:

1. Legal standards –by Govt. may be Central, State, Municipal etc.
2. Company/Voluntary label standards – by Segment of the food industry.
3. Industry Standard – where legal standard are not involved and it may be by organizations (marketing).
4. Consumers/Grade standard – Consumers demand.

Tests of food product:

S.N	*Factors*	*Tests Involved*
1	Colour	Colour difference meter Munsell colour system, Spectrophotometry.
2	Viscosity/consistency/ rheology	GOCUS or Ostwald, Viscometer, Rotating spindle.
3	Texture	Finger feel/by touching.
4	Tenderness	Mouth feel, Texture value(Tenderometer).
5	Container	By weight, volume, vaccum.
6	Symmetry, size and shape defects	By weight, volume, length, width and diameter count or size measurement.

(*Source* : Kalia M and Sood S. 2008)

Food standards:

1. PFA (Prevention of food Adultration) – 1954-55 revised 1968, 1973, 1981.

2. FPO (fruit product order) – 1955 mainly for fruits, vegetables and products.
3. AGMARK – 1937 includes vegetables oils, ghee, cream, butter, rice, gur, groundnuts, potatoes, fruits, pulses and spices. Regarding weights and correct selling practices.
4. BIS (Bureau of Indian standard) – 1986.
5. VOPO (Vegetable oil products (regulation) order) – 1998-order implemented by Directorate of vanaspati, vegetable oil and fats, Ministry of food and civil supplies; GOI (under section-3).
6. SEODMEFO (Solvent extracted oil, De-oiled meat and edible flour (Control) order)-1967-under Section 3 (Essential commodities act.-1955) Rule 50 under PFA rule.
7. MPCO (Meat product control order) – 1973(Ministry of rural areas and employment) under (Essential commodities act.-1955), licensing under PFA-1955.
8. EOPO (Edible oil packaging (Development and regulation order) – 1998 Ministry of consumer affairs has issued in 1998 during the period of dropsy in india - All edible vegetable oils shall be sold only in packed conditions and packed after testing by the manufacturers.
9. MMPO (Milk and milk product order) – 09/06/1992 Ministry of Agriculture, Department of Animal Husbandry and Dairying, GOI. (Essential commodities act.-1955).
10. SWAMA (Standard of Weights and Measures Act.) – 1976 to regulate inter-state trade
    - Packaged Commodities Rule Framed in 1977 revised in 2011.
11. Export (Quality Control and Inspection) Act – 1963 under central govt.
    - EIAs (Export Inspection Agencies) – at Chennai, Delhi, Kochi, Kolkata and Mumbai, EIAs were established by the Ministry of commerce, GOI-1963.
12. APEDA (Agricultural and Processed Food Export Development Authority) – 1985 Act, effect from 13 Feb. 1986.
13. CAC (Codex Alimentarius Commission) was created in 1963 by the FAO (Food and Agriculture Organization and WHO (World Health Organization) jointly to develop food standards programming by a resolution of United Nations.
14. Codex India – National Codex Contact Point (NCCP) for India, launched at Directorate of General of Health Services, Ministry of Health and family Welfare, New Delhi.
15. ISO (International Organization for Standard) established in – 1947 Geneva, Switzerland and it released ISO:9000 in 1987.
16. SGA (Sale of Goods Act) – 1930
17. Trade and Merchandise Marks act – 1958.
18. Dunnett test – to compare treatments against single control.

Weight and Measure Act

- The best time of the day for sensory testing is an hour after any normal meal viz. mid morning or mid afternoon, when the judges are neither too fed nor too hungry.
- Benzoic acid-C_6H_5COOH.

- Sodium benzoate- $C_6H_5COOHNa$.
- Sorbic acid-CH_3-CH=CH-CH=CH-COOH (2, 4-hexadienoic) best activity at pH 6.5. Naturally occurring compound first isolated from the oil of unripe rowanberries (Sorbapple/mountain ash tree) by the German chemist A.W.Von Hofmann- 1859, Antimicrobial property.
- Sulphur dioxide SO_2.
- Diglyceride and monoglycerides are just different due to presence of $C_{17}H_{35}$.
- When no. of $C_{17}H_{35}$ is one then it is called monoglycerides.
- Conduction is the method of heating in which the heat moves from one particle to another by contact (in solid/consistence matter).
- Convection the method of heating in which the heat moves from one particle to another by contact may be semiliquid or liquid matter/medium.
- Radiation is the method of heating in which the heat moves from one particle to another by air.
- Commercially and household refrigerators are usually operated at 4.5°C–7.0°C temperature.
- Freezing is possible for about 16°C to – 2.0°C temperature.
- Ice cream hardening done at (– 34°C).
- Cottage cheese contains moisture about – 79.5% and normally 30-50%.
- ISO-9000 quality system standards have had considerable impact on the evolution of quality activities on a global scale since the first set of standard were issued in 1987.
- The ISO 9000 quality system standards introduced in -1987 revised in the year 1994, 2000.
- **2000 Revision Important:**
  1. ISO 9000:2000 quality management system – Fundamentals and vocabulary.
  2. ISO 9001:2000 quality management system – For requirements.
  3. ISO 9004:2000 quality management system –guidelines for performance improvement.

SOFTEL: Strengthening of Food Testing Laboratories in order to strengthen and devlop a robust food testing laboratories network in India.

Principles of ISO 9000:2000 quality management system—(1) Customer focus, (2) Leadership, (3) Involvement of people, (4) process approach, (5) System approach to management, (6) Continual improvement, (7) Factual approach to decision making, (8) Mutually beneficial supplier relationship.

ISO 22000 : 2005– Specifies requirements for a food safety management system where an organisation in food chain needs to demonstrate its ability to control food safety hazards in order to ensure that food is safe at the time of human consumption.

GMP – Good Manufacturing Practices.

Prerequisite programs for the implementation of an HACCP system is – GMP.

HACCP covers – (1) Location (2) Grounds (3) Building exterior (4) Building interior (5) Access to permisess (6) Employee facilities (7) Cleaning and sanitizing facilities (8) Storage facilities (9) Waste collection/storage facilities (10) Water/steam/ice.

Principles of HACCP:

1. Conduct hazard analysis.
2. Determine critical control points
3. Establish critical limits
4. Establish monitoring procedure
5. Establish corrective action procedure
6. Establish verification procedure
7. Establish record – keeping and documentation procedure

Hazards are of three types:

1. Biological hazards 2. Chemical hazards 3. Physical hazards

- International standard for drinking water given by WHO 1971.
- CAC – Codex Alimentatius Comission.
- GSC – General Standard for Contaminants.

Group of food as per Annex A, complementary food categorization system for the GSC.

1. D – processed foods of plant origin(fermented/nonfermented, sole matter)
2. E – processed foods of animal origin(raw and cooked, sole or combination food)
3. F – multi ingredient manufactured foods (hybrid/combination food stuffs)
4. G – Other edible products (water, minerals and organic compound etc.)

- Adopted in 18, 2008 total quality management (TQM) by W.E. Deming 1987.
- Codex alimentarius Latin word food code/food book 1963 and published in Arabic, Chinese, English, French and Spanish.
- OSHA 18682, OHSAS – Occupational health safety assessment series, OHSAS 18001 released in 1999.
  - Encourage employers and employees to reduce workplace hazards and to implement new or improve existing safety and health programs,
  - Provide for research in occupational safety and health to develop innovative ways of dealing with occupational safety and health problems,
  - Establish ***separate but dependent responsibilities and rights*** for employers and employees for the achievement of better safety and health conditions
  - Maintain a reporting and record keeping system to monitor job-related injuries and illnesses,
  - Establish training programer to increase the number and competence of occupational safety and health personnel
  - Develop mandatory job safety and health standards and enforce them effectively, and
  - Provide for the development, analysis, evaluation and approval of state occupational safety and health programs.
  - Most OSHA standards cover hazards, which exist in a wide variety of industries. These are compiled as the **OSHA General Industry standards, OSH construction standards** and **OSHA maritime sectors standards.**
- ISO 45001 based on OSHAS 18001 is published in March 2018.
- SPS: Agreement on the application of sanitary and phytosanitary measure is an International treaty of WTO.
- Quality Council of India established in 1997 jointly by GoI and ASSOCHAM; CII; and FICCI.
- **WTO:** World Trade Organization (established on 1st Jan., 1995). Head Office at Geneva (Switzerland). It helps producers of goods and services traders, exporters, and importers to conduct their business safely.

CHAPTER 6

MILK, EGG, FISH & MEAT PRODUCTS

Milk as the normal mammary secretion derived from complete milking of healthy milch animal.
***Eggs** are the hard-shelled reproductive body produced by a bird and especially by the common domestic chicken.*
***Fish** are aquatic animals which lives and breathes in water and swims.*
***Meat**, the flesh or other edible parts of animals (usually domesticated) used for food, including not only the muscles and fat but also the tendons and ligaments.*

1. Milk contains several salts such as potassium and sodium phosphates which are responsible for its stability (Swaminathan, 1987).
2. When blood pH goes above 7.8 (acidosis) tetany disease occurs and excessive acidity (pH below 7.0) causes coma (Pattabiraman, 1994).
3. Milk also contains albumin (lactalbumin) at 0.5% and globulin (lactoglobulin) at 0.1%.
4. In sugar at high temperature caramelization takes place and while in protein (Amino acid) milard reaction.
5. Calcium, phosphorus, sodium and potassium are the main minerals which are present in milk at pH 6.5-6.6.
6. The centrifugal procedure used for removing bacteria from milk is known as bactofugation and this high speed centrifugation removes about 99% of spores and more than half the vegetative cells of bacteria pulse from milk.
7. Pasteurization reduces small amount of vitamin C that milk naturally contains.
8. Size of fat globules of milk is about 0.1-20 μ and homogenized milk is about average size 2 μ.
9. The centrifugal procedure used for removing bacteria from milk is known as bactofugation and this high speed centrifugation removes about 99% of spores and more than half the vegetative cells of bacteria plus from milk.
10. Low temperature preservation needs to cool milk at 7-10°C or less.
11. Butter, frozen cream are stored at (–) 17 to (–) 18°C or lower.
12. Process in which the quick frozen product is dried under a high vacuum is called lyophilisation.
13. Sour taste of curd is due to lactic acid and it is converted form of lactose.
14. Ghee is the butter by which all the moisture is evaporated/removed.
15. Up to 60% of moisture is evaporated in evaporated milk.
16. In condensed milk total milk solids are not less than 28% and milk fat not less than 9.5%.
17. On the basis of moisture content cheese is classified as hard, semi hard and soft cheese.
18. Cheese contains about 20-25% protein, 30-35% fat and 30-50% moisture, and about 150g. Cheese is equivalent in food value of 1 litre of milk.

19. In swiss cheese propionic acid contributes to nutty flavour and CO_2 forms collects in pockets within the ripening curd forming eyes.
20. Propionibacterium plays an important role in formation of swiss cheese and forms hole eyes and sweet nutty flavour.
21. Syrup for Gulabjamun is prepared from 8 parts of sugar and 12 parts of water.
22. Evaporated/concentrated milk should be stored at 4.4°C.
23. Dried whole milk contains 26% milk fat (NLT) and 5% moisture (NMT).
24. Homogenization is to break up the fat into much smaller globules which will remain dispersed.
25. Yoghurt is usually prepared from camels or mares milk.
26. Yolk of eggs contains high chlestrol and is not safe for patient suffering from cardiac and liver disease.
27. Waterglass is a 10% solution of sodium silicate which is used as preservative for egg preservation and solution is most effective at 23.9-26.7°C.
28. In thermo-stabilization or heat treatment method fertile and fresh eggs both can be preserved by destroying the viable germ.
29. Cold temperature storage should not be less than 28°F (–2.2°C).
30. At village conditions lime water method of egg preservation is best.
31. Pressure and temperature for dried eggs are 126.5-351.53kg/cm^2 and 110°C-148°C respectively which are employed similar to milk driers.
32. Phospholipids viz lecithin is known for their emulsifying quality present in the eggs.
33. Eggs are poured in simmering water to prepare poaching.
34. Scrambling is to cook in a pan.
35. Bubbles of gas encaved by thin layer of a liquid are called foam and egg white is a good foaming agent.
36. Veal is meat of slaughtered 3-4 weeks after birth.
37. **Beef:** meat of cattle over one year old.
38. **Stear:** a bovine mate animal castrated at very young age.
39. **Heifer:** a female bovine animal that has not born a calf.
40. **Cow:** a female bovine animal that has borne calf.
41. **Stag:** a male bovine animal that is castrated after maturing.
42. **Calf:** a male/female bovine animal upto 12 months of age, generally 3-8 months age.
43. **Mutton:** meat of sheep/sheep carcasses.
44. **Lamb:** both sexes up to 12 months sheep.
45. **Yearling mutton:** up to 12-20 months sheep.
46. **Mature mutton:** 20 months age at the time of slaughter both male (castrated/uncastrated) and female.
47. **Pork:** swine's meat at 3-12 months age (Bacon: it is the cut from the belly portion of hog carcases and has a high percentage of fat).
48. **Organ meats:** are less expensive and more nutritive.
49. **Sausages:** the cooked and smoked sausages are known as table ready meats.

50. Meat contains 15-20% protein and 5-40% fat (mostly saturated).
51. Cathepsins protein- hydrolyzing enzymes are present in meat are responsible for the increased tenderness of it during ageing.
52. Conditioning of meat to tender is done at 0°C for 48 hrs.
53. Artificial tenderizing involves treatment with proteolytic enzymes.
54. Fungal protease, papain, Bromaline and trypsin are proteolytic enzymes used for artificial tenderizing and are injected into animal just before one hour of slaughter.
55. 148.9-176.7°C is the temperature of deep fat frying.
56. Denaturation of Myoglobin during cooking changes colour of meat.
57. Elastin does not undergo any change during cooking.
58. Inosine-5-mono-phosphate (mononucleotides) are substantially responsible for the flavour of meat during cooking.
60. Antibiotics, chlorine, nitrates or nitrites, polyphosphates, edible organic acids like sorbic, succinic and lactic acid are chemical preservatives used in preservation of poultry.
61. Sodium chloride, sodium nitrate and sodium nitrite are curing agents.
62. Fish from cold, clear and deep water are superior in quality and in flavour to fish from warm, muddy and shallow water.
63. Fatty fish contains 6-20% fat.
64. Fish meal contains 50-70% proteins, 2-5% fat, 10-12% minerals and 6-12% moisture.
65. Milk is a complex mixture of lipids, carbohydrates, proteins, and many other organic compound and inorganic salt dissolved or dispersed in water.
66. Gerber test is used to know the percentage of fat present in food.
67. Glutamic acid is present in casein as well as wheat.
68. Calcium % in casein is about 8.2%.
69. When milk is heated, lactose reacts with protein and develops brown colour (non enzymatic) called "Millard reaction" Given by Millard 1912.
70. Dispersed casein, calcium and phosphorus are responsible for white colour of milk.
71. Milk fat contains linoleic acid (2.1%) linolenic acid (0.5%) and Arachidonic acid (0.14%), and is easy to digest.
72. Milk is rich source of tryptophan while poor source of niacin.
73. Casein is present largely as calcium caseinate at pH 6.6.
74. There is no action occur below 10°C or above 65°C in milk of enzyme.
75. Rennin action does not occur in alkaline medium.
76. Freshly drawn milk should be cooled immediately to 4°C to arrest microbial growth either boil it at boiling point.
77. In pasteurization heat liable vitamins like thiamine and ascorbic acid are decreased slightly.
78. Pasteurization results approximately 99% of bacterial, yeast and moulds are destroyed.
79. Dr. Verghese Kurien (milk man of India) awarded by world food prize in 1989.

80. Upto 30-50% of the total milk production in the country is converted to milk products.
81. Evaporated milk is the milk from which about 50-60% water has been evaporated.
82. Fat % in buffalo's milk khoa is 46% and cow's milk khoa is 35%.
83. Sugar is added in rabri when the milk is reduced to 1/3 of the original volume.
84. Gelatin,sea weed or china grass and cellulose derivatives such as carboxymethyl cellulose are used as stabilizers in ice cream making to prevent formation of crystals.
85. Standardised milk contains 4.5% fat and 8.5% solid not fat.
86. Half and half is mixture of milk and milk fat of 10-12%.
87. Butylated hydroxyanisole (BHA) is effective as preservative to enhance the shelf life of butter at 0.02% level stored at 25°C and lower.
88. Nicin is naturally produced in cheese by a number of strains of cheese starter organisms.
89. Nisin is a bio-preservative and is generally recognised as safe.
90. Unripened cheese is called paneer while ripened is cheese.
91. In carrot halwa khoa is used as a binding agent.
92. In eggs the small holes are covered with a thin layer of gelatinous material mucoprtein called cuticle or bloom.
93. Egg shell is made up of protein polysaccharide complex and calcium carbonate.
94. Eggs contain little or no air cells in hen's body.
95. The yolk of the egg is enclosed in sac called the vitelline membrane.
96. Infertile eggs are also called lifeless or vegetarian eggs.
97. Egg white contains 8-12% protein and largely water not fat or carbohydrates.
98. An Ooporphyrins derivative of haemoglobin is the substance responsible for colour of egg shell (white).
99. Colour of egg white is due to small amount of ovoflavin.
100. Due to carotenoids and xanthophylls colour of egg yolk is pale yellow to brilliant orange.
101. Egg is one of the richest sources of lecithin a phospoholipid which forms a part of the structure of every cell wall in the body.
102. Vitamin C is totally absent in the egg.
103. Vitamin D deficiency in the hen reduces egg output.
104. Size and colour of eggs does not reflect the quality.
105. Good quality egg has 72 haugh units and height of thick white is measured by micrometer.
106. Disruption of protein occurs in the tertiary structure (or 3 dimensional structure) due to heat, chemicals or acidity is called "denaturation".
107. Eggs are stored at (–) 1.5 to 0°C at RH 85-90%
108. Dipping of eggs in light mineral oil reduces the loss of moisture.
109. Formation of dark greenish discoloration in hard eggs is due to iron and sulphur present in white and yolk.
110. The sulphur is present mostly as cysteine and methionine amino acid in eggs.

111. Boiled egg, poached egg, scrambled egg; fried egg and omelette are the food stuff made up by egg.
112. Ideal temperature to prepare fried egg is about 126-137°C.
113. Soufflés contain additional ingredients such as grated cheese, vegetable pulp or ground meat.
114. Meat refers to muscle of warm blooded four legged animals it is defined as skeletal muscle with naturally attached tissue.
115. Myosin, Actin, Tropomyosin, Troponin, Collagen and Elastin are muscle protein.
116. Fish protein has higher biological value than meat protein.
117. Fat penetrates between the muscle fibre bundles and this is known as "marbling".
118. Liver is rich in vitamin B_{12} and vitamin A and iron.
119. Ageing or ripening is done by holding meat at temperature at 0.5 °C to (–) 20°C in cold room and it takes 1-4 weeks.
120. Pork never ages because it's high fat content.
121. Papain is inactived at 55°C.
122. Salts used for tenderising are sodium chloride, sodium bicarbonate and, sodium and potassium phosphate.
123. Soaking beef for 48 hrs in concentrated vinegar increases its tenderness and juiciness.
124. Curing agents retard microbial growth and gives flavour to meat. And common salt, sodium nitrate or nitrite, sugar and spices are used for it.
125. As per Codex Alimentarins, the nitrate in meat products can be used 150-500 mg/Kg.
126. Commonly used meat in India (about 70%) comes from sheep and goat.
127. Melting of fat dissolution of collagen in hot liquids to become soft gelatin and softening and muscle fibre separation are three types of changes contribute to increase tenderness.
128. Meat cured with nitrite retains red throughout cooking.
129. Some 5-nucleotides (inosinic acid and guanylic acid) are used in meat and poultry products as flavour potentiators.
130. Broiling is carried out at temperature of 176°C.
131. Cooking losses are great in pressure cooking.

Broiler or fryer	- 8-10 weeks chicken
Rooster	- 3-5 months chicken
Stag	- 10 months chicken
Stewing chicken or fowl	- >10 months chicken
Cock	- mature male chicken over 10 months.

132. Refrigerated poultry has a shelf life of only a few days (6-10 days). Frozen poultry at (–) 23°C to (–) 18°C may be stored up to 9 months.
133. Chicken fat is more unsaturated than the fat of red meat (four legs animal).
134. Emu's meat is dark red in colour and fat free and low in cholestral.

135. Emu's meat is known as lean red meat.

136. Tandoori chicken is a well known and popular Indian chicken dish.

137. Moisture present in dried (dehydrated) meat is about 4 to 5%.

138. India has a total coast line of 7516.6 km (Mainland Coastline 6100 km and Islands coastline consists of 497 km)

139. Fish is rich in lysine and methionine hence it has supplementary value with cereals and pulses.

Fatty acids % in fish

1.	Saturated fatty acid		40
2.	Mono saturated fatty acid		25
3.	Polyunsaturated fatty acid	ω-3	25
		ω-6	10

140. Fresh water fish contains eicosapentaenoic acid and decosahexaenoic acid which are ω-3 poluunsaturated fatty acids.

141. Selenium is a powerful antioxidant found in fish.

142. Shell fishes such as oyster are among the nature's richest source of zinc and the bioavailability of iron and zinc is higher than from plant food.

143. Fish that is oven baked enclosed in a sort of oil paper is called "en papillote".

144. Fishy off odour is due to the production of Trimethylamine by the action of bacterial enzymes on phospholipids and choline present in fish.

145. Ascorbic acid and niacin are effective in returning the flesh to its normal pink colour.

146. Salting of fish is done with the addition of potassium sorbate, sodium benzoate and acid sodium phosphate (0.5%).

147. The chemical name for lactose is 4-0-β-D- galactopyranosyl –D- glucopyranose.

148. Lactose is cleaved to glucose and galactose in the intestine by an enzyme activity called lactose (or β-galactosidase).

149. The major whey proteins in cow milk are β-lacto globulin and α- lactalbumin.

150. Milk protein allergy is only one type of food protein allergy.

151. Lipase has a lipolytic action and contributes to development of desirable flavours in cheese but also rancid flavours in milk.

152. The morning milk contains less fat and water than evening milk in cattle.

153. If milking intervals are longer milk quantity in increased while fat percentage is lowered.

154. Bear and kangaroo have very little lactose in milk.

155. pH of normal milk about 6.6-6.9. Acidity decreases on standing due to loss of carbon-di-oxide and lactic bacteria.

156. a_w water activity of milk is about 0.993.

157. Freezing points of milk is about (–) 0.55°C, which decreases by (–) 0.0055°C on addition of 1% water. This fact is utilized to check the dilution.

158. Lysine is one of the most abundant amino acid presents in milk.

159. Processed milk food like khoa and Rabri contain a higher amount of iron as it is taken from the utensils used for cooking purpose.
160. Calcium, magnesium, phosphorus and citrate make casein resistant to heat and that's why it requires temperature above 100°C to form coagulum.
161. Heated milk tends to form smaller and renderer curds in the stomach compared to raw milk and it improves digestibility of milk.
162. Millard in 1912 observed the phenomenon that reducing sugar and amino acids react to impart brown colour and called Millard reaction.
163. Heating of milk in uncovered pan forms scum while in covered pan it does not occur and because of it milk to boil over from the pan.
164. At pH 6.6 casein is present largely as calcium caseinate.
165. When casein is precipitated by the action of rennet, the calcium is not released to the whey but remains attached to the casein; therefore cheese made with rennet is a much better source of calcium than cheese made by acid precipitation alone.
166. Cottage cheese is often made by acid precipitation.
167. Pasteurization temperatures do not affect the action of renin.
168. Salts either present in milk or added from outside can also curdle milk *e.g.* sodium chloride.
169. Louis Pasteur who discovered that spoilage organisms could be inactivated in wine by applying heat at temperatures below its boiling point, later applied to milk.
170. Rancidity of milk fat takes places due to the acceleration of lipase activity by homogenization.
171. Cheese whey contains fat, lactose, α-lactoglobulin, α-lactalbumin and water.
172. Skim Milk Powder (SMP) contains less milk fat (0.05-0.10%).
173. Without air, ice cream would be similar to a frozen ice cube.
174. % overrun = (wt/gallon of mix –wt/gallon of ice cream) × 100.
175. In khoa addition of 0.2% potassium sorbet and nisin (100 mg/g) prolongs the shelf life to 20 days at 30°C and 125 days in cold storage with no flavour deterioration.
176. Mozzarella is traditionally southern Italian cheese made from Italian buffalos' milk by the pasta filata method also called pizza cheese.
177. Calcium carbonate in egg shell is about –94%.
178. The shell surface of egg contains 7-17 thousand tiny pores.
179. Sometimes the main air cell ruptures, resulting in one or more small separate air bubbles floating beneath the main air cell. Which are known as bubbly air cells.
180. Proteins in egg white are ovalbumin, conalbumin, ovamucid, lysozymes, ovomucin, avidin, ovoglobulin and ovoinhibiter, 55%, 13%, 10%, 3.5%, 2%, 0.05% and 0.1% respectively.
181. Lysozyme in the food industry is related to its ability to selectively inhibit the uncontrolled growth of Clostridium tryobutyricum during the maturation of cheese.
182. Lipovitillins (16-18%), Livetin (4-10%), phosvitin (5-6%) and LDL (12% of granules) are present in egg yolk.
183. Yolk consist 3 types of fats viz. Triglycerides, phospholipids and lipoprotein.

184. Egg yolks are one of the few foods naturally containing Vitamin D.
185. Except riboflavin and niacin, the yolk contains a higher proportion of the egg's vitamins than the white.
186. Yolk is responsible for the eggs emulsifying properties.
187. The yolk is the site of embryo formation in fertilized eggs.
188. The breed of hen determines the colour of the shell.
189. Breeds with white feathers and ear lobes lay white eggs; breeds with red feathers and earlobes lay brown eggs.
190. Greenish ring around hard- cooked egg yolks may occur when eggs are over cooked or when there is a high amount of iron in the cooking water.
191. As the hen ages, her eggs increase in size.
192. Size of eggs is classified as follow jumbo, extra-large, large, medium, and small.
193. Excluding jumbo and small rest of the size are commonly available.
194. The nutrient content of eggs is not affected by whether or not the ration is organic.
195. Free range eggs are eggs produced by hens raised outdoors.
196. ω-3 enhanced eggs are from hens fed a diet containing 10-20% flax seed those eggs contain 10 times ω-3 fatty acids than the classic eggs.
197. Temperature range of 10-16°C is most commonly used to store eggs.
198. Salmonella is found in the intestinal tract of animals, birds, insects, reptiles, sea food and people.
199. Salmonella eateritidis (Se) will not grow at temperature below 4°C and is killed at 71°C.
200. Egg contains all the essential amino acids, and all of the vitamins except vit. C.
201. Eggs have a biological value (efficacy with which protein is used for growth) of 96%. Comparable values are 84.5% for milk, 76% for fish and 74.3% for beef.
202. Egg shell structure consist of three basic units: (*i*) Outer circle made of keratin, (*ii*) Middle sponges or calcareous layer, (*iii*) Inner mamalery layer
203. Yolks of fresh eggs have a slightly acidic pH of about 6.
204. Yolk index is equal to height of yolk/yolk width.
205. Hough's unit (HU) = Height of thick white/weight of the eggs.
206. If the value obtained is 72 the egg is of good quality. Deteriorating eggs give the HU value as low as 30-60.
207. Sodium silicoalmuniate added as a free flow agent to free flowing whole egg/yolks solids.
208. Dehydrated egg yolk with glucose removed is normally pasteurized in a hot room at 54°C for 7 days.
209. Sodium lauryl sulphate, an angel food cake volume enhancer, is added at a level of less than 0.1% on a solid basis.
210. The addition of salt to fresh egg white decreases the stability of foam and beating time is increased from 6-9 minutes.
210. Egg white coagulates at lower temperature (62 to 65°C), egg yolk at higher temperature

(65-70°C), and whole egg at intermediate temperature.

212. Eggs are used in hot liquid like broths, soups and coffee to remove foreign particle, this is achieved since egg white coagulates in hot liquid and traps the unwanted particle within the coagulates network which can be removed.
213. Fluffy omelettes are made by beating egg white separately till stiff and then mixed into the yolk.
214. Soufflés are popular as desserts and consists of a very well beaten egg mixture with essence and flavour which is later served cold originated in France.
215. Egg is broken and the contents poured into a dish already coated with fat are shirred eggs.
216. Water is heated in a pan and the egg is broken over it and poured into boiling water in poached egg.
217. Ideal temperature to prepare fried eggs is around 126-137°C.
218. Devilled eggs are a popular egg dish which consists of de- shelling the hard-boiled eggs and then cut in half.
219. Hard boiled egg spin wells, while raw egg wobble.
220. It is easier to separate the yolk from the white if egg is very cold.
221. "Meat as animal flesh used for food" oxford dictionary.
222. The muscle fibre is surrounded by a protective layer called the sarcolemma.
223. Connective tissue is made up from basic proteins collagen, elastin and reticulin. Collagens are weakened by heat and forms gelatine, which is soluble. This change helps the meat to become tender. The two other proteins are not weakened by heat, yet they provide elasticity and strength.
224. Marbling: - The penetration and deposition of fat in between muscle fibres from the deposits in between muscles and around organs as a subcutaneous fat.
225. Meats are excellent sources of some B complex vitamins particularly B12.
226. The liver is an excellent source of vitamin A.
227. Calcium and magnesium are the main minerals with important roles to play in the contraction of muscles.
228. Cathepsins protein hydrolysing enzymes help in the process of denaturation of the muscle proteins which in turn makes meal tender.
229. Rigor mortis is the phenomenon in animal after death due to interruption of cell metabolism and vital processes there is stiffening and hardening of the carcass.
230. After rigor mortis the meat once again becomes, soft with an improvement in flavour as well as juiciness in cold conditions, this is called resolution of rigor.
231. Curing is a traditional art practised primarily to preserve meat and retard spoilage.
232. Nitrites are thought to be carcinogenic when heated to high temperatures, posing a threat to the health of humans consuming cured meat.
233. Specifications of ISI assessment of quality of meat before using it for human consumption:
234. Healthy animals should only be slaughtered with the objective of procuring meat.

235. Slaughter house should be maintained under hygienic conditions with proper cleanliness in and around the slaughter area.

236. There should be a competent manager to supervise the functioning of the slaughter house.

237. Antemortem and post-mortem examination of the carcass should be conducted for eliminating any potentials contamination chances and selecting the best meat.

238. The commonly used meat is mutton (approx 70%) of all meat is derived from sheep or goat.

239. Smoking of fish and meats is a preservation process.

Objectives of cooking meat:

- Develop or improve flavour, colour and aroma.
- Make it delicious/appetising to eat.
- Make it tenderer.
- Make it easier to digest.
- Make it safe to eat *i.e.* kill any harmful bacteria it may have picked up during handling.

Chemical changes during cooking process of meat:

- Muscles proteins shrink and moisture is lost.
- Changes in colour.
- Connective tissue softens.
- Fat melts, browning occurs, and flavour develops.
- Seasoning develops flavour.
- Dry heat methods do not use liquid, but can use fat or oil while moist heat method uses liquid.
- Roasting temperature for meat (very lean/totally trimmed cuts):
- Slow roast: under 160°C (but NLT 100°C).
- Medium: 170-180°C.
- Fast: 200°C or over.

257. *Barbecue/Barbeque/BBQ/Barbie*: -A meal or gathering at which meat, fish or other food is cooked out of doors on a rack over an open fire or on a special appliance.

258. Braising (from the French word braiser) is a combination cooking method that uses both lit wet and dry hearts: typically, the food is first seared at a high temperature, then finished in a covered pot at lower temperature while sitting in some amount of liquid.

259. In freezing of meat temperature don't fluctuate by more than 0.5°C.

260. Meat analogues, which mimic the sensory properties of meat and can be used to replace or extended meat in traditional products *e.g.* textured vegetable protein (TVP) and myco-protein (*e.g.* TVP, Tofu, Temph, myco-protein, Fusarium graminearumis used in Myco-protein production.)

261. In 2008, Dr. Rajendra Pachauri, chair of the UN intergovernmental panel on climate change, urged people to have one meat-free day a week to help curb climate change.

262. The Food Standard Agency said that "any novel food, or food produced using a novel production process, must undergo a stringent and independent safety assessment before it is placed on the market".
263. Tandoori chicken is a very popular poultry preparation and has made India world famous.
264. Doner Kebab; A popular Turkish dish, it uses turkey meat as the main ingredient.
265. It is natural phenomenon for fish to struggle and try to escape when caught. As a result of this excessive activity all the glycogen is converted in to glucose and used up. With no glycogen available for conversion into lactic acid, pH doesn't decrease, since bacterial growth is retarded in low pH, this condition accelerates spoilage.
266. Selfish have lower protein content than fin fish.
267. Discolouration and dark colour of selfish in storage is attributed to the reaction between hydrogen sulphite (released from the fish) and iron (of the can) to form ferrous sulphite.
268. *To avoid this some steps can be taken:-*
269. Using zinc coated enamel cans to replace iron cans.
270. Dipping selfish in acids (acetic, citric, and tartaric) to increase the acidity and reduce the possibility of FeS formation.
271. Court-bouillon or court bouillon is a quickly cooked broth used for poaching other foods, most commonly fish or seafood or highly seasoned stalk to enhance the flavour.
272. Pasteurization of Milk is carried out at 72.7°C for 15 sec.
273. Milk fat is present in the form of emulsion.
274. Casein is present in milk in emulsion.
275. Minimum fat % in double toned milk is 1.5%.
276. Butter flavour is due to vallin herb.
277. By weight of 45% cream and 4% milk 5% fat, 1 part of 45% cream and 40 parts of 4% milk must be mixed to milk testing.
278. Yellow colour in cow milk is due to carotene.
279. Pasteurization efficiency of milk is checked by phosphates test.
280. Fat content of khoa should not be less than 20%.
281. The chief muscle pigment is myoglobin.
282. Bottom layer obtained during ghee making is impurities.
283. Component responsible for flavour in fermented dairy products is salt.
284. Hydrogenation of oil generally takes place in presence of catalyst such as nickle, palladium or platinum.
285. Major fat found in egg yolk is unsaturated 30%.
286. Cross contamination is possible in animals for meat production by through excreta blood and viscera and equipment used during processing.
287. Water holding capacity of meat is due to fat (due to marbling).
288. Preservatives used in meat Nitrites, Nitrates, Salt, ficin (fig), Bromelain (pineapple) and Papain (papaya).
289. Milk is deficient in Iron, phosphorus, Vitamin C, Iodine, Cu and methionine.
290. Pasteurized milk should be stored below 50 °C temperature.
291. In homogenization the particle size of fat globules is reduced by 0.02-0.2μ.

292. Lactose, or 0-4-D-galactopyranosyl- (1, 4)-glucopyranose, is the major carbohydrate of milk.
293. Oil of fish contains high amount of Vitamines.
294. White revolution initiated in the year 1970 by V. Kurien (Milkman of India).
295. NDDB Established in the year 1965.
296. For meat preservation which is used Na nitrate and $NaCl_2$ are used.
297. Mince meat and spices are filled and used to make sausages.
298. Cold shortening can be avoided by keeping the meat above 140°C for sufficient time to pass the rigor stage.
299. Per capita availability of milk in India in the year 2016-19 - 355 gm. per day.
300. When pre-rigor meat is frozen, a severe type of rigor mortis ensues during thawing called thaw rigor, where the shortening so produced may be 60 to 80% of the original length of the unrestrained muscle.
301. Milk production in India is 18.5 percent of world production, acheving an annual output of 165.1 million tones during 2016-19.
302. Myoglobin is carrier oxygen.
303. MSG is used in meat preservation Tenderization.
304. Candling is done to evaluate quality of egg
305. If the egg sinks in water it is of good of quality.

     Eggs are candled to determine the condition of the air cell, yolk, and white. It is also done to learn which eggs are fertile and will hatch into baby chicks. This process works by illuminating the inside of the egg so you are able to see what is inside shell.
306. In candling egg is hold under a strong light above or below to observe the embryo.
307. Freezing point of yolk is about 1°C and it may be stored at 6°C or below.
308. Defect of meat is due to lactic acid slumminess on surface.
309. NaCl is used as curing agent in meat.
310. Myoglobulin binds O_2 in muscles.
311. Collagen with water heating is gelatin.
312. Sausage are cured and packed meat.
314. KMS is used as Meat preservative.
315. On freezing yolk or whole egg becomes viscous and gummy called Gelation.
316. In tenderization of meat phosphate salts are more effective than common (table) salt.
317. Meat has 12% protein content.
318. Shrinkage of meat is greater at pH 5.8 because net charge on the main protein of muscle is zero.
319. After homogenization lypase is immediately deactivated.
320. Renin is an enzyme.
321. Tenderization is softening of meat.

322. Milk has been curdled and whey is liquid remaining after strained.
323. Meat products have pH of about - 5.5-6.
324. Biological value of egg protein is about 90%.
325. Fish protein is more digestible due to amount of connective tissues present is less than meat.
326. Animal cells are without chloroplast.
327. Cocoa in chocolate milk comes from seaweed.
328. Major constituents of milk are water, fat, protein, lactose and minerals.
329. Minor constituents of milk are phospholipids, sterols, vitamins, enzymes, pigments etc.
330. True constituents of milk are milk fat, casein and lactose.
331. Milk proteins are considered complete proteins as they contain all essential amino acids.
332. Milk is an excellent source of calcium and phosphorus. Milk is low in iron, copper and iodine.
333. Various types of milk depending on fat and SNF content are: standardized milk, recombined milk, toned milk, double toned milk and skim milk.
334. Different types of processed milk include pasteurized milk, flavored milk, sterilized milk and UHT milk.
335. Jersey breed cow milk contains highest fat content.
336. Murrah breed buffalo milk contains highest fat content.
337. Pearson's square method is used for standardization of fat and SNF in processed milk.
338. Phosphatase test is used to check adequacy of pasteurization.
339. Lactose is the sugar found only in milk and is 1/6th as sweet as sucrose.
340. Carotene (fat soluble) is responsible for yellow color of milk, ghee, cream, butter and other dairy products while riboflavin gives a greenish yellow color to whey.
341. The TA (Titratable acidity) of cow milk varies from 0.13 to 0.14% and 0.14 to 0.15% in buffalo milk.
342. Pasteurization of milk is done at 63°C/30 minutes, 72°C/15sec.
343. Standardized milk should contain a minimum of 4.5% fat and 8.5% SNF.
344. Toned milk should contain a minimum of 3.0% fat and 8.5% SNF.
345. Double toned milk should contain a minimum of 1.5% fat and 9.0% SNF.
346. Cream should contain NLT 25% milk fat.
347. Butter must contain NMT 1.5% by weight curd, NMT 3.0% by weight of common salt and NLT 80% by weight of milk fat.
348. The flavor of butter is chiefly due to diacetyl.
349. The color of butter is due to added coloring agent annatto.
350. Butter oil refers to fat concentrate obtained mainly from butter or cream by removal of practically all the water and SNF.
351. The percentage of butter fat in butter oil is 99.5-99.8%.

352. Ice cream is frozen dairy product and should contain NLT 10% milk fat, 3.5% protein, 36% total solids, NMT 0.5% stabilizers and emulsifiers by weight.
353. Cheese is a product obtained by draining after the coagulation of milk and may contain coagulating agent, sodium chloride and calcium chloride not exceeding 0.02% by weight.
354. Unsweetened condensed milk should contain NLT 8% milk fat and NLT 26% milk solids.
355. Sweetened condensed milk should contain NLT 9% milk fat, NLT 31% total milk solid and NLT 40% cane sugar
356. Unsweetened condensed skim milk should contain NLT 20% total milk soilds and NMT 0.5% fat by weight.
357. Sweetened condensed skim milk should contain NLT 26% total milk soilds, NLT 40% cane sugar and NMT 0.13% fat content by weight.
358. Whole milk powder should contain NMT 5% moisture, NLT 26% fat and NMT 1.2% total acidity.
359. Skim milk powder should contain NMT 1.5% milk fat, NMT 5% moisture and NMT 1.5% total acidity.
360. Milk powders are drum dried/roller dried and spray dried.
361. The maximum solubility index should be 15 for roller dried and 2 for spray dried powder.
362. Khoa, mawa, rabri and kulfi are concentrated whole milk products.
363. Dahi, shrikhand, paneer and chhana are coagulated milk products.
364. Makkhan, ghee, lassi and ghee residue are products of clarified butter fat industry.
365. Khoa should contain NLT 20% milk fat.
366. Pindi, dhar, danedar are varieties of khoa.
367. Chhana or paneer should contain NMT 70% moisture and NLT 50% milk fat of dry matter.
368. Ghee is the pure clarified fat derived solely from milk or from desi butter and should contain NLT 99-99.5% milk fat and NMT 0.5% moisture.
369. Ghee residue refers to the charred light to dark brown residue which is obtained after the filtration of ghee.
370. Ghee residue is the byproduct of ghee industry. Diacetyl content in butter should be NMT 4ppm. India is the leading producer of milk in the world.
371. Sanitizers and cleaning agents form an important part of the dairy industry for hygiene maintenance.
372. Major constituents of milk are water, fat, protein, lactose and minerals.
373. Minor constituents of milk are phospholipids, sterols, vitamins, enzymes and pigments etc.
374. True constituents of milk are milk fat, casein and lactose.
375. Milk proteins are considered complete proteins as they contain all essential amino acids.
376. Milk is an excellent source of calcium and phosphorus. Milk is low in iron, copper and iodine.

377. Various types of milk depending on fat and SNF content are: standardized milk, recombined milk, toned milk, double toned milk and skim milk.
378. Different types of processed milk includes pasteurized milk, flavored milk, sterilized milk and UHT milk.
379. Phosphatase test is used to check adequacy of pasteurization.
380. Milk plasma ais also called *skim milk.*
381. Canned meat blackening is due to *Clostridium nigrificans.*
381. Specific gravity of milk decreases with **rise of temperature**
382. Fat content of anhydrous milk fat should not be lower than 99.9%
383. Freezing point of milk is **– 0.55 °C**
384. Caesin content of milk represent about 80% of milk proteins
385. The pioneer of UHT milk processing is Dr. Harold Burton
386. Iodine solution is used to test the presence of **starch** in the milk.
387. Tomato ketchup is good example of Non Newtonian fluid and pseudoplastic.
388. Sodium benzoate is effective in pH range of 2.5-4.0.
389. Milk is pre-heated before UHT treatment to avoid **fouling**
390. Milk is an **emulsion** of fat in water
391. Tofu paneer is prepared from soybean.
392. Saffron is obtained from flowers.
393. The common adulterants of milk are urea, starch, sucrose, water, neutralizes detergents.
394. NDRI Karnal is the leading institute in dairy research in India.
395. White revolution is related to enhanced milk production in India by Dr. Verghese Kurien
396. Lipid is a major component of the carcass of a meat animal and is inversely proportional to the moisture content.
397. Immediately after slaughter, muscle normally contains a very small amount (nearly 1%) of glycogen.
398. The rate and amount of glycolysis influence the color, tenderness and water holding capacity of meat.
399. Most of the total body inorganic material is located in skeletal tissue primarily as salts of calcium and phosphorus and some other minerals especially magnesium.
400. The inorganic elements play an important role in the conversion of muscle to meat and cause the development of rigor mortis and alteration of fluid balance which cause a drop in pH and water holding capacity.
401. Water soluble vitamins are localized in lean tissues whereas fat-soluble vitamins in fatty tissues.
402. Pork contains 5-10 times more thiamine content as compared to mutton.
403. Stress and fatigue lower the quality of meat in several ruminant species due to depletion of glycogen in the muscle.

404. Due to low acid production, the ultimate pH of the muscle remains high causing a condition called dark cutting meat or dark, firm and dry (DFD) meat. In pigs, low ultimate pH is achieved within 45 minutes due to rapid glycolysis and results in pale, soft and exudative (FSE) pork that has higher drip and cooking losses.

405. Stunning is a process employed to create a state of immobility or unconsciousness at the time of slaughter for 1 minute.

406. Meat cutting refers to the skill of separation of carcass into wholesale primal cuts in order to facilitate requirements of meat trade, cater to the consumer preference and convenient handling by the butchers.

407. Postmortem inspection involves visual perception and palpation of organs and tissues, incisions where necessary and laboratory tests. Primal and sub-primal cuts of fresh meat are overwrapped with thermoplastic films having excellent optical properties.

408. Post slaughter, the accumulation of lactic acid due to anaerobic glycolysis lowers down the muscle pH which is an important postmortem change during the conversion of muscle to meat.

409. There is decline in postmortem pH of the meat from 7 to ultimately 5.5-5.7.

410. Rigor mortis refers to stiffening of muscles after death and is another important postmortem change in the process of conversion of muscle to meat.

411. The onset of rigor mortis is enhanced at ambient temperature above 200°C.

412. Pre-rigor meat is quite tender but its toughness keeps on increasing until rigor mortis is completed.

413. The onset of rigor mortis is also accompanied by a decrease in water holding capacity.

414. A rapid decline in muscle pH also causes denaturation of collagenous connective tissue.

415. The principal meat pigment is myoglobin.

416. Myoglobin content of more active species and muscles is higher than the passive ones.

In intact meat, iron in the heme ring of myoglobin exists in the reduced form. Upon cutting, grinding or exposure to air, myoglobin is oxygenated to form oxymyog-lobin which has a bright red color.

417. In conditions of less oxygen, partial vacuum or semi permeable package, myoglobin as well as oxymyoglobin is oxidized to brown colored metmyoglobin.

418. The capacity of meat to retain its water during the application of physical forces is known as water holding capacity (WHC).

419. Marbling refers to the intramuscular fat which can be visibly detected when the muscle surface is cut.

420. Fresh meat with a good water holding capacity is less prone to shrinkage during storage.

421. When prerigor meat is fast chilled below 150°C, there is shortening of muscles. This cold shortening or contraction is more at 0.0°C and still more at –2.0°C.

422. Raw milk quality is measured by Somatic Cell Count (SCC) and Standard Plate Count (SPC)

IMPORTANT POINTS

- Egg is poor source of Ca and Vitamin C.
- PER is 4.5 and NPU is 94° of egg. (Biological value 10°) (PER protein eq. ratio NPU (Net Protein Utilization)
- Egg (raw) albumin contains an antinutritional factor avidin which is destroyed by heat that's why eating raw eggs must be avoided.
- Avidin combines with Biotin (Vitamin B_7) to form a complex which is not absorbed from the intestine, when egg is cooked this complex is broken down and biotin is released for absorption in body.
- Egg injury – it is syndrome due to the deficiency of biotin.
- Kheer is considered as a good combination from nutritional point of view because it overcomes many deficiencies in rice.
- **Milk products:**
  (1) Fermented – Curd, Yoghurt, Lassi/Butter milk, Butter, Ghee, Cheese.
  (2) Unfermented – Skimmed milk, Skimmed milk powder, Toned milk, Cream, Malai (Cloted cream), Khoa, Channa (Cottage cheese) and Whey and Junket.
- Yoghurt is by *Lactobacillus bulgaricus* (a specific type of lactic acid bacteria) and it is a curdled milk product.
- Fat in Skimmed milk is 0.05-0.1 %
- Channa/cottage cheese – valuable source of phosphorus, fat.
- Khoa weight is less 20-30% from milk (khoa obtained from milk is 20–30% of milk).
- Toned milk – 3.0% fat, 8.0% SNF and Double toned – 1.5% fat, 9.0% SNF
- Whey – by product of butter and cheese making/production
- Junket – when milk is clotted with rennet

Meat products:

- Protein % 18-22.
- Meat does not contain Vitamin A, C and D and mineral Ca.
- Liver is the richest source of Vitamin A, D and B_{12} complex and Protein viz. 18-22%.
- Fish contains protein 18-22%.

Meat and Sea Food Processing:

(1) *Curing*– The classic meat cure ingredients are NaCl, Nitrites/Nitrates and Sugar (Sucrose/glucose) with the combination of NaCl, Additionally phosphates, Sodium ascorbate or erythrobate, potassium sorbate, monosodium glutamate, hydrolized vegetable proteins, lactose etc.

(2) *Smoking*–liquid smoke contains all the essential ingredients of wood smoke but it is free of the carcinogen benzopyrene.

- **Bacon** – the salted and often smoked meat of pig.
- **Sausage** – stuffed into a prepared intestine or other casing.
- **Jerky** – is a dried self stable product made from lightly salted and spiced of meat or fish most often beef.
- **Fish** – Water 63-83%, Protein 9-20%, Fat 0.4-16.5%, Ash 1-2.5%, Carbohydrates 1-1.5%.
- **Shellfish** – The most widely consumed Shellfish with in this group are shrimp, lobsters, crabs and crayfish.
- **Crustaceans** – catheptic like marine enzymes rapidly breaks protein (munida).
- **Mollusks** – Carbohydrates in the form of glycogen.
- **Milk and milk products:**
- Pasteurization at 150-155 °F/65.5-68.3 °C for 30 minutes or 166-175 °F/74.4-79.4 °C for 15 seconds and cooling at 4 °C.
- Evaporated milk by removal of up to 60% water from whole milk which result 11.5% of lactose.
- Sweetened milk (sweetened condensed milk)–by the addition of sucrose/glucose before evaporation sugar content finally reaches about 54% or > 64% in solution.
- Skim milk fat 0.5% produced by high speed centrifugation at the rate of 100°F.
- Chocolate milk processed at slightly higher temperature at 75°C for 15 seconds.
- **Meat is classified as follow:**

  (1) Mutton—(a) Lamb (b) Yearling mutton (c) Mature mutton

  (2) Pork

  (3) Organ meats

  (4) Sausages

  (5) Fish (finfish/shellfish).
- FPC–fish protein concentrate.
- Smoked fish not popular in India.
- Salting (pickling) is widely used in India.
- For the enhancement of shelf life of fish some chemicals like acids viz. Sodium benzoate, ethylene oxide and antibiotic Aureomycin are used, preservatives are not permitted in country.
- About 20-25 days (life) storage achieved by irriadiation of γ (Gama) radiation.
- About 3-10% of fish flour may be incorporated in variety of dishes with 85-90% high quality protein.

- Roasted white meat (without skin) 64% water, 32% protein, 3.5% fat.
- In yolk iron is about 1.42mg/egg and mineral 1% in egg.
- Egg is the excellent source of vit. A while yolk is source of vit D (commonly not found in other food)
- Weight of an egg is about 49-70g and in Indian conditions it is about 45g.
- Small eggs contain large yolk than large eggs.
- Glucose of egg white results browning by combining with egg protein at temperature of above freezing or normal after dehydration and it may be prevented by glucose exclusion by glucose oxidase or by fermentation with yeast prior to drying
- Ratio of yolk to egg white in egg is 2:3.
- **Halal** is the Arabic word which means permissible items/stuff/action relevant to food and other things.
- Potatoes, rice, corn and soy flour used as sausage binders, the binders used in sausage is meat fibres together and prevent shrinkage by absorption of meat juice.
- Preservatives used in meat – nitrites, nitrates, salt or fig(ficin), pineapple(bromaline) and papaya(papain) with the help of proteolytic enzyme.
- Injection of an enzyme into the animal before slaughter is done for enzymatic meat tenderization of meat.
- Due to growth of Escherichia coli the fishy flavours in eggs is seen
- **Composition of Ghee :** Ghee is clarified butter fat it contains 99.0-99.5% fat, < 0.5% moisture, solid at 15-28°C melt at 28-44°C, specific gravity - 0.93- 0.94. saponification value < 2.0, iodine value 24-36 units.
- Iodine value is used to determine degree of unsaturation in fatty acids.

  (It is the mass of iodine in grams that is consumed by 100 gm of a chemical substance.)
- **Khoa** : Shelflife 4-5 days, moisture 19-20%, fat 25-45%, protein 19-25%, lactose 25-30%, ash 3-5%.
- About 20-30 kg of khoa will be obtained from 100 kg of milk.
- Fat percentage in meat is 5-40%, mostly saturated.
- When fat penetrates between the muscle fibre bundles and this is called as Marbling desirable with some meats.
- Water holding capacity of meat depends on fat percentage and it influences the juiciness of meat.
- Purpose of curing is to produce the unique flavoured meat and products.
- Uncured meat becomes brown after cooking.
- Cured meat remains red after cooking.
- Salt retards microbial growth and gives flavour.
- Nitrite fixes the red colour of myglobin and also inhibits *Clostridium botulinum* and improves flavour.

Table 1: List of meat products available in markets

– Meat sausage and loaves (fermented)
– Packed meat
– Frozen meat – RTE chicken, salamon, meat balls, bacon, seekh kebabs
– Cured meat – Ham, bacon
– Precooked frozen meat products – Keema, hamburger, hot dog
– Luncheon meat – From pork (in Army), sandwiches (comminuted product)
– RTE compressed meat formulations
– Mutton pickle (partially fermented)
– Dehydrated mutton mince
– Meat patties
– Fast food (meat based)
– Meat protein concentrate (MPC)

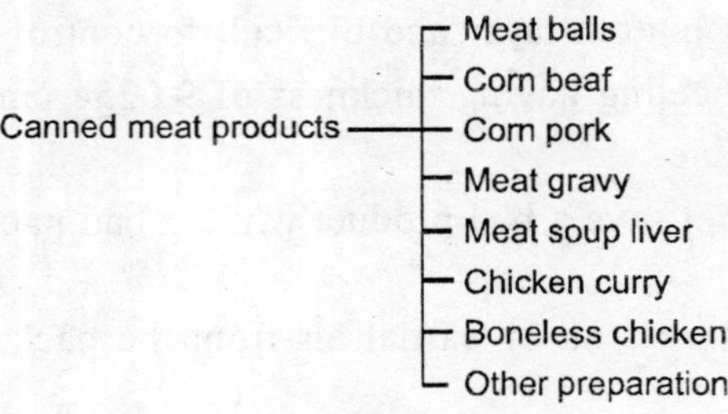

- **Lard:** Lard is pig fat in both its rendered and unrendered forms. Lard was commonly used as a cooking fat or shortening, or as a spread similar to butter.
- **Tallow:** Animal edible tallow is normally obtained from beef but also from sheep and goats, processed from suet. Unlike suet, tallow can be stored for extended periods without the need for refrigeration to prevent decomposition, provided it is kept in an airtight container to prevent oxidation.
- **Collagen:** Collagen is a substantial part of connective tissue and is found in ligaments, tendons, skin and many other types of tissue serving mechanical and structural functions. Collagen accounts for almost one third of the total protein and is made from several different proteins.

CHAPTER 7

FOOD PACKAGING

***Food packaging** is defined as enclosing food to protect it from physical, chemical, and biological factors, with active packaging being the most common packaging system used for preserving food products.*

1. Cellophane, resins of polyesters and polyethylene are more important plastics and film of food packaging.
2. The use of wood pulp in paper making was introduced in 1867.
3. The first paper making machinery, in which fibres were laid down on a moving wire cloth, began production in 1799 in England.
4. Glass containers include-1. Bottles 2. Jars 3. Trumblers 4. Jugs 5. Carbys 6. Vials and ampoules.
5. Due to overloading the container compact injury may take place.
6. Impact injury result in bottom layer and difficult to control for such type of damage.
7. Thin flexible plastic sheeting having thickness of 9.0254 cm or less are film.
8. First film was cellophane.
9. Good packaging may not save a bad product while a bad packaging can definitely derail a good product.
10. Vacuum packaging removes all or partial air from the package to prevent oxidation of foods.
11. Points to be considered before designing a packaging system are as follow – product details, distribution, handling, destination market and packaging cost etc.
12. Regional Centres of Indian Institute of Packaging are situated at Kolkata, Delhi and Chennai while Head quarter is at Mumbai.
13. Slogan of World Packaging Organisation is "Better quality of life through better packaging".
14. Government has made "Best Before Date" mandatory w.e.f. July 1999.
15. Green and brown colours for vegetarian and non-vegetarian respectively doted labels on packaging made mandatory w.e.f. 04.10.2001 by GOI.
16. IFOAM stand for International Federation of Organic Agriculture Movement.
17. National Standard for Organic Products (NSOP)-2000.
18. National Programme for Organic Products (NPOP).
19. OFAI stands for Organic Farming Association of India.
20. Packaging can be arbitrarily classified into Primary, Secondary and Tertiary Packaging.
21. Secondary packaging is outside the primary packaging, so as to group the primarily packed objects.

22. Food Authenticity means the food should match the description on the labels.
23. Incorrect Origin, Incorrect Quantitative Description and Extending the food are all forms of mis-description.
24. Risk assessment is applied to data on toxicity and human exposure to: Estimate the likelihood, or probability, of a toxic effect on exposed humans.
25. Food allergies: Usually occur only after an individual has been sensitized by prior exposure
26. It is a clause that the writing on the label of the container has to be clear.
27. Codex Alimentarius is an international commission for food labeling.
28. Coffee, Tea and Spices have been exempted from food labelling.
29. WVTR stands for water vapor transfer rate.
30. WVTR is expressed as $g/cm^2/24$ hr at 90% Rh. 38 °C.
31. OTR stands for oxygen transfer rate.
32. IPP stands for Institute of Packaging Professional's.
33. Gas mostly used in packaging is carbon dioxide.
34. In bread packaging the packaging material should have low WVTR.
35. Fillers in paper improve gloss, brightness and opacity.
36. In controlled Atmospheric packaging which is controlled is CO_2 and O_2.
37. Resin is used in packaging material for printability.
38. Packaging contains information and security for consumers.
39. Packaging material for soft drink is PET.
40. Packaged food may be affected by light intensity and wavelength of light.
41. Laminates are made up of polythene and paper.
42. CAP involves monitoring and adjustment of the gases.
43. Aluminium foils used in food packaging are essentially impermeable to water vapor and gas.
44. Vacuum skin packaging and shrink and non shrink bag methods are used for vacuum packaging of meats.
45. Non enzymatic browning is principal cause of deterioration in dehydrated vegetables.
46. 'C' enamels contain FeS and used for non acidic foods.
47. Most suitable packaging material" for cut flowers is cardboard boxes.
48. Thickness of tin can is 0.5-2.0μ.
49. A polythene/packaging material should have bursting strength, tear resistant and grease resistant quality.
50. Storage of food under reduced pressure is termed as hypobaric storage.
51. Sizers in paper improve strength, printability and resistance to water.
52. MAP involves introduction of a gas mixture other than air into a package.

53. For high acidic foods 'I' type cans are used.
54. Headquarter of Indian Institute of Packaging is located in Mumbai.
55. Flex resistance test is used to evaluate the seal strength of a flexible packaging material.
56. Ethylene vinyl alcohol is an excellent oxygen barrier.
57. Neilson prior to 1913 carried out first aseptic packaging of food in Denmark
58. Alkaline process is Kraft process of chemical pulping.
59. Moisture is major concern to coffee from packaging point of view.
60. Retort pouches are heat sterilizable flexible packs.
61. Combination of Nylon - paper - plastic or metal foiles can be used for making a retort pouch.
61. China clay is used in paper manufacture as filler.
62. Aluminium silicate, Calcium sulphate and Magnesium silicate is/are used as filler in paper.
63. Aluminium foil acts as good barrier for vapour, light and oxygen.
64. Glass is the packaging material which has perfect barrier properties.
65. Kraft's process is the major chemical process used for pulping of wood during paper manufacturing.
66. ASTM stands for American Society for Testing and Materials.
67. Heat shrink ability is one of the production properties of flexible packaging materials.
68. To protect the product is the technical function of package.
69. Controlled atmosphere packaging (CAP) involves monitoring and adjustment of the gases.
70. A secondary-package is that contains the primary package.
71. Industrial packaging usually contains goods or materials for further processing.
72. The test used to evaluate the seal strength of a flexible packaging material is Flex resistance test.
73. In case of CAP and MAP Oxygen, nitrogen and carbon dioxide gases are introduced, monitored or adjusted.
74. PET is good oxygen barrier compared to PVC, PP and PS.
75. First things the consumer notices about a package are what is this and what is it going to do for me and who guarantees that.
76. EVOH stands for Ethylene vinyl alcohol. SWAMA (1976) stands for Standard Weight and Measure Act.
77. Nylon can be steam sterilized at 140 °C.
78. Vinyl chloride monomer in PVC is carcinogenic.
79. Diastatic activity is combined activity of α and β amylase.
80. Packaging material for coffee, tea and confectionary goods contains paper /aluminium/ low density polyethylene.
81. 'C' enamel cans contain FeS and are used for Non Acidic foods.

82. Screen, Flexography and lithography are the typical methods used in printing of packages.
83. TAPPI stands for Technical Association of Pulp and Paper Industry. Polystyrene can be used for increasing the shelf life of citrus fruits.
84. Cryovac is Polyolefin shrink film with high oxygen and aroma borne properties.
85. PVA stands for Polyvinyl Alcohol.
86. Impact and vibration are the transportation hazard.
87. Polystyrene is used for Acidic foods.
88. Lacquering of cans helps in preventing cans from discolouration.
89. Lamination is combination of two or more materials into a single homogenous packaging web by means of adhesive, solvent or heat.
90. Paper-Al-LDPE lamination combination is preferred to pack coffee.
91. Misbranding and use of ambiguous statements on package labels are prevented by Standard Weight and Measure Act, 1976.
92. Shrink wrapping is method of packaging the material to give skin tight wrap.
93. Natural Kraft paper is used wherever maximum strength is needed.
94. Virgin Kraft papers that have been treated plasticizer to make them more pliable are known as pouch paper.
95. The actual material used to make a tin more is low carbon steel.
96. Polypropylene has lower crystallinity than polyethylene.
97. Starch and starch based products animal glue, hot melts, synthetic emulsions are common classes of packaging adhesive.
98. The Meat Food Product Order was promulgated in 1973.
99. A means of binding two or more webs together and bonding them with an adhesive or by heating is lamination process.
100. Sulphite process of pulping is a chemical method.
101. General purpose enamels are often used for more acidic products.
102. The first commercial aseptic filling plant was bought by Dole Company.
103. Indicator organism used in testing of packaging material sterilization by hydrogen peroxide and heat is *Bacillus stearothermophilus*.
104. Per acetic acid as a sterilant used in aseptic packaging is produced by oxidation of acetic acid by hydrogen peroxide.
105. The first commercial use of sub-sectors was done by Pillsbury for pizza.
106. A low oxygen MAP system is unsuitable for red meats because of discoloration of meat.
107. Use of high oxygen MAP is not widespread for prolonged storage of meat because it results in off odours and rancidity in meat
108. Nitrogen is convenient for gas packaging because it influence neither the colour of meat nor its microbiological quality.
109. Microbial spoilage, change in colour, lipid oxidation and moisture loss are the major problems related to the packaging of restructured meats.

110. The storage life of horticultural produce under MAP is frequently less than that of CAP.
111. The appearance of molds and bacteria is the limiting factor in MAP of horticultural produce.
112. In case of milk, transparency of packaging material is a key to the protection of flavor qualities and nutritional qualities.
113. The plastic tubes used for packaging of cream are usually made from high impact.
114. Transparent brown glass packaging materials was found to offer superior protection against light and oxygen.
115. Aluminium foil laminate packaging materials used for butter is good to prevent oxidation induced deterioration.
116. In recent years biscuits, cookies and crackers are packed in OPP (Oriented Polypropylene) either plane or co extruded.
117. In case of confection, cast PP is better than BCE because it holds the twist better than RCF.
118. The most common packaging material used for tea is a paperboard carton with either an aluminium foil liner or an over wrap of PE.
119. Laminates used in aseptic packaging of fruit juice and concentrates have sequence as Plastic film/aluminium foil/paperboard.
120. The filling of a commercial sterile product into sterile containers under aseptic conditions and hermetically sealing of the containers can be defined as Aseptic packaging.
121. The chemicals used in aseptic packaging of food are Hydrogen peroxide, per acetic acid and ethylene oxide.
122. The two mechanisms by which microwaves produce heat in foods are Dipole rotation and tonic polarisation.
123. In case of aseptic packaging, dry heat in the form of hot air is used because high temperature can be reached at atmosphere pressure.
124. Vinyl chloride, a potential migrant from PVC was found to be a cardiac irritant.
125. Styrene oxide, a metabolite from styrene monomer was found to be a potent mutant and central nervous depressant.
126. The vast majority of plasticizers incorporated into a packaging material are Ester of phthalic acid.
127. The possible migrant from paperboard carton is Dioxin.
128. Activities carried by the company to design and produce a differentiated container for particular product is classified as packaging.
129. Formal statement by the manufacturer of the product regarding its performance is classified as warranty.
130. Fruits grown locally and native to ones area has to be consumed. Some other factors which have given the impetus to the packaging industry *e.g.* *a*) Consumers acceptability, *b*) Transport, *c*) Quality, *d*) Storage, *e*) Invert nature, *f*) Odour proof and *g*) Strength.
131. Tetra pack boxes and milk bottle are examples of aseptic packaging.

IMPORTANT POINTS

- The population strength of cannery wastes is ten times greater than domestic sewage and it is due to high sugar and starch.
- The strength is expressed in terms of biochemical oxygen demand (BOD) in ppm.
- Alum or ferrous sulphate plus lime, soluble aluminium or iron salts are used as flocculent precipitate formation by chemical treatment of disposal management.
- For apple juice, berries, cherries and pickles Type L (steel base) most strongly corrosive food highly and mildly acidic.
- Apricots, fig, grape, peaches, Type MS and MR (steel base) moderately corrosive acidified fruits and vegetables.
- Pea canned Type MR and MC are low acid mildly corrosive.
  [where MS - Mild Steel, MR - Low metallic steel (mostly for thin base plate), MC - Similar to MR steel high in phosphorous to give mechanical strength, L- High purity steel with low metalloid and residuable content.
- Maize, meat, fish, dehydrated soups, frozen foods ghee (shortening) and nuts Type MR and MC low acid product and mostly dry and nonprocessed food mildly noncorrosive.
- The temperature difference of inside and out side of glass container must be 44°C (or upto) with respect to thermal shock.
- CFB stands for corrugated fibre boxes.
- The principal/largest part of the container is called body.
- Seamer. Double seam is also called closing machine.
- External inspection of seams is done visually and internal inspection by some tools....viz
  1. Seam micrometer
  2. Countersink gauge
  3. Can opner
  4. Nippers (mostly No. 5 and it is marketed by hardware merchants)
  5. Seam saw
  6. Seam projector
  7. Seams cope.
- **The main parts of glass containers are:**
  1. Sealing surface
  2. Finish
  3. Shoulder
  4. Body
  5. Bottom
  6. Bearing surface
- The side wall of glass container is called body.
- PT (Press ON Twist Off) is the criteria for evaluating the caps with respect to packing.
- For irradiation of potato and onion **Nasik (Maharashtra)** named as proton.
- Unit of GTR is cc/24hrs./m^2/atmp.@27°C.
- Unit of WTR is g/sqm./day@90% RH and 38°C.
- **Fick's law of diffusion:** According to Fick's law, a species can have a velocity relative to mass or molar average velocity only if gradients in the concentration exist.
  The rate equation for mass diffusion is known as *Fick's first law* which is a empirical relation defining the diffusion of species *A* as isothermal isobaric system. For diffusion only in *x*-direction, the Fick's rate equation is

$$J_{A,x} = -D_{AB}\frac{dC_A}{dx}$$

where, $J_{A,x}$ is molar flux of species *A* in the *x*-direction relative to the molar average velocity,

$\frac{dC_A}{dx}$ is the concentration gradient in *x*-direction and

D_{AB} is the mass diffusivity of species *A* diffusing though species *B*.

CHAPTER 8
APPLIED NUTRITION

***Applied nutrition** concentrates on improving the nutritional quality of foods; It may be defined as the science of food and its relationship to health. It is concerned with the part played by nutrients in body growth, development and maintenance.*

- Nutrition is a science which tells us about what happens to the food when it enters our body and thereafter.
- Nutrients are invisible chemicals in the foods which are necessary for keeping the body healthy.
- Fibre in food or diet aids in peristaltic movements and keeps the digestive system clear.
- **Oedema-A** condition characterized by an excess of watery fluid collecting in the cavities or tissues of the body.
- Phenyl (Ketonuria Commonly known as PKU) is an inherited disorder that increases the levels of a substance called **"Phenylalanine"** in the blood.
- Phenylalanine is a building block of proteins (an amino acid) that is obtained through the diet. People with PKU cannot break down the amino acid phenylalanine which then builds up in their blood and brain and lead to brain damage.
- Phenylalanine hydroxylase (PAH) enzyme is necessary to convert dietary phenylalanine to tyrosine.
- When PAH activity is reduced, phenylalanine accumulates and is converted into phenyl pyruvate (also known as phenyl ketone), which is detected in the urine.
- Cooking causes the destruction of toxins and undesirable substances present in pulses, etc. and make them nutritionally better.
- Symptoms of kwashiorkor include *cracked* and *scaly skin.*
- When the protein is deficient but calories or energy from carbohydrates is sufficient, the condition known as *Kwashiorkor occurs.*
- Loss of equilibrium in energy intake and energy expenditure results in *kwashiorkor.*
- Severe protein deficiency in children is known as *kwashiorkor.*
- Carbohydrates, proteins and lipids are three major components of any food system.
- Deficiency disease is a condition which occurs in the body when a particular portion in daily meals has been missing for a prolonged period.
- When there is lack of proteins and carbohydrates in the diet for a long time the deficiency disease known as Protein Energy Malnutrition (PEM) occurs.
- PEM deficiency occurs mainly in children below 5 years of age.

- When protein and energy both are insufficient for a prolonged period then a disease condition known as marasmus occurs.
- Beri Beri is quite prevalent in areas where polished rice is the staple food.
- Beriberi diseases originated in China.
- Beriberi disease is caused due to constant use of white rice and chicken.
- Damage to nervous system and limb paralysis is caused due to beriberi.
- Vitamin D can be created from a natural substance under the skin called as Ergosterol.
- Vitamin D can also be called **calciferol.**
- The only solution to goitre is to eat iodised salt and Vit. D intake in diet or by sunshine.
- Vitamins B complex and C may be leached into unused water while they are water soluble in nature.
- Those Vitamins which are soluble in water are known as *water soluble vitamins.* These are Vitamins of B Group and C.
- Catabolism is the metabolic reaction in cells undergo to extract energy.
- **Anabolism** is a biochemical process where the simple molecules combine to generate complex molecules
- In cold climate, more energy is required to maintain body temperature.
- Type of energy produced during movement is called kinetic energy.
- Energy reserves are normally stored as glycogen.
- Cereals form the bulk of our daily meals and are the main and also the cheapest source of energy.
- Amino acids are molecules containing an amine group, a carboxylic acid group and a side chain that varies between different amino acids.
- In enzymatic reactions, the molecules at the beginning of the process are called substrates, and they are converted into different molecules, called the products.
- Nuts are a rich source of protein and fat and a good source of Vitamin B and antioxidant Vitamin E.
- Tiredness is the type of nutritional anaemia.
- In ethanol (C_2H_5OH) emulsion test, the resulting emulsion is of cloudy white colour.
- Very few organisms can digest cellulose.
- Peristalsis is enabled through dietary fibre.
- Dietary fibre, also known as roughage, is the undigestible carbohydrate present in food.
- Fibre is present in foods of plant origin only.
- Lack of dietary fibre causes constipation.
- Bulk of undigested matter is made up of cellulose.
- Fibre is important for the proper functioning of large intestine.
- If iodine is applied to glycogen rich food, the resulting colour will be brown.
- In respiratory system, the dust particles are trapped due to mucus.

- During weight loss, an increased protein diet may increase the amount of nitrogen in body.
- Lactose can also be called as milk sugar.
- Dietary imbalances cause **malnutrition.**
- In case of malnutrition, the basic body needs are met through the consumption of stored fats and glycogen.
- In starvation, the first thing to be consumed to keep vital processes is fats and glycogen
- Basal metabolic rate shall be measured while a person is resting.
- Basal`metabolic rate measures how fast chemical reactions occur.
- Basal metabolic rate of a child is more than an old person.
- Basal metabolism refers to the amount of energy required to carry out all the vital processes.
- Basal metabolism, physical activity and heat all collectively determine the energy expenditures.
- Physically tiring jobs may result in basal metabolic rate of 2050 kJ.
- Cold climate vs. tropics, the basal metabolic rate is higher.
- Age, Gender, Body size and climate determine the basal metabolic rate.
- Across age, the basal metabolic rate decreases.
- Muscle wasting may seriously damage the heart. (Muscle wasting is loss of muscle mass weakening and shrinking)
- People experiencing muscle wasting are a case of starvation.
- Toxication may results from large consumptions of vitamins.
- Process of condensing many small molecules to form one large molecule is called **polymerization.**
- If Biuret solution is added to egg white, the resulting colour will be violet.
- In **Healthy Diet Pyramid,** fruits and vegetables are at the level 2.
- According to healthy diet pyramid, fat, salt and sugar shall be eaten least.
- In Healthy Diet Pyramid, meat and alternatives are at the level 3.
- In Healthy Diet Pyramid, bread and cereals are at the level 1.

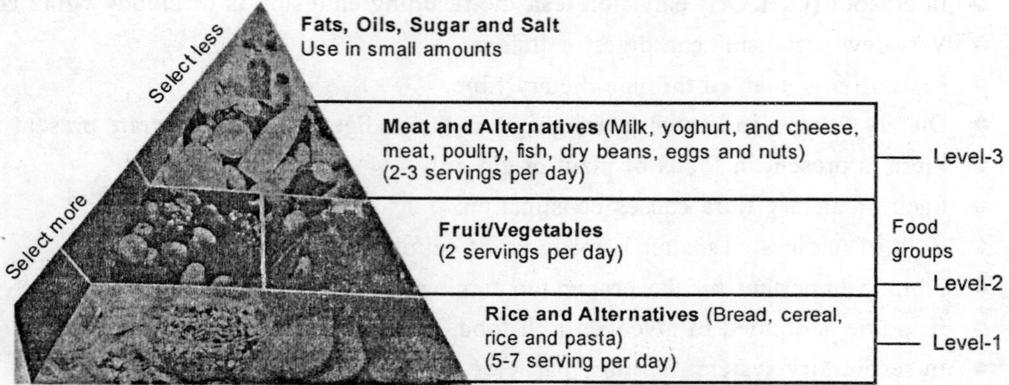

Fig. The food guide pyramid- a guide to daily food choice

- One way of managing a balanced diet is through a healthy pyramid way.
- Cellulose $(C_6H_{10}O_5)n$ is a form of polysaccharides.
- Butter, cheese and nuts are good source of fats.
- Most of the animal fats are saturated fats.
- Carbohydrates $(C_nH_mO_m)$ include all but dietary fibre.
- Rickets is caused due to the deficiency of Vitamin D (Calciferol), Calcium and Phosphorus
- Rickets is characterized by knocked knees and bowed legs.
- The softening due to inadequate levels of available phosphate, calcium, and vitamin D is osteomalacia.
- Cellulose cannot be digested by fish and mammals.
- Despite keeping a check on weight, an increase in weight may be due to more sodium in diet.
- Unequal food distribution results in malnutrition, starvation and over eating.
- Most of the vital activities are performed when we are asleep.
- Diseases like rickets, scurvy and beriberi occur due to the deficiency of vitamins.
- In digestion, peristalsis prevents the signs of constipation.
  (Peristalsis is a series of wave-like muscle contractions that moves food to different processing stations in the digestive tract).
- After fats and glycogen $(C_{24}H_{42}O_{21})$ are consumed in case of starvation, the next nutrient to be consumed is proteins.
- Potato contains 2% of protein, 0.2% of fat and 20% carbs.
- If sucrose $(C_{12}H_{22}O_{11})$ is heated in the presence of enzymes or catalysts, the output will be glucose.
- Sucrose $(C_{12}H_{22}O_{11})$ may be called as non reducing sugars.
- Weight reduction programs shall not increase protein intake.
- Number of glucose $(C_6H_{12}O_6)$ units in a starch $(C_6H_{10}O_5)$ n molecule may be up to 200.
- Essential constituent of protoplasm is water.
- Person's lower metabolic rate may be due to low production of thyroxin.
- Complete digestion of one gram of proteins results in 17 kilojoules of energy.
- Water acts as a reactant in hydrolysis.
- Obesity is a case of over nutrition.
- Age, activities, and lifestyle determine the amount of food materials.
- Starvation, malnutrition, and over nutrition are caused due to unequal food distribution.
- Muscle wasting includes cardiac muscles (*Cardiac cachexia*)
- Glycolysis is the name given to the series of biochemical reactions in which glucose is converted into pyruvate.
- The highly branched structure of glucose units results in polysaccharide glycogen.

- Condensation of glucose molecules ($C_6H_{12}O_6$) results in complex molecules glycogen.
- One gram of carbohydrate gives 4 kcal. An adult person needs 400-420 gm of carbohydrates every day.
- $C_{12}H_{22}O_{11}$ is the general formula of disaccharides.
- Fructose ($C_6H_{12}O_6$) is very uncommon in animals.
- Starch ($C_6H_{10}O_5$) n is broken down to form glucose ($C_6H_{12}O_6$) units when hydrolyzed by acidic base.
- Starch is commonly formed and stored in plants as **Polysaccharides**
- Common name of glycogen ($C_{24}H_{42}O_{21}$) is animal starch.
- Muscles are mostly made up of starch (glycogen)
- Water insolubility of glycogen makes it excellent for suitable for storage materials.
- Glucose ($C_6H_{12}O_6$) and fructose ($C_6H_{12}O_6$) can be obtained if sucrose ($C_{12}H_{22}O_{11}$) is heated in the presence of dilute hydrochloric acid.
- Lactose ($C_{12}H_{22}O_{11}$) can by hydrolyzed in glucose ($C_6H_{12}O_6$) and galactose ($C_6H_{12}O_6$) in the presence of enzyme lactase.
- As compared to carbohydrates, fats are lower in the proportion of oxygen.
- When one gram of carbohydrates $(C_nH_mO_m)_n$ is completely burnt, the released energy is 16 kilojoules.
- Bread and cereal group is rich in **carbohydrates.**
- Elements of carbon (C), hydrogen (H_2) and oxygen (O_2) are present in carbohydrates.
- Cereals, potatoes and tapioca are common sources of polysaccharides.
- Condensation reaction always results in the formation of complex sugar (disaccharide or polysaccharide) and water.
- Enzyme to digest starch $(C_6H_{10}O_5)$n to sugar maltose ($C_{12}H_{22}O_{11}$) is amylase.
- Blue black colour is produced when substance containing starch is mixed with iodine.
- An average daily intake of carbohydrates ($C_nH_mO_m$) shall be about 45-65% of calories required.
- Glyceryl Tristearate (triglyceride) can be hydrolyzed to form stearic acid and glycerol.
- Enzyme causing breakdown of sucrose into simple sugar ($C_6H_{12}O_6$) is sucrose.
- To test presence of reducing sugars in food, the test conducted is Benedict Test.
- Sugar results after the hydrolysis of carbohydrates.
- Carbohydrates are classified depending on the number of sugar or saccharide unit they contain.
- Combination of glucose ($C_6H_{12}O_6$) and fructose ($C_6H_{12}O_6$) molecules result in sucrose.
- When needed glycogen $(C_6H_{10}O_5)$n can be easily hydrolyzed to glucose.
- Lactose ($C_{12}H_{22}O_{11}$) is largely obtained from milk sugar.
- Simple and complex sugars may be called as reducing sugars.
- Glucose ($C_6H_{12}O_6$) can also be called as grape sugar.

- Galactose ($C_6H_{12}O_6$) and lactose ($C_{12}H_{22}O_{11}$) are commonly found in mammals.
- In order to get glucose ($C_6H_{12}O_6$), enzyme maltase shall be applied to maltose.
- If the generalized formulae of carbohydrates is $C_nH_{2m}O_m$, n and m for glucose are n=6 and m=6 respectively.
- On boiling with Benedict solution, the reducing sugar will form a precipitate of red colour.
- Galactose ($C_6H_{12}O_6$) is a component of lactose.
- Galactose is derived from the breakdown of lactose.
- Lactose is the disaccharide of milk and milk containing products.
- Lactose ($C_{12}H_{22}O_{11}$) can be commonly found in mammal's milk.
- Combination of glucose ($C_6H_{12}O_6$) and galactose ($C_6H_{12}O_6$) molecules result in lactose.
- Fructose ($C_{12}H_{22}O_{11}$) is commonly found in plants.
- Carbohydrate and protein, when combined, form mucus.
- Disaccharides ($C_{12}H_{22}O_{11}$) are also known as *complex sugar.*
- Carbohydrates, fats, proteins, vitamins, and minerals are the form of nutrients.
- Curculin or neoculin is natural low calorie sweetener was discovered in 1990 from fruit of *curculigo latifolia.*
- In carbohydrates ($C_nH_{2m}O_m$), the ratio of hydrogen (H_2) and oxygen (O_2) is 0.084027778.
- In animals and fungi, glycogen ($C_{24}H_{42}O_{21}$) is stored in the form of carbohydrates.
- Maltose, lactose and sucrose ($C_{12}H_{22}O_{11}$) belong to which class of carbohydrates-disaccharides.
- Animals store carbohydrates mainly in the form of glycogen.
- One of the simplest carbohydrates is sugar glucose.
- Common test for starch presence is Benedict Test.
- Glucose, fructose and galactose ($C_6H_{12}O_6$) are simple sugars.
- Mucus is made through carbohydrates.
- In order to break starch ($C_6H_{10}O_5$) n to form glucose ($C_6H_{12}O_6$) units, starch needs to hydrolyze with the assistance of water.
- Ability to do work is defined as energy.
- Stored energy found in most foods is called as potential chemical energy.
- Prevention of heat is attributed to the rate of heat production.
- Energy requirement of a sedentary person of 55 kg weight is 2400 kcal/day.
- In nutrition, Energy balance refers to the equilibrium between energy intake and energy expenditures.
- Amount of energy requires depends upon the body size.
- Energy is measured in units called joules.
- Energy reserves are normally stored as fat.
- Highest energy value is provided by fats.
- Trigylcerides have a glycerol backbone bonded to three fatty acids.

- In most naturally occurring unsaturated fatty acids, all are cis bonds.
- Obesity results if energy expenditure is less than the energy intake.
- Starch $(C_6H_{10}O_5)n$ is a most common storage form of carbohydrates.
- Cellulose $(C_6H_{10}O_5)n$ can be digested in herbivores through bacteria.
- Fats are present in the protoplasm especially in the protoplasmic membranes.
- An excess of fat soluble vitamins can cause demineralization of bones and calcification of soft tissues.
- Rate of heat lost depends upon the amount of fatty tissues in a body.
- The term "fats" can be used to refer to solid animal fats, liquid animal fats and plant fats.
- Common fat to cause heart attack is cholesterol.
- Saturated fatty acids chains are straight.
- Fats act as a solvent for fat soluble vitamins.
- Heart has to work harder to pump blood round the body in an obese person.
- People with gallstones in gall bladder should avoid fats.
- Fatty acids and glycerol $(C_3H_8O_3)$ are produced after hydrolysis of fats.
- If the fatty acids can take in no more of hydrogen atoms (H), it is known as saturated fats.
- The property of fat soluble vitamins is that it can be stored in the body for later use.
- When one gram of fat is completely burnt, the amount of energy released is 36-40 kilojoules or 9 kcal.
- Vegetables fats are unsaturated fats.
- Fats act as: an insulating material, a constituent of protoplasm and a substance that restricts water loss.
- Thyroxin is secreted from thyroid glands.
- An average daily intake of fats should be 0.25 g.
- Two essential fatty acids are linoleic acid (LA) and alpha-linolenic acid (ALA).
- Meat fats are rich in saturated fatty acids. The cholesterol content of meat is 75 mg/100 gm.
- One gram of fat gives you 9 kcal. An adult needs only 50-60 gm of fat every day.
- Animal fats increase the chances of heart related diseases.
- In hydrolysis, the larger molecules are broken down into smaller molecules by the addition of water.
- Fats found in food ar mixture of saturated and unsaturated fatty acids.
- Healthy consumption of fats is saturated fats.
- High level of LDL (Low-density Lipoprotein) cholestrol indicates a high risk of cardiovascular disease.
- Fish rich in fat include herring like fish.

- Fats commonly found inside liver of fish.
- Disadvantage of fats is reduction in the rate of heat loss.
- Fat soluble vitamins help in all, but it increases tooth decay.
- Most fish and white meat are fat free.
- Function of myoglobin is to aid in muscular contraction.
- Hydrolysis cannot be carried out without water.
- Unsaturated fatty acid chains bend at places of hydrogen molecules.
- Liver and muscles are the common places of storage of glycogen.
- An average polypeptide chain may contain up to 500 amino acids.
- The protein from animal sources is known as animal protein and the protein from plant sources is known as plant protein.
- One gram of protein gives 4 kcal. An adult needs 1 gm of protein for every kilogram of body weight.
- Linkage of amino acids is known as condensation reaction.
- Amino acids are joined to form proteins.
- Test of Proteins is known as Biuret test.
- Breakage of hydrogen bonds in protein coils results in denaturation of proteins.
- Very high protein intake is good for kidneys and liver.
- In digestion process protein molecules are water soluble.
- Average adult protein requirement is 50 to 100 g per day.
- An average daily intake of proteins shall be 0.15 gm of per kg of body weight (about 56 gm per day for men and 46 gm for women).
- In order to digest proteins, it is converted into polypeptides.
- Liver produces urea to remove excess nitrogen.
- Hydrolysis of polypeptides results in amino acids.
- Thyroid gland is found in the neck.
- Sulphur (S_8) and phosphorus (P_4) are often present in proteins.
- Most complicated food molecules are proteins.
- Synthesis of new protoplasm largely depends upon proteins.
- Coiled chains of proteins are linked through weaker bonds of hydrogen atoms.
- Heat, acids (H^+) or alkalis (OH^-) easily break the coils in proteins structure.
- Basic building block of proteins are amino acids.
- Types of amino acids present in proteins are 22. The body needs 20 amino acids to synthesize proteins of these 9 are essential and 11 are non-essential because body can produce them.
- Minerals are inorganic compounds.
- Average daily intake of iron for adults is about 0.02 grams.
- Trace elements do not include calcium.

- Calcium (Ca) and phosphorus (P_4) are essential for internal skeleton.
- Nutritional anaemia often occurs due to lack of iron.
- Average daily intake of calcium for growing children is about 1 gram/day.
- Internal skeleton is made up of bones and cartilage in mammals.
- Inorganic nutrients include water.
- The minerals calcium and phosphorus are found in bones and teeth.
- Minerals do not provide energy and are not destroyed during food preparation.
- Calcium and phosphorus are known as macro or major minerals, as they are present in the body in large amounts especially in bones and teeth.
- Milk and its products like butter and ghee are the best sources of calcium.
- Deficiency of iodine leads to a number of disorders like goitre, cretinism, mental retardation and deaf-mutes'.
- Minerals do not include iodine.
- Ossification (Bone formation) is the process by which new bone is produce. Bone is major storage site for calcium in the body.
- Anaemia is caused due to deficiency of iron.
- Structural component of haemoglobin is iron.
- Philodendrons are toxins and contain as much as 0.7% of oxalates in the form of calcium oxalate crystals.
- Minerals essential for the formation of skeletal structures include calcium.
- Element that is not a part of minerals is manganese.
- General feeling of irritability and tiredness may be due to lack of vitamins.
- Diabetic people do not require more water than those without. Although hydration is substantially more crucial for individuals with diabetes.
- Deficiency of Niacin (Vit. B_3) causes Pellagra.
- Vitamins are the substances which occur in very small amounts in foods, and are essentials for proper functioning of the body.
- Vitamins cannot be manufactured by the body, therefore must be supplied by the diet.
- Those vitamins which are soluble in fats are known as fat soluble vitamins. These are Vitamins A, D, E, and K.
- Deficiency of Vitamin A leads to dryness of conjunctiva (the white portion of the eye).
- Vitamin C deficiency disorder known as scurvy is endemic to people who do not eat fresh fruits and vegetables.
- Sprouting cereals help in improving their vitamin C content.
- Flesh foods including meat, poultry and fish are rich in proteins, Vitamin A and Vitamin B.
- Fruits especially citrus fruits, amla and guava, are good source of Vitamin C.
- The 5-carbon monosaccharide ribose is an important component of coenzymes (*e.g.*, ATP, FAD, and NAD).

- There are actually eight separate vitamins in the B family: thiamine (vitamin B_1), riboflavin (vitamin B_2), niacin (Vit. B_3), vitamin B_6, folate, vitamin B_{12}, biotin, and pyridoxine.
- Rich sources of Vitamin B are Liver.
- Water soluble vitamins are excreted by body.
- Lack of vitamin B may result in poor cellular respiration.
- Polar bear liver contains an enormous amount of Vitamin E.
- Vitamins do not generate energy inside the body but they are necessary for an array of biological processes.
- Vitamins can be soluble in fat and water.
- Sources of vitamin may include meat and eggs.
- An overactive thyroid gland may expedite the metabolic rate.
- Lack of fat soluble vitamins causes multiple fractures.
- In order to digest polypeptides, they are converted into amino acids.
- Peptone means the bond between 3 or more amino acids.
- Peptide bond is formed between two amino acids.
- Calcification of kidneys is caused due to excess of fat soluble vitamins.
- Water soluble vitamins need to be supplied daily.
- By nature, Vitamins are organic compounds.
- Processed foods generally lack vitamins. There are few vital elements in ultra-processed or processed foods, compared with whole or minimally processed foods.
- Light sensitive pigment in retina is created by Vitamin A.
- Water soluble vitamins are characterized as resistant to heat and high temperatures.
- Lack of ascorbic acid causes poor healing of wounds.
- Over consumption of Vitamins for long periods may result in death.
- 100% orange juice has all 3 provitamin A carotenoids that can form vitamin A in the body ß-carotene, α-carotene and ß-cryptoxanthin.
- It is believed that vitamin deficiency can be avoided by consuming limes.
- Rich source of vitamins include fresh raw vegetables.

IMPORTANT POINTS

- Function of food are mainly three

  (*a*) *Physiological*—(1) To supply energy.

  (2) To build and maintain the body tissues.

  (3) To regulate body process.

  Basic thing of all above is nutrient.

  (*b*) *Social* –In festivals, birthday, naming ceremony and marriage etc.

(*c*) *Psychological*- by whom and for whom the food is prepared, cooked the normal attachment to mothers cooking.

(*d*) *Special functions* — (1) Carbohydrates – Provides energy
(2) Protein – Tissues maintenance
(3) Fat – Concentrated source of energy
(4) Vitamins – Growth and regulation
(5) Minerals – Body building
(6) Water – Universal solvent, carrier and regulator

- RDA (Recommended Dietary Allowance) is defined as the nutrient present in the diet that satisfies the requirement of nearly all individuals in a population.
- **Adequate Intake (AI)** is a recommended average daily nutrient intake level, based on experiment.
- **Dietary Reference Intake (DRI):** is a system of nutrition recommendation from the National Academy of Medicine (NAM)
- **Estimated Average Requirement (EAR):** Average daily level of intake estimated to meet the requirements of 50% of healthy individuals used to assess the nutrient intakes of groups of people and to plan diets.
- **Tolerable Upper Intake Level (TUL):** Maximum daily intake unlikely to cause adverse health effects.
- RDA for Ca:P for infants is 1:5 and for others 1:1.
- RDA for Vit. A is 600 μg for adults in terms of β carotene 2400 μg and upper tolerable limit is 3000 mg/days.
- Conversion factor is 1 μg β carotene = 0.25 μg retinol.
- Per 100 Kcal in food should contain – Thiamine – 0.5 mg
  Riboflavin – 0.6 mg
  Niacin – 6.6 mg
- Kwashiorkar – (1-4 year) *-Sign* – Growth failure, mental change, Odema, muscle wasting, moon face, liver changes, Gastro-intestinal tract, skin and hair change and anaemia.
- Marasmus (Nutritional marasmus) – (0-1 year) *-Sign* – Growth retardation, wasting of muscle and subcutaneous fat.
- Bones get porous due to deficiency of calcium termed as **Osteoporosis**.
- Term fibre was coined by Hipsley in 1953
- Egg is poor source of Ca and Vitamin C. PER is 4.5 and NPU is 98 of egg.
- **Antivitamins:**
  1. In raw soybean (*Glycen max L.*) lipoxidase lowers the Vitamin A and D availability as well as amount.
  2. A Rajmash (*Phaseolus vulgaris*) raw seed feeding cause necrosis of liver and muscular dystrophy and inhibits availability of vitamin E.
  3. Sweet clover (*Meliolotus officinalis*) has Antivitamin K.

5. Ackee fruits contains Antiriboflavin factor.

6. Lineseed meal contains Antipyridoxine factor(1 amino –D-proline) and also called Linatine-1 amino –D-proline is 4 times active comparatively linatine and prevented by the addition of pyridoxine in diet.
7. Raw eggs (white) contains Avidin binds with Biotin and makes it unavailable, it is destroyed by heating/cooking at 80-100°C for 10 min.
8. Radioactive food poisoning matter – Iodine-131, Stronitium-90, Cesium-137.
9. Deficiency of Niacin/nicotinic acid (B_5) causes pellagra.
10. Deficiency of vitamins B_2 causes dwarfness.
11. In sugar beet sugar content is 15-16%
12. Potato is rich source of starch
13. Guava fruit is rich source of Pectin
14. Golden rice is rich in Vitamin A
15. Protein rich variety of rice is sabarmati.

"For the irradiation of any food, the minimum absorbed dose should be sufficient to obtain the technological purpose and the maximum absorbed dose should be less than that which does not affect the consumer safety. The maximum absorbed dose should not be greater than 10 kGy, except in some cases."

According Codex General Standard on Irradiated Food, retail food products are required to display the following Radura Symbol in green colour from showing treated with irradiation.

- **Nutraceuticals:** Nutraceuticals, as defined by Wildman (2000), are naturally occurring substances in foods that have been found to be effective in the prevention or treatment of one or more diseases, or the improvement of physiological performance, thereby enhancing human health.
- **Functional foods:** These are foods or food ingredient that may provide health benefit beyond the traditional nutrient it contain.

ROLES OF VITAMINS

- **Vitamin A (Fat soluble vitamin):** Important for vision, skin, bones and reproduction. Found in: carrots, sweet, potatoes, spinach (Retinol)
- **Vitamin B_1 :** Converts carbs into energy & is vital for glucose metabolism. **Found in :** Sunflower seeds, whole grains, pork (Thiamine)
- **Vitamin B_2 :** Plays a role in energy production, skin and eye health. **Found in:** Dairy, organ, meat, almonds. (Riboflavin)
- **Vitamin B_6:** Amino Acid. Metabolism and red blood cell production. **Found in :** Bananas, Chickpea, Salmon (Pyridoxine)
- **Vitamin B_5 :** Necessary for fatty acid synthesis. **Found in:** Avocado, chicken, broccoli (Pantothenic acid)
- **Vitamin B_3 :** DNA Repair, and metabolic functions as well as energy. **Found in:** Salt-water Fish, Poultry, Avacado. (Niacin).

- **Vitamin B_7:** It enables the body to metabolize proteins, fats, and carbohydrates. It also contributes to keratin, a structural protein in the skin, hair, and nails (Biotin).
- **Vitamin B_9 :** It is essential for making DNA and RNA. Deficiency: During pregnancy, this can affect the fetus's nervous system. Doctors recommend folic acid supplements before and during pregnancy (Folate).
- **Vitamin B_{12}:** It is essential for a healthy nervous system. Deficiency: Low levels may lead to neurological problems and some types of anemia. Good sources: Examples include fish, shellfish, meat, poultry, eggs, milk and other dairy products, fortified cereals, fortified soy products, and fortified nutritional yeast (Cobalamin).
- **Vitamin C: (Water soluble vitamin):** It contributes to collagen production, wound healing, and bone formation. It also strengthens blood vessels, supports the immune system, helps the body absorb iron, and acts as an antioxidant. (Ascorbic acid)
- **Vitamin D (Fat soluble vitamin):** It is necessary for the healthy mineralization of bone. Good sources: Exposure to UVB rays from the sun or other sources causes the body to produce vitamin D. Fatty fish, eggs, beef liver, and mushrooms also contain the vitamin.
- **Vitamin E:** Its antioxidant activity helps prevent oxidative stress, an issue that increases the risk of widespread inflammation and various diseases. **Good sources:** Wheat germ, kiwis, almonds, eggs, nuts, leafy greens, and vegetable oils. (Tocopherol).

  Vitamin E is the collective name for a group of fat-soluble compounds with distinctive antioxidant activities. Naturally occurring vit. E exits in either chemical form (alpha-beta-gamma and delta-tocotrienol). But alpha or α-tocotrienol is the only form that is recognized for human requirements.

  RDA of Vit. E for children (Infants) (9-13 years) - 11 mg and adult is 15 mg/day.
- **Vitamin K (Fat soluble vitamin):** Necessary for blood clotting. **Found in :** Dark leaf, grams, kale and spinach

Table 1: Classification of the essential minerals

Microminerals (> 100 mg/day)*	**Microminerals (< 100 mg/day)***
• Calcium	• Iron
• Phosphorus	• Zinc
• Magnesium	• Copper
• Sulphur	• Iodine
• Sodium*	• Fluoride
• Potassium*	• Manganese
• Chloride*	• Selenium
	• Chromium
	• Molybdenum

* Recommended intake are greater or less than 100 mg/day as indicated.

* One of the body's three primary electrolytes.

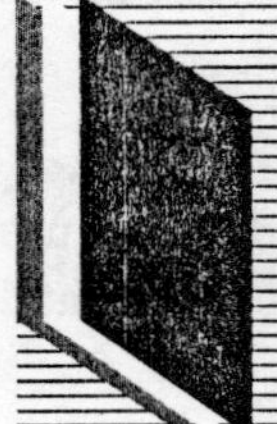

CHAPTER 9
FOOD BIOTECHNOLOGY

***Food biotechnology** is the use of technology to modify the genes of our food sources. With food biotechnology, we create new species of animals and plants that we eat. These new species have desired nutritional, production and marketing properties.*

- The first realisation that microorganisms were involved in food production processes was in 1837, when scientists discovered the role of yeast in an alcoholic fermentation.
- Later Louis Pasteur when trying to explain what happened during the production of beer and vinegar in the 1860es, he found that microorganisms were responsible.
- Louis Pasteur (1822-1895) is often called the father of modern microbiology because of his many scientific discoveries and contributions to the field.
- Food biotechnology is not new. For thousands of years people have been discovering that fruit juices ferment into wine, that milk can be used to develop products such as cheese or yogurt, or that beer can be made through the fermentation of malt and hops.
- Biotechnology is the use of biological processes, organisms, or systems to manufacture products intended to improve the quality of human life.
- Modern or 'new' biotechnology refers to the understanding and application of genetic information of animal and plant species. Genetic engineering modifies the functioning of genes in the same species or improves genes across species resulting in Genetically Modified Organisms (GMOs).
- Modern food biotechnology may help promote public health, providing fruits, vegetables and grains with more nutritional benefits. These include more proteins, vitamins and minerals, or less fat and saturated fat.
- For those with food allergies, biotechnology is seeking ways to reduce allergens in peanuts, wheat and other crops.
- Foods from biotechnology are just as nutritious as conventional foods, and some are higher in certain nutrients.
- There are two issues of primary concern to food consumers: (*i*) the potential introduction of food allergens and (*ii*) marker genes that would increase human resistance to antibiotics
- Today, in the arena of food, the primary goals of food biotechnology are to provide a more abundant, less expensive, and a more nutritious food supply in order to address the needs of our growing global population.
- .Modern food biotechnology techniques include the joining of two pieces of DNA from different organisms leading to a single piece of DNA. Core techniques in biotechnology are (*i*) Genetic engineering such as recombinant DNA Technology and (*ii*) Gene Cloning
- R-DNA is DNA from two different sources that has been combined in vitro (Outside living organism). It creates a protein product and multiple copies of genes and also insert foreign genes into other organisms of choice.

- In 1972 Stanley Cohen and Herbert Boyer invented the technique DNA cloning.
- Tools of R DNA technology are (*i*) Restriction Enzymes and (*ii*) Plasmids
- Restriction Enzymes recognize specific sequences of nucleotides in a DNA strand. Their use allows detection of point mutations in DNA and eliminates the need for subcloning and sequencing.
- Restriction Enzymes is a group of enzymes used to cleave or cut. DNA strands, each having a characteristic base sequence at which it cleaves.
- Plasmid is an extra chromosol, circular DNA molecule found in certain bacteria, capable autonomous replication.
- Modern bio-techniques are much faster and more precise. It is possible to quickly transfer a specific gene of interest rather than waiting on the random shuffling of genes over several generations.
- Examples of products developed through food biotechnology include corn varieties containing a bacterial gene that kills insects and soybeans inserted with gene that renders them resistant to weed killers such as Roundup. Cotton, squash, and papaya are other examples of commodities in which biotechnology was used to reduce pesticide use, increase profitability through greater yield,
- Cheese are made with a starter culture. As the culture grows in the milk, it converts the sugar lactose into lactic acid, which ensures the correct level of acidity and gives the cheese its moisture. As the cheese ripens, the culture gives it a balanced aroma, taste, texture. It is also responsible for the 'holes' in cheeses such as Emmenthal. Choosing the right mixture of culture is essential for a high-quality cheese.
- In yoghurt and other fermented milk products, the culture is responsible for the taste and texture of the final product
- Yeasts are responsible for the fermentation process which produces alcohol in wine.
- Fermentation processes can be classified as spontaneous and induced (*e.g.* making bread dough by the addition of baking yeast to flour)
- Fermentation of 1 molecule of glucose yields 2 molecules of ATP, in aerobic respiration 36 ATP molecules are formed.
- Lactiplantibacillus plantarum is a widespread member of the genus lactiplantibacillus and commonly found in many fermented food and is found to address neurodegenerative disease.
- IgA (Immunoglobulin A) is found in saliva, sweat, tears, nasal fluids and intestinal secretion.
- Type IV hypersensitivity is also called as cell mediated immunity.
- Parasites worm helminthes causes **Leishmaniasis disease.**
- Linus Pauling discovered helical structure of protein molecules.
- Epitopes are specific antibody binding sites on the surface of antigen also antigenic determinates.
- An organism in guinea pigs causes diphtheria is **Corynebacteria.**
- Immunity acquired the lifetime of an individual is known as **adaptive immunity.**
- An Inverted microscope is essential for examination of cell culture.
- Thyroid is involved in oxygen consumption and energy metabolism.
- Cryopreservation is the long term storage of sperms in liquid nitrogen at (minus)–196°C

- Saliva of ruminant has an alkaline pH viz. 8.1-8.9.
- The protozoa number in the rumen is about10^6/ml.
- Methanogenic bacteria are useful for the ruminants.
- Methanogenic bacteria help in removing H_2 by reducing CO_2 to CH_4.
- Composition of gas mixture in rumen is about 65% CO_2.
- Major product of ruminal fermentation is VFA (volatile fatty acids viz. acetate, propionate, and butyrate etc.).
- Ruminal pH ranges between 5.5-7.2.
- The name **single cell protein** was coined by Carroll L. Wilson of MIT
- Amyloytic organisms digest starch in rumen.
- DBS (Dibenzylidene-D-sorbitol) is added to culture medium to prevent sticking to the surface.
- Deamination in rumen leads to conversion of amino acids to NH_3.
- Propionic acid is the main product of glycerol fermentation.
- Omasum also called as true stomach.
- Aflatoxin is produced by fungus through the fermentation.
- Isotricha is an important example of rumen protozoa.
- Reagent used for determination of sugar adulteration in milk is **resorcinol.**
- Colchicines are used for arresting cell division of mitosis.
- The number of chromosomes present in *Bos taurus* is 60.
- Nucleic acids are large molecules made up of thousands of nucleotides.
- A distance between genes is measured by an arbitrary unit called **Map unit.**
- For DNA quantification spectrophotometer method is preferred when samples are prepared.
- B-Chromosomes are usually genetically silent and lack major functional genes and are called non-essential.
- Staining of Giemsa stain is also called as **G-Banding.**
- Dolly (sheep) was cloned by Keith Campbell, Ian Wilmut and cellageus on 5th July 1996.
- Transgenic animal are an important source for production of drugs of proteins for human therapy.
- DNA Sequence recognized by restriction enzymes are called *palindrome*.
- The gene battery model was developed by Britten Davidson.
- According to Chargaff law T = A and C = G. where, T = Thymine, A = adenine, C = Cytosine, G = Guanine.
- Shape of chromosome depends on position of blastomere.
- V-shaped chromosomes during metaphase are called telocentric.
- E.G. Balbiani (1881) discovered a polytene chromosome is found in salivary glands of animals.
- Trisomy at chromosome 21 results in Down's syndrome
- Genes constitute the physical basis of inheritance.
- Some of the viruses and bacteriophages have RNA as the genetic material.
- Genome contains haploid of chromosomes.

- Insulin is produced by transgenic bacteria.
- Super ovulation means generation of a number of ovum at time in ovary.
- During estrous stage, ovary is under the influence of hormone estrogen.
- In cattle the estrous cycle is typically of 21 days.
- The head quarter of Common Wealth Institute of Biological Control is situated at Trinidad.
- *Trichogrammo chilonis Ishii* is an egg parasitoid.
- *Epiricania meloanoleaca* (fletcher) is effective to control sugarcane pyrilla.
- Viruses are transmitted by insects as vector to cause viral diseases.
- Amino acid is commercially produced by micro-organisms and used by microbes during their growth and therefore is called primary microbial product or primary metabolite.
- *Penicillin* was isolated and discovered in 1928 by Scottish scientist Sir Alexander Fleming.
- Lyophilization method for culture preservation is also known as rapid drying in frozen state.
- DeBecza and Liebmann used first large scale (about 20 liter capacity) ferment for the production of yeast.
- Source of micro-organisms for alpha amylase production is *Bacillus*.
- Antibodies are the chemical substances secreted by some micro-organisms which inhibit the growth and development of other microbes.
- Streptomycin antibiotic is effective against tuberculosis causing organism *Mycobacterium tuberculosis*.
- Invertase enzyme is also known as Saccharase or sucrase.
- Rum is distilled liquor and it is produced from cane molasses.
- Mashing process consists of cooling, filtering and dispensing into bottles and cans in beer production.
- Calorimetric value of protein is 5.7 kcal/g.
- Vitamin A activity is expressed in terms of International unit (IU) and Retinal activity both.
- Vitamin C is water soluble vitamin.
- Polishing of rice removes Vitamin B_1.
- α-amylase enzyme hydrolyse 1-4 glycosidic bond from non reducing end stares.
- In dairy industries lipase enzyme is used for the controlled hydrolysis of milk fat to produce lipolysed milk fat.
- Galactose milk sugar-is sometimes abbreviated as Gal, is **65%** as sweeter as sucrose.
- Naringin primary bittering water soluble compound found in the citrus fruit membrane.
- Renin converts co-casein of the milk to the co-para caseinate which has curd like appearance.
- Invertase, also called beta-fructofuranosidase cleaving the terminal non-reducing beta-fructofuranoside residues, is a glycoprotein with an optimum pH 4.5 and stability at 50 °C.
- Entrapant techniques of immobilization are based upon occlusion of biocatalyst within the constraining structure tight enough to prevent the leakage of biocatalyst.
- Immobilization may lead to loss of enzyme activity due to which involvement of active site in mobilization.

- Papain the proteolytic enzyme is used in meat tenderization.
- In textile industries lipase, protease and amylase enzymes are used for the dry cleaning.
- Ascorbic acid into delydroascorbic acid is acidic condition.
- At about 4-6 pH most of the proteins are precipitated.
- Gluten is about 80% of wheat Protein.
- *Pelshenke value* gives the idea of flour strength through gas production and retention capacity of the wheat carbohydrate/protein complex.
- Protein concentrates contains 70% proteins.
- The gelatinization temperature in parboiling of grain is 65-75°C.
- Strong and elastic gluten contains 7-13% proteins.
- Parboiled rice contain 70% vitamin B.
- Microwave radiation is that part of the electromagnetic radiation spectrum that falls between the frequencies of 300-300000 MHz.
- For demineralization in membrane technology electrodialysis technique is used.
- Naringinase enzyme is used for debettering of fruit juices.
- Resorcinol reagent is used to detect the cane sugar adulteration in milk.
- Decomposition of carbohydrates with the help of micro-organisms is called fermentation.
- Ethanol, ethyl alcohol and alcohol are the end product of alcoholic fermentation.
- Sucrose in one of the major etiologic factor in dental caries.
- The daily consumption of fat in diet is about 80g/day/capita.
- Infant is born with a store of mineral up to six month age is Fe (Iron).
- In liposome mediated gene transfer DNA enters the protoplast due to endocytosis.
- Arabidopsis small subunit of Rubisco is a green tissue and specific promoter.
- *Agrobacterium* become an important tool in plant biotechnology to transfer foreign genes of interest plant cells to create transgenics with economically important traits.
- *Agrobacterium* known in plant pathogen in beginning of 20th century has been proved to have ability to transfer DNA to plant cells for the purpose of genetic engineering and prove to be natural genetic engineer for biotechnology.
- In agrobacterium mediated plant transformation Timetin is used to check the agrobacterium.
- Polynuclotide transfers enzyme is used for making DNA.
- Concatomer is a long continuous DNA molecule that contains multiple copies of the same DNA sequence linked in series by rolling circle replication (RCA).
- A cosmid is a type of hybrid plasmid that contains a Lambda phage cos sequence. The DNA sequences of Cosmids (cos sites + plasmid = cosmids) are originally from the lambda phage. They are often used as a cloning vector in genetic engineering.
- Lambda has short single stranded 5 projection of 12-nucleotide length
- Relaxed plasmid has multiple copies per cell.
- Restriction enzyme that cuts straight across the DNA produces blunt end.
- In vitro packaging is required for PAC (packaging site).

- Electrophoretic separation of DNA and RNA in agarose is based on charge and size.
- Ethidium bromide reagent is useful for visualizing DNA.
- Endochitinase can be used as an antifungal.
- Phaseolus vulgaris, bananas, chestnut, kiwifruit avocado, papaya and tomatoes contain significant level of chitinase as defense against fungal attacks. Endochinates are cell wall (chitin) binding enzymes.
- If adenine makes up 35% of DNA, cytosine well makes 15%.
- Bar gene is herbicide resistant gene.
- Cytoplasmic channels connecting adjacent cells are called **plasmodesmeta.**
- Homologous parts line up along equatorial plane during Metaphase-I.
- The browning of culture medium is induced by some explants can be prevented by addition of PVP (polyvinylpyrrolidone).
- In meiosis, as Mitosis the chromosomal materials are replicated during S phase.
- The gene transferred from *E. coli* to tobacco to increase the level of mannitol is mannitol dehydrogenase.
- The t-DNA region of all the Ti & Ri plasmids are flanked by direct repeat sequence 25 bp.
- The transgenic tomato plants showing delayed ripening due to suppression of ethylene was developed using methodology of antisense RNA.
- The direct DNA uptake by the protoplast is stimulated by the chemical PEG.
- The chemical used as an inducer of the vir operon is *Acetosyringene.*
- The vir region is organized into six operons viz, vir A, vir B, vir C, vir D, vir E and vir G out of these four Operon are required for virulence A, B, D, G.
- The large dark body in the nucleus is the nucleolus, which participates in the formation of RNA.
- Nuclear envelope breaks down in Metaphase-II.
- Most plant cells are surrounded by a rigid cell wall made primarily of polysaccharides.
- The organelle that functions in the breakdown of cells and tissues is the **lysosomes.**
- The function of nucleus includes housing the hereditary information.
- Batch system of culture is non steady state process.
- Bacculoviruses are DNA viruses.
- If meiosis does not occur, the chromosome, number would double in each generation.
- An example of naturally occurring auxin is IAA.
- Protoplast fusion can be achieved spontaneously.
- The Shine- Dalgarno (SD) sequence is known as ribosome binding site in bacterial RNA.
- An example of commercially important primary alcohol is ethanol.
- In PCR, the DNA is generally denatured by temperature.
- Anther culture provides a method for the production of homozygous line.
- Germplasm preservation of meristem and shoot tip culture involves Cryopreservation and slow growth.
- The term somaclonal variation was termed by Larken and Scowhoft in 1981.

- Somaclonal variation is the variation seen in plants that have been produced by plant tissue culture.
- **Callus culture** is an uneven, undifferentiated and unstructured mass of proliferating cells on agar media treated with plant growth regulators.
- **Suspension culture** is a liquid culture in which single or group of cells are suspended.
- Acridine orange is the organic compound that serves as a nucleic acid selective fluorescent dye with cationic properties useful for cell cycle determination
- $CaCl_2$ is used for preparation of competent cell.
- Transcription is directly involved in steps in the flow of genetic information from DNA to RNA.
- **Guanosine** is purine nucleosides have neuroprotective properties.
- Substance, such as tryptophan that decrease the amount of enzyme produced by a cell is known is *repressor.*
- Francois Jacob and Jacques Monod proposed **Operon hypothesis.**
- Large size is not a desired characteristic of a vector.
- Transcription factor controls gene expression in eukaryotes.
- Transformation is a means of transfer of gene in host without a biological agent.
- When genetic material is carried from one cell to another by a phage, the phenomenon is known as **transduction**.
- Mutation that involves only smallest change in base pairs is known as point mutation.
- In the case of maize crop monoecious condition occurs.
- *Protogyny* is found in the case of bajra.
- Single seed descent method was originally suggested in 1939 by Goulden.
- Self and often cross pollinated crop show considerable heterosis and additive variance.
- Mass selection is based on the maternal parent only.
- Triticale was developed from the cross between wheat and rye.
- Bread wheat has somatic chromosome number of Zn=42.
- Coupling and repulsion hypothesis was first described by Bateson.
- The phenomenon of crossing over occurs during pachytene.
- The phenomenon of gene interaction was first described by Bateson and Punnet.
- In case of a dihybrid cross, 4 types of gametes will be produced by F1.
- Frame- shift mutations are produced by base deletion and addition.
- LD_{50} is the most likely to be the optimum dose of a mutagen.
- *Raphanobrassica* was developed from the cross *Raphanus sativus* ×*Brassica oleracea.*
- Chromosome substitution is the easiest using Nullisomics.
- The chemical formula of colchicines is $C_{22}H_{25}O_6N$.
- A nucleoside is made up of a five-carbon sugar (ribose or 2'-deoxyribose) and a nucleobase, commonly known as a nitrogenous base.
- Gene for gene relationship was proposed by Flor.
- In meiosis the first Telophase is sometimes omitted.

- The term cell was coined by Robert Hooke in 1665 in the book Micrographia.
- .Segregation takes place during Anaphase-I.
- Mitochondria's are the power house of the cell.
- In dicot plant shape of the stomata is like kidney.
- The storage period of fruits can be increased by spraying with waxy emulsion
- The size of cell is increased due to addition of solute.
- The auxin is synthesized from its precursor tryptophan.
- The shape of growth curve in crops like sorghum is S.
- Because of photorespiration yields of C_3 plants are decreased up to 30-40%,
- The Krebs cycle takes place in mitochondria.
- The most commonly employed matrices are cellulose, polyacrylamide and sepharose.
- Improvement in the activity and usefulness of existing enzyme is enzyme engineering
- The term Chromatography was coined by Tswett.
- Normally nitrogen, argon and helium carrier gases are used in gas chromatography.
- The most widely used technique for analysis and characterization of protein and nucleic acid is PEG (Polyacrylamide Gel Electrophoresis).
- International unit for enzyme activity recommended by enzyme commission is Katal.
- The process during which the information in a sequence of DNA in used to construct an mRNA molecule transcription.
- The site on a DNA sequence at which transcription stop is Terminator.
- A length of DNA equal to 1000 nucleotides kb or kilobase (kb) is a unit of measurement equal to 1000 base pairs of DNA or RNA.
- Partial or total suppression of gene expression is gene silencing.
- Central dogma the original postulate that genetic information can be transferred RNA to protein, nucleic acid to protein and DNA to RNA.
- 1 angstrom (Å), unit of length, equal to 0.1 nanometre or 10^{-10} metre.
- The term pH was introduced by Sorensen.
- The combination of genes from two different cells is called recombination.
- Nutritionally deficient mutant organisms are auxotrops.
- Plasmid replication occurs by which enzyme polymerase-III.
- In nature competition occurs in the cells due to uptake of DNA.
- Chargff's rule states that in DNA structure the A=T and G=C molar equivalents exist.
- When an amino acid substitution has no detectable effect on phenotype is called silent mutation.
- The ability of a molecule to exist in more than one chemical form is called tautomerism.
- The DNA content of haploid eukaryotic cells ranges from 107 to 1011 bp.
- Animal cell communicates by means of integrins. (Integrins are transmembrane proteins found in all animal cells)
- Nod D gene is activated by flavonoids.
- Glutathione s-transferase is used in herbicide detoxification in plant.

- Isomerization of citrate in TCA cycle occurs by aconitase.
- Biosynthesis of carbohydrates from non carbohydrate precursors is called **citrate synthase.**
- The pH at which a solute has no net electric charge is **isoelectric point.**
- The aqueous content of cell or organelle with dissolved solute are called matrix.
- An antibiotic pumycin inhibits the plypeptide synthesis of a polypeptide chain.
- A contiguous and nonoverlaping set of the three nucleotide codons in DNA or RNA called reading frame.
- A highly repeated nontranslated segment of DNA is present in eukaryotes.
- Acridone dyes a chemical which inhibits plasmid replication not chromosomal DNA replication.
- A segment of DNA that can move from one position to another in the genome called transposon, jumping DNA and mobile DNA.
- A virus particle is called virion.
- A dipolar ion with spatially separated positive and negative charges is called *Zwitterions*.
- Ribosomal genes are repeated thousands of times in nucleolar organizer region (NOR) regime.
- RFLP (restriction fragment length polymorphism) technique is used for genetic characterization of DNA at molecular level.
- A Gierer (1916) and G. Schramm discovered RNA could alone initiate an infection of TMV (Tobacco Mosaic Virus) in Tobacco leaves.
- Positive charge will be present between at the metaphase involved chromosomes.
- In Glyoxylate cycle final step occurs in cytosol.
- Epinephrine glucagon is important for breakdown of glycogen.
- RNA polymerase enzyme catalyzed RNA synthesis.
- Enzyme commission appointed in 1955 and first version of enzymes was published in 1961.
- The inhibitor binds non-covalently with enzyme cause reversible inhibition.
- Lysozymes has bactericidal properties..
- Chymotrypsinogen is composed of a single polypeptide chain with 254 amino acid residues.
- Pepsin in an example for the class of enzyme hydrolase.
- The coded information that determines the sequence of amino acid in a protein residues in mRNA.
- The base that is never found in RNA genetic code is thymine.
- All the RNA has ACC trinucleotide sequence at 3 ends.
- The folding of polypeptide chain into tertiary structures occurs during translation.
- The bond in protein structure that are not broken on denaturation are peptide bond.
- Individuals used for production of biotech product are bioreactor.
- For a majority of mesophilic enzymes Q 10 value is 2 at 0°C to 40°C.
- Temperature coefficient (Q_{10}) provides the rate of a reaction increases for every 10°C rise in temperature.
- In most of the organisms satellite DNA contains AT-rich sequence.
- Most globular proteins undergo denaturation when heated above 60-70°C.

- Genetic information flows in the direction DNA → RNA → protein.
- There are 64 possible combinations of AVGC to specify 20 amino acids.
- In 80s ribosomes the ratio of the RNA protein is-1:1.
- Methionine is the sulphur containing amino acid.
- Ergosterol on irradiation changes to Vitamin B_2.
- Site of protein biosynthesis is Ribosome.
- The width (diameter) of a double helix DNA is 20 Å.
- Beer's Law states that a chemical solution's concentration is directly proportional to its light absorption. Beer's Law may be written simply as: $A = ebc$. where A is absorbance (no units), e is the molar absorptivity with units of L mol^{-1} cm^{-1} (formerly called the extinction coefficient), b is the path length of the sample, usually expressed in cm, c is the concentration of the compound in solution, expressed in mol L^{-1}
- In transcription initiation occurs at promoter site on the DNA.
- Prostaglandins are biologically active molecules that are polycyclic.
- The enzyme that is used to make the first strand cDNA from mRNA is reverse transcriptase.
- Riboflavin and cobalamine is the pair of vitamins participates as cofactors in the cellular oxidation reduction reaction.
- Most accurate method to determine the molecular weight of a given polypeptide is SDS-PAGE.
- Shape of the cholesterol is globular.
- Bacteriophages or simply phages, are viruses which infect bacteria.
- Majority of all bacteriophages known exhibit a double-stranded DNA genome inside the virion capsid and belong to the order of tailed phages.
- **Acclimatization:** The adaptation of a living organism (plant, animal or micro-organism) to a changed environment that subjects it to physiological stress. Acclimatization should not be confused with adaptation (q.v.). cf acquired.
- **Adventitious:** A structure arising at sites other than the usual ones, *e.g.*, shoots from roots or leaves, and embryos from any cell other than a zygote.
- **Allopolyploid;** A polyploid organism (usually a plant) having multiple sets of chromosomes derived from different species.
- **Amplification:** 1. Treatment (*e.g.*, use of chloramphenicol) designed to increase the proportion of plasmid DNA relative to that of bacterial (host) DNA. 2. Replication of a gene library in bulk. 3. Duplication of gene(s) within a chromosomal segment. 4. Creation of many copies of a segment of DNA by the polymerase chain reaction (PCR)
- **Amplified fragment length polymorphism (AFLP):** A type of DNA marker, generated by digestion of genomic DNA with two restriction enzymes to create many DNA fragments, ligation of specific sequences of DNA (called adaptors) to the ends of these fragments, amplification of the fragments via PCR (using a set of primers with sequences corresponding to the adapters, plus various random combinations of three additional bases at the end), and visualization of fragments via gel electrophoresis.
- **Biotechnology:** A set of biological techniques developed through basic research and now applied to research and product development. Biotechnology refers to the use of recombinant DNA, cell

fusion and new bioprocessing techniques

- **Callus:** A mass of unorganized regenerated cells in culture medium
- **Cell:** The lowest denomination of life thought to be possible. Most organisms consist of more than one cell, which become specialized into particular functions toenable the whole organism to function properly. Cells contain DNA and many other elements to enable the cell to function.
- **Cell culture:** Regeneration of whole plant from a single cell in a nutrient medium. It may include somatic cells or germinal cells (pollens).
- **Chromosomes:** The self-replicating genetic structure of cells containing the cellular DNA. Humans have 23 pairs of chromosomes. Cry1A: A protein derived from the bacterium Bacillus thuringiensis that is toxic to some insects when ingested. This bacterium occurs widely in nature and has been used for decades as an insecticide, although it constitutes less than 2 percent of the overall insecticides used.
- **Cultivar:** Synonymous with variety; the international equivalent of variety.
- **Double helix:** The twisted-ladder shape that two linear strands of DNA assume when complementary nucleotides on opposing strands bond together.
- **DNA (deoxyribonucleic acid):** The genetic material of all cells and many viruses. The molecule that encodes genetic information. DNA is a double-stranded molecule held together by weak bonds between base pairs of nucleotides. The four nucleotides in DNA contain the bases adenine (A), guanine (G), cytosine (C) and thymine (T). In nature, base pairs form only between A and T and between G and C; thus the base sequence of each single strand can be deduced from that of its partner
- **Embryogenesis:** The process of differentiation of root and shoot from somatic embryos.
- **Enzyme-linked immunosorbent assay (ELISA):** A technique using antibodies for detecting specific proteins. Used to test for the presence of a particular genetically engineered organism
- **Gene cloning:** A technique of genetic engineering where a gene sequence with several identical copies can be replicated
- **Gene flow:** The exchange of genetic traits between populations by movement of individuals, gametes or spores. It involves the spread of new variants among different populations through dispersal.
- **Gene expression:** The result of the activity of a gene or genes which influence the biochemistry and physiology of an organism and may change its outward appearance.
- **Gene gun:** A device invented at Cornell University that allows genetic material to be introduced into a new organism. The genetic material from the donor is "shot" into cells of the recipient and the material is incorporated into its DNA.
- **Gene sequencing:** The method of determining the order of bases of DNA molecules which constitute a gene.
- **Gene splicing:** The isolation of a gene from one organism and then the introduction of that gene into another organism using techniques of biotechnology.
- **Genetic engineering:** The technique of removing, modifying or adding genes to a DNA molecule in order to change the information it contains. By changing this information, genetic engineering changes the type or amount of proteins an organism is capable of producing, thus enabling it to make new substances or perform new functions.

- **Genetically modified organism (GMO):** Often the label GMO and the term "transgenic" are used to refer to organisms that have acquired novel genes from other organisms by laboratory "gene transfer" methods.
- **Genetics:** The study of the patterns of inheritance of specific traits.
- **Genome:** All the genetic material in the chromosomes of a particular organism; its size is generally given as its total number of base pairs.
- **Genomics:** The mapping and sequencing of genetic material in the DNA of a particular organism as well as the use of that information to better understand what genes do, how they are controlled, how they work together, and what their physical locations are on the chromosome
- **Genotype:** The genetic identity of an individual. Genotype often is evident by outward characteristics, but may also be reflected in more subtle biochemical ways not visually evident.
- **Hybrid:** Seed or plants produced as the result of controlled cross-pollination as opposed to seed produced as the result of natural pollination. Hybrid seeds are selected to have higher quality traits, *e.g.* yield or pest tolerance
- **Meristem culture:** Regeneration of plants from tissues of actively dividing organs like stem tip
- **Micropropagation:** Regeneration of plants from isolated meristematic cellsor tissues.
- **Mutation:** Any inheritable change in DNA sequence. Mutation breeding: Commonly used practices in plant breeding and other areas in which chemicals or radiation are applied to whole organisms, *e.g.* plants, or cells so that changes in the organism's DNA will occur. Such changes are then evaluated for their beneficial effects, such as disease resistance.
- **Natural selection:** The concept developed by Charles Darwin that genes which produce characteristics that are more favorable in a particular environment will be more abundant in the next generation.
- **Nucleotide:** A subunit of DNA or RNA consisting of a nitrogenous base (adenine, guanine, thymine or cytosine in DNA; adenine, guanine, uracil or cytosine in RNA), a phosphate molecule, and a sugar molecule (deoxyribose in DNA and ribose in RNA). Thousands of nucleotides are linked to form a DNA or RNA molecule.
- **Organ culture:** Regeneration of complete plant from an organlike apical bud, root or shoot.
- **Organogenesis:** The process of differentiation of root and shoot from somatic embryos.
- **Outcrossing:** Mating between different populations or individuals of the same species that are not closely related.
- **Ovule:** An outgrowth of the ovary of a seed plant that encloses an embryo.
- **Phenotype:** The visible and/or measurable characteristics of an organism (how it appears outwardly).
- **Pollen:** The cells that carry the male DNA of a seed plant.
- **Polymerase chain reaction (PCR):** A technique used to create a large number of copies of a target DNA sequence of interest. One use of PCR is in the detection of DNA sequences that indicate the presence of a particular genetically engineered organism.
- **Protoplast culture:** Regeneration of whole plant from naked single cell in culture medium.
- **Random Amplified Polymorphic DNA (RAPD)** markers are DNA fragments from PCR amplification of random segments of genomic DNA with single primer of arbitrary nucleotide sequence.

- **Recombinant DNA molecules (rDNA):** A combination of DNA molecules of different origin that are joined using recombinant DNA technologies.
- **Recombinant DNA technology:** Procedure used to join together DNA segments in a cell-free system (an environment outside a cell or organism). Under appropriate conditions, a recombinant DNA molecule can enter a cell and replicate there, either autonomously or after it has become integrated into a cellular chromosome.
- **Recombination:** The process by which progeny derive a combination of genes different from that of either parent.
- **RFLP (Restrictive Fragment Length Polymorphism)** is a difference in homologous DNA sequences that can be detected by the presence of fragments of different lengths after digestion of the DNA samples in question with specific restriction endonucleases. RFLP, as a molecular marker, is specific to a single clone/restriction enzyme combination.Most RFLP markers are co-dominant (both alleles in heterozygous sample will be detected) and highly locus-specific.

  An RFLP probe is a labeled DNA sequence that hybridizes with one or more fragments of the digested DNA sample after they were separated by gel electrophoresis, thus revealing a unique blotting pattern characteristic to a specific genotype at a specific locus. Short, single- or low-copy genomic DNA or cDNA clones are typically used as RFLP probes.
- **Selectable marker**: A gene, often encoding resistance to an antibiotic or an herbicide, introduced into a group of cells to allow identification of those cells that contain the gene of interest from the cells that do not. Selectable markers are used in genetic engineering to facilitate identification of cells that have incorporated another desirable trait that is not easy to identify in individual cells.
- **Selective breeding:** Making deliberate crosses or matings of organisms so that the offspring will have a desired characteristic derived from one of the parents
- **Somoclonal variation:** The variability generated by the use of tissue culture.
- **Somatic hybridization:** Crossing of plants through fusion of somatic cells *i.e.* protoplasts.
- **Sub culturing:** Transfer of tissues or callus from old culture medium to fresh culture medium
- **Tissue culture:** A process of growing a plant in the laboratory from cells rather than seeds. This technique is used in traditional plant breeding as well as when using techniques of agricultural biotechnology.
- **Transgene**: A gene from one organism inserted into another organism by recombinant DNA techniques.
- **Transgenic:** Containing genes altered by insertion of DNA from an unrelated organism. Taking genes from one species and inserting them into another species in order to get that trait expressed in the offspring. Or organism which contain foreign gene.

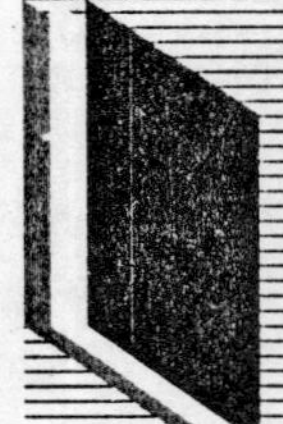

CHAPTER 10

HOME SCIENCE

Home science is an integrated field of study that provides scientific and systematic knowledge about various aspects of family living and the art of effectively allocating your resources.

1. The recommended dietary allowance (RDA) of energy (ICMR, 2020) for a moderately active pregnant woman is 2720 + 350 (3070) kcal.
2. Butter is an example of 'water - in - oil' type of emulsion.
3. Menu for 'meals on wheels' is selective type.
4. Methylene blue is a soluble blueing agent.
5. Wool fibres can be confirmed by performing microscopic test.
6. The list of human values was given by Parker.
7. The specialization of functions of the two hemispheres of the cerebral cortex is called lateralization.
8. Flat puppets which are operated against the rear of a tightly stretched white cloth screen with a light behind are called shadow puppets
9. 'Distrust' between a sender and a receiver in communication is a type of socio-psychological barrier.
10. A cumulative percentage curve with an s - shaped figure is called an Ogive.
11. Diarrhoea, dermatitis and dementia are the symptoms of niacin deficiency.
12. Bread, white sauce and beer foods have gluten present in them.
13. A guest relation program adopted in a restaurant should include anticipate customer need, use pleasant and reassuring words, observe customer behaviour.
14. The characteristics of individuality are personal signature, rejecting styles that are in fashion and doing own thinking
15. Pina and abaca are leaf fibres.
16. ????
17. The emergence of the following adaptive behaviours occur during the sensorimotor period between 8-12 months as given by Jean Piaget's goal directed behaviour, object permanence and intentionality.
18. Extension aims at human resource development for multiplier effect by imparting knowledge, imparting skills and bringing desirable changes in behaviour.
19. Aspects of non-verbal communication are body language, facial expressions and posture.
20. The Mann-Whitney test is a test of difference between two independent samples, uses measurements on an ordinal scale and small sample size

21. Foods which have higher amounts of amylose have a lower glycemic index.
22. Including oats and its' products in the diet helps in reducing the risk of cardiovascular, diseases in populations.
23. β-glucan helps in normalising the lipid profile.
24. RDA of vitamin A for 10 year old boy as per ICMR, 2010 is 600 μg retinol
25. Crystallization of sugar occurs in chenna murki
26. Milk is not allowed in a clear fluid diet while black tea, coconut water and carbonated beverage are allowed.
27. Quick service restaurants offer the nutritive value of their menus on website.
28. Drop feed is not considered as a sewing machine feed mechanism.
29. Salt is added in dyeing for exhaustion.
30. Red goods identify the American expression for fast moving consumer goods, consumed and replaced at a rapid rate.
31. Operation chart technique in time and motion studies considers movement of both the hands.
32. 'People born in one period of time are influenced by particular historical and cultural conditions', this is called. cohort effect.
33. A child rearing style that is high in acceptance and involvement, emphasizes firm control with reasoning is termed as *authoritative style*
34. News headlines are not a form of feedback in mass communication.
35. An interactive plan tool to collect data for planning an extension programme is seasonal diagramming.
36. NFHS, NSSO and CBHI agencies provide data for nutrition monitoring in India.
37. Retrospective methods of diet assessment are 24 hours dietary recall food frequency questionnaire and food balance sheets.
38. Ascorbic acid is essential for maintaining the following functions in the body collagen formation, acts as an antioxidant and acts as a reducing agent
39. Serum triglycerides more than 150 mg/100 ml, waist circumference more than 80 cm. in females and BMI more than 23 kg/m^2 are the diagnostic criteria for metabolic syndrome.
40. Equipments found in the production area are. griddle, charbroiler, and deck oven and clambell cooker.
41. Some tools needed for problem solving are pareto chart, check sheet, cause and effect diagram and process chart.
42. Neoprene and spandex fibres are stretch fibres.
43. Structural jamming pucker can be prevented by using chain stitch, using thinner thread and reinforcing the seam
44. Plasma technology optimizes hydrophobic, UV protection and flame retardency properties in textiles.

45. Benefits of ergonomics include safer jobs, increased efficiency and productivity and fewer injuries.
46. Ergonomics indicate the factors contributing to improved working conditions sufficient lighting, good housekeeping and personal protective equipments.
47. The exercise of planning in management is future oriented and is based on analysis of goals achieved.
48. Two prominent perspectives for the decline in social interaction in late adulthood are disengagement theory and activity theory.
49. According to Piaget children's thinking during the pre-operational period is characterized by concentration, irreversibility and egocentrism
50. Memory strategies used to store and retain information during school years include rehearsal, organisation and elaboration.
51. Seating arrangement, use of artefacts and use of colour are important aspects of using para language in communication.
52. Problems connected with entrepreneurship development can be identified in the following domains viz. procuring of raw material, marketing of products and procuring of capital.
53. Glycoside found in green olive leaves is oleuropein.
54. Untreated gum disease leads over time to bad breath, expensive dental bills and tooth loss.
55. Addiction's most confounding symptom is denial.
56. From smoking, from eating too much and you catch it from your parent's one get a chronic disease.
57. One pound (0.45kg) of fat is equal to how many calories (3,500).
58. The group of highly aggressive adolescent girls is most at risk of developing an eating disorder.
59. A myocardial infarction is coronary heart failure.
60. The recommended serving size of milk, yogurt or cheese is 3/4 cup low-fat or non fat milk or yogurt; 2 ounces low fat natural cheese.
61. A disease marked by low bone mass and deteriorating structure of bone tissue is called osteoporosis.
62. Proteins build enzymes, muscles, tissues, hormones and red blood cells hence they are important.
63. The foods or combinations of sashimi (raw fish) and steak, eggs and beans and brown rice foods provide good quality protein.
64. Joint inflammation is the symptoms of arthritis.
65. Angina occurs when not enough oxygen is reaching your heart muscle.
66. So many people have chronic diseases because they don't eat a healthy diet.

67. Inactivation of enzymes in food is the primary reason for blanching food.
68. Salt is added in dyeing for exhaustion.
69. Bending and carrying respectively belong to Torsal and manual kind of effort.
70. Vanaspati is an adulterant in ghee and butter.
71. Moderate hearing loss is indicated when a child can hear only at 41-55 decibel.
72. Disability in reading is called dyslexia.
73. One of the motifs used in bandhani is ladoo-jalebi.
74. Principles of design are, repetition, balance, harmony and rhythmic.
75. 'GOTS' stands for global organic textile standards
76. RDA's for Indian women are based on reference woman who has body weight 55 kg and height 1.61 m.
77. HDL is synthesized and secreted from liver
78. Degree of polymerization for polyester ranges between 115-140.
79. Bluish green, blue and green colours are cool colours.
80. Tunnel finisher can finish hundreds of garments at one time by a single operator.
81. Type of fabric governs the selection of needle.
82. Rotary is not a design repeat.
83. Yogurt and cheese foods are produced by involving lactic acid fermentation.
84. Oscillating hook holds the bobbin in the sewing machine?
85. Aari does not represent kasuti embroidery while menthi, gavanti and represent murgi.
86. The symptoms viz GFR 20 ml or less/min, oliguria and oedema are found in kidney failure patients.
87. Therbligs are 18 kinds of elemental motions, used in the study of motion economy in the workplace, the word therblig was the creation of Frank Bunker Gilbreth and Lillian Moller Gilbreth
88. Releasing spent up emotional energy is emotional catharsis.
89. The correct sequence of producing synthetic fibres is polymerization, dissolving in solution, treatment with finishing chemicals and extrusion.
90. Planning, organisation, implementation, feedback are the correct sequence of activities in the home management process.
91. Urinary iodine, haemoglobin estimation and serum retinol are method of nutritional assessment using biochemical method.
92. Principle of operation of an electric water heater is by induction.
93. The period of human embryo is 2 – 8 weeks
94. Test to assess PEM in children in early stages is by anthropometry
95. Low sodium diet is recommended in CHF (Congestive Heart Failure) and liver cirrhosis.

96. Level of intelligent quotient (IQ) of educable mentally challenged child is 75 – 100.
97. Isoelectric point at which maximum coagulation of milk protein takes place. 4.6 pH.
98. The fortificants used in iodized salt is potassium iodate.
99. Serum vitamin D level < 10 ng/mL is indicative of sub-clinical vitamin D deficiency.
100. Sociometry is a tool to measure child's relationship with peers.
101. There must be alteration between active play and quiet play.
102. To avoid diaper rash change wet diapers immediately and clean and dry the area before putting a fresh diaper.
103. A clear fluid diet supplies only carbohydrates and calories and only minerals and vitamins.
104. Duplex is not a hand printing technique.
105. Tunnel garment finishers are used for finishing number of garments together.
106. Electromyography is a method used for measuring electric phenomenon occurring in the muscle.
107. International literacy day is celebrated on 8th September every year.
108. Persian carpets are divided into three groups viz farsh/qali, qalichech and gelim/zilu.
109. The homogenization of milk is done to disperse fat molecules.
110. Requirements of iron and folic acid for pregnant women is 30-60 mg of elemental iron and 400 µg (0.4 mg) folic acid respectively, recommended for pregnant women to prevent maternal anaemia, puerperal sepsis, low birth weight, and preterm birth.
111. Centralised system food delivery system is used for hospital in patients.
112. Widal Test is used for the diagnosis of Tuberculosis.
113. Epidiascope is also known as opaque projector.
114. Components of implementing are facilitating and controlling.
115. Language development in children is promoted through. storytelling, conversation and social participation.
116. Aspects of a good lesson plan are objectives, teacher's activities, learning experiences, teaching aids and appraisal.
117. Job description and work schedule tools are used for personal management.
118. Sustainable fashion includes environment friendly material, methods socially responsible and products that could last multiple seasons.
119. Correct layouts of unidirectional fabrics for garment cutting are lengthwise fold, double fold and open.
120. Conversation is an expressive skill.
121. Bouclé yarn, slub yarn and flock yarn are novelty yarns.
122. The emulsifier used in mayonnaise is lecithin.
123. Milk is a rich source of retinol.

124. When black colour is added to any colour it is called shade.
125. Exhibition is a systematic arrangement and display of visual materials under a roof to create awareness and arouse interest in the minds of the learners about an idea.
126. Textured is not a simple yarn.
127. Intrinsic value is also called terminal value.
128. Gluten free diet (GFD) is given to patients with celiac disease.
129. Tube feeding is also known as enteral nutrition.
130. The process of cutting materials by means of a high velocity jet of high temperature ionized gas (argon) is called plasma cutting.
131. Leaf stands for latest ecologically approved fashion and labelling ecologically approved fabrics.
132. A bedspread used for ceremonial occasions made with kantha embroidery is sujani.
133. Anaemia caused by vitamin B_{12} deficiency is pernicious.
134. Attitudes, feelings and interests are. affective component.
135. The ideal size for flash card is 10 × 12 inches.
136. Vitamin B_6, vitamin B_{12} and folate nutrients play an important role in the metabolism of homocysteine.
137. Fleece is sheared from a living sheep.
138. Components of the national vitamin a prophylaxis programme are distributing mega doses of vitamin A and encouraging consumption of fruits and vegetables.
139. Colostrums are very good as it is rich in proteins and antibodies.
140. Band is a stationary knife.
141. Normal BMI for adult Asians as suggested by WHO is 18 – 23 kg/m^2
142. Traditional costumes of egypt include gallebaya, seblah and yelek
143. Generally visually impaired persons have visual acuity of 20/200.
144. The female sex hormone is estrogen.
145. Fish is a double pointed dart.
146. A portion of output re-entered as input to affect succeeding output is feedback
147. Eliminating or combining parts of jobs is suggested by incorporating changes in production sequence
148. Family directly influences personality of the child by communication and moulding.
149. The recommended height of the work surface in the kitchen for efficient operation is 3 inches below elbow level
150. Disciplining is a way of improving. mannerisms, aesthetic sense and educational values
151. Right to survival of children includes right to birth and registration and right to health and nutrition.

152. A group of persons whom an individual consults before taking an important decision is known as reference groups.
153. Tetra pack boxes and milk bottle are examples of aseptic packaging.
154. Approaches to understand women's participation in development have gone through the following phases. welfare, women in development, gender and development
155. Chlorine compounds and azo compounds chemicals used in the textile industry are hazardous.
156. Putting the last as first, means reversals in learning.
157. The effects of mental fatigue are decreased attention, decreased motivation and impaired perception and thinking.
158. Polyuria, glycosuria and polyphagia are the symptoms of diabetes mellitus.
159. Fanda, bijli and pechni stitches are used in chikankari embroidery.
160. As per the human development report, the dimensions for measuring 'human development' in any country are longevity, knowledge and decent standard of living.
161. Japanese traditional costumes include kimono, yukata and zanshi
162. the objectives of non-formal education are to raise the extent of functional, literacy, to provide life-long education and to prepare individuals for self-employment
163. Digital printing leads to. economic short runs, sampling in multiple colours and mass customization.
164. The equipment Bain-Marie is used for keeping cooked food warm in a cafeteria.
165. Determining need, internal source, advertisement, interview, and establishment of wage, appointment letter and orientation is right sequence for the procedure used in selecting a food service employee.
166. Recommendations for visible dietary fat intake for an adult Indian woman (moderate worker) as suggested by ICMR is 25 g per day
167. Viscose is not a stretch fibre.
168. The gas that is found in compressor of refrigerator is Freon-12.
169. The primary reason for parboiling is to conserve nutrients.
170. Arrange the stages of child development in correct sequence. prenatal, antenatal, neonatal, infancy and toddlerhood.
171. Cumulative frequency distribution should be used in order to find out where certain scores rank relative to all others.
172. Immunization is necessary for children. to develop defence mechanism in the body and to reduce incidence of viral and infectious diseases.
173. The retinol requirement (μg/day) age group in school child- 400, pregnant woman- 800, lactating woman-950 and adolescent boy-600 respectively.
174. Anthropometric is concerned with structural dimensions which are; weight, height and waist circumference.

175. To meet the individual differences the curriculum should be. formal and flexible.

176. Operant conditioning is also known as instrumental conditioning.

177. Fatty fish, mustard seeds and walnuts foods are rich in omega 3 fatty acids.

178. HACCP and GHP terms are associated with sanitation.

179. Developmental period from birth to 8 to 12 months known as infancy.

180. The target group for national literacy mission is 15-35 years.

181. Iron and sulphur nutrients are responsible for green ring formation in boiled egg.

182. Campaign is an intense educational activity for motivating and mobilizing a community to action.

183. Electronic and microprocessor controlled alternatives in weaving have resulted in better and assured quality fabrics, higher rate of production and consistency and reliable performance.

184. Plan of work and calendar of work aspects are closely related to programme planning.

185. Credibility in communication means. trustworthiness and complete.

186. Dominant emotions are always. pleasant, unpleasant and strong.

187. The causes of increasing social evils are. lack of creative parenting, the concept of education for job not for life, unhealthy mass and multimedia communication and no emphasis is given regarding human values, civic responsibilities and learning life skills.

188. Types of traction (important in the development of goal character in activities) include operation traction, batch traction, process traction, machine traction and line traction.

189. Public service is a service intended to serve all members of a community.

190. Job vacancy and matrimonial are advertised under 'classified category'.

191. The menu is the heart of the entire establishment on which all activities are centred.

192. Goals of the elderly include. family relations and good health

193. Post mature babies are generally long and thin as they receive insufficient blood supply towards the end of gestation.

194. Painting walls and ceiling with light colour, matt finish paint will reduce the size of the room.

195. The matt finish even though the colour is light will absorbs the light by creating illusion of advancing effect.

196. Marker efficiency can be enhanced by pattern engineering.

197. The correct sequence in the manufacturing of viscose rayon is conditioning of wood pulp, steeping process, ageing process and churning process.

198. Marriage laws are designed to protect safety of the individual and safety of the society.

199. Foods in increasing order according to their sodium content per 100g is tomato>spinach>musk melon>banana>egg>meat.

200. Antistatic finish on a textile fabric produces the following effects. improves the surface conductivity and develops an electric charge opposite that of a fibre.

201. "The protection of children from sexual offences act" was enacted in 2012.
202. β-carotene in the body changes into retinol in liver.
203. Total parenteral nutrition involves use of the large central vein to deliver life sustaining nourishment.
204. The common type of warp knitting is double knitting.
205. Floats formed by weft yarns are sateen.
206. Spinning is the process of convert fibres into yarn.
207. Cotton is the world's major textile fibres.
208. Bending of yarn without breaking is flexibility.
209. Wool can absorb moisture up to 30 percent of its weight.
210. Spinning quality is otherwise termed as cohesiveness.
211. Filament fibre can be measured in miles or kilometre.
212. Azlon refers to man-made proteins from natural sources such as soy, peanut, milk or corn fibre
213. Cotton is the fibre which has the smell like burning paper when it burns.
214. Lanolin is wool grease recovered and purified during the scouring process and used in cosmetic industry.
215. Flyer spinning is the oldest method which produces smooth and lustrous yarns.
216. The primary properties of textile fibres are breadth ratio, tenacity, spinning quality.
217. Length to breadth ratio of wool is 3000 : 1.
218. Wool producing sheep may classify in to 4 types according to the wool quality.
219. The first fleece sheared from a lamb about six to eight months old is called as lamb's wool or fleece wool.
220. Thread count/fabric count is determined by counting the number of wrap (ends) and weft (picks).
221. While planning the home makers may see to it that plans are realistic and flexible.
222. Implementation refers to putting the plan into action.
223. Social qualities imply that the home maker vitality and polite.
224. Selection of standard is based on fundamental goal.
225. Energy refers to the ability to do work.
226. Ironing comes under moderate work.
227. Accumulation of lactic acid and carbon dioxide is the cause of muscular tension.
228. A good manager will balance the time by work, rest and leisure.
229. Home maker must be conscious about menu planning, keeping household clean and time plan.
230. According to WHO the energy expenditure for heavy work for men is about 300 kcal.

231. Routine task at home is called mental effort.

232. Total calories requirement for an average adult woman (sedentary) in a day is 1900 kcal.

233. Aversion of any work leads to stress.

234. Process chart drawn up to show the flow of movement of the work and worker.

235. Operation chart techniques are help to redtice wasteful expenditure of time and energy in all activities.

236. Commodities and facilities which are available to the family without the use of money is family income.

237. In cooking area the height of the area should be about 90 cm from the floor and about 55 cm deep.

238. Imaginative thinking occurs at the age of 12 years.

Imaginative thinking the process we use to remember something we know; or combine two or more of our five senses to create something we have never seen.

239. The study about different approach in human development is known as cross sectional study.

240. FED stands for feeding and eating disorders.

241. Dyslexia can be identified among child at the age of two years.

242. Person's special mental abilities can be notable at the age of 26 year.

243. The Rorschach test was developed in the year of 1921's by Swiss psychologist Hermann Rorschach.

244. The union department of social welfare was created in the year of 1964.

245. Central social welfare board was set up in the year 1953.

246. Pre–vocational training programme offered in the age group 11-14 year and the duration of it should be three year.

247. Nativist proposed that human infants are equipped at birth with a language acquisition device.

248. Hallow needle inserted through abdominal wall to obtain amniotic fluid in uterus is called amniocentesis. Amniotic fluid is the fluid that surrounds and protects a baby during pregnancy.

249. Psychosomatic disorders are explained by Sylee is called *general adaptation syndrome*.

Psychosomatic disorder is a disease which involves both mind and body. It is related to stress in everyday life. Examples include, eczema, psoriasis, high blood pressure, ulcers and heart diseases.

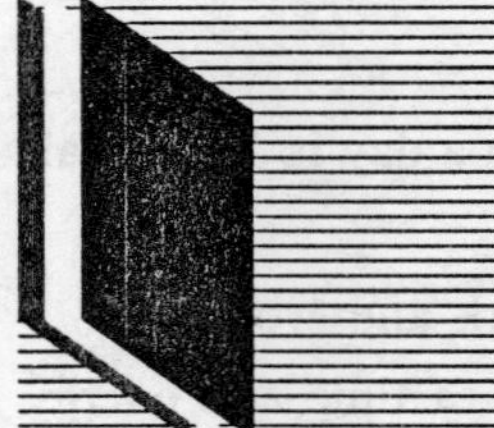
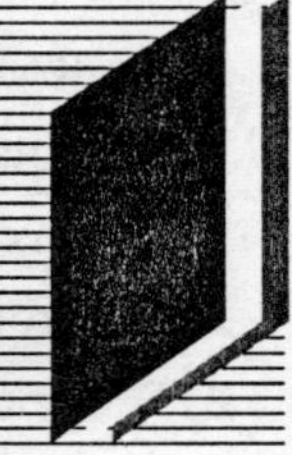

CHAPTER 11
STATISTICS

Statistics, the science of collecting, analyzing, presenting and interpreting the datas.

(A) IMPORTANT CONCEPTS AND FORMULAE

I. MEASURES OF CENTRAL TENDENCY

1. MEAN

A. Arithmetic Mean (A.M.)

It is the most popular and widely used measure. It may be either (*i*) *simple arithmetic mean* or (*ii*) *weighted arithmetic mean.*

Simple arithmetic mean of a set of observations is arithmetic mean of their sum divided by the number of observations.

(*i*) ***Arithmetic mean of discrete series***

$$\bar{x} = \frac{1}{n}\sum_{i=1}^{n} x_i \qquad (i = 1, 2... n)$$

In case of frequency distribution

(*a*) *Direct method*

$$\bar{x} = \frac{1}{N}\sum f_i\, x_i\,,\; N = \Sigma f_i \qquad (i = 1, 2, 3...n)$$

$\bar{x}$ is mean, f_i is frequency, N is total number of observations.

(*b*) *Short cut method*

If data contain big figures we may use *short cut method*

$$\bar{x} = A + \frac{\Sigma f_i d_i}{\Sigma f_i}$$

where A is assumed mean (generally mid term in x_i) and $d = x_i - A, f_i$ is respective frequency.

(*c*) In *weighted arithmetic mean* relative importance of the different items are different. The weighted arithmetic mean is calculated as

$$\bar{x}_w = \sum_{i=1}^{n} \frac{w_i\, x_i}{\sum_{i=1}^{n} w_i}$$

where $\bar{x}_w$ represents the weighted arithmetic mean x_i represent the variable values and w_i represents the weights attached to variable values.

(ii) Arithmetic mean of continuous series: We find the midpoint of class mark or mid point (x_i) and than can use any of the following method.

(a) Direct method

$$\overline{x} = \sum_{i=1}^{n} f_i x_i$$

(b) Short cut method

$$\overline{x} = A + \frac{\Sigma f_i d_i}{\Sigma f_i}$$

where $d_i = x_i - A$, where, A being assumed mean.

(c) Step deviation method

$$\overline{x} = A + \frac{\Sigma f_i d_i'}{\Sigma f_i} \times i$$

where, A is assumed mean,

$$d_i = \frac{x_i - A}{i}$$

where i is the class size.

(d) The *weighted arithmetic mean* is calculated as

$$\overline{x}_w = \sum_{i=1}^{n} \frac{w_i x_i}{\sum_{i=1}^{n} w_i}$$

where $\overline{x}_w$ represents the weighted arithmetic mean x_i represent the variable values and w_i represents the weights attached to variable values.

(e) Combined Arithmetic Mean

$$\overline{x}_{12} = \frac{n_1\overline{x}_1 + n_2\overline{x}_2}{n_1 + n_2}$$

where,

$\overline{x}_{12}$ = combined mean of two groups,

$\overline{x}_1$ = Arithmetic Mean of first group

$\overline{x}_2$ = Arithmetic Mean of second group

n_1 and n_2 are number of items in first and second group respectively.

B. Geometric Mean

(i) Geometric mean of a set of n observations is the nth root of their product.

Geometric mean $(G) = (x_1, x_2, x_3 \; .... \; x_n)^{1/n}$

If the data contains only two values, the square root of the product of the two values is the geometric mean (*i.e.* $G = \sqrt{x_1 x_2}$). For three values, the cube-root is used, and so on.

Note: Geometric mean does not accept negative or zero values, e.g. all values must be positive.

When the number of items is three or more logarithms are used for simpler calculation.

(ii) For *individual data*

$$\log G = \frac{\Sigma \log X}{N} \quad \text{or} \quad G = \text{Anti log}\left(\frac{1}{n}\sum_{i=1}^{n} \log x_i\right).$$

(*iii*) *For discrete series*

$$= \left(\frac{\Sigma f \log X}{N}\right) = \left(\frac{\Sigma f \log X}{N}\right)$$

(*iv*) *For continuous series*

$$G = \text{Anti log}\left(\frac{\Sigma f \log m}{N}\right)$$

where, m is the mid point value

(*v*) *Weighted G.M: Like A.M. is also calculated as*

$$G_w = \sqrt[n]{x_1 w_1 \times x_2 w_2 \times \ldots . x_n w_n}$$

C. Harmonic Mean (H.M.)

(*i*) Harmonic mean of a number of observations, none of which is zero, is the reciprocal of the arithmetic mean of the reciprocals of given values.

For individual data

$$H.M = \frac{1}{\frac{1}{n}\sum_{n=1}\left(\frac{1}{x_i}\right)} \quad \frac{n}{\frac{1}{x_i}+\frac{1}{x_2}+\ldots .+\frac{1}{x_n}}$$

Used to calculate rate like average speed, velocity, displacement and rate.

Note: The harmonic mean does not take rates with negative or zero value.

D. Relationship Between Three Means

AM ≥ GM ≥ HM.

Note: We have reviewed three different ways of calculating the average or mean of a variable or dataset.

The arithmetic mean is the most commonly used mean, although it may not be appropriate in some cases.

Each mean is appropriate for different types of data; for example:

- If values have the same units: Use the arithmetic mean.
- If values have differing units: Use the geometric mean.
- If values are rates: Use the harmonic mean.

The exceptions are if the data contains negative or zero values, then the geometric and harmonic means cannot be used directly.

2. MEDIAN AND QUARTILES

Median

Median of a distribution is the value of the variable which divides it into two equal parts.

Method of Computation

Computation From the Raw Data.

(a) *Median for Raw Data:* When all the observations are arranged in ascending or descending order of magnitude, the middle one is known as the *median*.

If n is the total number of observations, the value of the $\left(\frac{n+1}{2}\right)^{th}$ item will be called *median* $\left(\frac{n+1}{2}\right)$, which stands for the serial order of the median is known as *median number*.

(b) *Median for grouped data*: We first prepare the cumulative frequency table. Let the total number of observations be N. We determine the median class *i.e.*, the class in which $(N/2)^{th}$ observation lies, then we use the formula

$$\text{Median} = l+\left(\frac{N-c.f}{f}\right)\times i$$

where,

l = is the lower limit of the median class,

N = is the total frequency,

i = is the range (upper limit – lower limit) of the median class; or class interval.

$c.f$ = is the cumulative frequency of the class just before the median class and f_1 is the frequency of the median class.

Quartiles

(i) Sample Quartiles. When individual observations are ordered then

1. *First quartile,* $Q_1 = 25\ th$ percentile

$$Q_1 = \frac{(n+1)}{4} th \text{ item, when } n \text{ is odd}$$

$$= \frac{\frac{n}{4} th \text{ item} + \left(\frac{n}{4}+1\right) th \text{ item}}{2}, \quad \text{when } n \text{ is even}$$

2. *Second quartile or median* $Q_2 = 50\ th$ percentile

$$Q_2 = \left(\frac{n+1}{2}\right) th \text{ item, when } n \text{ is odd}$$

$$= \frac{\left[\frac{n}{2} th \text{ item} + \left(\frac{n}{2}+1\right) th \text{ item}\right]}{2}, \quad \text{when } n \text{ is even.}$$

3. *Third quartile* $Q_3 = 75\ th$ percentile

$$= \frac{3(n+1)}{4} th \text{ item, when } n \text{ is odd}$$

$$= \frac{3n}{4} th \text{ item} + 3\left(\frac{n}{4}+1\right) th \text{ item, when } n \text{ is even}$$

4. *Interquartile range* : The amount of variation in the middle half of the data is described by the *Interquartile range* = *third quartile* (Q_3) – first quartile (Q_1).

3. MODE

(i) Mode for Raw Data: It is the value which occurs most frequently in a set of observations and around which the other items of the set cluster densely. In other words, mode is the value of the variable which is predominant in the series.

(ii) Mode for Grouped Data

$$\text{Mode} = l + \frac{f_2}{f_1 + f_2} \times i$$

where,

l = Lower limit of class preceding modal class

f_1 = Frequency class succeeding modal class

f_2 = Frequency of the next higher class

i = width of the class interval

4. RELATION BETWEEN MEAN, MEDIAN AND MODE

A distribution in which values of mean, median and mode coincide (*i.e.*, mean = median = mode) is known as *symmetrical* and when do not coincide then they are called *asymmetrical distribution*.

The relationship between mean, median and mode for two type of distribution are as follows:

Symmetric Distribution

Mean = Median = Mode

Asymmetric Distribution

Karl Pearson has expressed relationship are as follows

Mean – Mode = 3 (Mean – Median)

or Mode = 3 Median – 2 Mean

and Median = Mode + 2/3 (Mean – Mode)

II. MEASURES OF DISPERSION

"*The degree to which numerical data tend to spread about an average value is called the dispersion*".

– ***Spiegel***

A. Absolute Measures of Dispersion

1. Range: It is difference between two extreme observations of a distribution.

- Largest item – Smallest item = Range.
- It is simplest measure of dispersion.
- Coefficient of range (% of range and sum of maximum and minimum) = $\frac{L_{max} - S_{min}}{L_{max} \times S_{min}} \times 100$

2. QUARTILE DEVIATION (Q.D.)

- **First Quartile Deviation (Q_1)**: It is that value of the variate below which one-fourth of the values lie and above which the remaining three-fourth of the values lie when the values are arranged in ascending order of magnitude.
- **Third Quartile Deviation (Q_3)**: It is that value of the variate below which three-fourth of the values lie and above which the remaining one-fourth of the values lie when the values are arranged in ascending order of magnitude.
- First and third quartiles are also called as *lower* and *upper quartiles* respectively.

Quartile range = $Q_3 - Q_1$

Quartile Deviation is given by the formula.

$$\text{Q.D.} = \frac{Q_3 - Q_1}{2}$$

3. MEAN DEVIATION

(a) Mean Deviation for Mean

$$M.D. = \frac{1}{\Sigma f_i} \cdot f_i \,|\, D_i \,| = \frac{1}{N} f_i \,|\, x_i - \overline{x} \,|$$

where,

D_i = Deviation from the mean = $x_i - \overline{x}$

$|D_i|$ = Absolute deviation

N = Number of observations.

f_i = frequency.

(b) Mean deviation from median: In this case we take deviation from median then it is called mean deviation from median.

$$\text{M.D. (median)} = \frac{1}{N} f_i \,|\, D_i \,| \quad \text{where, } D_i = x_i - M$$

M. D. is least when deviations are taken from the Median.

4. STANDARD DEVIATION (S.D.)

The concept of Standard Deviation was introduced by Karl Pearson in 1893. It is by far the most important and widely used measure of dispersion.

- It is defined as the square root of the mean or the squares of the deviations taken from Arithmetic mean.
- Denoted by σ (for population) and S (for sample)

(a) S.D. For Ungrouped data

It is defined by the following formula

$$\text{S.D.} = \sqrt{\frac{\Sigma(x - \overline{x})^2}{N}}$$

where, x = An observation or variate value, $\overline{x}$ = Arithmetic mean of the population

N = Number of given observations.

(b) S.D. For frequency distribution (Discrete series)

$$\text{S.D. }(\sigma) = \sqrt{\frac{\sum_{i=1}^{n} f_i x_i^2}{N}}, \quad \text{where } x_i = X_i - \bar{x}$$

Alternatively,

$$\text{S.D. }(\sigma) = \sqrt{\frac{\sum d_i^2}{N} - \left(\frac{\sum d_i}{N}\right)^2}$$

where $d_i = x_i - A$ (A is assumed mean)

(c) S.D. For continuous series

$$\text{S.D. }(\sigma) = i\sqrt{\frac{\sum f_i d_i^2}{N} - \left(\frac{\sum f_i d_i}{N}\right)^2}$$

where $d_i = \frac{x_i - A}{i}$, x_i is midpoint and A is assumed mean.

For sampling distribution we find sample standard deviation

(d) Sample Standard Deviation

(i) For ungrouped data $\quad s = i\sqrt{\frac{\sum (x - \bar{x})^2}{N - 1}}$

For practical purposes, the formula can be written as

$$s = \sqrt{\frac{\sum x_i^2 - \frac{\left(\sum x_i\right)^2}{N}}{N - 1}}$$

(ii) For grouped data $\quad s = \sqrt{\frac{\sum f_i x_i^2 - \left(\sum f_i x_i\right)^2}{N - 1}}$

Alternatively, $\quad s = i\sqrt{\left[\frac{\sum f_i x_i^2 - \frac{\left(\sum f_i d_i\right)^2}{N}}{N - 1}\right]}$

- Sample standard deviation (s) are used to estimate population standard deviation.
- It gives minimum value when the deviations are taken from the mean.
- Range is 0 to ∞

(e) Combined Standard Deviation

$$\sigma_{12} = \sqrt{\frac{N_1\sigma_1^2 + N_2\sigma_2^2 + N_1 d_1^2 + N_2 d_2^2}{N_1 + N_2}}$$

where,

σ_{12} = Combined standard deviation

σ_1 = Standard deviation of first group

σ_2= Standard deviation of second group

$$d_1 = |\bar{x}_1 - \bar{x}_{12}|\ ,\ d_2 = |\bar{x}_2 - \bar{x}_{12}|$$

(f) Standard deviation of first n natural numbers

$$\sigma = \sqrt{\frac{1}{12}(n^2 - 1)}$$

(g) Relation Between Measure of Dispersion

- Quartile Deviation = $\frac{2}{3}\sigma = 0.67$ SD
- Mean Deviation = $\frac{4}{5}\sigma = 0.8$ SD

5. VARIANCE

Term given by R.A. Fisher and concept by Galton.

Variance: It represents the dispersion of data about the mean: It is actually the minimum value of mean square deviation

$$s^2 = \frac{1}{n}\sum(x_i - \bar{x})^2 = \frac{\sum f_i(x_i - \bar{x})^2}{N} \quad \text{(In case of frequency distribution)}$$

$$\text{Variance} = \sigma^2 = \left\{\frac{\Sigma f u_i^2}{n} - \left(\frac{\Sigma f_1 u_i}{n}\right)^2\right\} \times i^2$$

where, $u_i = \frac{\bar{x} - A}{i}$ and i = class size, A is assumed mean

The smaller the value of σ the lesser the variability or greater the conformity in the population.

Variance and standard deviation compared

Both the variance and standard deviation are measures of variability in a population. These measures are closely related as variance = (standard deviation)^2. Variance is the averaged squared deviations from the arithmetic mean and standard deviation is square root of variance. Analysis of variance is (ANOVA) is important tool in statistics. Standard deviation is used in test of hypothesis/ sampling etc.

Correcting incorrect values of mean standard deviation

We have already discussed, how to find correct mean when some data is wrong.

Correct ΣX^2 = Incorrect ΣX^2 – Square of wrong data + Square of correct data

Correct standard deviation

$$\sigma = \sqrt{\frac{\Sigma X^2}{N} - (\bar{X})^2} \quad \text{when } \bar{X} \text{ is correct mean.}$$

B. Relative Measure of Dispersion

(*i*) ***Coefficient of Q.D.*** $= \dfrac{Q_3 - Q_1}{Q_3 + Q_1}$

(*ii*) ***Coefficient of M.D .*** $= \dfrac{\text{Mean Deviation}}{\text{Median or Mean or Mode}}$

(*iii*) ***Coefficient of variation***: (*Coefficient of variability*) It is a dimensionless parameter. It is generally used to compare the variability of two series which differ widely in their averages or which are measured in different units. The coefficient of variation is equal to the ratio of standard deviation and the mean

$$C.V = \frac{\sigma}{\bar{x}} \times 100$$

III. MEASURE OF SYMMETRY

1. SKEWNESS (β_1)

It measures how the data is scattered about mean. If the data is exactly symmetrically displaced about the mean, the measure of asymmetry should be zero.

For symmetrical distribution.

Mean = Mode = Median and the curve is bell shaped. (Fig. 1).

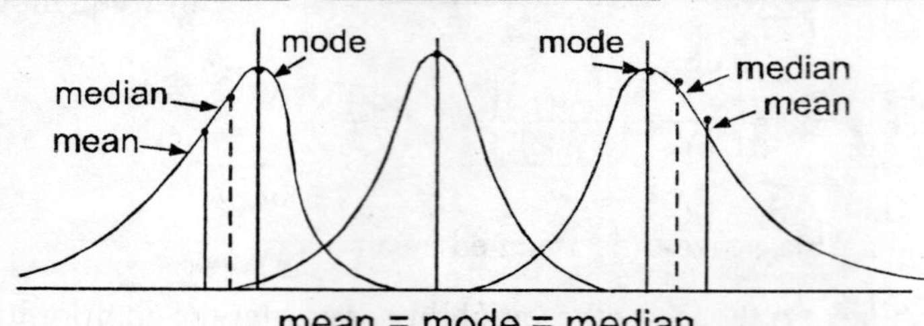

Fig. 1. Symmetrical and skewed distribution

For asymmetrical distribution.

If the data to the right of the mean are more spread out from the mean then those on the left then, by convention, the asymmetry is positive and the distribution is said to be *positively skewed* but if data to the left of mean are more spread out from mean than those on the right then, asymmetry is negative and distribution is said to be *negatively skewed.*

Symmetrical (Skewness is zero)	*Asymmetrical/Skewed*	
	Positively Asymmetrical	*Negatively Asymmetrical*
Mean = Median = Mode	Mean > Median > Mode	Mean < Median < Mode
Bell Shaped curve	The curve bending towards left from the mean and having long tail towards right.	The curve bending towards right from the mean and having a long tail on left.

1. Absolute Measure of Skewness

Absolute $S_{kp} = \bar{x}$ – Mode

If value of mean is greater than mode, skewness will be positive and if the value of mode is greater than mean it is negative sign and we say that distribution is negatively skewed.

2. Relative measures of skewness:

(*i*) *Karl Pearson's coefficient of skewness:*

$$Sk_p = \frac{\text{Mean} - \text{Mode}}{\text{Standard Deviation}}$$

This formula cannot be used where mode is ill defined. However in moderately skewed distribution

$$Sk_p = \frac{\bar{X} - \left[3Med - 2\bar{X}\right]}{\sigma} = \frac{\bar{X} - 3Med + 2\bar{X}}{\sigma} = \frac{3\left(\bar{X} - Med\right)}{\sigma}$$

(*ii*) *Bowley's Coefficient of Skewness*

$$Sk_B = \frac{(Q_3 - Med) - (Med - Q_1)}{(Q - Med) + (Ned - Q)} \quad \text{or} \quad \frac{Q_3 + Q - 2med}{Q_3 - Q_3}$$

(*iii*) *Kelly's coefficient of skewness*

$$S_{kk} = \frac{P_{10} - P_{90} - 2Med}{P_{90} - P_{10}}$$

Also $$S_{kk} = \frac{D_1 + D_9 - Med}{D_9 - D_1}$$

where, *P* and *D* stand for percentile (division into 100 groups) and Decile (division into 10 equal subsections.)

3. Difference between dispersion and skewness : Dispersion is concerned with the *amount of variation* rather than with its direction. Skewness tells about the direction of the variation or departure from symmetry. In fact, the measures of skewness are dependent upon the amount of dispersion.

3. KURTOSIS (β_2)

The Kurtosis in Greek word means '*bulginess*'. In statistics kurtosis refers to the degree of flatness or peakedness in the region about the mode of frequency curve. The degree of kurtosis of a distribution is measured relative to the peakedness of normal curve. In other words, measures of kurtosis tell us the extent to which a distribution is more peaked or flat-topped than the normal curve. If a curve is more peaked than normal curve, it is called '*leptokurtic*'. In such a case the items are more closely related to bunched around the mode. On the other hand, if a curve is more flat topped than normal curve, it is called '*platykurtic*'. The normal curve itself is known as *mesokurtic* and in this case mean = mode = median. The condition of peakedness or flat-toppedness

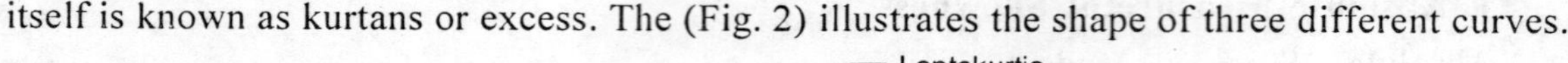
itself is known as kurtans or excess. The (Fig. 2) illustrates the shape of three different curves.

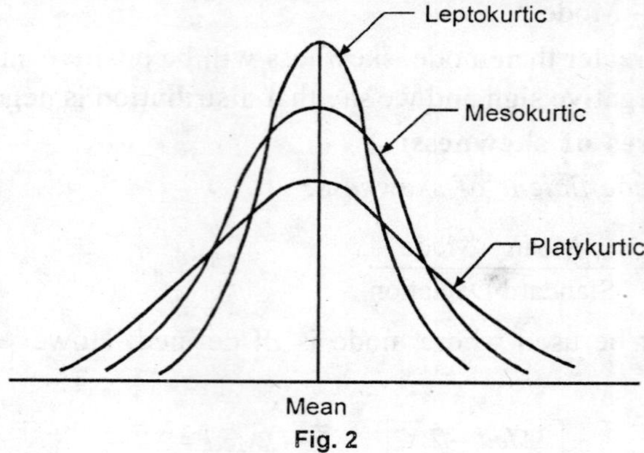

Fig. 2

For leptokurtic curve $\beta_2 > 3$

For platykurtic curve $\beta_2 < 3$ and for mesocurtic (normal curve)

$$\beta_2 = 3.$$

For a moderately skewed distributions. The averages has the following relationship.

$$\text{Mode} = 3\ \text{Median} - 2\ \text{Mean}$$

- Kurtosis is simply a measure of how pointy or flat the peak of your distribution curve is.

Platykurtic	*Mesokurtic*	*Leptokurtic*
The peak or vertex of the curve is flatter.	The peak of the curve is normal	The peak of the curve is narrow
The tails on both sides are long compared to normal curve	The tails on both sides are also normal	the tails on both sides are short compared to normal curve.
$\beta_2<3$	$\beta_2=3$	$\beta_2>3$
Tortoise shaped	Bell shaped	Kangaroo shaped.

IV. CORRELATION

In a bivariate distribution we may be interested to find out if any change in one variable affects a change in other variable? If one variable change with change in other variable then the two variables are said to be *correlated.*

"*Correlation is an analysis of variation between two or more variable*" —***A. M. Tuttle***

1. Types of Correlation

(*i*) Based on direction

a) **Positive Correlation:** Variables are varying in same direction ↑↑ or ↓↓

b) **Negative Correlation:** Variables are varying in opposite direction ↑↓ or ↓↑

***(ii)* Based on number of variables**

a) **Simple Correlation-** only 2 variables are studied

b) **Partial Correlation-** More than two variables are studied but consider only 2 to be influencing each other, the effect of other influencing variable being kept constant.

c) **Multiple Correlation–** 3 or more are studied simultaneously.

***(iii)* Based on consistency of ratio of change between variables**

a) **Linear–** If the amount of change in one variable tends to bear a **constant ratio** to the amount of change in the other variable

b) **Non-linear / curvilinear–** If the amount of change in variable doesn't bear a constant ratio to the amount of change in other variable.

In the most of the practical situations we find a nonlinear relationship between variables.

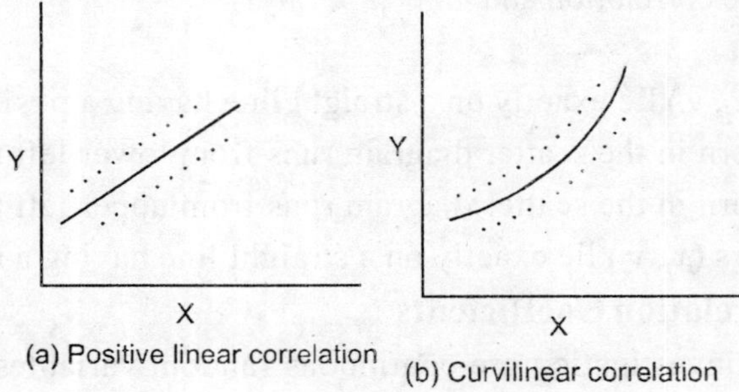

(a) Positive linear correlation (b) Curvilinear correlation

Fig. 3

2. Karl Pearson's coefficient of correlation

As a measure of intensity or degree of correlationship between two variables, Karl Pearson a British Biometrician, developed a formula called correlation coefficient.

Correlation coefficient between two random variable *X* and *Y*, usually denoted by *r* is a numerical measure of linear relationship between them and is defined as

$$r = \frac{Cov.(x, y)}{\sigma_x, \sigma_y}$$

where, *Cov*, (*x*, *y*) is the covariance of *x* and *y* and σ_x and σ_y variable are standard deviation of *x* and *y* respectively

If (x_i, y_i), $i = 1, 2, \ldots.. n$ is the bivariable distribution, then *Cov* (*x*, *y*)

$$= \frac{1}{n}\Sigma(x_i - \bar{x})(y_i - \bar{y}) = \frac{1}{n}\Sigma x_i y_i - \Sigma\bar{x}\ \Sigma\bar{y}$$

$$\sigma_x = \sqrt{\frac{1}{n}\Sigma(x_i - \bar{x}_i)^2} = \sqrt{\frac{1}{n}\Sigma x_i^2 - (\bar{x})^2}$$

and $$\sigma_y = \sqrt{\frac{1}{n}\Sigma(y_i - \bar{y})^2} = \sqrt{\frac{1}{n}\Sigma y_i^2 - \bar{y}^2}$$

The correlation coefficient

$$r = \frac{\Sigma xy}{n\sigma_x \cdot \sigma_y} = \frac{\Sigma xy}{\sqrt{\Sigma x^2 \Sigma y^2}}$$

where, σ_x and σ_y are standard deviation and n is the number of pairs of observations.

$$x = x_i - \bar{x} \text{ and } y = (y_i - \bar{y})$$

The correlation coefficient is independent of change of origin and scale.

The value of correlation coefficient obtained from above formula lies between ± 1. Conclusions from values of r are as follows.

(*i*) when $r = +1$, perfect positive correlation.

(*ii*) when $r = -1$, perfect negative correlation.

(*iii*) $0 < r < 1$, Direct or positive correlation

(*iv*) $-1 < r < 0$, negative correlation and

(*v*) $r = 0$, no correlation

If $r = +1$, all pairs (x_i, y_i) lie exactly on a straight line having a positive slope.

If $r > 0$ then the pattern in the scatter diagram runs from lower left to upper right.

If $r < 0$ then the pattern in the scatter diagram runs from upper left to lower right.

If $r = -1$ then the pairs (x_i, y_i) lie exactly on a straight line having a negative slope.

3. Assumptions of Correlation Coefficients

i) The variables under investigation are continuous random variables and they are normally distributed

ii) The association between variables is linear.

iii) Each pair of observations are independent.

- Coefficient of determination = r^2
- Coefficient of non-determination = $1 - r^2$
- Coefficient of alienation = $\sqrt{1 - r^2}$

4. Rank Correlation

Spearman's rank correlation coefficient is defined as

$$R = 1 - \frac{6\sum D^2}{n^3 - n}$$

where, R denotes rank coefficient of correlation and D refers to difference of ranks between paired item in two series.

In case ranks are repeated

$$R = 1 \frac{6\left(\sum D^2 + \frac{1}{12}(m^3 - m) + \frac{1}{2}m^3 - m + ...\right)}{n^3 - n}$$

where, m stands for the number of items with common rank, this value is added as many times the number of such groups.

V. REGRESSION

'The term regression analysis refers to the method by which estimates are made of the values of a variable from a knowledge of the values of one or more other variables and to the measurement of the errors involved in this estimation process" — ***Morris Hamberg***

A. LINEAR REGRESSION

If the variable in a bivariate distribution are related, we will find that the points in scatter diagram will cluster round some curve called the "*curve of regression*". If the curve is a straight line, it is called the *line of regression* and therefore, is said to be *linear regression.*

The linear regression equation in this case,

$$y_i = a + bx_i + \in_i, \quad i = 1, 2, ... ,n$$

where $\in_i$, a random variable, y_i is the ith value of dependent or regressed variable. The regression line crosses the y-axis at point 'a' and has a slope 'b'.

1. The Line of Regression

Let us suppose that in a bivariate distribution (x_i, y_i), $i = 1, 2, 3, ...n$ where, y is dependent variable and x is independent variable. Let the line of best fit (or regression line) be

$$y = a + bx \qquad (i)$$

The above equation represents a family of straight lines for different values of arbitrary constants 'a' and 'b'.

The problem is to determine 'a' and 'b' so that line is *line of best fit.*

The working procedure for line of *best fit* from given paired observations are as follows:

Step I: From normal equations

$$(i) \quad \sum_{i=1}^{n} y_i = na + b\sum_{i=1}^{n} x_i \qquad (ii) \quad \sum_{i=1}^{n} x_i y_i = a\sum_{i=1}^{n} x_i + b\sum_{i=1}^{n} x_i^2$$

Step II: Solve the above two equations for a and b.

Step III: Substitute for a and b in the line $y = a + bx$ which will be required line of best fit.

Two types of regression lines.

The regression line y on x is given by

$$y - \overline{y} = b_{yx}(x - \overline{x})$$

where, b_{yx} is slope of the line of y on x and known as regression coefficient of y on x and is given by

$$b_{yx} = r\,\frac{\sigma_y}{\sigma_x}$$

where, σ_y and σ_x are standard deviations

Thus *regression line of y on x, is given by*

$$y - \overline{y} = r\frac{\sigma_y}{\sigma_x}(x - \overline{x})$$

Similarly the regression line of x on y is given by

$$x-\bar{x}b_{xy}=r\frac{\sigma_x}{\sigma_y}(y-\bar{y})$$

where, b_{xy} is the slope of line x on y and known as regression coefficient of x on y,
It is given by

$$b_{xy}=r\frac{\sigma_x}{\sigma_{xy}}$$

∴ Thus equation of line of regression of x on y is given by

$$x-\bar{x}=r\frac{\sigma_x}{\sigma_y}(x-\bar{y})$$

The two regression line passes through $(\bar{x},\bar{y})$, hence intersection of $\bar{x},\bar{y}$

2. Properties of Regression Coefficients

(i) Correlation coefficient is the geometric mean between regression coefficients

Proof: $$b_{xy}\times b_{yx}=r\frac{\sigma_x}{\sigma_y}\times r\frac{\sigma_y}{\sigma_x}=r^2$$

or $$r=\pm\sqrt{b_{xy}\times b_{yx}}$$

Clearly the two regression coefficients must have same sign and sign of r is taken same as that of b_{xy} and b_{yx}.

(ii) Both the regression coefficients cannot be greater than unity.

Proof : We have

$$r=\pm\sqrt{b_{xy}\times b_{yx}}\ \text{ but } |r|\le 1$$

$$\therefore\quad |b_{xy}\times b_{yx}|\le|1$$

Thus both b_{yx} and b_{xy} cannot be greater than one.

(iii) Regression coefficients are independent of the change of origin but not the scale.

(iv) Angle between two regression lines

$$\tan\theta=\left|\frac{b_{yx}-b_{xy}}{1+b_{yx}\cdot b_{xy}}\right|\left|\frac{r\cdot\frac{\sigma_y}{\sigma_x}-\frac{\sigma_y}{r\sigma_y}}{1+\frac{r\sigma_y}{\sigma_x}\frac{1\sigma_y}{r\sigma_x}}\right|=\left|\frac{r^2-1}{r}\right|\left(\frac{\sigma_x\sigma_y}{\sigma_x^2+\sigma_y^2}\right)=\frac{1-r^2}{|r|}\left(\frac{\sigma_x\sigma_y}{\sigma_x^2+\sigma_y^2}\right)(\because r^2\le 1)$$

$$\therefore\quad \theta=\tan^{-1}\left\{\frac{1-r^2}{|r|}\left(\frac{\sigma_x\sigma_y}{\sigma_x^2+\sigma_y^2}\right)\right\}$$

Special cases

(*i*) If $r = 0$, $\tan\theta = \infty \Rightarrow \theta = \frac{\pi}{2}$, thus if the two variables are uncorrelated, the lines of regression become perpendicular to each other.

(*ii*) If $r = +1$, $\theta = 0$ or π. In this case two lines of regression either coincide or they are parallel to each other. But since both lines passes through $(\bar{x}, \bar{y})$ then can not be parallel. Hence in case of perfect correlation (positive or negative) the two lines of regression coincide. The above discussed properties are illustrated in Fig. 4.

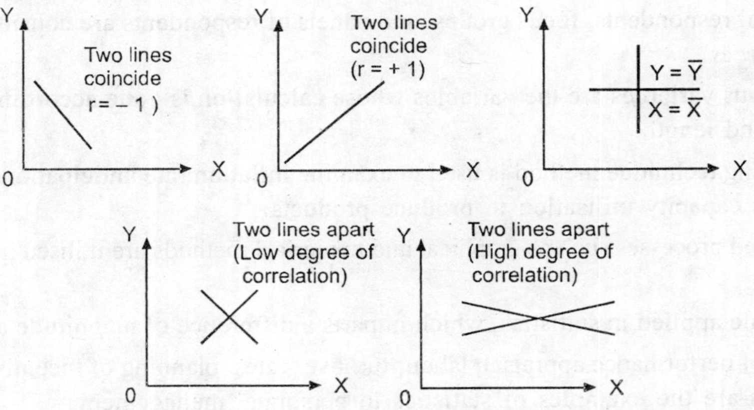

Fig. 4. Properties of regression lines

4. Standard Error of Estimate:

With the help of regression equations perfect prediction is practically impossible. So it is needed a measure which indicate how precise is the prediction of Y is, based on X or, conversely, how inaccurate the prediction may be. The measure is called ***standard error of estimate*** and calculated as.

$$S_{yx} = \sqrt{\frac{\Sigma(Y - Y_c)^2}{N}} \quad i.e., \quad \sqrt{\frac{\text{Unexpected variation}}{N}}$$

also $S_{yx} = \sigma_y \sqrt{1 - r^2}$

where, S_{yx} = the standard of regression of values from Y_c.

The more convenient formula is

$$S_{yx} = \sqrt{\frac{\Sigma X^2 - a\Sigma Y - b\Sigma XY}{N}}$$

Similarly, the standard error of regression of X value from X_c.

$$S_{xy} = \sqrt{\frac{\Sigma(X - X_c)^2}{N}} \quad \text{or} \quad S_{xy} = \sigma_x \sqrt{1 - x^2}$$

Also $$S_{xy} = \sqrt{\frac{\Sigma X^2 - a\Sigma X - b\Sigma XY}{N}}$$

B. IMPORTANT ONE LINERS

1. Sample statistic values are used as a summary measure for a sample, such as a sample mean.
2. Descriptive statistics and inferential statistics are the branch of statistics.
3. The control charts and procedures of descriptive statistics which are used to enhance a procedure can be classified into *Statistical tools categories.*
4. Roman letters can also be represented as sample statistics.
5. Individual respondents, focus groups, and panels of respondents are considered as *primary data sources*
6. Continuous variables are the variables whose calculation is done according to the weight, height, and length.
7. Forecasting technique method is used to examine inflation rate anticipation, unemployment rate, and capacity utilisation to produce products.
8. Specialised processes such as graphical and numerical methods are utilised in the Descriptive statistics.
9. Ratio scale applied in statistics, which imparts a difference of magnitude and proportions.
10. Review of performance appraisal, labour turnover rates, planning of incentives, and training programs are the examples of statistics in personnel management.
11. In five One-Day Internationals, a batsman has scored 31, 97, 112, 63, and 12 runs. the standard deviation is- **37.89**
12. The mode of the decision received seven days in a row: 11,13,13,17,19,23,25 will be 13.
13. Median of the following 7 days: 11, 13, 17, 13, 23, 25, 19 is 17.
14. Calculate the average of four coins tosses is 2.
15. Variance of a relentless 'x' is 0.
16. $E(X) = \lambda$ is employed that distribution is Poisson's distribution.
17. Two unbiased coins are tossed the probability of having access to most one head is 3/4.
18. A and B are two independent event specified $P(A) = 0.4$ and $P(A \cap B) = 0.2$. Then $P(B)$ is 0.5
19. The mean mode and median of the messages received on 7 consecutive days 7,13,5,9,6,5,10 are 8,5,7 respectively.
20. The mean deviation from the mean per the Mean of the given data sets 7, 47, 8, 42, 47, 95, 42, 96, 3 is 25.1.
21. The mean deviation from median of the given data sets 7, 47, 8, 42, 47, 95, 42, 96, 3 is 25.
22. The variance of the given data sets 7, 47, 8, 42, 47, 95, 42, 96, 3 is 1029.78.

23. The quality deviation of the given data sets 7, 47, 8, 42, 47, 95, 42, 96, 3 is 32.78.
24. For the Poison's distribution is used random variable on a regular basis is discrete Random Variable (DRV).
25. The arithmetic mean of the following set of numbers: 9, 11, 10, 10, 5. 15, and 10, is 10.
26. Variance $V(X) = k(X^2) - (k(X))^2$
27. The mean value of the Hyper geometric distribution is $E(X) = n^2k / N$
28. Output of the range of the data sets 61, 22, 34, 17, 81, 99, 42, 94 is 82.
29. A parameter is a measure which is computed from Population data.
30. Questionnaire survey method is used to collect Primary data.
31. The number of accidents in a city during 2010 is Discrete variable
32. The mean of a distribution is 23, the median is 24, and the mode is 25.5. It is most likely that this distribution is: Negatively Skewed.
33. A constant variable can take values is Fixed.
34. A variable that assumes any value within a range is called *Continuous variable.*
35. According to the empirical rule, approximately what percent of the data should lay within $\mu \pm 2\sigma$ is 95%.
36. Census reports used as a source of data is *Secondary source.*
37. A specific characteristic of a population is called *Parameter.*
38. The grouped data is also is not same as *secondary data.*
39. A chance variation in an observational process is *Random error.*
40. The listing of the data in order of numerical magnitude is called *Arrayed data.*
41. Primary data and ungrouped data are not same.
42. The mean of a distribution is 14 and the standard deviation is 5, the value of the coefficient of variation will be 35.7%.
43. Sum of dots when two dice are rolled is a discrete variable.
44. Given $X_1 = 12$, $X_2 = 19$, $X_3 = 10$, $X_4 = 7$, then $\sum_{i=1}^{4} X_i$ equals 48.
45. Data collected by NADRA (National Database and Registration Authority) to issue computerized identity cards (CICs) are Primary data.
46. The first hand and unorganized form of data is called Primary data.
47. If a distribution is abnormally tall and peaked, then is can be said that the distribution is: Leptokurtic.
48. The data which have already been collected by someone are called Secondary data.
49. You asked five of your classmates about their height. On the basis of this information, you stated that the average height of all students in your university or college is 67 inches. This is an example of: Inferential Statistics.

50. In statistics, a sample means a portion of the population.
51. In inferential statistics, we study the methods to make decisions about the population based on sample results.
52. Statistic is a numerical quantity, which is calculated from: Sample.
53. Mode is not based on all the observations.
54. The data which have not undergone any statistical treatments are called primary data.
55. The mean is affected by the change of both origin and scale.
56. In statistics, a population consists of: all subjects or objects whose characteristics are being studied.
57. Standard Deviations do not divide a set of observations into equal parts.
58. Descriptive Statistics deals with the techniques that are used to organize, summarize, and present the data.
59. If there is no gap between the consecutive classes, the limits are called Class boundaries.
60. Data in the Population Census Report is: Secondary data.
61. In descriptive statistics, we study the methods for organizing, displaying and describing data
62. If any value in a series is zero then we cannot compute the Geometric mean.
63. If all the items in a variable are non-zero and non-negative then AM>GM>HM.
64. When data are collected in a statistical study for only a portion or subset of all elements of interest we are using: a sample.
65. In statistics, conducting a survey means collecting information from elements.
66. Which one is the not measure of dispersion 50th Percentile.
67. The algebraic sum of deviations from mean is: Minimum.
68. The height of a student is 60 inches. This is not an example of qualitative data.
69. If $Y = -8X - 5$ and SD of X is 3, then SD of Y is 24.
70. The lowest value of variance can be 0.
71. If a and b are two constants, then $Var(a + bX)$ is $b^2Var(X)$.
72. The variance of 5 numbers is 10. If each number is divided by 2, then the variance of new numbers is 2.5.
73. The measure of Dispersion can never be Negative.
74. The standard deviation is always greater than the mean deviation.
75. If the standard deviation of the values 2, 4, 6, 8 is 2.24, then the standard deviation of the values 4, 6, 8, 10 is also 2.24.
76. If all values are same then the measure of dispersion will be 0.
77. The sum of squares of deviation is least if measure from Mean.
78. Standard deviation is never calculated from the Harmonic Mean (HM).
79. Mean Deviation, Variance and Standard Deviation of the values 4, 4, 4, 4, 4, 4 is 0.

80. Variance is always calculated from Mean.
81. The measure of dispersion is changed by a change of scale.
82. For the symmetrical distribution, approximately 68% of the cases are included between $\bar{X} - S$ and $\bar{X} + S$.
83. Coefficient of variation is a relative measure of dispersion.
84. The sum of squared deviations of a set of n values from their mean is least.
85. The mean deviation of the values, 18, 12, 15 is 2.
86. Variance remains unchanged by the change of Origin.
87. The range of the values – 5, – 8, –10, 0, 6, 10 is 20.
88. Var $(2X + 3)$ is 4 Var(X).
89. A measure of dispersion is always positive.
90. If X and Y are independent then $SD\ (X - Y)$ is $SD(X) + SD(Y)$.
91. Suppose for 40 observations, the variance is 50. If all the observations are increased by 20, the variance of these increased observations will be 50.
92. The percentage of values lies between $X - \pm 2SD$ is 95.45%.
93. The variance of a constant is Zero.
94. The measure of central tendency to be used to study average rate of change in population is Geometric Mean.
95. To find the average size of shoes sold in .the market we should use Mode.
96. To find the average speed .of a vehicle when the same distance is covered with different speeds, the suitable measure is Harmonic mean.
97. To find the average of quantity prices, the measure of central tendency to be used is Harmonic mean.
98. To find the average height of plants we should use Arithmetic mean.
99. The first step of summarizing the data is Classification.
100. We study measure of central tendency to represent the whole data by only single value.
101. The suitable measure to find average speed when time for each speed is fixed would be Arithmetic mean.
102. In industries for quality control, the most important measure of dispersion is Range.
103. The formula for Geometric mean for n values $X_1, X_2 \ldots . X_n$ is $(X_1, X_2 \ldots\ldots X_n)^{1/n}$.
104. If all the variate values are negative the standard deviation will be Positive.
105. A quantitative or qualitative characteristic that varies from observation to observation in the same group is called *variable*.
106. The standard deviation for the values 4, 5, 6, 7, 8 will be $(2)^{1/2}$.
107. The degree of freedom for error in R.B. design with 10 treatments and 4 replication will be 27.

108. Under the assumption for analysis of variance, the parent population should be Normal.
109. For any two values *a* & *b* the relationship among Arithmetic mean (*A*), Geometric mean (*G*) and Harmonic mean (*H*) is - $G^2 = A.H.$
110. For testing the significance of correlation coefficient we use 't' test.
111. A figure acquired by dividing sum of all factor by total number of factors. - **Averages/ Arithmetic Mean**
112. **AM** is influenced by change in starting point and scale both.
113. Value of Regression Coefficient varies between- **1 to 1**
114. Range of multiple correlation coefficient is- **0 to + 1**
115. In confounding, the precision on the main effects and certain interaction of lower order: - **Increase**
116. Validity of regression coefficient is tested by **- *Z*-test or *t*-test**
117. Rank correlation is tested by **- *t*-test**
118. Which test is applied for the test significant b/w two variance: **-*F*-Test**
119. Relationship between AM, Median and Mode in asymmetrical distribution - **Mode = 3 Median - 2 Mean.**
120. The best measures of central tendency - **Arithmetic Mean (AM)**
121. The ratio of no. of observations to the sum of the reciprocal of the value of the different observations. - **Harmonic Mean**
122. The order of three averages for a given data - **AM > GM > HM**
123. Mean applied when deals with rate, price and speed of a vehicle - **HM**
124. The average of the sum of squares of the deviation about mean - **Variance**
125. The regression coefficient is independent of change of **- origin**
126. Which transformation is most appropriate for percentage: **-Arc sine**
127. For test of significant of difference between two means which test is used: **- Z-test**
128. For χ^2 (chi square test) **N** should be at least: **- 50**
129. The degree of scatterness or variation of the variable about a central tendency. - **Dispersion**
130. The best measure of Dispersion is - **Standard Deviation (SD)**
131. SD ranges from - **0 to ∞**
132. Coefficient of variation calculated by. - **CV = (SD / Mean) × 100**
133. The variation used to compare the variability between two series - **CV**
134. The measures of the direction and degree of asymmetry - **Skewness**
135. Coefficient of skewness for normal distribution is **- 0**
136. An idea about the flatness/peakedness of the curve - **Kurtosis**
137. The term 'Kurtosis' was introduced by- **Karl Pearson (1906)**

138. The curve has $\beta_2 > 3$ or $\gamma_2 > 0$ is - **Leptokurtic curve**
139. The curve has $\beta_2 = 3$ or $\gamma_2 = 0$ is - **Mesokurtic curve**
140. **Regression** is used to measure the average relationship between two or more variables.
141. Regression coefficient is independent of - **Origin**
142. The distribution in which Mean > Variance - **Binomial distribution**
143. The distribution in which Mean = Variance - **Poisson distribution**
144. Probability ranges from - **0 to 1**
145. Students *t*-test is used when Small samples size and SD is **unknown**
146. Students *t*-test was proposed by - **W.S. Gosset**
147. To test the proportions and variance, we use - ***F*-test**
148. To test the goodness of fit or homogeneity, we use - **Chi-square test**
149. Index number was given by - **Pearson**
150. Logical constructions of the experiments in which the degree of uncertainty with which the inference (Result/confusion) or may be well defined. - **Design of Experiments**
151. The objects of comparison, which an experiment has to try in the field for assessing their value. - **Treatment**
152. The 3 basic principles of field experimentation. - **Replication, Randomization and Local control**
153. Repeated application of treatments - **Replication**
154. Allocation of treatments to the different experimental units by a random process - **Randomization**
155. Which principle of experimentation eliminates human biases - **Randomization**
156. Local control helps in reducing the - **Experimental error**
157. The transformation required when data not follow normal distribution - **Data transformation**
158. The most appropriate transformation for percentage - **Angular transformation**
159. Which transformation is applied when mean is a variance - **Square root transformation**
160. The hypothesis under test - **Null hypothesis**
161. The variation due to uncontrolled factors - **Experimental error**
162. **Type 1st error:** Rejected H_0 (null hypothesis) when it is - **true** or accepted H_1 (Alternative hypothesis) when it is - **false**
163. **Type II error:** Accepted H_0 (null hypothesis) when it is - **false** or rejected H_1 (Alternative hypothesis) when it is - **true**
164. The error in which hypothesis is true but our test rejects it - **Type I error**
165. Out of the two types of error in testing, the more severe error is - **Type II error**
166. If the number of rows = number of column = number of treatment, which design is used: - **LSD**

167. **Analysis of Variance (ANOVA):** This is a statistical technique by which source of variation of any attribute is **- estimated.**
168. In order to find out the reliability of the experiment. The **coefficient of variation** is used. It is computed as.

$$CV = \frac{\sqrt{\text{Error MS}}}{\text{Overall mean}} \times 100$$

169. If a simple random sample of size n is drawn without replacement from a finite population of size N with mean μ and variance σ^2 the covariance between any two members of the sample is - $\frac{\sigma^2}{N-1}$
170. The simplest experimental design - **Complete Randomized Design (CRD)**
171. The experimental design which provides maximum degree of freedom for error - **CRD.**
172. The design which is applied when experimental material are limited and homogenous - **CRD**
173. The error degree of freedom in CRD is formulated as - ***N* - *t*.**
174. The most commonly used design - **Randomized Block Design (RBD)**
175. **RBD** is also called as One-way elimination of heterogeneity design/Two-way classification of ANOVA
176. When fertility gradient in one direction, the statistical design to be used - **RBD**
177. The maximum no. of treatments adopted in RBD - **20**
178. In RBD, the number of blocks is equal to - **No. of replications ($b = r$)**
179. The error degree of freedom of RBD is formulated as - **$(t-1)(r-1)$**
180. The design in which fertility gradient is in two-way direction - **Latin Square Design (LSD)**
181. **LSD** is also known as Two-way elimination of heterogeneity design/Three-way classification of ANOVA
182. The optimum number of treatments studied in Latin square design - **5 to 12**
183. The error degree of freedom of LSD is formulated as - **$(t-2)(t-1)$**
184. The design which provides main effects and interactions - **Factorial RBD**
185. The technique of reducing the size of replication over a number of blocks at the cost of losing some information on same effect -**Confounding Design**
186. The difference between sample estimate and its corresponding population parameter is called - **Sampling error**
187. Confounding Design is adopted when the number of treatments is - **10**
188. If an interaction effect is confounded with all the replicates of the treatment - **Complete/ total confounding**
189. The most appropriate design, when all factors are not equally important in experimentation. - **Split Plot Design (SPD)**

190. To study two factors with different level of precision, which design is used - **Split plot design**
191. The factor requires larger units to be applied and may produce larger differences - **Main plot**
192. The COV (XY) of the random variable x and y can be written in terms of expectation as - **COV (X,Y) = E(XY) – E(X) E (Y)**
193. If sub treatments are laid out in strips then the design is called - **Strip Plot Design**
194. Number of error variance applied in Strip Plot Design - **3**
195. In Strip Plot Design, which one is to be tested with higher precision - **Interaction**
196. If X and Y be independently and identically distributed with parameters μ and σ^2 then the mean and variance of X/Y is - **0 and $2\sigma^2$**
197. For testing the homogeneity of several population variance, we use - **Bartlett's test**
198. The value of χ^2 when all frequency of classes are same is - **zero**
199. Joint cumulative distribution $F(x, y)$ takes values with the limits - **0 and λ.**
200. Coefficient of contigency lies between - **0 and 1.**
201. Indian National Statistics Day is celebrated on- **29th June**
202. RA Fisher is known as - **father of statistics**
203. The intelligence, ability or efficiency can be measured by use of - **Mode**
204. One condition for application of χ^2 test is that no cell frequency **should be less than five.**
205. In a Latin Square design the number of rows will be equal to- **No. of columns and number of treatments**
206. CRD can be adopted only when the experimental material is- **homogenous.**
207. In a Latin Square design with 5 treatments the number of experimental units will be equal to - **25**
208. In a factorial experiments factor refers to a set of - **related treatments.**
209. For calculation of χ^2, N should be at least- **50**
210. The error degrees of freedom for an experiment with one factor at 2 levels and another at three levels and 3 replications will be - **10**
211. Indian Agricultural Statistics Research Institute is established at - **New Delhi**
212. The curve which are highly peaked and have value $\beta_2 > 3$ are called - **Leptokurtic**
213. In field experimentation local control is used for- **Diminution of error**
214. The accuracy of a measurement signifies the closeness with - **True value**
215. Mean deviation is least when calculated about (minimal property) - **Median**
216. For valid conclusions we should have - **Unbiased estimate**
217. The minimum error of degree of freedom should be at least - **12**
218. When the correlation coefficient $r = +1$, then the two regression lines - **Coincide**
219. If the three factors are A, B and C are tried with three levels the total number of combinations will be - **twenty-seven.**
220. Ogives for more than type and less than type distribution intersect at - **Median**

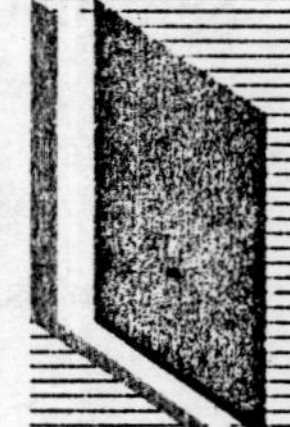

CHAPTER 12

MISCELLANEOUS

1. Mushroom contains 85-95% moisture, 3% protein, 4% carbohydrates, 0.3-0.4% fat and 1% minerals and vitamins.
2. While mushroom (*Agaricus bisporus*), paddy straw mushroom (*Volvariella spp.*), oyster mushroom (*Pleurotus spp.*) and shiitake (*Lentinus edodes*) are most popular mushroom in India.
3. Moisture content of dried mushroom should not be more than 5%.
4. 0.5% $NaHSO_3$ or 2% NaCl solution (for 30 min.) are used for blanching.
5. Micro-algae contains protein 45-70%.
6. Single - cell proteins are proteins derived from bacteria, yeasts, moulds and algae.
7. The length of algae is 300-500μm while width is 6-8mm.
8. Incorporation of algae upto 30% in diet/food is considered as safe. (UNID, document, Chamorre 1982).
9. Spirulina contain 18 times more β-carotene than carrot.
10. Biolipistic is made up by spirulina pigment phycocyanin.
11. Quality standard by (BIS) (IS: 12895:1990) is for algae.
12. Leaf protein concentrates (LPC) contains 60-65% protein and 0.1-0.2% β-carotene.
13. "Analogue" is a food product which is designed as an alternative to traditional animal foods such as meat, poultry, sea foods or dairy products.
14. Meat analogues were developed by John Harvey Kellogg in 1898.
15. 1 curie is equal 3.7×10^{10} disintegration/sec.
16. ACINF: Advisory Committee on Irradiated and Novel Foods
17. FDA stands for Food and Drug Administration.
18. H_2O_2 is a strong oxidizing agent and a toxicant to microorganisms.
19. IAEA stands for International Atomic Energy Authority. Head Office of IAEA is at Geneva (Switzerland)
20. Gamma rays are emitted by Cobalt 60.
21. Wet –dog-odour occurs in high protein foods that are meat becomes darker and burnt off flavour by irradiation.
22. IPCL Baroda (Indian Petrochemical Corporation Limited estd. 22nd March 1969)
23. **Nutraceutical:** The word nutraceutical was coined in 1989 by "De Felice" any substance that may be considered as food or part of food and provides medical and health benefits, including the prevention and treatment of disease.

24. Caffeic acid and ferulic acid acts as analgesic, anticancer, ant mutagenic and antioxidant rich in plums, blueberries and pineapple.
25. Isoflavones from soya products have nutraceutical function as antioxidant and in addition possesses phytoestrogenic properties that can be effective for menopausal symptoms and to promote bone density in post –menopausal women.
26. Isoflavones such as hesperidin and rutin are present in citrus fruits and grape fruits and these combined with vitamin C can help to reduce hot flushes in menopausal women.
27. Food source of fructooligosaccharides (prebiotics) include honey, beer, onion, banana and oats.
28. All the skin functions and maintenance of membrane stability are done by ω-6 fatty acids.
29. Extrusion (Latin word) means to force press or push out or to shape by forcing through die.
30. The extruder was first produced by "Wenger" (USA).
31. Retort processed foods also known as "Ready to Eat" foods.
32. Nuts are "one seeded indehiscent fruit".
33. Nuts and oilseeds are good sources of B-vitamins and groundnut is especially rich in thiamine and nicotinic acid.
34. **Marzipan:** A sweet or small cake made of or coated with marzipan or a soft, yellow or white food made from almonds, sugar and eggs used for decorating cakes and making sweets.
35. Groundnut is also called as "time pass nut" or "common man's nut", monkey nuts.
36. Groundnut is deficient in lysine and Methionine.
37. Coconut sap received by tapping or cutting the stalk of young flower bunches are rich in sucrose called toddy (consumed fermented or unfermented both).
38. Pistachios (pistachio) is not growing in India mainly produced in Afghanistan.
39. Cashew is native of Brazil; fruit borne by the tree are called cashew apple.
40. It is believed that vitamin deficiency can be avoided by consuming lime.
41. Cell theory states that cells are fundamental structure units of living organisms
42. Nucleus was discovered by Robert Brown.
43. Each turn of α-helix contains 3.6 amino acids.
44. α-helix is stabilized by hydrogen bonds.
45. Transamination is a reversible process.
46. Helical structure of DNA was found by Watson and Crick.
47. Watson and Crick were awarded noble prize for their finding that DNA is double stranded.
48. World leader in fruit production - China, India ranks (second)
49. International Institute of Horticulture is situated in Brazil.
50. China ranked highest in vegetables production.
51. de Candolle is the father of systematic pomology.
52. ?????
53. The yellow pigment in papaya fruit is due to *caricaxanthin*.
54. ?????

55. Climateric fruit are those which releases ethylene gas.
56. Non-climateric fruit are those which absorbes ethylene gas.
57. In the world best quality tea is grown at Darjeeling (W. B.) in India and it has been geographical patented.
58. Kalipak is the most processed product from arecanut.
59. Central Institute of Post Harvest Engineering Technology (CIPHET) is situated at Ludhiana (Punjab).
60. Wine made from pea is known as perry.
61. Grape guard is a craft paper coated with potassium metabisulphite and plastic polymer.
62. Among cucurbites water melon contains more iron and its TSS is 9-10 %.
63. Marmelosin is present in bael.
64. King of fruit is mango.
65. Queen of fruit is mangosteen.
66. Apple of tropics is guava.
67. Queen of beverages is tea.
68. King of spices is black pepper.
69. Queen of spices is small cardamom.
70. Fancy fruit is mandarin.
71. King of nuts is walnut.
72. Carambola fruit cum ornamental tree and its root extract is used as antidote in poisoning.
73. Limolin is glycocide responsible for bitter taste of citrus fruit juice.
74. Mg deficient is universal in grape.
75. Sikkim is only place where mandarins are packed in wooden boxes.
76. Fig has highest fibre among fruits.
77. Almond contains 49% oil, 32% oleic acid, 13% linoleic acid and 10% palmatic acid respectively.
78. "Kirschwascer" distilled from pulp of cherry is a European wine. Rich source of Vitamin K.
79. Monolaurin content of coconut oil has anti HIV property.
80. Broma dryer commonly used drier for drying kernel at 2-4% moisture.
81. Main objective of withering is removal of moisture about 15-20% from the leaves of tea.
82. Coffee contains niacin and it cures dermal problem.
83. Betel vine contains Vitamin A about 9600 IU.
84. Toddy is regarded as a natural alcohol and a health beverage, with an approximate 5-8.1% alcohol level.
85. Mahua oil contains linoleic acid which is useful to reduce blood cholesterol level.
86. Dry chilli contains 06% stalk, 40% pericarp and seeds 54%.
87. Kanji beverage is prepared by black carrot.
88. Onion is rich source of Vitamin B.
89. Green chillies retard cancer due to natural enzyme asparaginase.
80. Storage protein in beans is phaseolin

91. Fragnance is controlled by Polygen while colour is controlled by additive gene.
92. Good jelly should contain 1.0% pectin, 60-65% sugar, 10.0% fruit acid and 33-38% water.
93. Only sugar acts as preservative in jam.
94. Sodium benzoate is added for the preservation of fruit juice in the concentrate of 0.06-0.10%.
95. Permissible limit of synthetic colour in food preservation is 200ppm.
96. Minimum fruit content and TSS for fruit jelly according to FPO is 45% and 65° Brix respectively.
97. Maximum level of SO_2 permitted in squash is 350 ppm.
98. The aroma in fruits is caused due to formation of Esters.
99. Best method for preservation is dehydration.
100. The separate ministry of food processing in India was established in the year 1999.
101. Guava jelly is preserved by sodium benzoate.
102. Ber fruits become available in the market when no other fruit arrives.
103. First international symposium on plantation crops was held in India.
104. Colour of tea is due to theoflavin while flavour is due to linalool.
105. Ficin is present in fig which is dormant in rainy season.
106. Mango pickle is national pickle.
107. Vine yard of India is Nasik (M. S.).
108. Ethyl acetate extract of guggal is named as guggulipids.
109. Kewda is used in headache and rheumatism.
110. Guggal is used in perfumery as incense and fixative.
111. Lemongrass is used in drugs for headache and toothaches.
112. Per capita availability of milk in India - 459 gm/day/ person IN 2022-23

IMPORTANT POINTS

- NCL – National Chemicals Laboratory, Pune.
- CFTRI – Central food technology research institute, Mysore (Karnataka)
- IISR – Indian Institute of Spices Research Kozhikode (Kerala).
- CID – Commercial Item Description.
- AMS – Agricultural Market Services.
- TQM – Total Quality Management.
- HACCP – Hazards Analysis and Critical Control Point.
- GMP – Good Manufacture Practices.
- GHP – Good Hygienic Practices.
- MRL – Maximum Residual Limit.
- FAC – Food Aduletration Cases.
- IQF – Individual Quick Freezing.
- HFCS – High Fructose Corn Syrup.
- GRAS – Generally Recognised as Safe.

- CIP – Cleaned in Place.
- CDC – Centre for Disease Control.
- SCP – Single Cell Protein *e.g.* Spiralling Maxima.
  - Breaking down of food by chewing is called **mastication**
  - Human masseter muscle is the main power source used for crushing or grinding foods
  - Post harvest losses of fruits and vegetables in India are about 20–30%.
  - Fruits are rich in vitamins while vegetables are rich in minerals.
- **ASTM** – American Society for Testing Materials.
- **CAP** – (Controlled Atmospheric Packaging) involves monitoring and adjustment of the gases.
- **MAP** – Modified Atmosphere Packaging
- Food Corporation of India established in the year 1964.
- **CWC** – Central Warehousing Corporation established in the year 1957.
- Indian Standard Institute established in the year 1946 (New name Bureau of Indian Standard came in to existence on 23rd Dec., 1986)
- Milk mission funded by IDD (Indian Dairy Authority) and GOI in the year 2012.
- **NDDB** – National Dairy Development Board.
- **WFC** – World Food Council.
- Total Livestock Population in India (20th census 2019) – 535.78 million (Growth percentage 4.63%)
- Total Poultry Population in India (20th census 2019) – 851.81 million. (Growth percentage 16.4%)
- Indian Tea Board established in the year 1954.
- *Clodosporium* green mold in fruits and cladosporium herbarum black spot on the surface of the meat in cold storage as it can survive below freezing.
- Stearic acid yields 148 molecule of ATP.
- Salt balance theory was given by Sommer and Hart.
- pH of jam is 5.0 and of jelly is 3.0.
- Thamnidium is responsible for whiskers (spoilage seen in meat under aerobic condition at the freezing point) but recommended for flavour development in meat in controlled growth.
- Canned meat is generally spoiled by *Clostridium*.
- Flat sour spoilage of canned foods is due to *Bacillus*.
- Spoilage of canned fruits due to *Bassochlamys fuva*.
- Spoilage of clove is by *Clostridium.*
- *Saccharomyces cerevisae var. carlsbergensis* used in beer manufacturing.
- 4 myoglobin = 1 haemoglobin.
- **PDCAAS** – Protein Digestibility Corrected Amino Acid Score.
- **PAGE** – Polyacrylamide Gel Electrophoresis.
- Domestic demand for edible oilseeds/oil in India is short of about 50 percent.
- WDRA stands for Warehousing Development and Regulatory Authority
- NFSA stands for National Food Security Act. launched since 2013.
- India ranks first in milk production, accounting for about world production of 2023-24.
- The average year on year growth rate of milk in India is 4.04 percent. Contribution of milk industry to GDP 4%.

- India shares about 5.4 percent of global fish production.
- Milk contributes largest to the livestock GDD (more than 70%) followed by meat dung and egg.
- **Total milk production** in the country during **2022-23 was 230.58 million tonnes** with a increase of 3.83% from 2021-22. Per capita valability of milk was **459g/day in 2022-2023**
- **Top 5 major milk producing states in 2022-2023 are:** U.P. (15.72%), Rajasthan (14.44%), MP (8.73%), Gujrat (7.49%) and A.P. (6.70%)
- Total egg production in India during 2022-2023 was **138.38 billion numbers**
- **Top 5 major egg producing states are:** A.P. (20.13%), T.N. (15.58%), Telengana(12.77%), West Bengal (9.94%) and Karnataka (6.5%)
- In terms of **Annual Growth rate** top state is West Bengal (20.10%) followed by Sikkim (18.53%) and UP (12.80%)
- **Per capita availability of egg during** 2022-23 was **101 nos/ annum**
- **Total meat production 2022-2023 is estimated to 9.77 million tonnes) gain of 5.15% from 2021-22**
- **Top contributing states are:** UP (12.20%), W.B. (11.95%), MH (11.50%). AP (11.20%) and Telengana (11.06%).
- In terms of AGR sikkim has recorded growth(63.08%) followed by Meghalaya (38.34%) and Goa (22.98%).
- **Per capita availability of meat in 2022 was 6.82 kg/ annum**
- National Bureau of animal Genetic Resources, Karnal is the nodal agency for registeration of breeds and total number of breeds registered in the country are - **222**
- Union Minister of Fisheries, Animal Husbandry & Dairying, launched **Nandi - NOC Approval for New Drug and Inoculation System portal on 26th June 2023** at New Delhi. With this portal, DAHD will facilitate the regulatory approval process with transparency to assess and examine veterinary product proposals will be more streamlined through seamless integration with the SUGAM portal of Central Drugs Standard Control Organization.
- **Wool production in 2022-2023- 33.61 million kgs** (a negative growth of 16.84%) over the last 5 years . But a positive growth over 2021-22 of 2.12%
- **Top 5 states are:** Rajasthan (47.98%), J&K(22.55%), Gujrat (6.01%), MH (4.73%) and H.P.(4.27%) in terms of AGR is Arunachal Pradesh(35.75%) Rajasthan (6.06%) and Jharkhand (2.36%)

Inland Fisheries In India

- Out of total inland fisheries percentage share of fresh water aquaculture is 95% in recent years.
- Area under Reservoirs - 3.15 million ha
- Area under Ponds & Tanks - 2.36 million ha
- Area under Brackish water - 1.24 million ha
- Length of Rivers & Canals - 195,210 km
- Flood plain lakes and derelict water, brackish water - 1.240 million ha
- Length of rivers and canals - 0.19 million km
- Estuaries. - 0.29 million ha

- India stands at third position of **fish production in 2022-23** in the world with a contribution of **8%** of the global production
- Contribution of fisheries sector to GVA was **1.09%** and contribution to the GVA of agriculture was **6.72% in 2022-2023**
- Leading state in inland fish production is Andhra Pradesh followed by West Bengal.
- **Kisan Credit Scheme extended to fishercies and AH sector** in the year 2018-2019
- PMMSY (Pradhan Mantri Masya Sampada Yojna launched in 2020 aims to enhance fish production to **220 lakh tonnes by 2024-2025**
- A new sub scheme PMMKSSHY(Pradhan Mantri Matsaya Kisan Samridhi Sah Yojna) started in 2023 2024 under PMMSY central sector scheme.
- Announcement of **Seaweed Park** in Tamilnadu state in 2022-2023.
- Announcement of Development of 5 major fishing harbours as hub of economic activity
- **The National Surveillance Programme for Aquatic Animal Diseases (NSPAAD)** has launched a mobile app called **'Report Fish Disease'.** This app is designed to help fish farmers across India to track and monitor fish diseases.

Marine Fisheries In India

- Length of the Coast Line - 8,129 km
- Continental Shelf - 0.53 million Sq.km
- Number of Fish landing Centers - 1547
- Number of Fishing Villages - 3477
- Exclusive Economic Zone 2.02 million Sq.km comprising 0.86 million sq km on west coast, 0.56 million sq km, 0.60 million sq km around Andaman and Nicobar island.
- Central Institute of Fisheries Technology (CIFT)- headquarters in Matsyapuri, Willingdon Island, Kochi, setup in 1957
- **Central Institute of Brackishwater Aquaculture (CIBA** on 1-4-1987, HQ is Chennai
- Central Institute of Fisheries Education (CIFE)- 6th June 1961, HQ- Mumbai, Maharashtra
- Central Institute of Fisheries Nautical and Engineering Training (or CIFNET) formerly known as the Central Institute of Fisheries Operatives (CIFO), is a marine studies centre located at Kochi- 1963
- Central Institute of Freshwater Aquaculture (CIFA-1987, Bhubaneswar, Odisha
- National Fisheries Development Board (NFDB): FDB was set up in September, 2006, Hyderabad
- **Coastal Aquaculture Authority:-** CAA was established under the Coastal Aquaculture Act, 2005 vide Gazette Notification dated 22 December 2005 at Chennai.
- Fisheries Survey of India (FSI) Mumbai.
- **India being the second largest silk producing country in the world, next to China,** provides employment to over 8.5 million people in the entire silk production value chain from farm to **fabric.**
- FSSAI notifies standards for honey and its products recently, it will address the honey adulteration. FSSAI notification is of 18 parameters to be complied, like that of sucrose content, glucose ratio, pollen count, foreign oligosaccharides among others.

  The FSSAI has fixed maximum 5 per cent limit for sucrose content in the honey, while 10 per cent for carviacallosa and Honeydew honey. The moisture percentage should be maximum 20 per cent and pollen count should be 25,000 per gram.

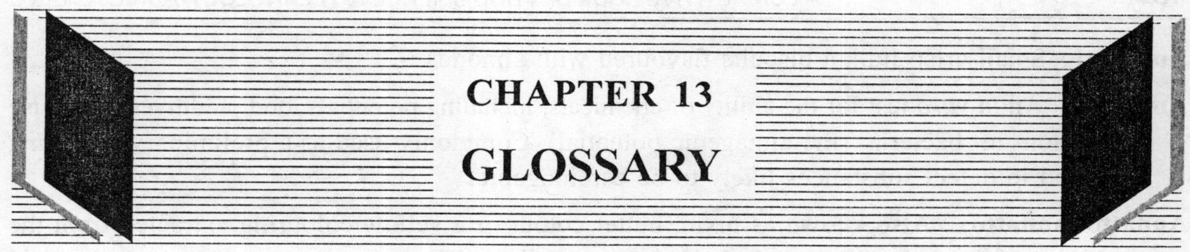

A

Abattoir Any premises or facility where live animals are slaughtered or and any or all of the following take place: meat is cut, wrapped, frozen, cured, smoked or aged.

Abscisic acid Plant hormone responsible for shedding of leaves by deciduous trees. In herbaceous plants can lead to dwarf or compact plants with normal or enhanced fruit production.

Acetone One of the ketone bodies formed in the body in fasting. Also used as a solvent.

Acids fruit Organic acids such as citric, malic and tartaric which give the sharp or sour flavour to fruits, often added to processed foods for taste.

Acid fast staining A staining that differentiates between bacteria based on their ability to retain a dye when washed with an acid alcohol solution.

Acidity Sourness or tartness in a food product.

Acrolein An aldehyde formed when glycerol is heated to a high temperature; responsible for the acrid odour produced when fats are overheated.

Actinomycete An aerobic, gram positive bacterium that forms branching filaments (hyphae) and asexual spores.

Actomyosin A combination of the two main proteins, actin and myosin, present in all muscle tissues.

Aerate To incorporate air into a mixture

Aflatoxin Carcinogenic mycotoxins formed by *Aspergillus avus*, *A. parasiticus* and *A. nominus* growing on nuts, cereals, dried fruit and cheese, especially when stored under damp warm conditions.

Akpiti West African; fried doughnuts made from maize (and sometimes plantain flour) the dough is left to undergo a lactic acid bacterial fermentation.

Albedo A measure of how much light that hits a surface is reflected back without being absorbed.

Almond oil Essential oil from the seeds of either the almond tree (*Prunus amygdalis*) or more commonly the apricot tree (*P. armeniaca*), containing benzaldehyde, hydrogen cyanide and benzaldehyde cyanohydrin.

Amaretti Small crisp Italian biscuits flavoured with almonds

Ames test An *in vitro* test for the ability of chemicals, including potential food additives, to cause mutation in bacteria (the mutagenic potential). Commonly used as a preliminary screening method to detect substances likely to be carcinogenic.

Annatto (annatto) Also known as bixin, butter colour or a yellow colouring extracted from the pericarp of the fruit of the tropical shrub *Bixa orellana*. The main component is the carotenoid bixin, which is fat soluble.

Antimicrobial agents Compounds used to preserve food by preventing growth of micro-organisms (bacteria and fungi).

Antimicrobial constituents The stability of some foods against attack by microorganisms is due to the presence of certain naturally occuring substances that have been shown to have antimicrobial activity. *Nisin* and other *bacteriocins* are good examples.

Antimony Toxic metal of known metabolic function, so not a dietary essential. Antimony compounds are used in treatment of some parasitic diseases.

Antioxidant A substance that retards the oxidative rancidity of fats in stored foods. Many fats, and especially vegetable oils, contain naturally occurring antioxidants, including vitamin E (E-306-309), which protect them against rancidity for some time.

Aspartame 200 times as sweet as sucrose, Stable for a few months in solution, then gradually breaks down. Used in soft drinks, dessert mixes and as a 'table top sweetener.

Atomiser Apparatus for atomisation of liquids or slurries.

Authentic The term "authentic" has a different meaning to "traditional". It may imply either that a product has remained unchanged through the passage of time, or that it actually originates from the area implied by its name (*e.g.* "authentic Lancashire Hot Pot") when the generic description of the product has passed into wider usage.

Auxin A plant hormone produced by shoot tips, responsible for controlling cell growth and differentiation, and frequently used as a rooting hormone for cuttings. Chemically indoleacetic acid and related compounds.

Avidin Protein in white of eggs that binds biotin with very high affinity.

Avicel *Azotobacter* Genus of free-living soil bacteria of family Bacteriaceae which can reduce nitrogen gas to ammonia and hence fix nitrogen for incorporation into amino acids etc.

B

Bacillus cereus *Bacillus cereus* (from Latin, meaning waxy rod) is a spore forming bacteria which produces a toxin when growing in food. This toxin, when eaten with the food, causes inflammation of the stomach, hence stomach pains and vomiting. Cooked rice is the food most commonly associated with this type of food poisoning.

Bacteria Unicellular micro-organisms, contains prokaryotic cells with primarily diacyl glycerol diesters in their membranes and with eubacterial rRNA.

Bacteriophage The virus which infects bacteria and causes the lysis of bacterial cells.

Baguette A French bread, a long thin loaf about 60cm long, weighing 250g, with a crisp crust.

Baker's yeast *Saccharomyces cerevisiae*, used as an emulsifier and thickener.

Banana Dessert bananas have a high sugar content (17-19%) and are eaten raw; plantains (sometimes known as green bananas) have a higher starch and lower sugar content and are picked when too hard to be eaten raw.

Banian days Days on which no meat was served; named after Banian (Hindu) merchants who abstained from eating meat. An obsolete term for days of short commons.

Bar code The technical definition for a barcode is a machine readable form of information on a scannable, visual surface. The information is then transmitted into a database where it can be logged and tracked. Barcodes are very useful for maintaining accurate information about inventory, pricing and other important business related data.

Barges A long flat bottom boat used for cocoa shipment where 500 tonnes of cocoa can be loaded into the holds of it.

Baron of beef The pair of sirloins of beef, left uncut at the bone.

Basal metabolic rate (BMR) The energy cost of maintaining the metabolic integrity of the body, nerve and muscle tone, respiration and circulation. For children the BMR also includes the energy cost of growth. It depends on the amount of metabolically active body tissue, and hence can be calculated from body weight, height and age.

Baseline A measurement, calculation, or location used as a starting point or condition against which to measure future changes.

Basmati Long-grain Indian variety of rice, much prized for its delicate flavour (the name means 'fragrant' in Hindi).

Bean, broad *Vicia faba a*lso known as fava or horse bean, Composition/100g:water 11g, 1427kJ (341 kcal), protein 26.1 g, fat 1.5g, carbohydrate 58.3g, fibre 25g, ash 3.1g.

Beastings The first milk given by the cow after calving, the colostrums, rich in immunoglobulins.

Bee wine Wine produced by fermentation of sugar, using a clump of yeast and lactic bacteria which rises and falls with the bubbles of carbondioxide formed during fermentation, hence named 'bee'.

Betanin Red-purple betacyanin pigment in beetroot; permitted food colour E-162.

Bezoar Foods with a high content of pectin can form bezoars if swallowed without chewing. The name is derived from the Arabic meaning protection against poison, since bezoars were formerly believed to have protective properties.

Biological Hazard Any danger to food safety by the contamination of food with illness or disease-causing organisms.

Biological value (BV) A measure of the proportion of absorbed protein from a food which is incorporated in the proteins of organisms body.

Biosensor The coupling of a biologically mediates process with production of an electrical signals to detect the presence of particular substances.

Blanching Fruits and vegetables are cooked before dehydrating or freezing, to soften the texture, shrink the food or remove air, destroy enzymes that may cause spoilage when frozen, and remove undesirable flavours. Blanching is also performed to remove excess salt from preserved meat, and to aid the removal of skin, e.g. from almonds and tomatoes.

Bloom Fat bloom is the whitish appearance on the surface of chocolate which sometimes occurs on storage. It is due either to a change in the form of the fat at the surface or to fat diffusing outwards and being deposited as crystals on the surface. Sugar bloom is due to the deposition of sugar crystals on the surface, but is less common than fat bloom.

Bonito Any of the various species of tuna fish.

Brander Scottish name for grid iron or grill.

Brandy A spirit distilled from wine and containing 37-45% (most usually 40%) alcohol by volume. The name is derived from the German *brandtwein*, meaning burnt wine, corrupted to brandy wine.

Brining The process of soaking vegetables in brine before pickling in vinegar, in order to remove some of the water, and retain a crisp texture.

Brix It is used to refer to the concentration of sugar syrups used in canned fruits. The specific gravity based on the balling tables, calculated in grams of cane sugar in 100g of solution at 20°C; degree Brix° percentage sugar.

Bromelain Enzymes present in pineapple, papaya and figs which hydrolyse proteins. It can be used to tenderise meat.

Bullace Fruit of the wild damson, *Prunus insititia*; similar to sloe, very acidic.

Burstin Orkneys, historical; barley grains toasted by placing in a pot beside the fire, then ground and used to make a porridge.

Cachou Small scented tablets for sweetening the breath.

Caffeine An alkaloid found in coffee and tea, also known as *theine*. It raises blood pressure, acts as a diuretic and temporarily averts fatigue, so has a stimulant action. coffee beans contain about 1% caffeine, and the beverage contains about 70mg/100mL. Tea contains 1.5-2.5% caffeine, is about 50-60mg/100mL of the beverage.

Calbindin An intracellular calcium binding protein induced by vitamin D; it is involved in calcium transport.

Calf's foot jelly Gelatine, stock made by boiling calves' feet in water; it sets to a stiff jelly on cooling.

Campylobacter A type of bacterial food poisoning.

Canbra oil Oil extracted from selected strains of rapeseed containing not more than 2% erucic acid.

Candy Sugar confectionery crystallised sugar made by repeated boiling and slow evaporation.

Canola Oilseeds of the brassica family that contain less than specified amounts of glucosinolates and erucic acid. Canola oil is 7% saturated, 62% mono-unsaturated, 31% polyunsaturated, vitamin E 17.1mg, K 122mg.

CAP Controlled atmosphere packaging.

Capon A castrated cockerel (male chicken), which has a faster rate of growth, and more tender flesh, than the cockerel. Surgery has generally been replaced by chemical caponisation, the implantation of pellets of oestrogen.

Caramels A chewy sweet similar to toffee but boiled at a lower temperature; may be soft or hard.

Caraway Dried ripe fruit of *Carum carvi*, an aromatic spice.

Carbonised food Carbonised food is food which is burnt in frying, roasting or baking. In industry carbonised food can accumulate on heat exchangers. These burnt food stains cling to surfaces and are difficult to clean.

Cariogenic Causing tooth decay (caries) by stimulating the growth of acid-forming bacteria on the teeth; the term is applied to sucrose and other fermentable carbohydrates.

Casson value A measure of the rheological properties (shear stress and viscosity) of chocolate.

Caul Membrane enclosing the fetus; that from sheep or pig used to cover meat while roasting.

Celiac disease Caused by intolerance of the protein gluten present in the cereals wheat, barley and rye.

Cellophane The first transparent, non-porous film, made from wood pulp (cellulose), patented in 1908 by Swiss-French chemist Jacques-Edwin Brandenburger; waterproof cellophane for food wrapping developed by Du Pont in 1926. Still widely used for wrapping foods and other commodities.

Central Kitchen A central kitchen is a place where the food is prepared, cooked, portioned then either chilled or frozen in a Cook-chill or Cook-freeze operation. A central kitchen normally also has a chilled storage area for Cook-chill or Cook-freeze food.

Champagne Sparkling wine made by a secondary fermentation in the bottle, adding sugar, citric acid and a champagne yeast starter to bottles of a previsiouly prepared selected table wine.

Cheese, whey Made from whey by heat coagulation of the proteins (lactalbumin and lactoglobulin).

Chemical Sanitizing A method of sterilizing a surface using a chemical that has been approved by the Canadian Food Inspection Agency at a specified concentration and contact time.

Chewing gum Based on chicle and other plant resins, with sugar or other sweetener, balsam of Tolu and various flavours. (Main ingredients gum base, sweeteners, plasticizers, flavors, colors and polyols)

Chinese restaurant syndrome Flushing, palpitations and numbness associated at one time with the consumption of monosodium glutamate, and then with histamine, but the cause of these symptoms after eating various foods are not known.

Cholesterol Free Contains fewer than 2 mg of cholesterol and 2 grams or less of saturated fat per serving.

C.I.P. C.I.P. is short for 'Cleaning In Place' and is an automatic cleaning system used for cleaning industrial equipment and machines without having to dismantle the equipment. The C.I.P. is normally controlled by a computer or microprocessor and the program should not be short cutted or altered without expert advice.

Clean As You Go Clean As You Go makes it the responsibility of all food handlers to keep their work area clean and wipe up spillages as soon as they occur, before they become engrained.

Clostridium perfringens *Clostridium perfringens* is an anaerobic, spore forming rod which produces a toxin during spore formation. This toxin causes a form of food poisoning, which is normally mild but it may be more severe in the very young, elderly or infirmed. The foods most commonly associated with this type of food poisoning are large pots of stews and curries or large joints of meat where the heat penetration is poor or where the cooling time is too long.

Cocoa butter The fat from the cocoa bean, used in chocolate manufacture and in pharmaceuticals; it has a sharp melting point, between 31 and 35°C, so melts in the mouth.

Co-enzyme A coenzyme is a cocatalyst that is converted to a new product concomitant with each turnover of substrate.

Cold spots Cold spots are localised areas which receive insufficient microwave energy during microwave cooking. Thus the temperature in cold spots is often too low to kill microbes. Cold spots can be reduced by; turning the food; stirring the food; allowing standing time during and after cooking and not overloading the microwave oven.

Colocasia Colocasia esculenta is a tropical plant grown primarily for its edible corms, the root vegetables most commonly known as *taro.*

Conformity Ability to meet set standards.

Cook-chill In Cook-chill, food is prepared, cooked, portioned then chilled to 3°C in a central kitchen. The food is taken to a feeder kitchen where it is reheated prior to being eaten. Cook-chill is used in large scale catering operations such as hospital food or school dinners.

Cook-freeze In Cook-freeze the food is prepared then cooked in a central kitchen, portioned then frozen to -20°C. The food can be stored for up to eight weeks, before it is reheated in a feeder kitchen before being eaten.

Culture A culture is a way of life of a group of people—the behaviors, beliefs, values, and symbols that they accept, generally without thinking about them, and that are passed along by communication and imitation from one generation to the next.

Colocasia esculenta is a tropical plant grown primarily for its edible corms, the root vegetables most commonly known as ***taro***. It is believed to be one of the earliest cultivated plants. Linnaeus originally described two species which are now known as *Colocasia esculenta* and *Colocasia antiquorum* of the cultivated plants that are known by many names including eddoes, dasheen, taro and madumbi, but many later botanists consider them all to be members of a single, very variable species, the correct name for which is *Colocasia esculenta*

Culture A population of microorganisms cultivated in medium is called culture.

Codex Alimentarius Originally Codex Alimentarius Europaeus; since 1961 part of the United Nations FAO/WHO Commission on Food Standards to simplify and integrate food standards for adoption internationally. Web site: http://www. codexalimentarius.net/.

Corrosion Deterioration due to the chemical reaction of water, air or acid (A metal or alloy that is likely to be damaged or destroyed, especially by oxidation or chemical action, is 'corrodible').

Crawfish Crustaceans (without claws), family Palinuridae, also called spiny lobster, rock lobster, sea crayfish.

Crumb softeners Derivatives of mono-acylglycerols (monoglycerides) added to bread as emulsifiers to give a softer crumb and retard staling (E-430-436); also called polysorbates.

Curing A method of preserving meat and fish by treating with sodium nitrite or nitrate and sodium chloride.

Curry Name given by the British (it means *sauce* in Tamil) to an Indian dish of stewed meat or vegetables. It is served with a pungent sauce whose components and pungency vary.

Cytochromes Haem containing proteins. Some react with oxygen directly; others are intermediates in the oxidation of reduced coenzymes. Unlike haemoglobin, the iron in the haem of cytochromes undergoes oxidation and reduction.

Cytosine One of the pyrimidine bases of nucleic acids.

Cytoplasm The cytoplasm, or protoplasm, of bacterial cells is where the functions for cell growth, metabolism, and replication are carried out. It is a gel-like matrix composed of water, enzymes, nutrients, wastes, and gases and contains cell structures such as ribosomes, a chromosome, and plasmids. The cell envelope encases the cytoplasm and all its components.

D

Dagé Indonesian; fermented presscake from various oilseeds or legumes or starch crops, soaked in water and left to undergo bacterial fermentation (mainly *Bacillus* spp.) to form a glutinous mass bound by bacterial polysaccharides.

Daily values The Percent Daily Values on the Nutritional Facts label is a guide to the nutrients in one serving of food. For example, if the label lists 15 percent for calcium, it means that one serving provides 15 percent of the calcium you need each day.

Damson Small dark purple plum (*Prunus damascena*); very acid, mainly used to make jam. Introduced into Europe by Crusaders returning from Damascus (early 13th century).

Danger zone The danger zone is the temperature range in which food (especially high risk food) is at the greatest risk from microbial attack. Food containing active (or potentially active) microbes should be stored or held within the danger zone for the shortest possible time. The danger zone is between 5°C and 63°C.

Date *Phoenix dactylifera* are of three types: 'soft' (about 80% of the dry matter is invert sugar, *see* sugar, invert); semi-dry (about 40% invert sugar, 40% sucrose); and dry (20-40% invert sugar, 40-60% is sucrose).

Deglutition The act of swallowing.

Denaturation A normally irreversible change in the structure of protein by heat, acid, alkali or other agents which results in loss of solubility and coagulation. Denatured proteins lose biological activity (*e.g.* as enzymes), but not nutritional value. Indeed, digestibility is improved compared with the native structure, which is relatively resistant to enzymic hydrolysis.

Depositor Machine for depositing a precise amount of food into a mould or onto a conveyor belt.

Detoxication The metabolism of (potentially) toxic compounds to yield less toxic derivatives that are more soluble in water and can be excreted in the urine or bile.

Deviation A variation from the standard or norm. In a food safety system, a failure of or departure from the standard operating procedures (SOP), is one example.

DHA Docosohexaenoic acid, a long chain polyunsaturated fatty acid. *See* fish oils.

Diastatic activity A measure of the ability of flour produce maltose from its own starch by the action of its own amylase (diastase).This sugar is needed for the growth of the yeast during fermentation.

Dietary Reference Values A set of standards of the intakes for most nutrients needed for good health

Digestibility It is measured as the difference between intake and faecal output, with allowance being made for that part of the faeces that is not derived from undigested food residues (such as shed cells of the intestinal tract, bacteria, residues of digestive juices).

Disinfection (milk) When milk is disinfected it is heated to 100°C for about 10 seconds. Disinfected milk is not sterile as spores can survive the disinfection process but disinfected milk is more stable than pasteurised milk. Disinfected milk is mainly used for milk products such as dried milk or yoghurt.

Dockage Name given to foreign material in wheat which can be removed readily by a simple cleaning procedure.

Dosa Indian; shallow-fried pancake made from a mixture of rice and a legume; the dough is left to undergo bacterial fermentation before cooking. The principal bacteria involved are *Leuconostoc mesenteroides* and *Streptococcus faecalis*, introduced with a starter of an earlier batch of fermented dough.

Dry weight basis (dwb) The composition of a wet food based on the mass of dry solids it contains.

Dunlop Scottish cheddar type cheese.

Due Diligence The degree of prudence that might be expected from a reasonable person, group or organization in the same circumstances.

D-Value The time in minutes at a specified temperature required to destroy 90% of the total organism in a population. Thus, the D-value or decimal reduction time, decrease the surviving population by one log cycle.

Dyspepsia Any pain or discomfort associated with eating; may be a symptom of gastritis, peptic ulcer, gall-bladder disease, etc.; functional dyspepsia occurs when there is no obvious structural change in the intestinal tract. Treatment includes a bland diet.

E

***E. coli* (*Escherichia coli*)** Group of bacteria including both harmless commensals in the human gut and strains that cause food poisoning by production of enterotoxins.

Ectomorph Description given to a tall, thin person, possibly with underdeveloped muscles.

EDTA Ethylene diamine tetra-acetic acid, a chelating agent that forms stable chelation complexes with metal ions. Also called versene, sequestrol and sequestrene. It can be used both to remove metal ions from a solution (or at least to remove them from activity) and also to add metal ions, for example in plant fertilisers (E-385).

Effective freezing time Time required to lower the temperature of a food from an initial value to a predetermined final temperature

Egg proteins What is generally referred to as egg protein is a mixture of proteins, including ovalbumin, ovomucoid, ovoglobulin, conalbumin, vitellin and vitellenin. Egg white contains 11% protein, mostly ovalbumin; yolk contains 16% protein, mainly two phosphoproteins, vitellin and vitellenin.

Einkorn A type of wheat, the wild form of which, *Triticum boeoticum*, was probably one of the ancestors of all cultivated wheat. Still grown in some parts of southern Europe and Middle East, usually for animal feed. The name means 'one seed', from the single seed found in each spikelet.

Electroporation Use of high-voltage electric pulses at low-voltage gradients to exchange genetic information between protoplast cells of micro-organisms, plants or animals. At high-voltage gradients (up to 30kV/cm) used to sterilise or pasteurise food by permeabilisation of bacterial cell membranes.

Elute To wash off or remove. Specifically applied to removal of adsorbed compounds in chromatography.

Emmental Swiss hard cheese, used in fondue.

Emulsification Reduction in droplet size of immiscible liquids to achieve a stable emulsion. Also known as homogenisation.

Endemic The usual cases of a particular illness in a community.

Endopeptidases Enzymes that hydrolyse proteins (*i.e.* proteinases or peptidases), by cleaving peptide bonds inside protein mole- cules, as opposed to exopeptidases, which remove amino acids from the end of the protein chain. The main endopeptidases in digestion are chymotrypsin, elastase, pepsin and trypsin.

Endospore A resting stage of some bacteria, during which the bacteria is resistant to unfavourable conditions. An endospore serves a purpose similar to the seed of a plant.

Endosperm The large interior section of cereal grains which provide starch, B vitamins and some protein.

Energy drinks Beverages containing glucose, vitamins, minerals, herb extracts and caffeine, and sometimes other ingredients, claimed to provide energy and to promote alertness and well-being. Some now contain artificial sweeteners instead of glucose, so negating the claims to be a source of (metabolisable) energy.

Energy Requirements These are calculated from the basal metabolic rate and the energy expenditure.

Enrichment The addition of nutrients to foods. Although often used interchangeably, the term fortification is used for mandatory (legally imposed) additions, and enrichment means the voluntary addition of nutrients beyond the levels originally present.

E numbers An 'E' number is used as a 'short form' definition for food additives found on food labels. The 'E' prefix indicates the additive is approved for the use in the European Union and has been tested for safety.

Enteropathy Any disease or disorder of the intestinal tract.

Enzyme Enzymes are proteins produced by living cells and utilized by these cells to catalyze specific biochemical reactions. It is capable of catalyzing a reaction in which substrate (S) are converted to product (P) through the formation of an intermediate enzyme-substrate complex.

Enzyme, immobilized Enzyme bound physically to glass, plastic or other support, so permitting continuous flow processes, or recovery and re-utilisation of enzymes in batch processes.

Enzyme repression Reduction in synthesis of enzyme protein in response to a stimulus such as a hormone or the presence of large amounts of the end-product of a pathway.

Epiphysis The end of a long bone; it develops separately from the shaft (diaphysis) and later undergoes fusion to form the complete bone. This fusion is impaired in rickets.

ESR Electron spin resonance.

Ethane Hydrocarbon gas (C_2H_6) formed in small amounts by metabolism of oxidised linolenic acid and exhaled on the breath; used as an index of oxygen radical damage to tissue lipids, and indirectly as an index of antioxidant status. *See also* fatty acids; pentane.

Ethyl formate Used as a fumigant against insects such as raisin moth, dried fruit beetle and fig moth and as a flavour, an ingredient of artificial lemon, strawberry and rum flavours.

Exchange list List of portions of foods in which energy yield, fat, carbohydrate and/or protein content are equivalent, so simplifying meal and diet planning for people with special needs.

Exhaustion Exhaustion is the process whereby air is removed from cans before they are sealed. Removing the air reduces the stress on the metal during heat processing and cooling as well as reducing the risk from undesirable chemical changes inside the can such as the vitamin loss.

Extra lean Less than 5 g fat, less than 2 g saturated fat, and less than 95 mg cholesterol per serving and per 100 g.

Extrusion cooking Ingredients are heated under pressure, then extruded through fine pores, when the superheated water evaporates rapidly, leaving a porous textured product.

Exudative diathesis Vascular disease of vitamin E-deficient chicks, characterised by accumulation of greenish fluid under the skin of the breast and abdomen.

F

Faggot Traditional British meatball made from pig offal and meat. Or Bundle of herbs.

Fairtrade The Fairtrade mark is an independent consumer label which appears on products as an independent guarantee that disadvantaged producers in the developing world are getting a better deal.

Fasting Going without food. The metabolic fasting state begins some 4h after a meal, when the digestion and absorption of food are complete and body reserves of fat and glycogen begin to be mobilised. In more prolonged fasting the blood concentration of ketone bodies rises, as they are exported from the liver for use by muscle and other tissues as a metabolic fuel.

Fat free EU regulations restrict use of the term 'fat free' to foods that contain less than 0.15g of fat/100g; in the USA low-fat foods must state the percentage of fat; thus a product described as 95% fat free contains only 5g of fat/100g.

Fatty acid: Any of the group of a long chain of hydrocarbon with a carboxylic acid at the beginning and a methyl end, and derived from the breakdown of fats (through hydrolysis)

Fat, saturated Fats containing only or mainly saturated fatty acids.

Favism Acute haemolytic anaemia induced in genetically sensitive people by eating broad beans, *Vicia faba*, or in response to various drugs, including especially antimalarials.

Feeder kitchen A feeder kitchen is a place where Cook-chill or Cook-freeze food is reheated before it is eaten. The feeder kitchen should be next to the dining area, or in a hospital on the ward, as the food should be eaten within 15 minutes, after being reheated.

Fehling's reagent Alkaline cupric tartrate solution used for detection and semi quantitative determination of glucose and other reducing sugars.

Fermentation Anaerobic metabolism, used generally of alcoholic fermentation of sugars, also production of acetic, lactic, and citric acids by micro-organisms in pickling and manufacture of vinegar.

Ferric ammonium citrate The form in which iron is sometimes added to foods. Occurs as brown-red scales (16.5-18.5% iron) and as green scales (14.5-16% iron).

Fibrinogen One of the proteins of the blood plasma responsible for coagulation. When prothrombin is activated to thrombin in response to injury, it hydrolyses fibrinogen to fibrin, which is deposited as strands that trap red cells and platelets, forming the clot.

FIFO First In, First Out Policy An effective food rotation system in which the first lot of product received is used up before using lots received on later dates.

Fish hame Japanese product made from a red fish such as tuna or marlin, pickled with salt and nitrite, mixed with whale meat and pork fat and stuffed into a large sausage-type casing.

Fistula An abnormal connection between two hollow organs, or between a hollow organ and the external environment; may occur as a result of infection, injury or surgery.

Flash point With reference to frying oils, the temperature at which the decomposition products can be ignited, but will not support combustion; ranges between 290° and 330°C.

Fatulence (atus) Production of gas in the intestine - hydrogen, carbon dioxide and methane.May be caused by a variety of foods that contain atogens.

Flavour Enhancers Flavour enhancers are used to bring out the flavour in a wide range of savoury and sweet foods without adding a flavour of their own.

Favour profiles A method of judging the flavour of foods by examination of a list of the separate factors into which the flavour can be analysed, the so-called character notes.

Fluorine A mineral that occurs in the form of fluorides (salts). It is generally thought to protect teeth and gums against decay especially in young children.

Foams Formed when gas is mixed into a liquid (e.g. air whisked into egg white creates a foam).

Flagella Flagella (singular, flagellum) are hairlike structures that provide a means of locomotion for those bacteria that have them. They can be found at either or both ends of a bacterium or all over its surface. The flagella beat in a propeller-like motion to help the bacterium move toward nutrients; away from toxic chemicals; or, in the case of the photosynthetic cyanobacteria; toward the light.

Fow, streamline (or laminar) Flow of liquids in layers without significant mixing between layers.

Food balance A national account of the annual production of food, changes in stocks, imports and exports, and distribution of food over various uses in the country. Permits estimation of *per capita* food availability, but not consumption.

Food debris Food debris are bits of food which are formed by flaking or falling off the main body of food, *e.g.* bread crumbs from a loaf of bread.

Food handler Food handlers are people involved in the manufacturing, processing, distribution and retailing of food as well as catering. Food handlers may be in direct contact with food such as food production and catering staff or indirectly such as designers of food equipment or food production areas.

Food handlers The microbiota on the hands and outer garments of handlers generally reflect the environment and habits of individuals, and the organisms in question may be those from soil, water, dust, and other environmental sources.

Food science The study of the basic chemical, physical, biochemical and biophysical properties of foods and their constituents, and of changes that these may undergo during handling, preservation, processing, storage, distribution and preparation for consumption.

Food technology The application of science and technology to the treatment, processing, preservation and distribution of foods.

Foreign bodies This is a technical term referring to any extraneous matter, whether of a physical, chemical or biological nature found in food. Examples of foreign bodies are particles of paint, cleaning fluid and human hair. Usually foreign bodies render the food unfit for human consumption.

However foreign bodies also include particles of the wrong food such as a butter bean found in a tin of peas.

Free flow agents Alternative name for anticaking agents.

Free range The term "free-range" is typically used to refer to any animal that is permitted to roam free through fields, rather than being confined to a cage or enclosure. Free-range chickens are chickens that have access to grass for at least some of the day, and free-range eggs are the eggs that free-range chickens produce.

Freeze drying A method of drying in which the material is frozen and subjected to high vacuum. The ice sublimes off as water vapour without melting and also known as lyophilisation.

Freezing agents Compounds that reduce the temperature of foods through direct contact.

Fruitarian A person who eats only fruits, nuts and seeds; an extreme form of vegetarian.

Fudging Unplanned crystallization of sugar in a confection.

Fumaric acid Unsaturated dicarboxylic acid, used as an acidulant.

Functional foods Foods eaten for specified health purposes, because of their (rich) content of one or more nutrients or nonnutrient substances which may confer health benefits.

Furcellaran Danish agar; an anionic, sulphated polysaccharide extracted from the red alga, *Furcellaria fastigiata*, structurally similar to carrageenan; used as a gelling agent.

Fussol Monouoroacetamide, a systemic insecticide for treating fruit.

***F*-Value** It is defined as the number in minute at a specific temperature required to destroy a specified number of organisms having a specific *Z*–value. The *F*-value is a measure of the capacity of heat treatment to sterilize.

G

Galactans Polysaccharides composed of galactose derivatives; a major constituent of carageenan.

Galactorrhoea Abnormal secretion of milk, due to excessive secretion of prolactin.

Galactose A six-carbon monosaccharide (hexose), differing from glucose in orientation of the hydroxyl group on carbon-4. About one-third as sweet as sucrose. The main dietary source is the disaccharide lactose in milk, important in formation of the galactolipids (cerebrosides) of nerve tissue. *See also* carbohydrates; galactosaemia.

Galactosidase Enzyme (EC 3.2.1.23) that hydrolyses A. β-galactans in non-starch polysaccharides; responsible for loss of firmness during ripening and storage of fruits.

Gallates Salts and esters of gallic acid, found in many plants. Used in making dyes and inks,and medicinally as an astringent.Propyl, octyl and dodecyl gallates are legally permitted antioxidants in foods (E-310-312).

Gall bladder The gland in the liver that stores the bile before secretion into the small intestine.

Garam masala A mixture of aromatic spices widely used in Indian cooking; contains powdered black pepper, cumin, cinnamon, cloves, mace, cardamom seeds and sometimes also coriander and/or bay leaf.

Garlic mustard A common wild plant of hedgerows and woodland (*Alliaria petiolata*); the leaves have a garlic-like flavour and can be used in salads or cooked as a vegetable.

Gastrin Peptide hormone secreted by G-cells of the antrum of the stomach; stimulates parietal cells to secrete acid.

Gastroplasty Surgical alteration of the shape of the stomach without removing any part. Has been used to reduce the physical capacity of the stomach as a treatment for severe obesity.

Gastrointestinal tract: The intestinal biota consists of many organisms; notable among these are pathogens such as Salmonella, Compylobacter, E. coli 0157:H7, and other microorganism. Any or all of the Enterobacteriaceae may be expected in feces of livestock and poultry.

Gean Scottish name for the fruit of *Prunus avium*; also known as wild cherry, sweet cherry and mazzard.

Gelatine sugar Obsolete name for glycine.

Gellan gum A polysaccharide produced by fermentation of the bacterium *Sphingomonas elodea* (*Pseudomonas elodea*), used in some foods.

Gelling agents The most common gelling agent is pectin (E440), which is used to make jam. Gelling agents are used to change the consistency of food.

Gelatinization of starch It is a process of irreversible swelling of starch granules in water at suitable temperature, accompanied by a loss of birefringence and crystalinity. Galatinization is also known as the thickening of a liquid.

Giardiasis Intestinal inflammation and diarrhoea caused by infection with the protozoan parasite *Giardia lamblia*.

Gluten free Only foods which contain less than 20ppm of gluten can be labelled 'gluten-free'. This will include naturally gluten-free foods, specialist substitute products which may contain Codex wheat starch and pure, uncontaminated oats.

Glutelins Proteins insoluble in water and neutral salt solutions but soluble in dilute acids and alkalis, *e.g.* wheat glutenin.

Glycaemic Index The Glycaemic Index is a dietry index that is used to rank carbohydrate-based foods. The index forecasts the rate at which the food we eat will increase blood sugar levels. Low GI foods include brown rice, pulses, orange juice and porridge.

Glycosides Compounds of a sugar attached to another molecule; called glucosides when glucose is the sugar.

Good manufacturing practice (GMP) Part of a food and drink control operation aimed at ensuring that products are consistently manufactured to a quality appropriate to their intended use (detailed in Food and Drink Good Manufacturing Practice, IFST 1998).

Graham bread Whole sapce wheat bread in which the bran is very finely ground. Graham cakes are made from wholemeal flour and milk. The name is that of a miller of wholemeal flour who advocated its use in the USA (*Treatise on Bread and Bread Making*, 1837).

Grist Cereal for grinding.

Gums Substances used in food manufacture to stabilize emulsions.

Gustin Zinc-containing protein associated with taste.

GYE Guinness yeast extract.

H

Hachis Minced or chopped mixture of meat and herbs.

Haematemesis (hematemesis) Vomiting bright red blood, due to bleeding in the upper gastrointestinal tract.

Haemin (hemin) The hydrochloride of haematin, derived from haemoglobin. The crystals are readily recognisable under the microscope and used as a test for blood.

Haemoglobinometer (hemoglobinometer) Instrument to measure the amount of haemoglobin in blood by colorimetry.

Hair analysis Measurement of various minerals, including chromium, selenium and zinc in hair has been proposed as an index of status, but interpretation of the results is confounded by adsorption of minerals onto the hair from shampoo,etc.

Halal Food conforming to the Islamic (Muslim) dietary laws. Meat from permitted animals (in general grazing animals with cloven hooves, and thus excluding pig meat) and birds (excluding birds of prey). The animals are killed under religious supervision by cutting the throat to allow removal of all blood from the carcass, without prior stunning. Food that is not halal is haram.

Halophiles (halophilic bacteria) Able to grow at up to 25% salt. The growth of colonic bacteria is inhibited at 8-9% salt, *Clostridia* at 7-10%, food poisoning staphylococci at 15-20% and *Penicillium* at 20%. Film-forming yeasts can grow in 24% salt.

Halphen test For the presence of cottonseed oil in other oils and fats.

Hammer mill Continuous process mill in which material is powered by impact from a set of hammers. A modified hammer mill using knives instead of hammers is used to shred food.

Hangover Headache and feeling of malaise resulting from excessive consumption of alcoholic beverages. but to the presence of higher alcohols and esters (collectively known as congeners or fusel oil), the substances that give different beverages their distinctive flavours.

Hazard Agents in or conditions of food that have the potential to cause an adverse health effect or injury in consumers. A biological, chemical, allergenic or physical agent that is reasonably likely to cause illness or injury in the absence of a control.

Hazard analysis Hazard analysis means assessing the risks in a catering or manufacturing process and predicting where in the process the risks from microbial, physical and chemical contamination are greatest.

Health foods Substances whose consumption is advocated by various reform movements, including vegetable foods, whole grain cereals, food processed without chemical additives, food grown on organic compost, 'magic' foods (bees' royal jelly, kelp, lecithin, seaweed, etc.).

Hedonic scale Term used in tasting panels where the judges indicate the extent of their like or dislike for the food.

Heparin Complex carbohydrate (glycosaminoglycan) from mast cells in liver, lung, muscle, heart and blood which prevents blood coagulation by activating antithrombin III, and so inhibiting the conversion of prothrombin to thrombin. *In vivo* cleared rapidly from the bloodstream, but *in vitro* 10mg prevents the coagulation of 100 ml of blood

Hess test A test for capillary fragility in scurvy. A slight pressure is applied to the arm for 5 min when a shower of petechiae (small blood spots) appear on the skin below the area of application in vitamin C deficient subjects.

Hexamic acid Cyclohexyl sulphamic acid, the free acid of cyclamate.

High risk food High risk foods are foods at the greatest risk from microbial contamination, as they readily support microbial growth when kept within the danger zone. Hence high risk food should be stored either below 5°C or above 65°C. Unless sterilised then aseptically packed high risk food should have a 'Use By' date.

Hominy Prepared from dried maize kernels, also known as samp. Lye hominy - pericarp and germ removed by soaking in caustic soda. Pearled hominy - degermed hulled maize. Corn grits are ground hominy.

Hontarako Japanese; salted and dried cod roe.

Hovis A mixture of brown flavour and wheat germ; from Latin *hominis vis*, strength of man; originally, in the 1880s, called Smith's Old Patent Germ Bread. Now a trade name for various types of bread and flour.

Hurdle technology The concept of mild but effective food preser vation based on considering all the different factors that inhibit (or act as hurdles to) the growth of spoilage organisms.

Hydrogenation Conversion of liquid oils to semi-hard fats by the addition of hydrogen across carbon-carbon double bonds; used for margarines and shortenings intended for bakery products. *See* fatty acids, unsaturated.

Hydrolyse To split a complex compound into its constituent parts by the action of water, either enzymically or catalysed by the addition of acid or alkali. Hence hydrolysis.

Hydrophilic A solute that will dissolve in water and other polar solvents.

Hydrophobic A solute that will dissolve in non-polar solvents, but not in water.

Hydroponics The practice of growing plants without soil in a solution of inorganic salts.

Hygiene Hygiene is derived from the Greek goddess for health (Hygeia). The purpose of food hygiene is to ensure that the food we eat is healthy and free from contamination. Food hygiene is about protecting food from microbes, pests, physical and chemical contamination. The most important factors are temperature, time, cleanliness and keeping the food covered.

Hypotonic A solution more dilute than the body fluids, *See* isotonic.

Hydrothermal treatment Hydrothermal treatment of grain refers to the addition of moisture and heat to the grain for improving the quality and quantity of their end product or to facilitate different milling operation for the desired product. Hydrothermal treatment is commonly called conditioning or pre-milling treatment. It can be used for improving shelling efficiency, nutritional quality and milling qualities of paddy and for facilitating degermination and dehulling of corn and wheat.

Hyssop Pungent aromatic herb, *Hyssopus officinalis*, used in salads, soups and in making liquers.

I

Ice cream A frozen confection made from fat, milk solids and sugar. Low-fat ice cream contains not more than 3 g, and non-fat ice cream less than 0.5 g milk fat per serving.

Idli S.E. Asian; small cakes made from a mixture of cooked rice and black gram, fermented with the aid of mould.

Ileocolitis Inflammation of the ileum and colon.

Immunoglobulins Specific antibodies produced in the blood in response to foreign proteins or other antigens. Five classes, IgA, IgE, IgG, IgM and IgI; present in circulating blood as a result of previous exposure to the antigens, and also present in breast milk to confer passive immunity.

Indian gum Ghatti gum, polysaccharide exudate from the stems of *Anogeissus latifolia*.

Induction period The lag period during which a fat or oil shows stability to oxidation because of its content of natural or added antioxidants, which are oxidised preferentially. After this there is a sudden and large consumption of oxygen and the fat becomes rancid.

Ingrained dirt Ingrained dirt refers to liquid which has dried onto a surface making it difficult to clean. Often ingrained dirt attracts other dirt and debris by sticking to it, thus causing an accumulation of dirt which attracts microbes and pests.

Instant foods Dried foods that reconstitute rapidly when water is added *e.g.* Tea, coffee, milk, soups, precooked cereal products, potatoes. The dried powders may be agglomerated to control particle size and improve solubility. 'Instant puddings' are formulated with pre-gelatinised starch and disperse rapidly in cold milk.

Insulin resistance Resistance of target tissues to the actions of insulin, leading to hyperinsulinaemia and hyperglycaemia, commonly associated with abdominal adipose tissue. Only the metabolic actions of insulin are affected;the slower actions mediated via map kinases are unaffected, so there is an exaggerated mitotic response to insulin, causing increased proliferation of vascular smooth muscle, leading to atherosclerosis and hypertension.

Integrated cleaning Integrated cleaning is incorporating cleaning into the job of all food handlers whose work involves direct contact with food. Integrated cleaning includes Clean As You Go and cleaning schedules.

Intermediate moisture foods These are semi-moist with about 25% (15-50%) moisture but with some of the water bound (and so unavailable to micro-organisms) by the addition of glycerol, sorbitol, salt or certain organic acids, so preventing the growth of micro-organisms.

IQF Individual quick frozen or freezing.

Iron A mineral present in the blood and stored in the liver .Absorption of non haem iron is aided by vitamin C. Absorption of iron is reduced by the presence of phytatic acid and phosphate. Prolonged lack of iron leads to anaemia.

Irradiation Ionising radiation (X-rays, α-rays and γ-rays) kills microorganisms and insects, so is used for sterilisation of foods; also inhibits sprouting of potatoes.

ISO 9000 Quality Standard The international standard for the management of quality, widely used in the food industry, catering and food distribution, but developed originally for the engineering industry. ISO 9001 covers the specification for design, manufacture and installation;ISO 9002 the specification for manufacture and installation; ISO 9003 the specification for final inspection and test.

Isoenzymes Enzymes that have the same catalytic activity, but different structures, properties and/or tissue distribution.

Isotonic Solutions with the same osmotic pressure (concentration of solutes); often refers to a solution with the same osmotic pressure as body fluids. Hypertonic and hypotonic refer to solutions that are respectively more and less concentrated.

J

Jaboticaba Fruit of the tree *Myrciaria cauliora* with purple astringent skin and sweet white pulp; the fruits grow straight from the trunk.

Jaggery (1) Coarse dark sugar made from the sap of the coconut palm. (2) Raw sugar cane juice, used in India as sweetening agent, also known as gur.

Jam A conserve of fruit boiled to a pulp with sugar; sets to a pectin jelly on cooling (known in the USA as jelly). Standard jam, with certain exceptions, contains a minimum of 35g of fruit per 100g; extra jam, with certain exceptions, contains 45g.

Jasmine tea A perfumed or scented tea made by adding petals of jasmine flowers to Chinese tea.

Jaundice A condition in which there is an excess of bile pigment in the blood, and in which the pigment is deposited in the skin and the whites of the eyes, which have a yellow colour.

Jellied Cooked or preserved in a jelly.

Jelly Clear jam made from strained fruit juice by boiling with sugar. Table jelly is a dessert made from gelatine, sweetened and Savoury gelatine jelly made from calf's foot or gelatinous stock.

Jellyfish seaweed South-east Asian; strips of dried and salted jellyfish.

Jonathan Calcined, ground oat chaff, used in 19th century as adulterant for maize and other cereals.

Jowar Indian name for sorghum (*Sorghum vulgare*), also known as great millet, kaffir corn, guinea corn.

Juniper The ripened berries of the bush *Juniperis communis*, used as a flavouring in gin.

Junk food Food of little nutritional value, *e.g.* high-fat processed snacks or salted snacks eaten between or instead of meals.

Junket Dessert made from milk by treating with rennet to curdle the protein. flavoured; known in North America as jello.

Joint A piece of meat, especially one suitable for roasting pieces of meat for cooking.

Joint Meeting on Pesticide Residues A committee of the FAO that produces reports on the long-term toxicological effects of pesticide use. Abbreviation JMPR.

Joule A unit of energy used to show the energy content of foods and energy expenditure.

Juice Extractor A device for extracting juice from a fruit or vegetable.

Jus Traditional gravy, the reduced juice from cooked meat, served ~~as an~~ accompanied to meat.

K

Kaffir beer African beer brewed from millet.

Kamut Variety of durum wheat (*Triticum durum*). The flour is claimed to be higher in protein, and to cause fewer allergic reactions, than ordinary wheat.

Kanji Indian; alcoholic beverage made by fermentation of carrot or beetroot juice.

Karasumi Japanese; preserved roe of grey mullet or tuna.

Karl Fischer method For determination of the moisture content of dehydrated foods. Water is extracted from the sample into anhydrous methanol, then titrated against the Karl Fischer reagent (sulphur dioxide, pyridine and iodine in anhydrous methanol) with electrometric determination of the end-point

Kasnudln Austrian; egg and flair dough with sweet or savoury filling, a type of ravioli.

Katsuobushi East Asian, Indian; tuna dried and fermented with the mould *Aspergillus repens*; may also be smoked.

Kamaboko Japanese; foods prepared from surimi, but generally excluding more recently developed seafood analogues. Strictly, kamaboko is steamed or grilled on a wooden plate.

Kcal Abbreviation for kilocalorie (1000 calories), sometimes shown as Calotine.

Kedgeree Indian; dish of rice and pulses. Modified to Victorian breakfast dish of flaked fish with egg and rice.

Keratin The insoluble protein of hair, horn, hoof, feathers and nails. Not hydrolysed by digestive enzymes, and therefore nutritionally useless. Used as fertiliser, since it is slowly broken down by soil bacteria. Steamed feather meal is used to some extent as a supplement for ruminants.

Ketchup (catsup or catchup) From the Chinese *koechap* or *kitsiap*, originally meaning brine of pickled fish. Now used for spicy sauce or condiment made with juice of fruit or vegetables, vinegar and spices.

Kibble To grind or chop coarsely.

Kid Young goat (*Capra aegragus*) usually less than three months old; similar to lamb, but with a stronger flavour.

Kimchi Korean; dish based on fermented cabbage with garlic, red peppers and pimientos, often with the addition of fish and other foods.

Kipfel (kipfl) Austrian; crescent shaped roll created to celebrate the lifting of the siege of Vienna (1683). Reputedly the precursor of the croissant, believed to have been introduced to France by Marie Antoinette.

Klippfisk Salted and dried cod, mainly produced in Norway, also known as bacalao or bacalhau.The fish is boned, stored in salt for a month, washed and dried slowly. *See also* stockfish.

Kneading To work dough by stretching and folding until it achieves the required consistency.

Koji Japanese; koji mould (*Aspergillus oryzae*) grown on roasted cereal to provide a starter for fermentation to produce natto and mirin. *See also* miso.

Kolatchen Eastern European; sour cream biscuit made with flour, butter, sour cream and yeast, served warm.

Konnyaku Chinese, Japanese; flour made from tubers of the devil's tongue plant, *morphallus rivieri.*

Kpokpoi West African; small (2–3 mm) steamed balls of fermented maize or yam flour; similar to couscous (which is not fermented).

Kumis Squishy fermented product traditionally made from Mare's milk used as drink or medium in Asian nomads.

Kosher Food which is selected and prepared in accordance with Jewish dietary law.

Kuru Or trembling disease; progressive degeneration of central nervous system cells, associated with cannibalism in Papua-New Guinea, and believed to be caused by a prion. More or less eradicated since ritual cannibalism was abolished.

Kuzu Starch from the tubers of the kuzu (or kudzu) vine (*Pueraria lobata* or *P. thunbergiana*) used as a thickening agent in Chinese and Japanese cuisine.

Kyphosis Excessive outward curvature of the spine, causing hunching of the back. May result from collapse of the vertebrae in osteoporosis.

L

Lacquer With reference to canned foods, a layer of synthetic resin is coated onto the tinplate and hardened with heat. The layer of lacquer protects the tin lining from attack by acid fruit juices.

Lactobacillus Genus of bacteria capable of growth in acidic medium, and producing lactic acid by fermentation of carbohydrates. Responsible for souring of milk, and production of flavour in yogurt and other fermented milk products.

Lactogen A drug or other substance that increases the production and secretion of milk. Lactogenic hormone is prolactin.

Lactosucrose A trisaccharide (galactosyl-glucosyl-fructose) formed from sucrose and lactose by fructosyl transfer catalysed by invertase (EC 3.2.1.6). Considered to be a prebiotic.

Landrace Variety of plant or animal, highly adapted to local conditions, often associated with traditional agriculture.

Lanolin The fat from wool. Consists of a mixture of cholesterol oleate, palmitate and stearate, not useful as food; used in various cosmetics.

Lard compounds Blends of animal fats, such as oleostearin or premier jus, with vegetable oils, to produce products similar to lard in consistency and texture. *See also* lard substitutes.

Lauric acid A medium-chain length saturated fatty acid (C12:0) in butter, coconut oil and palm oil.

Leaching The process of extracting soluble compounds from a food with water or another solvent; may be deliberate (as, *e.g.*, in water extraction of sugar from beet, or solvent extraction of oil from oilseeds), or accidental, when vitamins and minerals leach into cooking water and`are lost.

Leaker spoilage When a can leakes any part of its contents is called as "leaker". This type of spoilage is caused due to (*i*) Faulty seaming (*ii*) Excessive internal pressure due to microbial spoilage or corrosion, (*iii*) Mechanical damage during handling and (*iv*) Internal or external corrosion. Leaker spoilage can be prevented by: chlorinating the cooling water; using a good quality of can; and carefully controlling the temperature and pressure changes during heat processing and cooling.

Leathers, fruit Fruit purées dried in air in thin layers, 4–5 mm thick, then built up into thicker preparations.

Lecithin Chemically lecithin is phosphatidyl choline; a phospholipid containing choline. Commercial lecithin, prepared from soya bean, peanut and maize, is a mixture of phospholipids in which phosphatidyl choline predominates. Used in food processing as an emulsifier, e.g. in salad dressing, processed cheese and chocolate, and as an antispattering agent in frying oils. Is plentiful in the diet and not a dietary essential.

Leghaemoglobin Haem-containing protein in the root nodules of leguminous plants that binds O_2 for transport within the root, and so permits the growth of obligate anaerobic nitrogen-fixing micro-organisms, *Rhizobium* spp.

Lemon grass Herb, *Cymbopogon* spp., with lemon flavour, used in South-east Asian cuisine; dried leaves are sereh powder.

Leucopoenia Decrease in the number of leucocytes in the blood.

Levans Polymers of fructose (the main one is inulin) that occur in tubers and some grasses.

Lieberkühn, crypts of Glands lining the small intestine which secrete the intestinal juice. ($C_{18}H_{32}O_{16}$)

Limburger Originally Belgian, strong flavoured soft cheese.

Limonin The bitter principle in the albedo of the Valencia orange. Isolimonin in the navel orange. Both are present as a non-bitter precursor which is liberated into the juice during extraction and is slowly hydrolysed, making the juice bitter.

Liposuction Procedure for removal of subcutaneous adipose tissue in obese people using a tube inserted through the skin at different locations.

Liptauer Hungarian; cheese spread made from sheep and cow milk.

Lithium Metal not known to have any physiological function, although it occurs in food and water; lithium salts are used in the treatment of bipolar manic-depressive disease.

Loonzein Rice from which the husk has been removed; also known as brown rice, hulled rice and cargo rice.

Low Cholesterol Contains 20 mg or less cholesterol and 2 grams or less saturated fat per serving.

Low-Risk Food Food that is unlikely to contain pathogenic micro-organisms and that (normally) will not support their growth due to the characteristics of the food (*e.g.* un-cooked grains and cereals, bread, carbonated beverages, sugar-based confectionary, alcohol).

Lymphatics Vessels through which the lymph flows, draining from the tissues and entering the bloodstream at the thoracic duct.

Lyophobic A solute that has little or no affinity for the solvent medium. When the solvent is water the term hydrophobic is used.

Lyxoflavin An analogue of riboflavin isolated from human heart muscle, containing the sugar lyxose; its function is unknown.

M

Macedoine Mixture of fruits or vegetables, diced, or cut into small even-shaped pieces.

Maconochie A canned meat stew much used in the First World War; made by Maconochie Brothers.

Madeira wines Fortified wines from the island of Madeira: sercial (dry); verdelho (semi-dry); bual (semi-sweet); malmsey (sweet).

Magma Mixture of sugar syrup and sugar crystals produced during sugar refining.

Marinade Richly spiced liquid used to give flavour and assist in tenderising meat and fish.

Maize flaked Partly gelatinised maize used for animal feed. The grain is cracked to small pieces, moistened, cooked and flaked between rollers.

Maize quality protein (QPM) A hybrid derived from the Opaque II strain, with a 10% higher yield than conventional maize, and 70–80% more tryptophan and lysine.

Malai Indian; cream prepared by boiling milk, leaving it to cool and then skimming off the clotted cream.

Malnutrition Disturbance of form or function arising from deficiency or excess of one or more nutrients.

Manchego Spanish sheep's milk hard cheese.

Maple syrup Sap of the north American sugar maple tree, *Acer saccharum*. Evaporated either to syrup (63% sucrose, 1.5% invert sugar) or to dry sugar for use in confectionery.

Marine biotoxins Toxins in shellfish and marine fish, either produced naturally or accumulated by the fish from their diet (includes ciguatera and paralytic shellfish poisoning).

Marmalade The name comes from the Portuguese *marmalada*, the quince, which was used to make preserves. Used in French and German to mean jam or preserve in general.

Marshmallow Soft sweetmeat made from an aerated mixture of gelatine or egg albumin with sugar or starch syrup. Originally, the root of the marshmallow plant (*Althaea officinalis*), which contains mucilage as well as starch and sugar, was used.

Meat bar Dehydrated cooked meat and fat; a modern form of pemmican; 50% protein and 40% fat; provides 560 kcal (2350 kJ)/100 g.

Meat curing Pickling with the aid of sodium chloride (salt), potassium nitrate (saltpetre) and sodium nitrite, which permits the growth of only salt-tolerant bacteria and inhibits the growth of *Clostridium botulinum*.

Meat extenders Textured vegetable protein added to meat products in place of some of the meat.

Meat reformed Comminuted, flaked or ground meat that has been bound and shaped to resemble a cut of whole meat. In the UK even if it resembles a steak, it may not be so-called.

Medium-Risk Foods These foods may contain pathogenic micro-organisms but will not normally support their growth due to the characteristics of the food. Usually they are acidic, dried or high in salt (more than 20%) or sugar (more than 50%).

Melangeur Mixing vessel consisting of rollers riding on a rotating horizontal bed. Used to mix substances of pasty consistency (hence melangeuring).

Melting point The temperature at which a compound melts to a liquid. Often characteristic of a particular chemical and used as a means of identification, and as an index of purity, since impurities lower the melting point.

Methylene blue dye-reduction test When the dye methylene blue is added to milk, any bacteria present take up oxygen and decolourise the dye.A similar test uses resazurin, which changes from blue-purple to pink. The speed of the change indicates the bacterial content.

Microbial contamination Microbial contamination is the addition of harmful microbes, either pathogens or spoilage organisms, to food fit for human consumption, making it unfit for human consumption.

Micronutrient Vitamins and minerals which are needed in small quantities for health.

Microwaves Microwaves are a type of high frequency radiation which are absorbed by water molecules, causing them to vibrate and move faster, hence producing heat. This heat can be used to cook and reheat food in microwave ovens.

Miki South-east Asian; noodles made from wheat flour, eggs and soda ash.

Minamata disease Poisoning by organic mercurial compounds, named after Minamata Bay in Japan, where fish contained high levels of organic mercurials during 1953–1956, as a result of mercury-rich industrial waste entering the river estuary.

Miso Japanese sauce, prepared from autoclaved soya beans mixed with cooked rice and partly fermented with *Aspergillus oryzae* and *A. sojae* to form koji.

Mocca Mixture of coffee and cocoa used in bakery and confectionery products.

Monkey orange Fruit of the southern African tree *Strychnos cocculoides*.

Monosodium glutamate (MSG) The sodium salt of glutamic acid, used to enhance flavour of savoury dishes and often added to canned meat and soups. First isolated from seaweed by Tokyo chemist Kimunae Ikeda in 1908; he called it ajinomoto (aginomoto), meaning 'the essence of taste'.

Mucilage Soluble but undigested polymers of the sugars arabinose and xylose found in some seeds and seaweeds; used as thickening and stabilising agents in food processing by virtue of their water-holding and viscous properties. *See also* gum.

Mysore flour A blend of 75% tapioca and 25% peanut flour.

N

NAD, NADP Nicotinamide adenine dinucleotide and nicotinamide adenine dinucleotide phosphate, the coenzymes derived from niacin. Involved as hydrogen acceptors/donors in a wide variety of oxidation and reduction reactions.

Nan Indian flat bread, egg dough prepared with white flour and leavened with sodium bicarbonate, normally baked in a tandoor.

Nanofiltration A membrane filtration process to separate particles with molecular weights from 200–1000 gmol^{-1}. or amu, using lower pressures than reverse osmosis.

Naseberry Alternative name for sapodilla.

Natto Japanese; soya bean fermented using *Bacillus natto*. Composition /100g: water 55g, 887kJ (212 kcal), protein 17.7 g, fat 11 g, carbohydrate 14.4 g, fibre 5.4 g, ash 1.9 g, Ca 217mg, Fe 8.6 mg, Mg 115 mg, P 174 mg, K 729 mg.

Necrosis Death of cells or tissues in an unprogrammed manner, in response to toxicity or ischaemia.

Neomycin Broad spectrum aminoglycoside antibiotic isolated from *Streptomyces fradii* that is poorly absorbed from the gastrointestinal tract and is used to treat persistent intestinal bacterial infections.

Net protein ratio (NPR)/net protein utilisation (NPU) Measures of protein quality.

Ninhydrin test For proteins and amino acids (actually for the amino group). Pink, purple or blue colour is developed on heating the amino acid or peptide with ninhydrin (Triketohydrindene hydrate).

Nitrites Found in many plant foods, since they are rapidly formed by the reduction of naturally occurring nitrate. Nitrite is the essential agent in preserving meat by pickling, since it inhibits the growth of *Clostridia*; it also combines with the myoglobin of meat to form the characteristic red nitrosomyoglobin.

Nitrogen conversion factor Factor by which total nitrogen content of a material (measured chemically, e.g. by the kjeldahl determination) is multiplied to determine the protein; depends on the amino acid composition of the proteins concerned. Wheat and most cereals 5.8, rice 5.95, soya 5.7, most legumes and nuts 5.3, milk 6.38, other foods 6.25. Errors arise if part of the nitrogen is non-protein nitrogen.

Non-conformity Non-fulfilment of a requirement that is a stated, generally implied or an obligatory need or expectation.

Non-essential amino acids Those amino acids that can be synthesised in the body and therefore are not dietary essentials.

Non Starch Polysaccharide (Fibre) (NSP) The indigestible part of food; cellulose (the cell wall of plants).

Noni (Indian mulberry) Fruit of the south Pacific evergreen shrub *Morinda citrifolia*, with an unpleasant odour; the juice is claimed to have healing properties and to be beneficial in treatment of diabetes, heart disease and cancer.

Noodles pasta made with flour from various grains (*e.g.* rice, wheat, buckwheat, mung bean starch) and water; may have egg also added.

Nucleoproteins The complex of proteins and nucleic acids found in the cell nucleus.

Nutmeg Dried ripe seed of *Myristica fragrans*; mace is the seed coat (arillus). Both mace and nutmeg are used as flavourings in meat products and bakery goods.

Nutrification The addition of nutrients to foods at such a level as to make a major contribution to the diet.

Nutritional disorder Any morbid process or functional abnormality of the body due to the consumption of a diet not conforming to physiological requirements, or to failure in absorption or utilisation of the food after ingestion.

Nutrition surveillance Monitoring the state of health, nutrition, eating behaviour and nutrition knowledge of a given population for the purpose of planning and evaluating nutrition policy. Especially in developing countries, monitoring may include factors that may be potential causes of nutritional emergencies, in order to give early warning of such emergencies.

Nutro-biscuit Indian; biscuit baked from a mixture of 60% wheat flour and 40% peanut flour; contains 16–17% protein.

Nystagmus Rapid involuntary movement of the eyes, as when following a moving object; may also occur as a result of a congenital defect, and in the Wernicke–Korsakoff syndrome due to vitamin B_1 deficiency.

O

Obesity Excessive accumulation of body fat, a body mass index (BMI) above 30 kg/m^2 is considered to be obesity (and above 40 gross obesity).

Obstipation Extreme and persistent constipation caused by obstruction of the intestinal tract.

Octave A cask for wine containing one-eighth of a pipe, about 59 L (13 imperial gallons).

Odontoblasts Cells in teeth, lining the pulp and forming dentine.

Offal Corruption of 'off-fall'. (1) With reference to meat, the term includes all parts that are cut away when the carcass is dressed, including liver, kidneys, brain, spleen, pancreas, thymus, tripe and tongue. Known in the USA as organ meats or variety meat.(2) With reference to wheat, offal is the bran discarded when milled to white flour.

Ohmic heating Sterilisation by heat generated by passing an electric current through the food or mixture.

Oilseed A wide variety of seeds grown as a source of oils, *e.g.* cottonseed, sesame, groundnut, sunflower, soya, and nuts such as coconut, groundnut and palm etc. After extraction of the oil the residue is a valuable source of protein, especially for animal feeding stuffs, oilseed cake.

Olallie berry Cross between loganberry and youngberry.

Oleoresins In the preparation of some spices such as pepper, ginger and capsicum, the aromatic material is extracted with solvents which are evaporated off, leaving behind thick oily products known as oleoresins.

Olive *Olea europaea*; picked unripe when green or ripe when they have turned dark blue or purplish, and usually pickled in brine or used as a source of oil. Olives have been known since ancient times. The tree is extremely slow growing and continues to fruit for many years; there are claims that trees are still fruiting after 1000 years. Composition /100 g: water 75.3 g, 607 kJ (145 kcal), protein 1 g, fat 15.3 g, carbohydrate 3.8 g, fibre 3.3 g, ash 4.5 g, Ca 52mg, Fe 0.5mg, Mg 11mg, P 4mg, K 42mg,

Omega 3, 6 & 9 groups of fatty acids The Omega 3, 6 and 9 groups of fatty acids all contain essential fatty acids necessary for good health. Omega fatty acids are polyunsaturated fats. They are healthier than saturated fats and have many metabolic functions. There are many benefits of omega 3,6,9 supplementation. Omega 3 and omega 6 fatty acids are essential fatty acids (EFA's). Our bodies cannot manufacture them, and we must consume them in our diets. Omega 9 fatty acids are not essential. Our bodies need omega 9 fats, but we can manufacture them from other sources.

Omega-3 (ω, 3) marine triglycerides A mixture of triacylglycerols (triglycerides) rich in two long-chain polyunsaturated fatty acids, eicosapentaenoic acid (EPA, C20:5 ω, 3) and docosahexaenoic (DHA, C22:6 ω, 3).

Oncom Indonesian; fermented groundnut and soybean press cake with cassava, fermented with moulds: *Neurospora sitophila* to produce a red product or *Rhizopus oligosporus* for a grey product.

Onion Japanese bunching *Allium fistulosum*, similar to Welsh onion (*see* onion, welsh), but larger.

Oral rehydration Administration of an isotonic solution of salt and glucose (or sucrose) to replace fluid and electrolytes lost in diarrhoea.

Orange butter Chopped whole orange, cooked, sweetened and homogenised.

Organic foods Plants grown without the use of synthetic pesticides fungicides or organic fertilizers. They must have been prepared without preservatives.

Osmolality Concentration of osmotically active particles per kg of solvent.

Osmolarity Concentration of osmotically active particles per litre of solution.

Osmosis The passage of water through a semipermeable membrane, from a region of low concentration of solutes to one of higher concentration.

Osmosis, reverse The passage of water from a more concentrated to a less concentrated solution through a semipermeable membrane by the application of pressure. Also called as *hyperfiltration*.

Osteoporosis Degeneration of the bones with advancing age due to loss of bone mineral and protein, this is largely a result of loss of hormones with increasing age (oestrogens in women and testosterone in men).

Ovalbumin The albumin of egg white; comprises 55% of the total solids.

Oven spring The sudden increase in the volume of dough during the first 10–12 min. of baking, due to increased rate of fermentation and expansion of gases.

Overall heat transfer coefficient (OHTC) The sum of the resistances to heat flow due to conduction and convection.

Oxycalorimeter Instrument for measuring the oxygen consumed and carbon dioxide produced when a food is burned, as distinct from the calorimeter, which measures the heat produced.

Ozone O_3 It is a pale blue gas with a distinctively pungent smell. A powerful germicide, used to sterilise water and in antiseptic ice for preserving fish.

Oyster crabs American; small young crabs found inside oysters, cooked and eaten whole, including the soft shell.

P

Pacificarins Compounds present in foods that resist microorganisms; they may be of microbial origin or synthesised by the plant itself. Also known as phytoncides.

Packaging active Packaging that changes the condition of the packed food to extend its shelf life or improve safety or sensory properties, while maintaining quality. May include oxygen scavengers, desiccants and antimicrobial compounds.

Packaging, green Use of biodegradable materials to replace conventional plastics in food packaging.

Packaging, intelligent Packaging system that monitors the condition of packaged foods to give information about its quality during transport and storage.

Palestine soup English, 19th century, made from Jerusalem artichokes and named in the mistaken belief that the artichokes came from Jerusalem.

Palmitic acid A saturated fatty acid with 16 carbon atoms (C16:0), widespread in fats, waxes and oils.

Palmitoleic acid A omega-7 mono-unsaturated fatty acid that is found in plant lives.

Paneer Indian, Middle Eastern; soft mild-flavoured cheese.Milk is left to ferment for 6–12 hr, then heated to separate the curd.

Papain Proteolytic enzyme is obtained as the dried latex on the skin of the fruit by scratching it while still on the tree, and collecting the low.

Paratha Indian; wholewheat unleavened bread.

Parboiling Parboiling is a hydrothermal treatment followed by drying before milling for the product of milled parboiled grain. The objective of parboiling is to provide extra strength to the grain kernel consequently improving its milling characteristics.

Parnut foods Foods for particular nutritional used. For example, foods for people with coeliac disease.

Parity The number of pregnancies that a woman has had that have resulted in the birth of an infant capable of survival.

Paromomycin Antibiotic used to treat intestinal bacterial infections and amoebic dysentery.

Pasteurisation A means of prolonging the storage time of foods for a limited time, by killing the vegetative forms of many pathogenic organisms.

Pastry Baked dough of flour, fat and water. Six basic types: shortcrust in which the fat is rubbed into the flour; suet crust in which chopped suet is mixed with the flour; puff and flaky, in which the fat is rolled into the dough.

PDCAAS Protein digestibility corrected amino acid score; a measure of protein quality based on amino acid score, corrected for the digestibility of the protein.

Penicillamine Chelating agent used to enhance the excretion of copper in wilson's disease.

Peptide bond A link between amino acids used in the formation of dipeptides polypeptides and proteins.

Peptones Small polypeptides that are intermediate products in the hydrolysis of proteins. The term is often used for any partial hydrolysate of protein, e.g. bacteriological peptone, used as a growth medium for micro-organisms.

PER Protein efficiency ratio, a measure of protein quality.

Pericarp The fibrous layers next to the outer husk of cereal grains and outside the testa; of low digestibility and removed from grain during milling. The major constituent of bran.

Perishable Any food product or ingredient that is susceptible to deterioration or loss of quality when subjected to temperature abuse.

Persian berry Yellow colour obtained from the berries of the buckthorn, *Rhamnus* spp.; legally permitted in food in most countries. Contains the glucosides of rhamnetin and rhamnazin.

Physical contamination Strictly speaking physical contamination should refer to the addition of extraneous matter to food not directly of biological origin such as paper, paint or glass, but legally the term refers to all contamination of a non-microbial source, including human hair, parts of insects and cleaning fluids.

Pizza Originally Italian; savoury tart on a base of yeast dough, traditionally cooked in a wood-burning oven. The topping varies with region and may contain tomatoes, cheese, salami or seafood etc..

Pomes Botanical name for fruits such as apple or pear, formed by the enlargement of the receptacle which becomes fleshy and surrounds the carpels.

Potable Any liquid suitable for drinking.

Potassium sorbate Potassium salt of sorbic acid (E-202).

Preservatives Substances capable of retarding or arresting the deterioration of food; examples are sulphur dioxide, benzoic acid, specified antibiotics, salt; acids and essential oils.

Preserving food Preserving food involves indirect methods of protecting food from microbes whilst processing involves direct methods such as heat treatment. Pickling in vinegar, salting and adding sugar are methods used in preserving food.

Prickly pear Fruit of the *Opuntia* spp., also called Indian fig, barberry fig, tuna or sabra fruit, an important part of the diet in certain areas of Mexico.

Product tampering Product tampering is when people (human pests) deliberately and often maliciously add physical or chemical (or even microbial) contaminants to food either, for blackmail, revenge or other nefarious reason. Being more intelligent than other pests, human pests are often the hardest to control and protect food from them.

Potato starch Or farina, prepared from potato tuber and widely used as a stabilising agent when gelatinised by heat.

Prototype A sample product to be used for trial, test and market research.

Pure The term "pure" is mostly used on single ingredient foods (*e.g.* to indicate a single, named variety of rice) or to highlight the quality of ingredients of a food (*e.g.* "pure butter shortbread" to indicate the butter has not been blended with other fats).

Puri (poori) Indian; unleavened wholewheat bread prepared from a butter-rich dough, shaped into small pancakes and deep fried in hot oil.

Q

QPM Quality protein maize.

Quail A small game bird of the partridge family that resembles a small, plump chicken. Known also as "bobwhites" and "partridges." The flesh is white and delicately flavored. Most quail today are raised on bird farms.

Quality assurance The planned actions necessary to provide adequate confidence that a product will satisfy requirements for quality.

Quality control The operational techniques and activities that are used to fulfil requirements for quality.

Quality policy The overall quality intentions and direction of an organisation, formally expressed by management.

Quality system The organisational structure, responsibilities, procedures and resources for implementing quality management

Quantitative ingredient declaration (QUID) The requirement for the amount of a particular ingredient used in a foodstuff to be included on its labelling, in cases where this may be misleading or confusing, *e.g.* the actual amount of juice used in a 'juice drink'.

Quercitin A flavonol (*see* flavonoids) is found in onion skins, tea, hops and horse chestnuts and many fruits and vegetables leaves and grains. It has a bitter flavor and is used as an ingredient in dietary supplements, beverages and foods.

Quick breads Baked goods such as biscuits, muffins, popovers, griddles, cakes, waffles and dumplings, in which no yeast is used. The raising is carried out quickly with baking powder or other chemical agents.

Quick freezing Rapid freezing of food by exposure to a blast of air at a very low temperature. Unlike slow freezing, very small crystals of ice are formed, which do not rupture the cells of the food and so the structure is relatively undamaged. A quickfrozen food is commonly defined as one that has been cooled from a temperature of 0 °C to – 5° or lower, in a period of not more than 2h and then cooled to – 18°C.

Quiche A savoury tart made of a pastry case filled with a mixture of eggs and milk, with other ingredients such as onion, bacon, vegetables or cheese added.

Quid Most pre-packed foods have to be marked with an ingredients list. In addition foods which are characterised by particular ingredients or which have ingredients particularly mentioned in their name are required to have the percentage of those ingredients shown in the ingredients list.

Quiescent cooling, quiescent freezing Slow cooling and freezing of a food mixture without stirring, leading to the formation of ice crystals.

Quince This yellow-skinned fruit looks and tastes like a cross between an apple and a pear. Its texture and flavor make it better cooked than raw. Its high pectin content makes it ideal for use in jams, jellies and preserves.

Quinine Bitter alkaloid extracted from bark of the cinchona tree (*Cinchona officinalis*), formerly used to treat or prevent malaria and in apéritif wines, bitters and tonic water.

Quinoa Pronounced (KEEN-wah), Quinoa is a protein rich grain which is also high in unsaturated fat and lower in carbohydrates than most grains. It may be used in any dish in place of rice or similar grains. A tiny golden seed from South America that is similar to rice but has a higher protein content.

Quintal 100 kg (220 lb).

Quorn A product contains mycoprotein as an ingredient, which is derived from the Fusarium venenatum fungus and is grown by fermentation. Provides a good source of protein and which can be used as a meat substitute. A trade name for a vegetable protein used in cooking as a meat substitute.

R

Radappertisation Sterilisation of food by high-dose irradiation for destruction of (virtually) all organisms.

Radicidation Low-level irradiation treatment to kill non-spore forming pathogens and prevent food poisoning; less severe treatment than radappertisation.

Raffinose Trisaccharide, galactosyl-glucosyl-fructose, found in cotton seed, sugar-beet molasses and Australian manna; also known as gossypose, melitose or melitriose. 23% of the sweetness of sucrose. It is not digested easily.

Raisin Dried seedless grapes of several kinds. Valencia raisins

Raita A yogurt salad consisting of yogurt and a variety of chopped vegetables, fruits and flavored with garam masala, herbs and black mustard seeds. Raita originates from East India

Raftilose TM Fructo-oligosaccharide derived from inulin, a prebiotic.

Ragi *Eleusine coracana*, or **finger millet (Ragi)**, is an annual herbaceous plant widely grown as a cereal crop in the arid and semiarid areas in Africa and Asia. It is a tetraploid and self-pollinating species.

Rancidity The development of unpleasant flavours in oils and fats as a result of lipase action or oxidation.

Rasgulla Indian; dessert of small balls of milk curd, ground almond and semolina, boiled in syrup.

RDA Recommended daily (or dietary) allowance (or amount) of nutrients.

Razor clam A long, thin, razor-shaped clam, considered one of the most delicious of clams; eaten raw or cooked.

Recall Process of removing sold and unsold food products from market that do not meet legally required safety or company standards.

Recipe Sometimes called formulation in industry, it is the ratio and combination of ingredients required to make a successful product.

Red cooking Chinese method of cooking; meat or poultry is first stir fried, then simmered in broth or water.

Redox potential Oxidation/reduction potential, the potential of an electrode in a 1 mol /L solution of each of the oxidant and reductant, relative to a hydrogen electrode.

Reference man, woman An arbitrary physiological standard; defined as a person aged 25, weighing 65kg, living in a temperate zone of a mean annual temperature of 10°C. Reference man performs medium work, with an average daily energy requirement of 13.5MJ (3200kcal). Reference woman is engaged in general household duties or light industry, with an average daily requirement of 9.7MJ (2300kcal).

Reformed Reformed meat has the appearance of a cut, slice or joint of meat, formed by tumbling chopped meat; also finely comminuted meat and other ingredients may be added to bind the pieces together in a pre-ordained shape.

Relish Culinary term for any spicy or piquant preparation used to enhance flavour of plain food.

Remoulade This classic French sauce (or salad dressing) is made by combining mayonnaise (usually homemade) with mustard, capers and chopped gherkins, herbs and anchovies. It is served chilled as an accompaniment to cold meat, fish and shellfish.

Renin Proteolytic enzyme (angiotensin-forming enzyme, angiotensinogenase, EC 3.4.23.15) secreted by the kidney; specific for the leucine–leucine bond in angiotensinogen, yielding angiotensin I. This is then cleaved to yield active angiotensin II by the angiotensin converting enzyme (ace, EC 3.4.15.1), a peptidase in the blood vessels of the lungs and other tissues.

Rennet is a complex set of enzymes produced in the stomachs of ruminant mammals. Chymosin, its key component, is a protease enzyme that curdles the casein in milk. In addition to chymosin, rennet contains other enzymes, such as pepsin and a lipase.

Respiration: It can be described as the oxidative break down the most complex material normally present in the cell into simpler molecules or Metabolic activity of living animal or plant tissues.

Respiratory quotient (RQ) Ratio of the volume of carbon dioxide produced when a substance is oxidised to the volume of oxygen used. The oxidation of carbohydrate results in an RQ of 1.0; of fat, 0.7; and of protein, 0.8.

Rice noodles Noodles made with rice flour in very long strands and of varying thicknesses and widths, very common in Vietnam.

Rice vinegar Japanese; vinegar prepared from saké.

Ricing Culinary term: cutting into small pieces about the size of rice grains.

Ricotta Rich, fresh, moist cheese resembling cottage cheese, that may be made with whole or skim milk. Originally Ricotta was made from sheep's milk.

Rigor mortis The soft pliable muscle becomes stiff and rigid. If meat is hung in a cool place for a few days ('conditioned'), the meat softens again. Fish similarly undergo rigor mortis usually of shorter duration than in mammals.

Roll-on closure (RO) Aluminium or lacquered tinplate cap for sealing on to narrow-necked bottles with a threaded neck. The unthreaded cap is moulded on to the neck of the bottle and forms an airtight seal.

Roquefort Green-blue marbled French cheese made in Roquefortsur-Soulzon from ewe's milk; ripened in limestone caves where the mould, *Penicillium roquefortii* is present and inoculates the cheese.

Roughage Dietary fibre, fibrous indigestible material in vegetable foodstuffs which aids the passage of food and waste products through the gut.

Royal jelly The food on which bee larvae are fed and which causes them to develop into queen bees.

RPV Relative Protein value, a measure of protein quality.

Rum Spirit distilled from fermented sugar cane juice or molasses traditionally darker and more strongly flavoured.

Ryle tube A narrow rubber tube with a blind end containing a dead weight, with holes above this level, for removing samples of the contents from the stomach at intervals after a test meal.

S

Sabayon A frothy custard of egg yolk, sugar, and wine that is made by whisking the ingredients over simmering water. Served warm as a dessert or sauce.

Salination, salinization A process by which the salt concentration of soil or water increases, especially as a result of irrigation in hot climates.

Salmon A succulent fish that lives most of its life in the sea but returns to freshwater to spawn. Salmon is usually available whole, cut into steaks or fillets, or canned. Fresh salmon can be poached, grilled or baked.

Salt Cellar a small pot containing salt usually with a hole in the top so that it can be sprinkled on food.

Saltimbocca An Italian dish comprised of thin slices of veal, rolled around ham and cheese, seasoned with sage and braised in butter until tender.

Samosa An Indian dish consisting of a small triangular pastry containing spiced meat or vegetables, usually deep-fried and served as a starter or snack.

Sanitiser A sanitiser is a cleaner which contains both detergents and disinfectants. To sanitise is to reduce the number of microbes to a safe acceptable level. If the surfaces or equipment, to be cleaned, are very dirty or contain a very large number of microbes a separate detergent and disinfectant should be used.

Sauerkraut German, Dutch, Alsatian; prepared by lactic fermentation of shredded cabbage. In the presence of 2–3% salt, acid forming bacteria thrive and convert sugars in the cabbage into acetic and lactic acids, which then act as preservatives.

Sausage Chopped meat, commonly beef or pork, seasoned with salt and spices, mixed with cereal (usually wheat rusk prepared from crumbed unleavened biscuits) and packed into casings.

Sausage casings Natural casings are made from hog intestines for fresh frying sausages, and from sheep intestines for chipolatas and frankfurters, now mainly replaced by artificial casings made from cellulose, polyvinyl dichloride or collagen. Skinless sausages are prepared in cellulose casing, which is then peeled off.

Scaling up Increasing a recipe for bulk production while keeping the ratio and proportions the same.

Scup American term for various food and game fish of the sea bream family, especially *Senostomus* spp.

Sensitivity Of an assay; the smallest amount that can be determined with acceptable precision.

***Shigella* spp.** Food-poisoning organisms that invade intestinal epithelial cells and cause dysentery. Infective dose 102–105 organisms; onset 1–7 days; duration weeks; TX 4.1.4.1. The genus is named after Kiyoshi Shiga, who first discovered it in 1897.

Silica gel Sodium silicate, used as a drying agent in packaging. It can be regenerated by heating to drive off adsorbed water.

Single cell oil Fats produced by fungi or bacteria growing on a non-fat substrate.

Single cell protein Collective term used for biomass of bacteria, algae and yeast, and also (incorrectly) moulds, of potential use as animal or human food.

Sling Drink made from gin and fruit juice.

Soggy A cake that is damp and heavy in the centre due to excess moisture, lack of raising agent or incorrect baking temperature.

Smoke point The temperature at which the decomposition products of frying oils become visible as bluish smoke. The temperature varies with different fats, ranging between 160 and 260°C.

Sorbet A water-ice containing sugar, water and flavouring (commonly fruit juice or pulp). Also known as sherbet or granita.

Spillages Spillages are powders or liquids which escape from their container, causing a mess on floors, walls or work or equipment surfaces. If not cleaned up immediately food spillages attract microbes and pests and liquid food spillages become engrained onto surfaces making them harder to clean.

Spina bifida Congenital neural tube defect due to developmental anomaly in early embryonic development. Supplements of folic acid begun before conception reduce the risk.

Spinkganz German; goose breast, dry-brined and smoked.

Spores Spores are produced by some species, and they are resistant to hostile conditions such as heat and drying. They serve as survival mechanisms when environmental conditions are not suitable for growth and replication.

Sports drinks Solutions of glucose plus electrolytes to mimic those lost in sweat; generally isotonic with blood plasma to avoid potential problems of water intoxication. Sometimes known as 'bottled sweat'

Spoilage Food spoilage is the process whereby food fit for human consumption becomes unfit due to changes brought about either by microbes, pests or chemicals within the food. Microbes and pests can spoil food rapidly whilst chemical changes within food usually take longer time for spoilage.

Staling The crystalline structure of starch is lost during baking. Subsequently it recrystallises (undergoes retrogradation) and in bread the crumb loses its softness. Staling can be delayed by emulsifiers (crumb softeners) such as polyoxyethylene and monoglyceride derivatives of fatty acids. Retrogradation of starch also takes place in dehydrated potatoes.

Staph. aureus *Staphylococci aureus* is derived from the Greek, meaning golden bunches of grapes and berries, as *Staph. aureus* are small spherical clamps (which look like bunches under the microscope) which are non-spore forming but produce a heat resistant toxin. The toxin is responsible for a type of food poisoning which lasts between 6 and 24 hours. Fatalities from this food poisoning are rare. The main risk of Staph, aureus food poisoning comes from poor personal hygiene, especially the mouth or nose to hand to food route.

Starter Culture of bacteria used to inoculate or start growth in a fermentation, *e.g.* milk for cheese production, or butter to develop the flavour.

Steam baking An even temperature is maintained in the oven by means of closed pipes through which steam circulates. It is sometimes erroneously assumed that the bread is baked in steam.

Sterilization Sterilization is a heat treatment process in which we can destroy the microorganisms and harmful pathogens completely from product at specified time and temperature combination.

Sterilization of product is done at 121.1°C for 2 to 5 minute. The thermal conditions needed to produce commercial sterility depend on following factors;

* Nature of the food (*e.g.* pH)
* Storage condition of the food
* Heat resistance of the microorganisms or spores
* Heat transfer characteristics of the food, its container and the heating medium
* Initial load of microorganisms

Strain Horticultural term for seed-raised plants exhibiting certain characteristics, which are not stable or predictable enough when propagated to be a cultivar.

Stock rotation Stock rotation means using oldest stock first, to ensure that food is used within its 'Use By' or 'Best Before' date. This is to prevent stock losses and reduce the chance of pest attack.

Sucking pig Piglet aged 4–5 weeks, usually stuffed and roasted whole.

Syneresis Usually refers to eggs; if overcooked, the proteins shrink as they coagulate and separate from the watery liquid.

Syrup, high fructose Glucose syrup made by hydrolysis of starch and then half the glucose converted into fructose, similar to invert syrup produced from sucrose but cheaper. Also known as iso-syrups, high-fructose syrups (HFS), high-fructose corn syrups (HFCS). *See also* glucose isomerase.

T

Tamal (tamales) Mexican; maize meal pancake, similar to tortilla, but made with fat. Traditionally cooked inside the soft husks of maize.

Tandoori (tanduri) Indian term for food cooked in a clay oven (tandoor).The meat is marinated with aromatic herbs and spices before cooking.

Tankage Residue from slaughterhouse excluding all the useful tissues; used as fertiliser or (formerly) animal feed.

Tapas Spanish; small savoury dishes served with wine in bars.

Tapé Indonesian; sweet-sour alcoholic paste made from fermented cassava, millet or maize, using a ragi starter. Either sundried and used in soups and stews or deep fried as a snack.

Taro Corm of *Colocasia esculenta* and *C. antiquorum*; called eddo or dasheen in Caribbean, old cocoyam in W. Africa.

Tart A pastry case usually filled with sweet food, but sometimes also savoury bitter in flavour.

Tartaric acid Occurs in fruits, the chief source is grapes; used in preparing lemonade, added to jams when the fruit is not sufficiently acidic (citric acid is also used) and in baking powder (E-334).

Temperature Abuse A situation that arises when food is not held at the proper temperature (*e.g.* keeping raw meat at room temperature for more than two hours before cooking).

Tenderometer Instrument to measure the stage of maturity of peas to determine whether they are ready for cropping or the tenderness of meat. Measures the force required to effect a shearing action.

Tetraenoic acid Fatty acid with four double bonds, e.g. arachidonic acid.

Tetramine poisoning Paralysis similar to that caused by curare, caused by a toxin in the salivary glands of the red whelk, *Neptunea antiqua* (distinct from the edible whelk *Buccinum undatum*).

Texture Combination of physical properties perceived by senses of kinaesthesis muscle–nerve endings), touch (including mouthfeel), sight and hearing.

Textured Vegetable Protein (TPV) TVP is a meat substitute made from soya flour that has been processed and dried.

TGS Trichlorogalactosucrose. (WHO Food additive series 28)

Theaflavins Reddish-orange pigments formed in tea during fermentation; responsible for the colour of tea extracts and part of the astringent flavour.

Thawing is the process of taking a frozen product from frozen to a temperature (usually above 0°C) where there is no residual ice, *i.e.* "defrosting". ***Thawing*** is often considered as simply the reversal of the freezing process. However, inherent in ***thawing*** is a major problem that does not occur in the freezing operation. Thawing is not done at room temperature or in warm water.

Thermal centre The point in a food that heats or cools most slowly.

Thermal conductivity The rate at which heat moves through a substance.

Thermal runaway Thermal runaway is when the microwaves are focused, usually by round objects such as apples, causing localised burning whilst other areas receive insufficient heat. This problem can be reduced by turning the food and allowing standing time during and after cooking.

Thermography Technique for measuring and recording heat output by regions of the body, using a film or detector sensitive to infrared radiation.

Thiochrome Fluorescent product of the oxidation of thiamine (vitamin b_1) in alkaline solution; the basis of an assay of the vitamin.

Thrombin Plasma protein involved in the coagulation of blood, formed in the circulation by partial proteolysis of prothrombin.

Thyroglobulin The protein in the thyroid gland which is the precursor for the synthesis of the thyroid hormones as a result of iodination of tyrosine residues.The thyroid-stimulating hormone (thyrotropin) stimulates hydrolysis of thyroglobulin and secretion of the hormones into the bloodstream.

Tofu Soya bean curd, which can be used in stir fried meals and stews.

Tolerance levels The levels within which a process works safely and effectively.

TPN Total parenteral nutrition. Method of feeding that bypasses the gastrointestinal tract.

TQM Total quality management. It is a goal in which every individual in every department of an organization is dedicated to quality control and quality improvement.

Traditional The term "traditional" is widely used to describe a product or method of preparation when newer alternatives are available on the market. It implies more than "original" or "plain".

Trusoy Trade name of heat-treated full-fat soya flour.

Tuo zaafi African; sorghum or millet gruel left overnight to undergo a lactic acid fermentation.

Tyrosine An amino acid in protein that is a component of thyroxine and is a precursor to the catecholamines dopamine, noradrenaline and adrenaline.

Tyrosinosis Genetic disease due to lack of *p*-hydroxyphenylpyruvate oxidase (EC 1.13.11.27), affecting the metabolism of tyrosine and leading to excretion of *p*-hydroxyphenylpyruvate in the urine. Treatment is by restriction of dietary intake of phenylalanine and tyrosine.

Tyramine An enzyme found in cheese, beans, tinned fish, red wine and yeast extract that can cause high blood pressure if found in excessive quantities in the brain, monoamine oxidase.

U

Udon Japanese; fine transparent noodles made from wheat.

Ugli fruit A naturally occurring hybrid of the grapefruit and mandarin with a very rough blemished peel and soft juicy orange flesh, found growing wild in Jamaica in 1914.

Ulcerative colitis Inflammation of the rectum and colon with ulcers.

Ulcerative gingivitis Painful inflammation of the gums accompanied by the formation of ulcers, a condition associated with bacterial infection and malnutrition.

Ullage Air space left in cask or bottle after some liquid has been removed.

Ultrafiltration Procedure for removal of low molecular weight compounds from plasma, protein solutions, etc., using a semipermeable membrane and either hydrostatic pressure or centrifugation.

Ultra high temperature Ultra heat treated something such as milk that has undergone a process of sterilisation at very high temperatures for a very short time. Abbreviation UHT.

Ultrapasteurised Milk that has undergone UHT pasteurisation.

Ultrasound Sound above the normal range of human hearing, commonly above 20kHz.

Ultraviolet The range of invisible radiation wavelengths just greater than those of the visible spectrum. Abbreviation UV.

Ultra Violet Irradiation Used for surface sterilization, for tenderising and ageing meat, curing cheese and preventing the growth of moulds on the surface of baked products.

Umami Name given to the special taste of monosodium glutamate, some other amino acids, protein and the ribonucleotides (inosinate and guanylate). The Japanese name for a savoury flavour, now considered one of the five basic senses of taste.

Uncoupling proteins Proteins in mitochondria that act to uncouple the processes of electron transport and oxidative phosphorylation, so permitting more or less uncontrolled oxidation of metabolic fuels, with production of heat.

Uundernutrition The fact of not receiving enough nutrients in the diet.

Undressed 1. Not fully prepared for cooking or eating 2. Not covered with a dressing or sauce.

Universal product codes (UPC) Standard multidigit numbers that represent product, size, manufacturer and nature of contents, on food and other labels as machine-readable bar codes.

Unfit food Unfit food is food which is unsafe to eat either because it is contaminated or because it is decomposing. Food which is passed its shelf life, *i.e.* 'Use By' or 'Best Before' date is deemed unfit. It is an offence (Warning UK only) to have unfit food on food premises unless the unfit food is clearly in a refuse container.

Unpasteurised Not treated with heat so as to remove harmful bacteria.

Untreated Milk that has not been processed in any way

UPC abbreviation Universal Product Code.

Uperisation The sterilisation of milk using pressurised steam.

Urea $CO(NH_2)_2$, the end-product of nitrogen metabolism in most mammals, excreted in the urine. Synthesised in the liver from ammonia (arising from the deamination of amino acids) and the amino acid aspartic acid. It is the major nitrogenous compound in urine, and the major component of the non-protein nitrogen in blood plasma.

Uric acid is a waste byproduct. It's formed when body breaks down purines, which are found in some foods. Purines show up when cells die and get taken apart. Most of the uric acid leaves our body when we pee, and some when we poop. If you have high levels of uric acid, it can be a sign of disease such as gout.

Urine A yellowish liquid, containing water and waste products, mainly salt and urea, that is excreted by the kidneys and passed out of the body through the ureters, bladder and urethra.

Urogastrone Name given to a peptide found in urine that inhibits gastric secretion, (nearly) identical to epidermal growth factor.

Urokinase An enzyme formed in the kidneys that begin the process of breaking down blood clots.

V

Vacuum cooling a method of chilling food in a vacuum drying a method of drying foods by subjecting them to a vacuum so that the water evaporates at ambient temperatures, used with frozen food.

Vacuum contact drying a way of drying food using hot plates that maintain contact with the food as it shrinks cooling.

Vada Indian; spiced, deep fried balls of legume flour that has been left overnight to undergo a lactic acid bacterial fermentation, together with *Leuconostoc mesenteroides*, which produces carbon dioxide as a leavening agent.

Validation Validation involves obtaining confirmation that the elements of the HACCP system, including critical control points are complete and effective in controlling biological, chemical, and physical and allergen hazards.

Value or economy Terms such as 'value' and 'economy' mean different things to different people, and currently there is no legal definition for these terms. Some people might feel they mean high quality at a low price, and others might take them to mean basic standard at a basic price.

Vanaspati Indian; purified hydrogenated vegetable oil; similar to margarine and usually fortified with vitamins A and D. Also used to prepare ghee (vanaspati ghee).

Vanilla Extract of the vanilla bean, fruit of the tropical orchid *Aracus* (or *Vanilla*) *aromaticus* and related species. The major flavouring principle is vanillin (chemically methyl protocatechuic aldehyde), but other substances present aid the flavour.

Vasoamine substances such as histamine that are naturally present in some foods and can trigger an allergic reaction in large quantities.

Vasodilatation The relaxation of blood vessels, especially the arteries, making them wider and leading to increased blood flow or reduced blood pressure.

VDP Volatile decomposition products.

Vegan The term 'vegan' should not be applied to foods that are, or are made from or with the aid of animals or animal products including products from living animals.

Vegetable protein products General term to include textured soya and other bean products, often made to simulate meat (*see* textured vegetable protein). The basic material is termed flour when the protein content is not less than 50%; concentrate, not less than 65%; isolate, not less than 90% protein.

Vegetable shortening Shortening made from hydrogenated vegetable oil, with a bland flavour.

Vegetarian The terms 'vegetarian' or 'suitable for vegetarians' should not be applied to foods that are, or are made from or with the aid of products derived from animals that have died, have been slaughtered, or animals that die as a result of being eaten.

Vein A blood vessel that takes deoxygenated blood containing waste carbon dioxide from the tissues back to the heart.

Venado Antelope or deer meat; a lean meat, it needs moist heat to keep it tender. (Spanish) venison.

Verbascose A non-digestible tetrasaccharide, galactosylgalactosyl glucosyl-fructose, found in legumes; fermented by intestinal bacteria and causes flatulence.

Verjuice A very acidic juice made by pressing unripe grapes or crab apples, used as a flavouring.

Vermifuge A substance that removes worms from the intestine.

Vinegar A solution of acetic acid (not less than 4%); the product of two fermentations, first with yeast to convert sugars into alcohol; this liquor, called gyle (6–9% alcohol), is then fermented with *Acetobacter* spp. to form acetic acid.

Vinegar, cider Made from apple juice, and known simply as vinegar in the USA.

Vinification The process of fermentation of sugars in grape juice to make wine.

Virgin pastry Puff pastry after it is first made, not after rerolling, used for vol-auvents and other items that require an even rise or lift.

Volvulus Twisting of part of the gastrointestinal tract, leading to partial or complete obstruction.

Votator A machine used in the manufacture of margarine.

VP Vacuum packaging.

VSP Vacuum skin packaging.

W

Wafer A thin sweet biscuit eaten with ice cream.

Waffle A type of thick crisp pancake cooked in an iron mould and eaten with syrup.

Waffle Iron A device used to transform batter into crisp, golden waffles; available in electric or stove-top models.

Warfarin Clinically used to impair blood clotting in patients at risk of thrombosis, and as a rodenticide.

Wari Indian, Pakistani; dried balls of legume and cereal flour that has undergone yeast fermentation can be stored for some months and then deep fried or boilled for eating.

Warming cupboard A specially heated cupboard in a kitchen, where food can be kept warm.

Wasabi Also called Japanese horseradish, a pungent green paste made from a rhizome of the watercress family.

Wasabe Japanese; pungent condiment

Water activity Water activity is denoted by (a_w) ratio between vapour pressure of water in the food and that of pure water at the same temperature.

Water-binding agent Salt or sugar used for preserving foods by reducing their water activity.

Water brash The sudden filling of the mouth with acidic juices from the stomach, usually accompanied by heartburn and often resulting from indigestion, a condition that is common in pregnancy but may also be an indication of a disorder of the digestive tract.

Water-glass Sodium silicate; used at one time to preserve eggs, by forming a layer of insoluble calcium silicate around the shell, so sealing the pores.

Water hardness Soap-precipitating power of water due to the formation of insoluble calcium and magnesium salts of the soap.

Waste Management The collection, transport, processing or disposal of waste materials – including solid, liquid, gaseous or plasmic waste.

Waxing Coating fruits and vegetables with a thin layer of edible wax to increase shelf life.

Weak flour Flour of any type with a lower protein content than strong flour, used for making biscuits and cakes, but not suitable for bread-making.

Weaning foods Foods specially formulated for infants aged between 3 and 9 months for the transition between breast or bottle feeding and normal intake of solid foods.

Weld The seam along the length of a can that is vulnerable to corrosion.

Well-hung Meat that has been hung up long enough to mature and be good to eat.

Wellcome classification Categories of malnutrition in children, based on the ratio of actual weight to expected weight and on the presence or absence of oedema.

Whey The residue from milk after removal of the casein and most of the fat (as in cheese-making) also known as *lactoserum.*

Whipped cream Cream that is beaten until it is stiff, flavoured with sugar and vanilla.

Whipping cream a heavy cream containing a high proportion of butterfat that causes it to stiffen when whipped.

Whiskey, whisky A grain spirit distilled from barley, rye, maize or other cereal that has first been malted and then fermented. The distilled spirit is diluted to about 62% alcohol and matured in wooden casks.

Wholegrain Using the whole of the grain of wheat or other cereal.

Wholesome Wholesome is a term used to describe food which is safe and nutritious. Sometimes the term wholesome is used to describe fresh food which is free from additives and preservatives, whilst other people use the term in contrast to junk food. However as far as the food hygienist is concerned wholesome means safe, nutritious and of high quality.

White wine Wine made without leaving the grape skins in the fermenting mixture, making the wine pale yellow or green instead of deep red.

Wine Fermented juice from grapes (varieties of *Vitis vinifera*), also made with other fruits and even vegetables with the addition of sugar.

Withdrawal A period during which a person who has been addicted to a drug stops taking it and experiences unpleasant symptoms.

Winterization Process involving slow cooling of oils and removal of the precipitated fats with a relatively high melting point, so that the final product remains clear when refrigerated.

Wood pigeon A wild pigeon that is used as food

Worcester berry American species of gooseberry, *Ribes divaricatum.*

Wuntun (wonton) Chinese; small dough parcels containing meat, boiled or deep fried. Also known as chiao tzu or wraplings.

X

Xanthophylls It occurs in all green leaves together with chlorophyll and carotene, also present in egg yolk and Cape gooseberry etc.

Xanthan gum Polysaccharide produced by bacterial fermentation and used as a thickening agent to form gels and increase viscosity.

Xanthosis Yellowing of the skin associated with high blood concentrations of carotene.

Xerophagia The practice of eating only dry food.

Xerophonia A dry-sounding voice caused by diabetes medication.

Xerophthalmia Severe vitamin A deficiency leading to ulceration of the cornea.

Xerosis Abnormal dryness of an organ or tissue.

Xerostomia Dryness of the mouth caused by medication that arrests the salivary glands.

Xoconostle A cactus fruit grows at the end of nopales, or cactus paddles, sometimes in clusters of up to a dozen on one paddle.

XXX; XXXX Label symbols used for confectioners' (powdered) sugar.

Xylitol A type of alcohol somewhat sweeter than sugar, used in sugar-free chewing gum.

Xyloascorbic acid Term used for ascorbic acid (vitamin C) to distinguish from isoascorbic acid, which is araboascorbic acid and has only slight vitamin C activity.

Xyloglucan One of the hemicelluloses in plant cell walls, linking cellulose fibres.A component of non-starch polysaccharide.

Xylose Pentose (five-carbon) sugar found in plant tissues mainly as polysaccharides (xylans); 40% as sweet as sucrose. Also known as wood sugar. Mainly excreted unmetabolised, and used to test carbohydrate absorption.

Xylulose Pentose (five-carbon) sugar occurring as a metabolic intermediate in the pentose phosphate pathway.

Y

YAC Yeast artificial chromosome, a specialised cloning vector that can carry large DNA inserts.

Yakitori A dish of Japanese origin skewered chicken. Its preparation involves skewering the meat with *kushi*, a type of skewer typically made of steel, bamboo, or similar materials. Afterwards, they are grilled over a charcoal fire. During or after cooking, the meat is typically seasoned with tare sauce or salt.

Yakult TM yogurt containing live *Lactobacillus* spp. which are probiotics. Originally Japanese name for yoghurt fermented with *L. casei*.

Yam Tubers of perennial climbing plants of a number of species of *Dioscorea*, *D. rotundala* white yam and *D. Cayenensis*. A major food in parts of Africa and also the Far East.

Yeast Unicellular organisms, sometimes grouped with the fungi; eukaryotic organisms with more complex subcellular organisation than bacteria. Some types are of major importance in the food industry. *Saccharomyces cerevisiae* and *S. carlsbergensis* are used in brewing, wine-making and baking.

Yeast extract A thick sticky brown food obtained from yeast and eaten as a spread or used in cooking.

Yeast fermentation, bottom Or deep fermentation; fermentation during the manufacture of beer with a yeast that sinks to the bottom of the tank. Most beers are produced this way; ale, porter and stout being the principal beers produced by top fermentation.

Yeheb A nut, fruit of *Cordeauxia edulis*, originally from the Horn of Africa.

Yellow Chiles The general term to describe these is "Guero chiles" which refers to varieties such as the Santa Fe grande and Hungarian wax chiles. These chiles are medium flashed and slightly sweet with a bold flavor and waxy texture.

Yerba dulce The leaves of the Paraguayan shrub, *Stevia rebaudiana*, the source of stevioside and rebaudioside.

Yersinia enterocolitica A strain of bacteria that causes yersiniosis, found in raw pork products.

Yield Weight of food after processing as a percentage of unprocessed material.

Yoghurt Milk (from a variety of animals but usually cows) coagulated and fermented with two types of bacteria, *Streptococcus thermophilus* and *Lactobacillus bulgaricus*. Stirred yoghurt is prepared in bulk set yoghurt is fermented in the plastic containers in which it will be sold.

Yolk index Index of freshness of an egg; ratio between height and diameter of yolk under defined conditions. As the egg deteriorates, the yolk index decreases.

Yolk greening The formation of a greenish-grey film on the outside of a hard-boiled egg yolk, caused by the deposition of ferrous sulphur.

Youngberry Cross between blackberry and dewberry.

Yo-yo dieting A situation in which a person repeatedly loses weight through dieting and then regains the weight that he or she has lost.

Yucca Plant native to Latin America and the Southwest; petals, fruit and root can all be eaten; root is also used as a thickener for soups and stews.

Yukwa Korean; snack food made by deep frying dried dough prepared by steeping waxy rice for 1–2 weeks.

Yusho disease Caused by leakage of polychlorinated biphenyls which contaminated edible oil on the Japanese island of Kyushu in 1968.

Z

Zabaglione (zabaione) Italian; frothy dessert made from egg yolks, sugar and wine (usually Marsala) whisked over gentle heat until thick. French sabayon is similar.

Zampone Italian; pork sausage in which meat is stuffed into a boned pig's trotter instead of casing.

Zander A freshwater fish of the perch family, native to central Europe (NOTE: Its scientific name is *Stizostedion lucioperca*).

Zaatar An herb mixture composed of savory, thyme, sumac, and sesame seeds. A prepared mixture of this herb mixture can be found at most Middle Eastern groceries. The quality of zaatar can differ greatly.

Zearalenone A type of mycotoxin that is produced by fungus on cereals in storage.

Zeaxanthin A type of carotenoid found in eggs and citrus fruit that contribute to eye health.

Zébrine Variety of aubergine with purple and white stripes.

Zedoary root Root of the Indian plant *Curcuma zedoaria*, a member of the ginger family. Used in the manufacture of flavours and bitters.

Zen macrobiotics A very strict form of macrobiotic diet that avoids, *e.g.*, eating foods that are out of season or foods that have been transported a long distance.

Zein A prolamin, the major protein of maize (*Zea mays*), very poor in lysine and tryptophan.

Zester A small utensil with a row of tiny sharpened holes or edges at its tip for cutting strips of zest from oranges, lemons and other citrus fruits.

Zone diet Dietary plan in which 40% of daily calories should come from carbohydrates, 30% from proteins and 30% from fats.

Zest Outer skin of citrus fruits and is in sense of much tasty.

Zucchini Italian variety of marrow developed to be harvested when small. American and Australian name for courgette.

Zucker rat A genetically obese strain of rat used in research.

Zuppa Inglese A refrigerated dessert similar to the British favorite, trifle (Tipsy cake or Tipsy pudding). It is made with rum sprinkled slices of sponge cake layered with a rich custard or whipped cream (or both) and candied fruit or toasted almonds (or both).

Zwieback German twice baked bread or rusk.

Zwitterions An ionised molecule with both positive and negative charges, *e.g.* the amino acids.

Zwyieka A Polish sausage.

Zygosaccharomyces Yeasts that grow in high concentrations of sugar (osmophilic) that causes spoilage of honey, jams and syrups.

Zymase Obsolete name for the mixture of enzymes in yeast which is responsible for fermentation.

Zymogens The inactive form in which some enzymes, especially the protein digestive enzymes, are secreted, being activated after secretion. Also called proenzymes or enzyme precursors.

Zymology The branch of chemistry concerned with the action of enzymes.

Zymotachygraph An instrument that measures the gas produced in fermenting dough and the amount escaping from the dough, as an index of bread-making properties.

Zymurgy The branch of chemistry concerned with brewing and distilling.

***Z*-Value** The *Z*-value is the number of degree required for a specific thermal death time curve to pass through one log cycle (change by a factor of 10). It is also negative slope index of the thermal death rate curve. Different organisms in a given food have different Z-value.

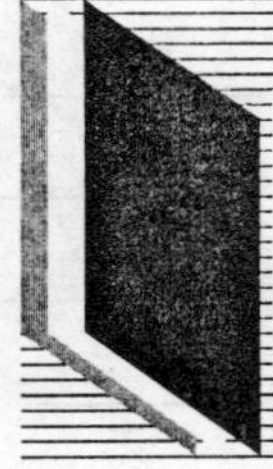

CHAPTER 14
BOTANICAL NAMES OF SOME CROPS

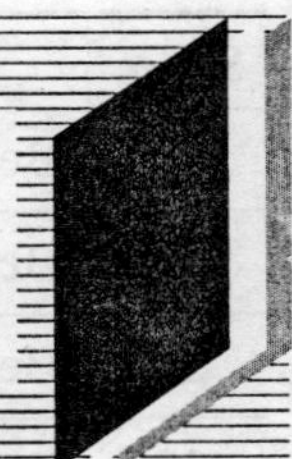

S.No.	Crop Name	Botanical Name
01	Abaca (Manila hemp)	*Musa textilis*
02	Alfalfa for fodder	*Medicago sativa*
03	Alfalfa for seed	*Medicago sativa*
04	Almond	*Prunus dulcis*
05	Anise seeds	*Pimpinella anisum*
06	Apple	*Malus sylvestris*
07	Apricot	*Prunus armeniaca*
08	Areca (betel nut)	*Areca catechu*
09	Arracha	*Arracacia xanthorrhiza*
10	Arrowroot	*Maranta arundinacea*
11	Artichoke	*Cynara scolymus*
12	Asparagus	*Asparagus officinalis*
13	Avocado	*Persea americana*
14	Bajra (Pearl millet)	*Pennisetum americanum*
15	Bambara groundnut	*Vigna subterranea*
16	Banana	*Musa paradisiaca*
17	Barley	*Hordeum vulgare*
18	Beans, dry, edible, for grains	*Phaseolus vulgaris*
19	Beans, harvested green	*Phaseolus and Vigna spp.*
20	Beet, fodder (mangel)	*Beta vulgaris*
21	Beet, red	*Beta vulgaris*

S.No.	Crop Name	Botanical Name
22	Beet, sugar	*Beta vulgaris*
23	Beet, sugar for fodder	*Beta vulgaris*
24	Beet, sugar for seeds	*Beta vulgaris*
25	Bergamot	*Citrus bergamia*
26	Betel nut	*Areca catechu*
27	Black pepper	*Piper nigrum*
28	Black wattle	*Acacia mearnsii*
29	Blackberries of various species	*Rubus spp.*
30	Blueberry	*Vaccinium spp.*
31	Brazil nut	*Bertholletia excelsa*
32	Breadfruit	*Artocarpus altilis*
33	Broad bean, dry	*Vicia faba*
34	Broad bean, harvested green	*Vicia faba*
35	Broccoli	*Brassica oleracea var. botrytis*
36	Broom millet	*Sorghum bicolor*
37	Broom sorghum	*Sorghum bicolor*
38	Brussels sprouts	*Brassica oleracea var. gemmifera*
39	Buckwheat	*Fagopyrum esculentum*
40	Cabbage (red, white, Savoy)	*Brassica oleracea var. capitata*
41	Cabbage, Chinese	*Brassica chinensis*
42	Cabbage, for fodder	*Brassica spp.*
43	Cacao (cocoa)	*Theobroma cacao*
44	Cantaloupe	*Cucumis melo*
45	Caraway seeds	*Carum carvi*
46	Cardamom	*Elettaria cardamomum*
47	Cardoon	*Cynara cardunculus*
48	Carob	*Ceratonia siliqua*
49	Carrot, edible	*Daucus carota ssp. sativa*

S.No.	Crop Name	Botanical Name
50	Carrot, for fodder	*Daucus carota ssp. sativa*
51	Cashew nuts	*Anacardium occidentale*
52	Cassava (manioc)	*Manihot esculenta*
53	Castor bean	*Ricinus communis*
54	Cauliflower	*Brassica oleracea var. botrytis*
55	Celeriac	*Apium graveolens var. rapaceum*
56	Celery	*Apium graveolens*
57	Chayote	*Sechium edule*
58	Cherry (all varieties)	*Prunus spp.*
59	Chestnut	*Castanea sativa*
60	Chickpea (gram pea)	*Cicer arietinum*
61	Chicory	*Cichorium intybus*
62	Chicory for greens	*Cichorium intybus*
63	Chili, dry (all varieties)	*Capsicum spp. (annuum)*
64	Chili, fresh (all varieties)	*Capsicum spp. (annuum)*
65	Cinnamon	*Cinnamomum verum*
66	Citron	*Citrus medica*
67	Citronella	*Cymbopogon citrates/ Cymbopogon nardus*
68	Clementine	*Citrus reticulata*
69	Clove	*Eugenia aromatica (Syzygium aromaticum)*
70	Clover for fodder (all varieties)	*Trifolium spp.*
71	Clover for seed (all varieties)	*Trifolium spp.*
72	Cocoa (cacao)	*Theobroma cacao*
73	Coconut	*Cocos nucifera*
74	Cocoyam	*Colocasia esculenta*
75	Coffee	*Coffea spp.*
76	Cola nut (all varieties)	*Cola acuminata*
77	Colza (rapeseed)	*Brassica napus*

S.No.	Crop Name	Botanical Name
78	Corn (maize), for cereals	*Zea mays*
79	Corn (maize), for silage	*Zea mays*
80	Corn (sweet), for vegetable	*Zea mays*
81	Corn for salad	*Valerianella locusta*
82	Cotton (all varieties)	*Gossypium spp.*
83	Cottonseed (all varieties)	*Gossypium spp.*
84	Cowpea, for grain	*Vigna unguiculata*
85	Cowpea, harvested green	*Vigna unguiculata*
86	Cranberry	*Vaccinium spp.*
87	Cress	*Lepidium sativum*
88	Cucumber	*Cucumis sativus*
89	Currants (all varieties)	*Ribes spp.*
90	Custard apple	*Annona reticulate*
91	Dasheen	*Colocasia esculenta*
92	Dates	*Phoenix dactylifera*
93	Drumstick tree	*Moringa oleifera*
94	Durra (sorghum)	*Sorghum bicolour*
95	Durum wheat	*Triticum durum*
96	Earth pea	*Vigna subterranea*
97	Edo (eddoe)	*Xanthosoma spp.; Colocasia spp.*
98	Eggplant	*Solanum melongena*
99	Endive	*Cichorium endivia*
100	Fennel	*Foeniculum vulgare*
101	Fenugreek	*Trigonella foenum-graecum*
102	Fig	*Ficus carica*
103	Filbert (Hazelnut)	*Corylus avellana*
104	Fique	*Furcraea macrophylla*
105	Flax for fibre	*Linum usitatissimum*

S.No.	Crop Name	Botanical Name
106	Flax for oil seed (linseed)	*Linum usitatissimum*
107	Formio (New Zealand flax)	*Phormium tenax*
108	Garlic, dry	*Allium sativum*
109	Garlic, green	*Allium sativum*
110	Geranium	*Pelargonium spp.; Geranium spp.*
111	Ginger	*Zingiber officinale*
112	Gooseberry (all varieties)	*Ribes spp.*
113	Gourd Lagenaria spp;	*Cucurbita spp.*
114	Gram pea (chickpea)	*Cicer arietinum*
115	Grape	*Vitis vinifera*
116	Grapefruit	*Citrus paradisi*
117	Grapes for raisins	*Vitis vinifera*
118	Grapes for table use	*Vitis vinifera*
119	Grapes for wine	*Vitis vinifera*
120	Grass esparto	*Lygeum spartum*
121	Grass, orchard	*Dactylis glomerata*
122	Grass, Sudan	*Sorghum bicolor var. sudanense*
123	Groundnut (peanut)	*Arachis hypogaea*
124	Guava	*Psidium guajava*
125	Guinea corn (sorghum)	*Sorghum bicolor*
126	Hazelnut (filbert)	*Corylus avellana*
127	Hemp fibre	*Cannabis sativa ssp. indica*
128	Hemp, Manila (abaca)	*Musa textilis*
129	Hemp, sun	*Crotalaria juncea*
130	Hempseed	*Cannabis sativa (marijuana)*
131	Henequen	*Agave fourcroydes*
132	Henna	*Lawsonia inermis*
133	Hop	*Humulus lupulus*

S.No.	Crop Name	Botanical Name
134	Horse bean	*Vicia faba*
135	Horseradish	*Armoracia rusticana*
136	Hybrid maize	*Zea mays*
137	Indigo	*Indigofera tinctoria*
138	Jasmine	*Jasminum spp.*
139	Jerusalem artichoke	*Helianthus tuberosus*
140	Jowar (sorghum)	*Sorghum bicolor*
141	Jute	*Corchorus spp. (over 30 spp.)*
142	Kale	*Brassica oleracea var. acephala*
143	Kapok	*Ceiba pentandra*
144	Kenaf	*Hibiscus cannabinus*
145	Kohlrabi	*Brassica oleracea var. gongylodes*
146	Lavender	*Lavandula spp. (over 15 sp.)*
147	Leek	*Allium ampeloprasum, Allium porrum*
148	Lemon	*Citrus limon*
149	Lemon grass	*Cymbopogon citratus*
150	Lentil	*Lens culinaris*
151	Lespedeza (all varieties)	*Lespedeza spp.*
152	Lettuce	*Lactuca sativa var. capitata*
153	Lime, sour	*Citrus aurantifolia*
154	Lime, sweet	*Citrus limetta*
155	Linseed (flax for oil seed)	*Linum usitatissimum*
156	Liquorice	*Glycyrrhiza glabra*
157	Litchi	*Litchi chinensis*
158	Loquat	*Eriobotrya japonica*
159	Lupine (all varieties)	*Lupinus spp.*
160	Macadamia (Queensland nut)	*Macadamia spp. ternifolia*
161	Mace	*Myristica fragrans*

S.No.	Crop Name	Botanical Name
162	Maguey	*Agave atrovirens*
163	Maize (corn)	*Zea mays*
164	Maize (corn) for silage	*Zea mays*
165	Maize (hybrid)	*Zea mays*
166	Maize, ordinary	*Zea mays*
167	Mandarin	*Citrus reticulata*
168	Mangel (fodder beet)	*Beta vulgaris*
169	Mango	*Mangifera indica*
170	Manioc (cassava)	*Manihot esculenta*
171	Maslin (mixed cereals)	*Mixture of Triticum spp.; Secale cereale*
172	Medlar	*Mespilus germanica*
173	Melon (except watermelon)	*Cucumis melo*
174	Millet broom	*Sorghum bicolor*
175	Millet, bajra	*Pennisetum americanum*
176	Millet, bulrush	*Pennisetum americanum*
177	Millet, finger	*Eleusine coracana*
178	Millet, foxtail	*Setaria italica*
179	Millet, Japanese	*Echinochloa esculenta*
180	Millet, pearl (bajra, bulrush)	*Pennisetum americanum*
181	Millet, proso	*Panicum miliaceum*
182	Mint (all varieties)	*Mentha spp.*
183	Mulberry for fruit (all varieties)	*Morus spp.*
184	Mulberry for silkworms	*Morus alba*
185	Mushrooms	*Agaricus spp.; Pleurotus spp.; Volvariella*
186	Mustard	*Brassica nigra; Sinapis alba*
187	Nectarine	*Prunus persica var. nectarina*
188	New Zealand flax (formio)	*Phormium tenax*
189	Niger seed	*Guizotia abyssinica*

S.No.	Crop Name	Botanical Name
190	Nutmeg	*Myristica fragrans*
191	Oats, for fodder	*Avena spp. (about 30 sp.)*
192	Oats, for grain	*Avena spp. (about 30 sp.)*
193	Oil palm	*Elaeis guineensis*
194	Okra	*Abelmoschus esculentus*
195	Olive	*Olea europaea*
196	Onion seed	*Allium cepa*
197	Onion, dry	*Allium cepa*
198	Onion, green	*Allium cepa*
199	Opium	*Papaver somniferum*
200	Orange	*Citrus sinensis*
201	Orange, bitter	*Citrus aurantium*
202	Palm Palmyra	*Borassus flabellifer*
203	Palm, kernel oil	*Elaeis guineensis*
204	Palm, oil	*Elaeis guineensis*
205	Palm, sago	*Metroxylon sagu*
206	Papaya (pawpaw)	*Carica papaya*
207	Parsnip	*Pastinaca sativa*
208	Pea, edible dry, for grain	*Pisum sativum*
209	Pea, harvested green	*Pisum sativum*
210	Peach	*Prunus persica*
211	Peanut (groundnut)	*Arachis hypogaea*
212	Pear	*Pyrus communis*
213	Pecan nut	*Carya illinoensis*
214	Pepper, black	*Piper nigrum*
215	Pepper, dry	*Capsicum spp. (over 30 sp.)*
216	Persimmon	*Diospyros kaki; Diospyros virginiana*
217	Pigeon pea	*Cajanus cajan*

S.No.	Crop Name	Botanical Name
218	Pineapple	*Ananas comosus*
219	Pistachio nut	*Pistacia vera*
220	Plantain	*Musa sapientum*
221	Plum	*Prunus domestica*
222	Pomegranate	*Punica granatum*
223	Pomelo	*Citrus grandis*
224	Poppy seed	*Papaver somniferum*
225	Potato	*Solamum tuberosum*
226	Potato, sweet	*Ipomoea batatas*
227	Prune	*Prunus domestica*
228	Pumpkin, edible	*Cucurbita spp. (over 25 sp.)*
229	Pumpkin, for fodder	*Cucurbita spp. (over 25 sp.)*
230	Pyrethum	*Chrysanthemum cinerariaefolium*
231	Quebracho	*Aspidosperma spp. (more than 3 sp.)*
232	Quince	*Cydonia oblonga*
233	Quinine	*Cinchona spp. (more than 6 sp.)*
234	Quinoa	*Chenopodium quinoa*
235	Radish	*Raphanus sativus (inc. Cochlearia armoracia)*
236	Ramie	*Boehmeria nivea*
237	Rapeseed (colza)	*Brassica napus*
238	Raspberry (all varieties)	*Rubus spp. (over 360 sp.)*
239	Red beet	*Beta vulgaris*
240	Redtop	*Agrostis spp.*
241	Rhea	*Boehmeria nivea*
242	Rhubarb	*Rheum spp.*
243	Rice	*Oryza sativa; Oryza glaberrima*
244	Rose	*Rose spp.*
245	Rubber	*Hevea brasiliensis*

S.No.	Crop Name	Botanical Name
246	Rutabaga (swede)	*Brassica napus var. napobrassica*
247	Rye	*Secale cereale*
248	Ryegrass seed	*Lolium spp. (about 20 sp.)*
249	Safflower	*Carthamus tinctorius*
250	Sainfoin	*Onobrychis viciifolia*
251	Salsify	*Tragopogon porrifolius*
252	Sapodilla	*Achras sapota*
253	Satsuma (mandarin/tangerine)	*Citrus reticulata*
254	Scorzonera – black salsify	*Scorzonera hispanica*
255	Sesame	*Sesamum indicum*
256	Shea butter (nut)	*Vitellaria paradoxa*
257	Sisal	*Agave sisalana*
258	Sorghum	*Sorghum bicolor*
259	Sorghum, broom	*Sorghum bicolor*
260	Sorghum, durra	*Sorghum bicolor*
261	Sorghum, Guinea corn	*Sorghum bicolor*
262	Sorghum, jowar	*Sorghum bicolor*
263	Sorghum, sweet	*Sorghum bicolor*
264	Soybean	*Glycine max*
265	Soybean hay	*Glycine max*
266	Spelt wheat	*Triticum spelta*
267	Spinach	*Spinacia oleracea*
268	Squash	*Cucurbita spp. (over 25 sp.)*
269	Strawberry	*Fragaria spp. (over 30 sp.)*
270	Sugar beet	*Beta vulgaris*
271	Sugar beet for fodder	*Beta vulgaris*
272	Sugar beet for seed	*Beta vulgaris*
273	Sugarcane for fodder	*Saccharum officinarum*

S.No.	Crop Name	Botanical Name
274	Sugarcane for sugar or alcohol	*Saccharum officinarum*
275	Sugarcane for thatching	*Saccharum officinarum*
276	Sunflower for fodder	*Helianthus annuus*
277	Sunflower for oil seed	*Helianthus annuus*
278	Sunhemp	*Crotalaria juncea*
279	Swede	*Brassica napus var. napobrassica*
280	Swede for fodder	*Brassica napus var. napobrassica*
281	Sweet corn	*Zea mays*
282	Sweet lime	*Citrus limetta*
283	Sweet pepper	*Capsicum annuum*
284	Sweet potato	*Lopmoea batatas*
285	Sweet sorghum	*Sorghum bicolor*
286	Tangerine	*Citrus reticulata*
287	Tannia	*Xanthosoma sagittifolium*
288	Tapioca (cassava)	*Manihot esculenta*
289	Taro	*Colocasia esculenta*
290	Tea	*Camellia sinensis*
291	Tef	*Eragrostis abyssinica*
292	Timothy	*Phleum pratense*
293	Tobacco	*Nicotiana tabacum*
294	Tomato	*Lycopersicon esculentum*
295	Trefoil	*Lotus spp. (about 100 spp.)*
296	Triticale for fodder Hybrid of	*Triticum aestivum and Secale cereale*
297	Tung tree	*Aleurites spp.; Fordii*
298	Turnip, edible	*Brassica rapa*
299	Turnip, for fodder	*Brassica rapa*
300	Urena (Congo jute)	*Urena lobata*

S.No.	Crop Name	Botanical Name
301	Vanilla	*Vanilla planifolia*
302	Vetch for grain	*Vicia sativa*
303	Walnut	*Juglans spp. (over 20 spp.), ep. regia*
304	Watermelon	*Citrullus lanatus*
305	Wheat	*Triticum aestivum*
306	Yam	*Dioscorea spp. (over 120 spp.)*
307	Yerba mate	*Ilex paraguariensis*

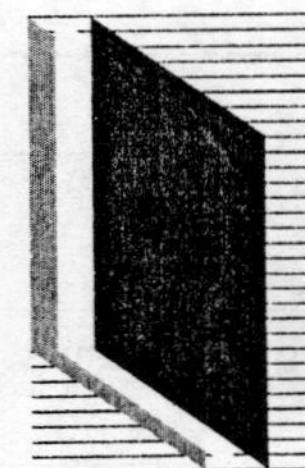

CHAPTER 15
IMPORTANT TABLES

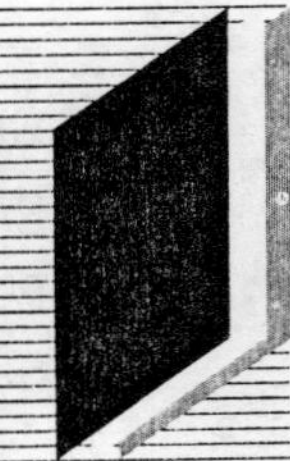

NUTRITIVE VALUE OF INDIAN FOODS (Per 100 gram)

S No.	Food	Energy	Pro-tein	Fat	Carbo-hydrates	Calc-ium	Iron	Caro-tene	Thia-mine	Ribof-lavin	Niacin
		Kcal.	g.	g.	g.	Mg.	Mg.	mcg.	Mg.	Mg.	Mg.
1	Bajra	361	11.6	5.0	67.5	42	8.0	132	0.33	0.25	2.3
2	Jowar	349	10.4	1.9	72.6	25	4.1	47	0.37	0.13	3.1
3	Maize, dry	342	11.1	3.6	66.2	10	2.3	90	0.42	0.10	1.8
4	Maize, tender	125	4.7	0.9	24.6	9	1.1	32	0.11	0.17	0.6
5	Ragi	328	7.3	1.3	72.0	344	3.9	42	0.42	0.19	1.1
6	Rice, parboiled, hand pounded	349	8.5	0.6	77.4	10	2.8	9	0.27	0.12	4.0
7	Rice, parboiled, milled	346	6.4	0.4	79.0	9	1.0	-	0.21	0.05	3.8
8	Rice, raw, hand pounded	346	7.5	1.0	76.7	10	3.2	2	0.21	0.16	3.9
9	Rice, raw, milled	345	6.8	0.5	78.2	10	0.7	0	0.06	0.06	1.9
10	Wheat flour (whole)	341	12.1	1.7	69.4	48	4.9	29	0.49	0.17	4.3
11	Wheat flour (refined)	348	11.0	0.9	73.9	23	2.7	25	0.12	0.07	2.4
12	Wheat bread (white)	245	7.8	0.7	51.9	11	1.1	-	0.07	-	0.7

(*Source* : Gopalan C., B. V. Rama Sastri and S. C. Balasubramanian, 1991)

APPLICATION OF ENZYMES

S.No.	Enzymes	Used in	Action
1	Endogenous proteases	Meat	Tenderisation of meat and flavour development
2	Subtilisin	Soya protein	Partial hydrolysis and increase whipping organisms on and emuls capacity
3	Papain	Meat	Injection into jugular vein shortly before slaughter, after slaughter enzyme is activated tenderizes the meat
4	Meat liable fungal process	Dough from high glutein wheat varieties	Hydrolysis of glutein makes the dough suitable for biscuits pasty making.

(*Source* : Notes ANGRAU, Hyderabad, 2012)

(ACCEPTABLE DAILY INTAKE) OF CERTAIN NON GRAS FOOD ADDITIVES

S.No.	Additives	ADI, Mg/kg/day	Function
1	EDTA	2.5	Preservative, Sequestrants
2	BHA	0.5	Antioxidant
3	BHT	0.5	Antioxidant
4	Sodium nitrate	5.0	Curing agent,Colour fixation
5	Sodium stearyl fumarate	—	Stabilizing is non yeast leavened. Conditioning agent is yeast leavened.
6	Glycine	25	Stabilizer
7	Succinylated monoglycerides	—	Emulsifier, Dough conditioner
8	Polysorbate	25	Emulsifiers
9	Propylene glycolalginate	25	Stabilizer, Emulsifier

(*Source* : Notes ANGRAU, Hyderabad, 2012)

PRACTICAL STORAGE LIFE (MONTHS) OF FOOD ITEMS AT DIFFERENT STORAGE TEMPERATURE

S.No.	Product	– 12°C	– 18°C	– 24°C
1	Beef carcasses	8	15	24
2	Beef steaks/cuts	8	18	24
3	Ground beef	6	10	15

...Cond.

S.No.	Product	– 12°C	– 18°C	– 24°C
4	Veal carcass	6	12	15
5	Veal steaks/cuts	6	12	15
6	Lamb carcasses	18	24	>24
7	Lamb steaks	12	18	24
8	Pork carcases	6	10	15
9	Pork steaks/cuts	6	10	15
10	Sliced bacon (vac.)	12	12	12
11	Chicken, whole	9	18	>24
12	Chicken parts/cuts	9	18	>24
13	Turkey, whole	8	15	>24
14	Ducks, Geese, whole	6	12	18
15	Liver	4	12	18

(*Source* : Judith A. Evans, 2008)

FREEZING RATE OF DIFFERENT METHODS

S.No.	Freezing methods	Freezing rate (cmh^{-1})
1	Ultra rapid freezing	Over 10
2	Rapid freezing	1–10
3	Normal freezing	0.3–1
4	Slow freezing	0.1–0.3
5	Very slow freezing	Less than 0.1

(*Source* : Judith A. Evans, 2008)

TYPES OF FUNGAL SPOILAGE OF FRUITS

S.No.	Product	Type of spoilage	Mold Involved
		Citrus fruits	
1	Oranges	Blue rot	*Penicillium italicum*
2	Tomatoes, citrus fruits	Sour rot	*Geotrichum candidum*
3	Citrus fruits	Green mold rot	*Penicillium digitatum*

S.No.	Product	Type of spoilage	Mold Involved
4	Citrus fruits	*Alternaria* rot	*Alternaria sp.*
5	Citrus fruits	Stem end rot	*Phomopsis citri, Diplodia natalensis, Alternaria citri*
		Peaches/apricots	
6	Peaches	Brown rot	*Monilinia fructicola*
7	Peaches	Pink rot	*Trichothecium sp.*
8	Peaches, apricots	Black mold rot	*Aspergillus niger*
9	Peaches, cherries	*Cladosporium* rot	*Cladosporiumherbarum*
		Apples/pears	
10	Apples	Soft rot	*Penicillium expansum*
11	Apples, pears	Lenticels rot	*Cryptosporidium malicorticus, Phyletanea vagabuna*
12	Apples/pears	Black spot/scab	*Venturia inaequalis*
13	Apples/pears	Brown rot	*Monilinia fructigena*
14	Pears	Erwinia rot	*Erwiniacartovora*
		Bananas	
15	Bananas	Bitter rot (Anthracnose)	*Colletotrichum musae*
16	Bananas	Finger rot	*Pestalozzia, Fusarium, Gleosporium sp.*
17	Bananas	Crown rot	*Colletotrichum musae, Verticillum theobromae*
		Other fruits	
18	Pineapples	Pineapple black rot	*Ceratocystis paadoxa*
19	Water melons	Anthracnose	*Ceratocystislagenarium*
20	Strawberries	Grey mold rot	*Botrytis cinerea*
21	Grapes	Grey mold rot	*Botrytis cinerea*

(*Source* : Y. H. Hui *et. al.* 2006)

VITAMIN CONTENT OF FRUITS
(VALUE PER 100 gm OF EDIBLE PORTION)

S. No.	Fruits	Vitamin C	Vitamin E (mg) (α-toc opherol	Vitamin A	Thiam in	Ribofav in	Niacin (mg)	Pyrido xine (mg)	Foalte (μg)
1	Apple	4.6	0.18	3	0.017	0.026	0.091	0.041	3
2	Apricot	10.0	0.89	96	0.030	0.040	0.600	0.054	9
3	Avocado	10.0	2.07	7	0.067	0.130	1.738	0.257	58
4	Banana	8.7	0.10	3	0.031	0.073	0.665	0.367	20
5	Cherry	7.0	0.07	3	0.027	0.033	0.154	0.049.	4
6	Grape	10.8	0.19	3	0.069	0.070	0.188	0.086	2
7	Guava	183.5	0.73	31	0.050	0.050	1.200	0.143	14
8	Kiwi fruit	75.0	-	9	0.020	0.050	0.500	-	-
9	Orange	53.2	0.18	11	0.087	0.040	0.282	0.060	30
10	Papaya	61.8	0.73	55	0.027	0.032	0.338	0.019	38
11	Passion fruit	30.0	0.02	64	-	0.130	1.500	0.100	14
12	Peach	6.6	0.73	16	0.024	0.031	0.806	0.025	4
13	Pear	4.2	0.12	1	0.012	0.025	0.157	0.028	7
14	Pineapple	36.2	0.02	3	0.079	0.031	0.489	0.110	15
15	Plum	9.5	0.26	17	0.028	0.026	0.417	0.029	5
16	Raspberry	26.2	0.87	2	0.032	0.038	0.598	0.055	21
17	Strawberry	58.8	0.29	1	0.024	0.022	0.386	0.047	24

(*Source* : Y. H. Hui *et. al.* 2006)

MINERAL CONTENT OF VARIOUS FRUITS (VALUE PER 100 gm OF EDIBLE PORTION)

S. No.	Fruits	Fe (mg)	Ca (mg)	P (mg)	Mg (mg)	K (mg)	Na (mg)	Zn (mg)	Cu (mg)	Se (μg)
1	Apple	0.12	6	11	5	107	1	0.04	0.027	0.0
2	Apricot	0.39	13	23	10	259	1	0.20	0.078	0.1
3	Avocado	0.55	12	52	29	485	7	0.64	0.190	0.4
4	Banana	0.26	5	22	27	358	1	0.15	0.078	1.0
5	Cherry	0.36	13	21	11	222	0	0.07	0.060	0.0
6	Grape	0.36	10	20	7	191	2	0.07	0.127	0.1
7	Guava	0.31	20	25	10	284	3	0.23	0.103	0.6
8	Kiwi fruit	0.41	26	40	30	332	5	-	-	-
9	Orange	0.10	40	14	10	181	0	0.07	0.045	0.5
10	Papaya	0.10	24	5	10	257	3	0.07	0.016	0.6
11	Passion fruit	1.60	12	68	29	348	28	0.10	0.086	0.6
12	Peach	0.25	6	20	9	190	0	0.17	0.068	0.11
13	Pear	0.17	9	11	7	119	1	0.10	0.082	0.1
14	Pineapple	0.28	13	8	12	115	1	0.10	0.099	0.1
15	Plum	0.17	6	16	7	157	0	0.10	0.057	0.0
16	Raspberry	0.69	25	29	22	151	1	0.42	0.090	0.2
17	Strawberry	0.42	16	24	13	153	1	0.14	0.048	0.4

(*Source* : Y. H. Hui *et al.* 2006)

CLASSIFICATION OF FLAVONOIDS AND THEIR PRESENCE IN FRUITS

S.No.	Subclasses	Flavonoids	Fruits
1	Flavones	Apigenin, luteolin	Apples, blueberries, grape fruit, grapes, orange
2	Flavonols	Quercitin, kaempferol, myricetin	Apples, berries, plum
3	Flavonols	Catechin, epicatechin, epigallocatechin gallate	Apples, berries, grapes, plum
4	Flavones	Hesperetin, naringenin	Citrus fruit
5	Anthocyanins	Cyaniding, pelargonodon, malvidin	Berries, grapes
6	Isoflavones	Genistein, daidzein	Currants, passion fruit

(*Source* : Y. H. Hui *et. al.* 2006)

RECOMMENDED STORAGE TEMPERATURE AND RELATIVE HUMIDITY FOR SELECTED FRUITS

S.No.	Fruit	Temperature (°C)	Relative humidity (%)	Storage life (weeks)
1	Apple	– 1.4/4.0	90-95	5-52
2	Apricots	– 0.5/0.0	90-95	1-3
3	Banana	13/14	90-95	-
4	Berries (other than cran berries)	2/4	90-95	1-5
5	Fig	– 0.5/0.0	85-90	1-2
6	Grape fruits	10-15	85-90	6-8
7	Grapes, vinifera	– 1/-0.5	90-95	4-31
8	Kiwis	– 0.5/0.0	90-95	14-25
9	Oranges	3-9	85-90	8-12
10	Passion fruit	7-10	85-90	3-5
11	Peaches	– 0.5/0.0	90-95	2-4
12	Pears	– 1.5/-0.5	90-95	2-7
13	Pineapples	7/13	85-90	2-5
14	Plums and prunes	-0.5/0.0	90-95	2-4

(*Source* : Hardenburg *et al.* 1986 and Hanson 1976)

AVERAGE AIR COMPOSITION

S. No.	Air components	Symbol	Volume (dry air)
1	Nitrogen %	N_2	78.08
2	Oxygen %	O_2	20.95
3	Argon %	Ar	0.93
4	Carbon dioxide (ppm)	CO_2	350
5	Neon (ppm)	Ne	18.2
6	Helium (ppm)	He	5.24
7	Methane (ppm)	CH_4	2
8	Krypton (ppm)	Kr	1.1
9	Hydrogen (ppm)	H_2	0.5
10	Nitrous oxide (ppm)	N_2O	0.3
11	Xenon (ppm)	Xe	0.08
12	Carbon monoxide (ppm)	CO	0.05-0.2
13	Ozone (ppm)	O_3	0.02-0.03

*Dry atmosphere below 80 Km (ppm = parts per million)

EFFECTS OF COOKING ON VITAMINS

S.No.	Vitamin	Soluble in Water	Stable to Air Exposure	Stable to Light Exposure	Stable to Heat Exposure
01.	Vitamin A	no	partially	partially	relatively stable
02.	Vitamin C	very unstable	yes	no	no
03.	Vitamin D	no	no	no	no
04.	Vitamin E	no	yes	yes	no
05.	Vitamin K	no	no	yes	no
06.	Thiamine (B_1)	highly	no	no	> 100 °C
07.	Riboflavin (B_2)	slightly	no	in solution	no
08.	Niacin (B_3)	yes	no	no	no
09.	Pantothenic Acid (B_5)	quite stable	no	no	yes
10.	Vitamin (B_6)	yes	?	yes	?
11.	Biotin (B_7)	somewhat	?	?	no
12.	Folic Acid (B_9)	yes	?	when dry	at high temp
13.	Cobalamin (B_{12})	yes	?	yes	No

(*Source*: NIN, 2011.)

RECOMMENDED LEVELS OF VITAMINS

S.No.	Nutrient	U.S. EAR	Highest U.S. RDA or AI	Highest EU PRI or AI	Upper limit (UL)			Unit
					U.S.	EU	Japan	
01	Vitamin A	625	900	1300	3000	3000	2700	µg
02	Vitamin C	75	90	155	2000	ND	ND	mg
03	Vitamin D	10	15	15	100	100	100	µg
04	Vitamin K	NE	120	70	ND	ND	ND	µg
05	α-tocopherol (Vitamin E)	12	15	13	1000	300	650-900	mg
06	Thiamin (Vitamin B1)	1.0	1.2	0.1 mg/MJ	ND	ND	ND	mg
07	Riboflavin (Vitamin B2)	1.1	1.3	2.0	ND	ND	ND	mg
08	Niacin (Vitamin B3)	12	16	1.6 mg/MJ	35	10	60-85	mg
09	Pantothenic acid (Vitamin B5)	NE	5	7	ND	ND	ND	mg
10	Vitamin B6	1.1	1.3	1.8	100	25	40-60	mg
11	Biotin (Vitamin B7)	NE	30	45	ND	ND	ND	µg
12	Folate (Vitamin B9)	320	400	600	1000	1000	900-1000	µg
13	Cyanocobalamin (Vitamin B12)	2.0	2.4	5.0	ND	ND	ND	µg

EAR Estimated Average Requirements.

RDA Recommended Dietary Allowances; higher for adults than for children, and may be even higher for women who are pregnant or lactating.

AI Adequate Intake; **PRI** Population Reference Intake is European Union equivalent of RDA.

ND Not been determined. **NE** Not been established.

(*Source:* NIN, 2011.)

NOMENCLATURE OF RECLASSIFIED VITAMINS

S.No.	Previous name	Chemical name	Reason for name change
01	Vitamin B_4	Adenine	DNA metabolite; synthesized in body
02	Vitamin B_8	Adenylic acid	DNA metabolite; synthesized in body
03	Vitamin BT	Carnitine	Synthesized in body
04	Vitamin F	Essential fatty acids	Needed in large quantities (does not fit the definition of a vitamin).
05	Vitamin G	Riboflavin	Reclassified as Vitamin B_2
06	Vitamin H	Biotin	Reclassified as Vitamin B_7
07	Vitamin J	Catechol, Flavin	Catechol nonessential; flavin reclassified as Vitamin B_2
08	Vitamin L_1	Anthranilic acid	Nonessential
09	Vitamin L_2	Adenylthiomethylpentose	RNA metabolite; synthesized in body
10	Vitamin M or Bc	Folate	Reclassified as Vitamin B_9
11	Vitamin P	Flavonoids	Many compounds, not proven essential
12	Vitamin PP	Niacin	Reclassified as Vitamin B_3
13	Vitamin S	Salicylic acid	Nonessential
14	Vitamin U	S-Methylmethionine	Protein metabolite; synthesized in body

(*Source*: NIN, 2011.)

THE DISCOVERY DATES OF THE VITAMINS AND THEIR SOURCES

S.No.	Year of discovery	Vitamin	Food source
01	1913	Vitamin A (Retinol)	Cod liver oil
02	1910	Vitamin B_1 (Thiamine)	Rice bran
03	1920	Vitamin C (Ascorbic acid)	Citrus, most fresh foods
04	1920	Vitamin D (Calciferol)	Cod liver oil
05	1920	Vitamin B_2 (Riboflavin)	Meat, dairy products, eggs
06	1922	Vitamin E (Tocopherol)	Wheat germ oil, unrefined vegetable oils
07	1929	Vitamin K_1 (Phylloquinone)	Leafy green vegetables
08	1931	Vitamin B_5 (Pantothenic acid)	Meat, whole grains, in many other foods
09	1931	Vitamin B_7 (Biotin)	Meat, dairy products, Eggs
10	1934	Vitamin B_6 (Pyridoxine)	Meat, dairy products
11	1936	Vitamin B_3 (Niacin)	Meat, grains
12	1941	Vitamin B_9 (Folic acid)	Leafy vegetables lentils, beans, nuts
13	1948	Vitamin B_{12} (Cobalamins)	Meat, organs (Liver), Eggs

(*Source:* NIN, 2011.)

MAJOR TYPES OF FATTY ACIDS IN FATS AND OILS

Saturated	Mono-unsaturated (MUFA)	Polyunsaturated (PUFA)		
Coconut	Red palm oil		**Linoleic (n-6)**	**α-Linolenic (n-3)**
Palm kernel	Palmolein			
Ghee/butter	Groundnut	**Low**	Red palm oil, Palmolein	Rapeseed,
Vanaspati	Rice bran	**Moderate**	Groundnut, Rice bran, Sesame	Mustard Soybean
	Sesame seed oil	**High**	Safflower, Sunflower, Cottonseed, Corn, Soybean	

(*Source:* NIN, 2011.)

Table–7: CLASSIFICATION OF FOODS BASED ON FUNCTION

S. No.	Major Nutrients	Other Nutrients	
01	**Energy Rich Foods**	***Carbohydrates & fats***	
		Whole grain cereals, millets	Protein, fibre, minerals, calcium, iron & B-complex vitamin
		Vegetable oils, ghee, butter	Fat soluble vitamins, essential fatty acids
		Nuts and oilseeds	Proteins, vitamins, minerals
		Sugars	Nil
02	**Body Building Food**	***Proteins***	
		Pulses, nuts and oilseeds	B-complex vitamins, invisible fat, fibre
		Milk and milk products	Calcium, vitamin A, riboflavin, vitamin B12
		Meat, fish, poultry	B-complex vitamins, iron, iodine, fat
03	**Protective Foods**	***Vitamins and minerals***	
		Green leafy vegetables	Antioxidants, fibre and other carotenoids
		Other vegetables and fruits	Fibre, sugar and antioxidants
		Eggs, Milk and milk products and flesh foods	Protein and fat

(*Source:* NIN, 2011.)

SOME GENERA OF BACTERIA POSSIBLY ASSOCIATED WITH MILK

S.No.	Family	Genus	Morphology	Motility	Gram reaction	Oxygen requirement
1	Micrococcaceae	*Micrococcus*	Coccus	—	+	Aerobic
		Staphylococcus	Clump of cocci	—	+	Aerobic
2	Lactobacillaceae	*Lactococcus*	Diplociccus	—	+	Aerotolerant
		Streptococcus	Chain of cocci	—	+	Aerotolerant
		Lactobacillus	Rod, chain	—	+	Aerotolerant
3	Bacillaceae	*Bacillus*	Rod, spore	—	+	Aerobic
		Clostridium	Rod, spore	—	+	Anaerobic
4	Enterobacteriaceae	*Escherichia*	Rod	+ (Peritrichous)	—	Facultative aerobic
		Salmonella	Rod	+ (Peritrichous)	—	Facultative aerobic
5	Pseudomonadaceae	*Pseudomona*	Rod	+ (Polar)	—	Aerobic

(*Source* : Chandan *et al.* 2006)

PROXIMATE COMPOSITION OF MILK OF MAMMALS USED FOR HUMAN CONSUMPTION

S No.	Mammal	% Total Solids	% Fat	% Total Protein	% Casein	% Whey Protein	% Lactose	% Ash
1	Cow	12.2	3.4	3.4	2.8	0.6	4.7	0.7
2	Cow, zebu	13.8	4.6	3.3	2.6	0.7	4.4	0.7
3	Buffalo	16.3	6.7	4.5	3.6	0.9	4.5	0.8
4	Goat	13.2	4.5	2.9	2.5	0.4	4.1	0.8
5	Sheep	19.3	7.3	5.5	4.6	0.9	4.8	1.0
6	Camel	13.6	4.5	3.6	2.7	0.9	5.0	0.7
7	Mare	11.2	1.9	2.5	1.3	1.2	6.2	0.5
8	Donkey	8.5	0.6	1.4	0.7	0.7	6.1	0.4
9	Yak	17.3	6.5	5.8	NA	NA	4.6	0.9

(*Source* : Chandan *et al.* 2006) NA: Not available

AMINO ACIDS

S. No.	Essential amino acids	Non essential amino acids
1	Methionine	Alanine
2	Arginine	Asparatic acid
3	Threonine	Glutamic acid
4	Tryptophan	Cysteine
5	Valine	Glycine
6	Isoleucine	Proline
7	Phenylalanine	Serine
8	Lysine	Tyrosine
9	Histidine – essential only for children	

(*Source* : Notes ANGRAU, Hyderabad, 2012)

PRESERVATIVES PERMITTED IN FOOD ITEMS

S.No.	Preservative	Concentration	Foods
1	Sulphurdioxide or salt of sulphurous acid	49-3,000 ppm	Sausages, fruit pulp, fruit juice concentrate, squashes, crushes, jams, syrups, cordial sugar, glucose, *khandsari*, corn flour and syrup, beer, cider, pickles, dehydrated vegetables, wines, ready –to-+ serve beverages, hard boiled confectionery
2	Propionic acid and its salts	5,000 ppm	Bread
3	Benzoic acid and its salts	50-6,000 ppm	Syrups, squashes, James, jellies, ready –to- serve beverages, pickles, chutney, ginger beer, tinned caviare
4	Sorbic acid and its salts	1,000-1,500 ppm	Cheese, bread, flour confectionery, smoked fish wrappers
5	Nisin	1,000 ppm	Cheese
6	Nitrites	200 ppm	Cooked pickled meat, ham and bacon
7	Nitrates	500 ppm	Cooked pickled meat, ham and bacon

(*Source* : Khader V. ICAR. 2001)

REMOVAL OF INSECTICIDES BY COMMON PROCESSING PROCEDURE IN VEGETABLES

S No.	Vegetables/insecticides	Washing with 2% salt water and cooking for 15 min.	Washing and steam cooking
		Beans	
1	Malathion	60%	69%
2	Monocrophos	42%	47%
3	Carbaryl	58%	69%
		Chillies	
4	Monocrophos	28%	30%
5	Quinolphos	22%	29%
		Tomatoes	
6	Carbaryl	67%	75%
7	Monocrophos	31%	32%
8	Quinolphos	29%	30%

(***Source*** : Khader V. ICAR. 2001)

IMPORTANT PROTEINS IN CEREALS

S. No.	Cereals	Prolamines	Glutelins	Globulins
1	Wheat	Gliadin	Glutenin	*
2	Rice	Gliadin	Oryzenin	*
3	Maize (corn)	Zein	Traces	*
4	Barley	Hordein	*	*
5	Millets	Panccin	*	*
6	Rye	Gliadin	Glutenin	Endestin
7	Oats	*	Evenin	Evenalin

(***Source*** : Khader V. ICAR. 2001) * = Minor

STEPS INVOLVED IN PREPARATION OF RICE BRAN OIL

S. No.	Steps involved in preparation of Rice bran oil	
1	Dewaxing	To remove wax
2	Degumming	To remove phospholipids
3	Neutralization or deacidification	To remove the fatty acids
4	Bleaching	To remove colour
5	Deodourization	To remove smell
6	Winterization	To remove saturated glycerides

(*Source* : Khader V. ICAR. 2001)

TYPES OF ALCOHOLIC DRINKS AND THEIR CALORIE VALUE

S. No.	Type	Alcoholic content%	Calorie value (cal/100ml)
		Beer	
1	Bitter	3	30
2	Mild	3	25
		Cider	
3	Dry	4	35
4	Sweet	4	40
		Wine	
5	White	9	70
6	Red	9	65
7	Fortified	16	135
		Spirit	
8	Whisky	40-50	220
9	Rum	40	200
		Liquor	
10	Benedictine	39	270

(*Source* : Khader V. ICAR. 2001)

CALORIES REQUIREMENT BASED ON WEIGHT/AGE

S. No.	Category	Calories requirement
1	Over weight	20 Kcals/Kg/day
2	Ideal weight	30 Kcals/Kg/day
3	Under weight	40 Kcals/Kg/day
4	Elderly person above 50 years	10% less calories for each additional decade
5	Children –Ist years	1000 calories
6	For girls 1-12 years	1000+100 calories per year of age upto 12 years
7	For boys 1-12 years	1000+125 calories per year of age upto 12 years

(*Source* : V. Vimla, 2009)

PROTEIN% IN DIFFERENT FOODS

1. Avocados	16	**4.** Egg yolk	31
2. Chocolate	35	**5.** Beef	41
3. Almond	58	**6.** Cheese	32

(*Source*: Khader V. 2001)

3R's OF COOKING TO CONSERVE NUTRIENTS

1. Reduce the amount of water used
2. Reduce the length of cooking period
3. Reduce the amount of surface area exposed

(*Source:* Shrilakshmi B. 2015)

19: NUTRIENT % IN MILK

1. Fat	3-6	**4.** Milk sugar	5
2. Protein	3-4 (casein)	**5.** Water	85.5-88.5
3. Ash	0.7	**6.** MSNF (milk solids not fat)	11.4-14.5

VARIOUS TYPES OF CONTAINERS

1. Tin cans	**2.** Electrolytic tinning
3. Steel base	**4.** Tin coating
5. Glass	**6.** Plastics and films
7. Paper	**8.** Laminations
9. Acrylic	**10.** Ceramic
11. Brushed copper	

THE DIFFERENT PLANTATION GRADES OF COFFEE ARE:-

1. Pea berry (oval shaped beans)
2. O or A (first size in flats- bold, heavy and well formed)
3. B (slightly smaller than O or A)
4. C (slightly smaller than B)
5. Triage (pale, discoloured, black spotted beans including bits)

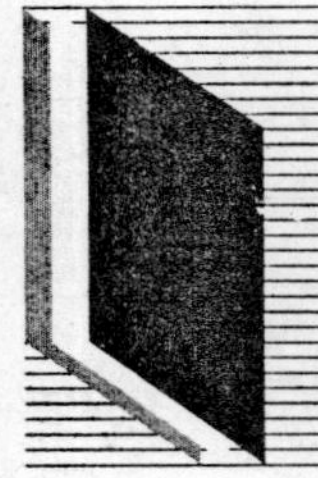

CHAPTER 16
GENERAL AGRICULTURE

HISTORY OF MODERN AGRICULTURE BEFORE INDEPENDENCE

S.No.	Years	Events
1	1871	Department of Revenue, Agriculture and Commerce (DRAC)
2	1874	Severe famine in Bihar
3	1875	Indian Meteorology Department (IMD) at Pune (Maharashtra)
4	1876	Famine in Madras and Bombay presidencies
5	1877	Famine in Punjab, Central province (approx 10 lac people died)
6	1878	Higher Education in agriculture at Coimbatore
7	1880	Famine commission appointed
8	1881	Government of India started Department of Revenue and Agriculture in provinces
9	1882	Veterinary college established at Lahore (Now in Pakistan)
10	1890	Higher Education in agriculture at Pune
11	1891	Dr J A Volcker's report on improvement of Indian Agriculture
12	1892	Agriculture chemist and an assistant chemist were appointed to look after research and teaching
13	1899-1900	Famine (Chhapaniya Kal)
14	1900	Forest Research Institute (FRI) established at Dehradun
15	1901-1905	Agriculture colleges were established at Pune, Kanpur, Sabour, Nagpur, Lyallapur and Coimbatore
16	1901	First Irrigation commission
17	1903	Model Village by Daniel Hamilton
18	1905	Establishment of Imperial (Now known as) Indian Agricultural Reseach Institute at Pusa (Bihar) shifted to New Delhi in 1936

...Cond.

S.No.	Years	Events
19	1906	Started Agriculture Journal India
20	1908	Tagore started Youth organization in the village in the Kaligram Pargana
21	1919	Constitutional Reforms made Agriculture as a state subject
22	1920	GURGAON Project by F L Bryne
23	1921	SHRINIKETAN Project by R N Tagore
24	1921	MARTHANDAM Project by Spencer Hatch
25	1921	SEVAGRAM Project by Mahatma Gandhi. Adarsh Seva Sangh, Pohari (Gwalior) by Col. Shitole (Wardha).
26	1921	Indian Central Cotton Committee
27	1926	Appointment of Royal Commission Agriculture headed by Lord Linlithgo
28	1929	Establishment of Imperial (Now Indian) Council of Agriculture Research (ICAR), at New Delhi.
29	1931	Indian Central Lac Committee
30	1932	Rural reconstruction movement by V T Krishnamachari in Baroda
31	1935	Rural Development Programme
32	1936	Indian Central Jute Committee
33	1940	Monthly Journal (Popular) Indian Farming started by Imperial (Indian) Council of Agriculture Research (ICAR), New Delhi
34	1942	Department of Food Created
35	1942	Grow More Food Compaign (Failed and again started in 1947 GMF)
36	1943	Great Bengal Famine (Caused by *Helminthisporium oryzae*)
37	1944	Indian Central Sugarcane Committee
38	1944	Dr W Burns report on Technological Possibilities of Agricultural Development in India
39	1945	Sir Pheroze Kharegat's memorandum on the development of Agriculture and Animal Husbandry in India
40	1945	Indian Central Coconut Committee
41	1945	Indian Central Tobacco Committee
42	1945	Indian Village Service by A T Mosher and B N Gupta, D Tharugad

...Cond.

S.No.	Years	Events
43	1946	Directorate of plant protection and quarantine
44	1946	Central Rice Research Institute (CRRI) at Cuttack, Odisha
45	1946-1947	Firka Development by Madras State by T Prakasham and D Tharugad
46	1947	Food Policy Committee
47	1947	Grow More Food Campaign (relaunched)
48	1947	Indian Central Oil Seeds Committee
49	1947	Fertilizers and Chemicals at Travancore
50	1947	Mazdoor Manzil at Nilokheri by S K Dey
51	1948	Etawah Pilot Project Lt.Col. Albert Mayer

Source : (Nem Raj Sunda. 2014 and M. S. Rathore, 2014)

DOMESTICATION OF PLANTS/ANIMAL IN VARIOUS REGIONS IN THE WORLD

S.No.	Estimated Time	Animal/Plant	Place
1	10,000 BC	Dog	Iraq and Israel
2	8,400 B C	Dog	North-Western America
3	9,000 B C	Sheep and Goat	Middle-East Region
4	7,000 B C	Pig	Turkey
5	6,300 B C	Cattle	Greece
6	6,000 B C	Wheat	Greece
7	6,000 B C	Lentil and Peas	Middle-East
8	6,000 B C	*Phaseolus lunatus*	Peru
9	6,000 B C	*Phaseolus vulgaris*	Peru
10	5,000 B C	Kidney bean	Peru and Mexico
11	5,000 B C	Maize	Mexico and South America
12	4,000 B C	Rice	China and Thailand
13	3,000 B C	Cotton	Africa and India
14	3,000 B C	Horse	Southern Russian Turkestan
15	3,000 B C	Ploughing began	Latin America and old world
16	25,00 B C	Buffalo	South Eastern Asia
17	18,00 B C	Sorghum	North Africa and India
18	Before 1,000	Sunflower	Central North America
19	4000 years ago	Potato (cultivated)	South America

Source : (Nem Raj Sunda. 2014)

INTERNATIONAL INSTITUTES

S.No.	Abbreviation	Full Name
1	AVRDC	Asian Vegetable Research and Development Centre, Taiwan
2	CABI	Commonwealth Agriculture Bureaux International
3	CABI	Centre For Agricultural Bioscience International Wallingford Oxfordshire OXIO 8DE
4	CIGAR	Consultative Group of International Agriculture Research, Washington DC (USA)
5	CIAT	Centro International de Agricultura Tropical (International centre for tropical agriculture), Coli - Columbia (South America)
6	CIDA	Canadian International Development Agency, Cubac
7	CIFOR	Centre For International Forestry Research, Indonesia
8	CIMMYT	International Centre For The Improvement of Maize and Wheat, Mexico
9	CIP	International Potato Centre, Peru, South America
10	FAO	Food And Agriculture Organization, Rome, Italy
11	IBPGR	International Board For Plant Genectics Resources, Rome, Italy
12	IBRD	International Bank For Reconstruction And Development (The World Bank), Washington DC (USA)
13	IBSNAT	International Benchmark Soil Network for Agro Technology, Transfer, Hawaii
14	ICARDA	International Centre For Agricultural Research in Dry Areas, Aleppo, Syria
15	ICRAF	International Centre For Research in Agro Forestry, Nairobi, Kenya
16	ICRISAT	International Cops Research Institute for the Semi-Arid Tropics, Hyderabad, (Telangana), India
17	IFAD	International Fund For Agricultural Development, Cubac
18	IFDC	International Fertilizer Development Centre, Alabama, USA
19	IFPRI	International Food Policy Research Institute, Washington DC
20	IIMI	International Irrigation Management Institute, Digana Village, Sri Lanka
21	IIRB	International Institute For Sugar Beet Research Rue Washington Brussels Belgium
22	IITA	International Institute of Tropicai Agriculture, Ibadan, Anigeria
23	IJSG	International Jute Study Group, Dhaka, Bangladesh

...Cond.

S.No.	Abbreviation	Full Name
24	ILCA	International livestock centre for Africa, Addis Ababa, Ethiopia
25	ILRAD	International Laboratory For Research on Animal Disease, Nairobi, Kenya
26	ILRI	International Livestock Research Institute, Nairobi.Kenya
27	IRRI	International Rice Research Institute, Manila, Philippines
28	ISANR	International Service For National Agriculture Rsearch, The Hague, Netherland
29	ISSS	International Society of Soil Science, Rome
30	IWMI	International Water Management, Digana Village, Sri Lanka
31	TPRI	Tropical Pesticide Institute, Arushan, Tanzania
32	WARDA	Western African Rice Development Association, Monrovia, Liberia
33	WMO	World Meteorological Organization, Geneva, Switzerland
34.	ICUC	International Centre for Underutilized Crops, Sri Lanka

Source : (Muniraj Singh Rathore. 2019)

ICAR INSTITUTES

1.	Central Island Agricultural Research Institute, Port Blair
2.	Central Arid Zone Research Institute, Jodhpur
3.	Central Avian Research Institute, Izatnagar
4.	Central Inland Fisheries Research Institute, Barrackpore
5.	Central Institute Brackishwater Aquaculture, Chennai
6.	Central Institute for Research on Buffaloes, Hissar
7.	Central Institute for Research on Goats, Makhdoom
8.	Central Institute of Agricultural Engineering, Bhopal
9.	Central Institute for Arid Horticulture, Bikaner
10.	Central Institute of Cotton Research, Nagpur
11.	Central Institute of Fisheries Technology, Cochin
12.	Central Institute of Freshwater Aquaculture, Bhubneshwar
13.	Central Institute of Research on Cotton Technology, Mumbai
14.	Central Institute of Sub Tropical Horticulture, Lucknow
15.	Central Institute of Temperate Horticulture, Srinagar
16.	Central Institute on Post-harvest Engineering and Technology, Ludhiana

...*Cond.*

17.	Central Marine Fisheries Research Institute, Kochi
18.	Central Plantation Crops Research Institute, Kasargod
19.	Central Potato Research Institute, Shimla
20.	Central Research Institute for Jute and Allied Fibres, Barrackpore
21.	Central Research Institute of Dryland Agriculture, Hyderabad
22.	National Rice Research Institute, Cuttack
23.	Central Sheep and Wool Research Institute, Avikanagar, Rajasthan
24.	Indian Institute of Soil and Water Conservation, Dehradun
25.	Central Soil Salinity Research Institute, Karnal
26.	Central Tobacco Research Institute, Rajahmundry
27.	Central Tuber Crops Research Institute, Trivandrum
28.	ICAR Research Complex for Eastern Region, Patna
29.	ICAR Research Complex for NEH Region, Barapani
30.	Central Coastal Agricultural Research Institute, Ela, Old Goa, Goa
31.	Indian Agricultural Statistics Research Institute, New Delhi
32.	Indian Grassland and Fodder Research Institute, Jhansi
33.	Indian Institute of Agricultural Biotechnology, Ranchi
34.	Indian Institute of Horticultural Research, Bengaluru
35.	Indian Institute of Natural Resins and Gums, Ranchi
36.	Indian Institute of Pulses Research, Kanpur
37.	Indian Institute of Soil Sciences, Bhopal
38.	Indian Institute of Spices Research, Calicut
39.	Indian Institute of Sugarcane Research, Lucknow
40.	Indian Institute of Vegetable Research, Varanasi
41.	National Academy of Agricultural Research & Management, Hyderabad
42.	National Institute of Biotic Stresses Management, Raipur
43.	National Institute of Abiotic Stress Management, Malegaon, Maharashtra
44.	National Institute of Animal Nutrition and Physiology, Bengaluru
45.	National Institute of Research on Jute & Allied Fibre Technology, Kolkata
46.	National Institute of Veterinary Epidemiology and Disease Informatics, Hebbal, Bengaluru
47.	Sugarcane Breeding Institute, Coimbatore
48.	Vivekananda Parvatiya Krishi Anusandhan Sansthan, Almora

...Cond.

49.	Central Institute for Research on Cattle, Meerut, Uttar Pradesh
50.	National Institute of High-Security Animal Diseases, Bhopal
51.	Indian Institute of Maize Research, New Delhi
52.	Central Agroforestry Research Institute, Jhansi
53.	National Institute of Agricultural Economics and Policy Research, New Delhi
54.	Indian Institute of Wheat and Barley Research, Karnal
55.	Indian Institute of Farming Systems Research, Modipuram
56.	Indian Institute of Millets Research, Hyderabad
57.	Indian Institute of Oilseeds Research, Hyderabad
58.	Indian Institute of Oil Palm Research, Pedavegi, West Godawari
59.	Indian Institute of Water Management, Bhubaneshwar
60.	Indian Institute of Rice Research, Hyderabad
61.	Central Institute for Women in Agriculture, Bhubaneshwar
62.	Central Citrus Research Institute, Nagpur
63.	Indian Institute of Seed Research, Mau
64.	Indian Agricultural Research Institute, Hazaribag, Jharkhand

Source : (Muniraj Singh Rathore. 2019)

TERMS AND they DERIVED FROM

S.No.	Term	Derived From
1.	Allelopathy	Greek
2.	Herbicide	Latin
3.	Extension	Latin
4.	Communication	Latin
5.	Pest	Latin
6.	Entomology (Entomo + lagus)	Greek
7.	Oleiriculture	Latin
8.	Agronomy	Greek I
9.	Agriculture	Latin
10.	Tillage	Anglosexon
11.	Genetics	Greek
12.	Entomology	Greek
13.	Horticulture	Latin
14.	Fungicide	Latin

Source : (Rammana Rao, 2019)

REVOLUTIONS IN AGRICULTURE

S.No.	Revolutions	Sector
1	Green Revolution	Food grain production
2	White Revolution	Milk production
3	Blue Revolution	Fish production
4	Brown Revolution	Food processing
5	Grey Revolution	Fertilizer production
6	Yellow Revolution	Oil seed production
7	Red Revolution	Tomato/Meat production
8	Pink Revolution	Prawn/Onion production
9	Golden Revolution	Fruit production
10	Round Revolution	Potato production
11	Silver Revolution	Egg/Poultry production
12	Black Revolution	Biofuel production
13	Rainbow Revolution	All/Allied sectors of Agriculture
14	Parbhani Revolution	Okra production

Source : (Nem Raj. Sunda. 2014; Muni Raj Singh Rathore, 2019)

TERMS ASSOCIATED WITH VARIOUS CROPS

S.No.	Crops	Term
1.	Oil palm	Stripping
2.	Rubber	Tapping
3.	Tea	Pruning and Skiffing
4.	Coffee	Stripping
5.	Cauliflower	Blanching
6.	French bean	Stalking
7.	Tomato	Stalking
8.	Tobacco and Tea	Curing
9.	Gram	Nipping
10.	Banana, Sugarcane	Propping
11.	Sunhemp	Degumming
12.	Tobacco	Desuckering, Topping, Rubbing, Priming
13.	Maize	De-tasseling
14.	Jute	Retting, Stripping
15.	Cotton	Ginning, Topping, Nipping
16.	Sugarcane	Ratooning Arrowing, Wrapping, Detrashing
17.	Rice	Parboiling
18.	Lucerne	Lopping
19.	Potato	Earthing up
20.	Groundnut	Pegging

Source : (Muniraj Singh Rathore. 2020)

IMPORTANT BOOKS AND THEIR AUTHORS

S.No.	Books	Authors
1	Disease of Cultivated Crop their Causes their Control	Kuhn
2	Rose in India	B P Paul (Father of Rose)
3	Bamboo farming	Shrikant Thatte
4	Peasant agriculture in Assam	Manmohan Das
5	Production technology of Exotic vegetables	Dr Arun Naphade, R Kharche
6	Principles and Practices of Agronomy	T Y Reddy
7	The Nature and Properties of Soil	Nyle C Brady
8	Soil fertility and fertilizers	Tisdale et al.
9	Horse hoeing husbandry	Jathrotull
10	Annals of Agriculture	Arthur Young

Source : (Arun Katyayan, 2011 ; S.R. Kantwa, 2012 and M.S. Rathore, 2019)

- Water is about 97% saline, 02.5% fresh and 0.5% only useful to human being.
- The water (prevention and control of pollution) Act-1974.
- The air (prevention and control of pollution) Act-1981.
- The environment (Protection) Act-1986.
- The motor vehicle Act-1988.
- YAP (Yamuna Action Plan) - 1963.
- GAP (Ganga Action plan) -1986.
- NRCP (National River Conservation Programme) - 1995, it includes about 34 rivers.
- The term biodiversity named by Walter G. Rosen in 1985.
- Biodiversity act -2002.
- National biodiversity authority was established with reference to Gazette 01/Oct (10)/2003.
- World Conservation Union (WCU) - Switzerland (Gland) has prepared a list in 1970 and published Red Data book and accordingly there are about 20,000 Endangered species.
- Koyoto protocol - Green house gas minimization.
- BSI (Botanical Survey of India) published a book - Threatened plants of India - A state of the Art Report (1980). Again BSI published Indian plant red data book - 1(1984) Editor S K Jain and ARK Sastry. (Botanical survey of India established in 1989)
- The term Ecology given by Earnt Haekel (1866) and Ecosystem A G Tansley (1935).
- Conservation of biodiversity may be achieved by In situ and Ex situ methods.
- World's first national park is Yellow stone park USA (1872).
- India's first national park is Hailey National park (old name) Jim Corbet (New name) Uttarakhand (1936).

- First national park in Madhya Pradesh is Kanha National park (1994).
- Wild life protection act - 1972.
- Indian forest act - 1865.
- Forest conservation act - 1980
- Father of modern plant pathology in India - E J Butler.
- Plant parasitic nematode first reported by Needham (1743) in England in wheat gall.
- K C Mehta discovered cereal rust disease cycle.
- Uncontrolled cell division is called Hyperplasia while abnormal cell elongation/enlargement (in size) called Hypertrophy.
- Fungicide is Latin word.
- Vitavax (Carbendazim) generally decomposed in 10-30 days after incorporation in soil.
- Tundu disease (Yellow Ear Rot) of wheat caused by *Clavibacter triticii* is usually associated with *Anguina triticii* (Nematode).
- The symptoms of powdery mildew of pea (caused by *Erisiphee polygoni*) first appears on leaves.
- Karnal bunt of wheat (*Neovossia indica*) 1931 by M. Mitra in Karnal (Haryana).
- *Trimethyl amine* the volatile compound causes foul smell in karnal bunt of wheat.
- Leaf rust of coffee was first time recorded in India (1870).
- Early blight of potato is soil born disease.
- Cochliobolin toxin compound is produced by *Drechslera oryzae* (Fungus) in rice is harmful to seeddling.
- Blast of rice is also known as rotten neck.
- *Penicillium roqueforti* is used in cheese making.
- Cause of spreading decline of citrus is Burrowing nematode *(Radopholus similisi.*
- Pest is Latin word.
- ETL (Economic Threshold Level) is given by Stern et al. (1959).
- Arthopoda means segmented.
- Insecticide act came in force in 1968.

S.No.	Particulars	Particle size
1	Dust	1-40 μ
2	Mist (A very thin fog)	50-150 μ
3	Granules	0.25-2.4 mm
4	Spray	100-400 μ
5	Fog (A thin cloud)	1-50 μ
6	Smoke	0.02 μ (0.001-0.1 μ)

Source : (Rammana Rao, Page. No. 30)

- High volume pressure: - 40-50 Kg/cm^2 pressure with 160-200 L. Water holding capacity.
- Ultra low volume: - 6L. /ha capacity.
- Droplet size for mosquitoes control should be 50-70 μ.
- Droplet size for spraying shade and orchard should be 80-100 μ.
- Brown plant hopper transmits the grassy stunt virus disease in rice.
- Green leaf hopper (Jassid) sucks juice of leaf and transmits Rice Tungro virus.
- LD-50 value shows toxicity of insecticides.
- Destructive Insect Pest Act (DIPA) – 1914.
- Directorate of plant protection quarantine and storage (DPPQS) -1946 at Faridabad, (Haryana)
- Sterile insect technique was first time proposed by Knipling in 1937.
- Bt discovered by S Ishiwata.
- Central insecticides Lab. (CIL) is at Faridabad (Haryana)
- In the world first field release of Bt cotton was in 1996. While in India first field release of Bt cotton was in 2002.
- Indian Grain Storage Institute - Hapur (UP).
- The newly hatched silk worms are known as Kegs/Ants/Chawaki.
- The stage of silk worm when it synthesizes silk is IVth and Vth instar larvae.
- The gland that helps in secretion of Lac to Lac insect is Resin gland.
- Vermicastin is excreta of earthworm.
- Study of animal behaviour is called Ethology.
- Strepsiptera is completely parasitic order.
- The attack of pea stem fly is maximum in November month.
- The term (IPM) Integrated pest management given by – Bertlet (1956).
- Pest management given by Geier (1970).
- Survival of insects ranges from 04-70 °C.
- Microbial control given by – E A Steinhaus (1949).
- Bio control of nematodes given by – Wilcox (1928).
- Father of insect physiology is Wiggelworth.
- Production function given by –LE Bishop
  viz. (A) Linear production function. (B) Quartratic production function
  (C) Square root production function (D) Cubic production function
- Most of the farmers in India belong to Irrational –I zone while farmer of Punjab, Haryana and western Uttar Pradesh belong to Irrational–II zone.
- National Agriculture Insurance Scheme launched in June 1999.
- The first Governer of Reserve Bank of India was Osborne Smith (British banker) while C.D. Deshmukh was the first India governer.
- Employment Guarantee Scheme was launched from Maharashtra.

AGRICULTURAL LOANS ACCORDING TO DURATION

S.No.	Type of Loan	Duration
1	Short term loan	1-1.5 year
2	Medium term loan	1-5 year
3	Long term loan	5-30 year

Source : (Arun Katyayan 2011)

- Crop loan recommended by – B L Mehta (1960) and first time sanctioned for cotton crop in Berar (Maharashtra).
- Directorate of Marketing and Inspection (DMI) Faridabad, (Haryana).
- The first Regulated market established in 1886 at Karanj in cotton market.
- World Standard Day 14 October.
- World Food Day 16 October.
- Single window system was recommended by Mohan Kanda.
- Speculate demand depends on interest rate.
- Overhead cost is also known as fixed cost.
- The term extension firstly used in USA (1873)
- Extension activity firstly conducted in USA.
- Father of DemonstrationlMethod Demonstration (1885) is Dr. Seeman A Knapp.
- Father of extension education in world/USA is James Stuart and in India K N Singh.
- Father of extension is J P Legans.
- Learning by Doing (1966) word used by John Dewey.
- Panchayati raj introduced first in TN while adopted in Rajasthan.
- Firka development programme was launched by Madras Gov. (1946-47) (T Prakasham and D Thorugad).

1. COMPONENTS OF EFFECTIVE LEARNING

Teaching material and plan

↓

Subject matter

↓

Physical facilities and environment

↓

Teacher or Instructor

↓

Learner

***Source* : (Arun Katyayao, 2011)**

2. STEPS OF TEACHING

Attention

↓

Interest

↓

Desire

↓

Conviction

↓

Action

Satisfaction

***Source* : (Arun Katyayao, 2011)**

3. ELEMENTS OF ADOPTION

Innovation

↓

Diffusion

↓

Motivation

↓

Adoption

***Source* : (Arun Katyayan, 2011)**

4. STEPS OF ADOPTION

Awareness

↓

Interest

↓

Evaluation

↓

Trial

↓

Adoption

***Source* : (Arun Katyayan, 2011)**

5a. KEY ELEMENTS OF COMMUNICATION

Sender
↓
Message
↓
Message treatment (Encoding)
↓
Channel/Medium
↓
Receiver
↓
Receiver's response

***Source* : (Arun Katyayan, 2011)**

5b. KEY ELEMENTS OF COMMUNICATION

Source
↓
Encoder
↓
Message
↓
Channel
↓
Decoder
↓
Receiver

***Source* : (Berio, 1960)**

6. LEGANS MODEL OF COMMUNICATION

Communication
↓
Message
↓
Channel
↓
Treatment
↓
Audience
↓
Audience Response

***Source* : (Arun Katyayan, 2011)**

CATEGORIES OF ADOPTERS

S. No.	Categories	Percent
1	Innovators	2.5
2	Early adopters	13.5
3	Late majority	34
4	Early majority	34
5	Laggards	16

Source : (Arun Katyayan, 2011)

- Kisan Bharti periodical is published from Pantnagar.
- A bulletin should contain 24-48 pages.
- National Rural Employment Programme started in 1977.
- Symposium is a short series of 2-5 lectures.
- National Agriculture science museum New Delhi inaugurated by Dr. A P J Abdul Kalam on 03/11/2004.
- Carotenoids are fat soluble and that are combination of carotene and Xanthophyll.
- Yellow colour of leaves is due to Carotenoids.
- Principal yellow pigment of maize is due to zeaxanthin.
- Phycobilins are found in blue, green and Red algae. It doesn't contain Mg.
- Pasteur Effect : Generally the increase in respiratory substrate or O_2 increases the rate of respiration But there are many cases where O_2 reduces the rate of sugar breakdown and even conserve it, is called Pasteur Effect.
- Enzyme is termed by W Kuhne (1878).
- Lock and Key theory was given by **Fischer (1894).**
- The term Vernalization was coined by **T D Lysenko (1920).**
- The term Self incompatibility was originally coined by **Stout in 1917.**
- Koelreuter in 1763 first reported male **sterility in flowering plants.**
- Astringent taste in Arecanut is due to **Polyphenol and Tennins.**
- Gelatinous substance in Ridge guard and Sponge guard is due to Luffein.
- Botanical Name of Harra (Harad) is *Terminalia Chebula* (Fruit of tree).
- Khaira disease of zinc deficiency reported by Y L Naine in IR-8 rice at Pantnagar in 1966

SYMPTOMS OF DIFICIENCY OF SOME IMPORTANT NUTRIENTS

Ca

- Blossem end rot in tomato, ber and water melon.
- Tip hooking in cauliflower.
- Cavities rot in carrot.

- Bitter pit and cracking in apple.
- Calyx end rot in grapes and persimmon.
- Pillow in cucumber.

Mg

- Sand drawn disease in tobacco.
- Reddening in cotton.
- Bronzing in citrus.
- Interveinal chlorosis in apple.

Sulphur

- Downward cupping of leaves in Tobacco and Tea.
- Tea yellow disease.

Zn

- Browning in guava.
- Bunchy top in peanut.
- White bud in maize.
- Khaira in paddy.
- Rossett leaf or little leaf in apple.
- Little leaf in brinjal, mango and litchi.
- Leaf molting and frenching in citrus.
- Little leaf in coconut.

Mn

- Grey speck in oat.
- Speckled yellow in sugar beet.
- Phahala blight and speckled yellow in sugarcane.
- Frenching in tung tree.

Fe

- Leaf bleaching in sugarcane.
- Ivory white in paddy.

Mo

- Whiptail in cauliflower.
- Yellow spot disease in citrus.

B

- Internal necrosis in Aonla and Mango.
- Top sickness of tobacco.
- Hard fruits of citrus.
- Hen and chicken disorder in grape.
- Hard rot in sugar beet.

- Water core in Apple.
- Crown chocking in coconut.
- Black tip of mango.
- Browning in cauliflower and Tip burn in lettuce.
- Hollow stem of cauliflower.
- Improper inflorescence development in wheat.

Cu

- Exanthema/Ammoniationl/dieback in citrus.
- Wither tip in apple.
- Reclamation disease in cereal and legume.

Se (Selenium)

- Wheat muscle disease or nutritional muscular dystrophy.

IMPORTANT POINTS

- Boron is one non metal micronutrient. (It is a metalloids)
- Chloride sensitive crop is tobacco, beans, citrus, potato, lettuce and gram.
- Application of KCl reduces the **hollow heart disease of potato.**
- Fungal disease in wheat has been found to be suppressed by application of **NH_4Cl.**
- Yellow rust in wheat is the first disease reported to be **suppressed by Cl.**
- Silicon is required for the development of strong roots, stem and leaves.
- Silicon reduces the lodging in rice and it involves in the biosynthesis of lignin.
- Rice straw and its compost is the available **organic source of silicon.**
- Ni containing mineral is **serpentine.**
- Water holding capacity of humus on mass basis is 4-5 times than that of the silicate clays.
- One hectare of water is equal to 1,00,000 L. or 100 tonnes water.
- Sprinkler irrigation is suitable for sandy soils.
- Khadins are the small water storage ponds for Agriculture
- Percentage of water available at wilting point is 10% and at field capacity it is 75%.
- Hydraulic conductivity of soil depends on **Porosity of soil.**
- Transpiration ratio of plants usually ranges from **250-1000.**
- **Misting and fogging system-** It is the application of water in the form of very fine spray in order to create humidity in the air at low level or overhead. Misting system has very low flow rate (10-30 lit/hr) and high pressure (3.5-10 kg/cm^2).
- Solar energy required to change the water into vapour from 560 Cal/g/25°C.
- For determination of CEC (Cation Exchange Capacity) IN NH40AC (Ammonium Acetate) is used as extract.
- Zn moves from soil to roots by root interaction, mass flow and diffusion in equal proportion.

- Maximum Nitrification takes place at 20% O_2.
- NH_4 fixation takes place in Vermicullite and Illite.
- Biuret content of urea applied as a foliar spray in citrus fruits should be more than 0.25%. (Biuret is toxic side product of Urea. It damages the germinating seeds)
- Inorganic and organic P in soil collectively called **Quantity factor.**
- Chemical formula of SSP is Ca (H_2PO_4).
- Diagnostic surface horizons are called **Epipedons.**
- Soil aeration limits the plant growth when percent pores filled with water are more than 50-60%.
- **Munsell colour chart** contains about 175 different coloured paper or chips.
- A mature and dry plant tissue contains 1-15% protein.
- Moisture equivalent is given by **Brigs and Mclane (1910)**
- Method of estimation of lime requirement- **Shoemaker et al.**
- Petrology, pedrography and pedogenesis are jointly known as **Pedology.**
- Term Catena was introduced by **Milne (1930).**
- Silica Sasquioxide ratio for tropical region is < 2.
- Chomozem soils are found in Russia.
- There are mainly seven soil deposit in India, alluvial soil, black soil, red soil, laterite soil, forest and mountainous soil and marsh soil.
- Humus forming fungi includes in *Alternaria* and *Aspegillus* genera.
- Coordinated project on long term fertilizer launched by ICAR in 1970-71.
- Total number of major horizons of soil is **5.**
- B horizon is generally absent in **black soil.**
- Most salt tolerant grass is **Karnal grass** (*Diplachne fusca*).
- Fertilizer control order issued on 1957.
- Gapons equation is widely used to describe the EC of soil.
- Stem noduling rhizobium spp. Is **Azo- rhizobium.**
- Father of soil testing is **Troug.**
- Principle of Stokes law is used for determination of particle size (mechanical analysis of soil).
- Interzonal soil with or surface developing under marsh or swamp condition called Bog soil.
- $CaCO_3$ is used to improve soil condition of water logged soil.
- Mineralogical composition of Feldspar is Na-38, Fe-12.
- Quasi stable small clods known as **clods.**
- Specific heat of soil, organic matter and water is 0.2, 0.5 and 1.0 respectively.
- Cat clays are extremely acidic due to oxidation of S compounds.
- Black soil falls under Vertisols, Inceptisol and Entisols and it is rich In Montmorelonite.
- Acidic soil fixes more phosphorus.

- Organic matter content of histosol and hydromorphic soil is 30-40%.
- Melon grows best in **sandy soil.**
- Toxic concentration of Fe^{2+} in the soil solution of latosol.
- Tarai soils are deficient in Zn.
- Negative charge in 2 : 1 type clay mineral is pH dependent and independent both.
- Average content of silica in soil is **27%.**
- Micro relief of soils produced by expansion and contraction with changes in moisture **Gilgai micro relief**
- **Aspergillus niger** is used to test the potash status in the soil
- In acid rains mainly NO_2 is present.
- Enzymes are chemically **proteins**
- Genes are composed of DNA
- Pungency in mustard oil is due to **Glucosinolates**
- Organism which is responsible for production of methane from Bio gas plant **Methanobacteria**
- Organic source of nicotine is Tobacco
- How many acres are in one hectare **2.47 Acre**
- Flood tolerant Rice verity **Scuba Rice**
- Yellow coloured fruits are rich in **Vitamin A**
- Which gas is responsible for ozone hole formation **Chlorofluorocarbon (CFCs)**
- The element constituent of chlorophyll is **Magnesium (Mg)**
- Water use efficiency is highest under which method **Drip irrigation (90%)**
- Lowest infiltration rate of soil **Sodic clayey soil**
- Tag colour of certified seed is **Blue**
- Shree Anna designated to millets by GoI to make India a global hub for millets.
- Element essential for osmotic and ionic balance in plants K (Potassium)
- Nitrogen content in anhydrous ammonia About 82%
- Ripening hormone for crops is **Ethylene**
- Chemical Oleoresins found in **Chillies and Capsicum**
- Precursors of Ethylene is Methionine
- The milk-solids-not-fat in skim milk should not be less than: **8.7%**
- Theoretically, the maximum overrun in butter can be : **25%**
- For production of sterilized cream, the fat content of fresh, sweet cream is first standardized to : **20%**
- A satisfactory temperature for separation of milk is : **40ºC**
- In India, for ice cream manufacture, the widely used stabilizer is **sodium alginate**
- RM (Reichert Meissl) value of ghee measures the steam volatile water soluble **fatty acids**
- The color pigment involved in flowering in plant is: **phytochrome**
- The Conversion of sugar to pyruvic acid is called: **glycolysis**
- The first product of photosynthesis in C_3 plant is: **phosphoglyceric acid**

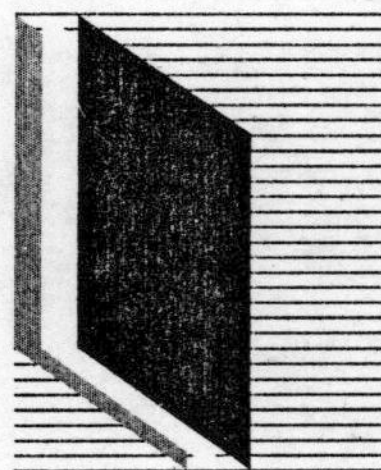
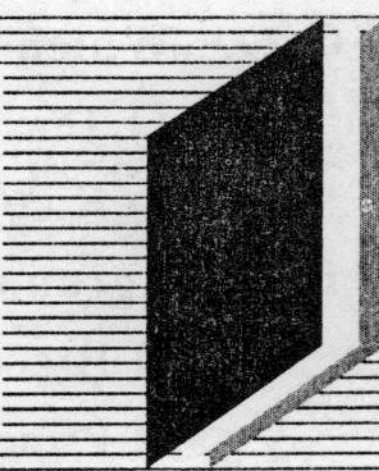

CHAPTER 17
MEMORY BASED QUESTION
(General Agriculture)

1. Q. Which of the following is not a nitrogenous fertilizer?

1) Ammonium sulphate — 2) Urea
3) Ammonium nitrate — 4) Super phosphate

2. Q. Rice crop needs

1) Warm and hot climate — 2) Dry and hot climate
3) Cold and humid climate — 4) Hot and humid climate

3. Q. The scientific study of soil is

1) Earth Study — 2) Soil Science
3) Pedology — 4) Soil Chemistry

4. Q. Prabhat is an early short duration variety of

1) Red gram — 2) Wheat
3) Maize — 4) Rice

5. Q. The Minimum Support Price for Food grains was introduced in the year

1) 1954-55 — 2) 1944-45
3) 1964-65 — 4) 1994-95

6. Q. Soil factors are otherwise known as

1) Climatic factors — 2) Edaphic factors
3) Biotic factors — 4) Physiographic factors

7. Q. Which of the following is a commercial crop?

1) Cotton — 2) Bajra
3) Jowar — 4) Paddy

8. Q. *Triticum aestivum*, the common bread wheat is

1) Tetraploid — 2) Hexaploid
3) Haploid — 4) Diploid

9. Q. Monoculture is a typical characteristic of

1) Shifting cultivation — 2) Subsitence farming
3) Specialized horticulture — 4) Commercial grain farming

10. Q. Which crop require water logging for its cultivation?

1) Tea 2) Coffee
3) Rice 4) Mustard

11. Q. Agronomy is a branch of Agriculture that deals with

1) Breeding of crop plants
2) Principles of field management
3) Principles and practice of crop production
4) Protection of crops from Diseases and Pests

12. Q. Soils of Western Rajasthan have a high content of

1) Aluminium 2) Calcium
3) Nitrogen 4) Phosphorus

13. Q. The Black rust of disease of wheat is caused by

1) *Xanthomonas graminis* 2) *Puccinia graminis*
3) *Puccinia recondita* 4) None of these

14. Q. A crop grown in zaid season is

1) Soyabean 2) Water melon
3) Jute 4) Maize

15. Q. The adoption of High Yielding Variety Programme in Indian Agriculture started in

1) 1966 2) 1965
3) 1968 4) 1969

16. Q. Which of the following is a food crop?

1) Palm 2) Jute
3) Cotton 4) None of the above

17. Q. Which of the following is an oilseed?

1) Cardamom 2) Garlic
3) Clove 4) Mustard

18. Q. Which one of the following makes a case for intensive, modern farming?

1) Cropping pattern 2) Higher output using organic method
3) Remunerative price 4) All the above

19. Q. Which of the following is not an agricultural product?

1) Alum 2) Cotton
3) Jute 4) Rice

20. Q. Crop rotation helps to

1) Lessen use of pesticides
2) Yield more crops
3) Produce a greater choice of plant products
4) Eliminate parasites which have selective hosts

21. Q. Potassium chloride (KCl) contains K

1) 18% 2) 48%
3) 44% 4) 60%

22. Q. Plant micronutrient is

1) Carbon 2) Boron
3) Magnesium 4) Sulphur

23. Q. Which gas is released from paddy fields?

1) CO_2 2) H_2S
3) CH_4 4) NH_3

24. Q. Which two crops of the following are responsible for almost 95% of pulse production in India?

1) Gram and pigeon pea 2) Gram and moong bean
3) Moong bean and lentil 4) Pigeon pea and moong bean

25. Q. Fire curing is followed in

1) Bidi tobacco 2) Hookah tobacco
3) Cheroot tobacco 4) Chewing type tobacco

26. Q. Groundnut pegs when developed in the soil from

1) Tubers 2) Fruits
3) Stems 4) Roots

27. Q. In Jute growing areas the usual alternate crop is

1) Cotton 2) Wheat
3) Sugarcane 4) Rice

28. Q. Neelum is a variety of

1) Grape 2) Papaya
3) Mango 4) Apple

29. Q. The Commission of Agricultural Costs and Prices (CACP) fixes the

1) Support price 2) Wholesale price
3) Retail price 4) None of these

30. Q. Vector of phyllody disease is

1) Thrips 2) Mite
3) White fly 4) Jassid

31. Q. Gynodioecious varieties of papaya produce

1) Only male plants 2) Female and hermaphrodite
3) Male and hermaphrodite plants 4) Only female plants

32. Q. Isolation distance for foundation seed of rice is

1) 30 metre 2) 3 metre
3) 35 metre 4) 50 metre

33. Q. Botanically pineapple is a

1) Pome 2) Baluster

3) Berry 4) Sorosis

34. Q. The basic unit of development under the Integrated Rural Development Programme is a

1) District 2) Family

3) Village 4) Community Development Block

35. Q. Black gram is originated in

1) Japan 2) Indonesia

3) China 4) India

36. Q. Seed rate of American cotton is

1) 20 kg/ha 2) 30 kg/ha

3) 35 kg/ha 4) 12 kg/ha

37. Q. Greening of potato results in

1) Increase in nutritional quality 2) Increase in disease resistance

3) Decrease in disease resistance 4) Decrease in nutritional quality

38. Q. Sugarbeet Nematode is

1) *Heterodera avanae* 2) *Heterodera cajani*

3) *Heterodera jae* 4) *Heterodera schacti*

39. Q. In medium term storage, material can be stored up to

1) 100 years 2) 3 to 5 years

3) 10 to 15 years 4) None of these

40. Q. Which is the saturated fatty acid of the following

1) Stearic acid 2) Arachidonic acid

3) Oleic acid 4) Linoleic acid

41. Q. Iron is an important component of

1) Siroheme 2) Ferredoxin

3) Cytochromes 4) All of these

42. Q. The chemical, which is used for controlling the mites, is known as

1) Fungicides 2) Mematicides

3) Acaricides 4) Insecticides

43. Q. WP abbreviates as

1) Wettable Paste 2) Wettable Powder

3) Water Paste 4) None of these

44. Q. Which of the following elements is not essential element of plants but proves to be beneficial for some plants?

1) Boron 2) Sodium

3) Iodine 4) Copper

45. Q. The pyrite is mostly found in

1) Bihar
2) Rajasthan
3) Andhra Pradesh
4) Maharashtra

46. Q. Parthenocarpy occurs in

1) Peach
2) Mango
3) Jackfruit
4) Banana

47. Q. Water use efficiency is the highest is case of

1) Border irrigation
2) Drip irrigation
3) Sprinkler irrigation
4) Flood irrigation

48. Q. Atmosphere is essential for

1) Winds
2) Cloud formation
3) Weather phenomena
4) All of these

49. Q. Which one of the following plants belongs to family Anacardiaceae?

1) Guava
2) Orange
3) Cashewnut
4) Papaya

50. Q. In India post harvest losses of fruit and vegetable is per cent of the total production.

1) 15-20
2) 50-50
3) 40-45
4) 25-30

51. Q. Which pH range is not suitable to grow the crop?

1) Oats- 5.0-9.5 pH
2) Cotton- 6.0-9.5 pH
3) Bean- 6.0-8.0 pH
4) Potato- 4.5-6.5 pH

52. Q. How much minimum temperature is essential for wheat germination and optimum temperature for crop growth in degree Celsius?

1) 3.5°C-5.5°C and 20°C-22°C
2) 5.6°C-9.5°C and 16°C-18°C
3) 8°C-10°C and 30°C-35°C
4) 10°C-12°C and 25°C-30°C

53. Q. The ideal temperature for most of the cultivable crops is

1) 30°C-50°C
2) 15°C-40°C
3) 35°C-40°C
4) 45°C-55°C

54. Q. Growth of early emerging leaves becomes faster because of

1) Cell division and celi enlargement
2) Stunt growth of plants
3) Faster photosynthesis
4) Low pressure of outer atmosphere

55. Q. How much percentage dry weight of crops should be at physiological maturity?

1) 40%
2) 35%
3) 25%
4) 20%

56. Q. To reduce the crop weed competition, at what stage are the herbicides used?

1) At germination
2) At tillering
3) At ear emergence
4) After first irrigation

57. Q. How does the supply of nitrogen in graïns take place?

1) From old leaves 2) From plant roots
3) From stem 4) By photosynthesis

58. Q. Which of the following points refers to the economic level of output?

1) MR < MC 2) MR > MC
3) MR = AC 4) MR = MC

59. Q. How much is the fat percentage in the milk of Bhadavari buffalo?

1) 15-18% 2) 8-13%
3) 13-16% 4) 6-10%

60. Q. A hen starts egg laying after how many weeks?

1) 15 weeks 2) 20 weeks
3) 18 weeks 4) 16 weeks

61. Q. Which is the Goat breed reared in the city?

1) Beetle 2) Surati
3) Marwadi 4) Barbari

62. Q. Makhdum is a variety for which crop?

1) Badam (Almond) 2) Date palm
3) Walnut 4) Coconut

63. Q. Generally during summer and kharif seasons annual plants produce bloom in how many days?

1) 60-90 days 2) 90-80 dyas
3) 90-95 days 4) 50-60 dyas

64. Q. Inarching method is used for culture of which fruits?

1) Mango and Guava 2) Mango and Grapes
3) Guava and Litchi 4) Phalsa and Guava

65. Q. How much tomatoes are required for one kg tomato seeds?

1) 50-300 kg 2) 300-350 kg
3) 160-210 kg 4) 200-250 kg

66. Q. What is the average annual production of European variety of honeybee colony?

1) 14 kg 2) 16 kg
3) 10 kg 4) 8 kg

67. Q. How much seed per hectare is needed for Berseem?

1) 18-22 kg 2) 25-30 kg
3) 30-35 kg 4) 15-20 kg

68. Q. Which is a variety of Oat?

1) K 12 2) Naveen
3) LD 491 4) Kent

69. Q. Sugarcane seed is required for sowing one hectare is-

1) 9000-9500 kg 2) 5500-6000 kg
3) 8000-8500 kg 4) 5200-5500 kg

70. Q. Which of the following is not matched?

1) Varuna-Irrigated or unirrigated condition
2) Vardan-Unirrigated condition
3) Narendra 85 Saline soil
4) K 88 Black grain

71. Q. Which disease is not related to Bajra?

1) Green Ear 2) Ergot
3) Wilt 4) Rust

72. Q. What is the suitable Rabi maize variety?

1) Sharadmani 2) Azad Uttam
3) Naveen 4) Ganga 5

73. Q. Which is not the symptom of Khaira disease?

1) Dark grey colour spots on leaves 2) Adverse effect on root growth
3) More diseases stop the crop growth 4) Stem of plants turn and fall down

74. Q. In case of availability of two irrigations for wheat, at which critical stage crop should be irrigated?

1) Tillering and Flowering 2) Crown Root Initiation and Milking stage
3) Crown Root Initiation and Flowering 4) Late joint and Dough stage

75. Q. From where is Krishak Bharati magazine published?

1) G. B. Pant University of Agriculture & Technology, Pantnagar
2) C. S. A. University of Agriculture & Technology, Kanpur
3) Narendra Dev University of Agriculture and Technology, Faizabad
4) Sardar Vallabh Bhai Patel University of Agriculture and Technology, Meerut

76. Q. More than how much percentage of loss of urea should not be during silage fermentation?

1) 20%-22% 2) 15%-18%
3) 10%-12% 4) 8%-10%

77. Q. Which is the perennial variety of Elephant Grass (Napier Grass)?

1) Pusa Giant 2) NB 21
3) Pusa Giant Napier 4) Napier 1

78. Q. Due to which reason is the Napier Grass mixed with Cluster bean or Cowpea for feeding?

1) Due to high crude fibre 2) Due to oxalic acid
3) Due to more carbohydrates 4) Due to more HCN content

79. Q. Approximately how much HCN dose is harmful for animal feeding?

1) 0.25 gm
2) 0.50 gm
3) 2.50 gm
4) 3.5 gm

80. Q. At which stage of crop, there is no competition for light, moisture and nutrients?

1) Node formation stage
2) Seedling stage
3) Grain formation stage
4) Before maturity stage

81. Q. At what stage are more nutrients essentially required in cereal crops?

1) Growth stage of plants
2) Formation of leaves
3) Panicle initiation
4) Maturity of crops

82. Q. What is the order of C_4 plants?

1) Sugarcane - Maize-Sudan grass - Bajra
2) Sugarcane - Cotton-Paddy - Maize
3) Sudan grass - Sugarcane - Paddy - Bajra
4) Cotton - Maize - Bajra - Sugarcane

83. Q. A.D.P. to A.T.P. change is called

1) Photosynthesis
2) Phosphorylation
3) Transpiration
4) Oxidation

84. Q. The monsoon airs in the country reaches at which bank first of all?

1) Coastal region of Orissa
2) Bay of Bengal region
3) Coastal region of Kerala of South Indian region
4) Kachchh region of Gujarat

85. Q. How much percentage of soluble salts is present in Alkali soils?

1) 1%-2%
2) 0.1%-0.2%
3) 1.5%-2.5%
4) 2%-3%

86. Q. Approximately how much area in lakh hectares of saline and alkali soils are there in Uttar Pradesh?

1) 15.00 lakh hectares
2) 12.4 lakh hectares
3) 10.4 lakh hectares
4) 14.4 lakh hectares

87. Q. Which is not natural factor affecting soil fertility?

1) Topography
2) Soil age
3) Air
4) Parent material

88. Q. The leaching loss of Nitrogen (N) is more in the form of

1) Ammonia
2) Nitrate
3) Nitrogen
4) Water solution

89. Q. The major fungi that effect food grains in storage are

1) Mucor
2) Rhizopus
3) Candida
4) Aspergillus

90. Q. Goal of extension education is

1) To promote income of the farmers
2) To promote production of the crops
3) To promote new crops
4) To promote scientific outlook

91. Q. How much area m^2 is required for a Goat?

1) 0.9-1.0 m
2) 1-1.5 m
3) 0.95-0.90 m
4) 1.5-1.95 m

92. Q. For how many years Sheep is able to breed?

1) 10 years
2) 9 years
3) 5 years
4) 12 years

93. Q. Which of the following is the cross of Karan Swiss?

1) Sahiwal × Brown Swiss
2) Sahiwal × Holstein
3) Hariyana × Brown Swiss
4) Hariyana × Jersey

94. Q. Which species of honeybee is not Indian?

1) *Apis florea*
2) *Apis dorsata*
3) *Apis dorsata*
4) *Apis mellifera*

95. Q. How much Brinjal seed may be obtained from one hectare area?

1) 150-200kg
2) 100-150kg
3) 200-300kg
4) 95-125kg

96. Q. Which elements are useful in energy storage, transfer and bonding?

1) NPK
2) NSP
3) NKS
4) None of these

97. Q. Which states are the highest & lowest producers of Potato crop?

1) Uttar Pradesh and Jharkhand
2) Gujarat and Assam
3) Uttar Pradesh & Himachal Pradesh
4) Bihar & Kashmir

98. Q. Which is not correct in the following?

1) X-rays and Gamma rays - 9% of energy
2) Visible lighting rays - 41% of energy
3) Infrared rays - 50% of energy
4) Ultraviolet rays - 10% of energy

99. Q. Effective cause of atmospheric pressure is not

1) Temperature
2) Altitude from the sea level
3) Rotation of earth
4) Soil erosion

100. Q. Where and when was World Meteorological Organization established?

1) New York -1980
2) Washington -1998
3) Geneva -1998
4) Rome -1996

101. Q. Sulphur coated Urea contains N

1) 21% 2) 33%

3) 40% 4) 26%

102. Q. Granite is a .... rock.

1) Metamorphic 2) Igneous

3) Sedimentary 4) None of these

103. Q. Chemical formula of pyrite is

1) FeS 2) CuS

3) MnS 4) FeS_2

104. Q. Soil fertility is reduced due to

1) Over irrigation 2) Poor drainage

3) Imbalanced use of fertilizers 4) Continuous cropping

105. Q. Anemometer measures

1) Wind direction 2) Relative humidity

3) Net radiation 4) Wind velocity

106. Q. Damping-off disease of vegetable nursery can be controlled by

1) Solarization 2) Mixing of fungicides in soil

3) Seed treatment 4) All of these

107. Q. Whiptail is a disorder of cauliflower due to deficiency of

1) Zinc 2) Boron

3) Potassium 4) Molybdenum

108. Q. The colour of tomato is due to the presence of

1) Carotene 2) Lycopin

3) Anthocyanin 4) Xanthomonas

109. Q. Mastitis is a disease of which organ?

1) Uterus 2) Heart

3) Udder 4) Lung

110. Q. Colostrum should be fed to newborn calves for

1) 1/2 day 2) 1 day

3) 4 day 4) 10 day

111. Q. Toda is breed of

1) Cattle 2) Goat

3) Buffalo 4) Sheep

112. Q. Mastitis in animals is due to

1) Worms 2) Virus and Worms

3) Fungi and dry hand milking 4) Bacteria and Virus

113. Q. Asexual reproduction includes

1) Amphimixis
2) Apomixis
3) Allogamy
4) Autogamy

114. Q. In India gene bank of wheat is located at

1) Kanpur
2) Ludhiana
3) Karnal
4) IARI, New Delhi

115. Q. TPS technique is related to

1) Tomato
2) Sugarcane
3) Potato
4) All of these

116. Q. SRI is a techniqu used in

1) Maize
2) Groundnut
3) Wheat
4) Rice

117. Q. Numbers of agro climate and ecological zones classified by ICAR respectively are

1) 15,131
2) 131, 8
3) 8,131
4) 21, 15

118. Q. The Green Revolution has mainly been successful for

1) Wheat
2) Rice
3) Maize
4) Gram

119. Q. Guttation occurs in plants through

1) Stomata
2) Hydathodes
3) None of these
4) Both (1) and (2)

120. Q. Stomata open at night in

1) C_4 plants
2) C_3 plants
3) CAM plants
4) None of these

121. Q. Living Cells are not essential for

1) Transpiration
2) Evaporation
3) Guttation
4) All of these

122. Q. α & β-tubulins are protein components of

1) Actin filaments
2) Microtubules
3) Intermediate
4) All of these

123. Q. 'First blight' of sugarcane is due to deficiency of nutrient

1) Mn
2) Zn
3) P
4) Fe

124. Q. Percentage of P_2O_5 in 'Pelofas' fertilizer is

1) 12
2) 16
3) 11
4) 18

125. Q. Which one of the following is not a primary nutrient?

1) S 2) N

3) K 4) P

126. Q. Which group of plant nutrients involves in N_2 fixation?

1) P, S, Mo 2) P, S, Co

3) P, Mo, Co 4) All of these

127. Q. Which one of the following fertilizers is known as 'Kisan Khad'?

1) Urea 2) Calcium Ammonium Nitrate

3) None of these 4) Ammonium Sulphate

128. Q. Zoological name of white grub is

1) *Holotrichia consanguinea* 2) *Helicoverpa armigera*

3) *Spodoptera litura* 4) *Bamisia tabaci*

129. Q. Botanical name of nobel cane is

1) *Saccharum officinarum* 2) *Saccharum* [illegible] *beri*

3) *Saccharum spontaneous* 4) *Saccharum sinensis*

130. Q. Nullisomics produce which type of gametes?

1) n – 1 2) n + 1

3) n 4) n + 1 – 1

131. Q. The crossing over occurs during

1) Diplotene 2) Zygotene

3) Leptotene 4) Pachytene

132. Q. 'Pusa Jai Kisan' is a somaclone of

1) Indian Mustard 2) Khesari

3) Citronella java 4) Basmati Rice

133. Q. Which one of the following countries, the farm gate value of milk price per liter (Rs.) is the highest?

1) U.S.A 2) Canada

3) Japan 4) New Zealand

134. Q. This is one of the best 'poultry feed stuff' and having good source of animal protein as it contains 34-55 percent protein

1) Groundnut Cake 2) Fishmeal

3) Soyabean-meal 4) Linseed-meal

135. Q. Which one of the following Indian breeds of sheep , you will suggest meat and carpet wool production?

1) Deccani 2) Nellore

3) Gaddi 4) Mandya

136. Q. Under the head 'Informatics in Agriculture' which institute has developed Grape Expert System, Cabbage Pest Expert System?

1) National Institute of Agriculture Extension Management (MANAGE), Hyderbad
2) Indian Institute of Horticultural Research (IIHR), Bengalurru
3) Indian Agriculture Research Institute (IARI), New Delhi
4) Centre for Informatics Research and Advancement, Kerala (AGREX)

137. Q. The 'Eri' Silkworm (*Philosamia recini*) which feeds on common casto-plant, is mainly raised in which of the following states, for producing eri-silk?

1) West Bengal
2) Bihar
3) Odisha
4) Himachal Pradesh

138. Q. The Jawahar, Amber are considered as important and good varieties of maize used for

1) Fodder
2) Quality Protein Maize
3) Odisha
4) Pop-Corn

139. Q. Which one of the following Rice varieties you will recommend for growing in saline areas of Haryana State?

1) Panvet-1
2) CSR 30
3) CST 9-1
4) HKR 126

140. Q. Which of the Following states developed 'Uzavaar Santhai- an innovative model in agricultural marketing which involved direct sale of farm produce to the consumers?

1) Andhra Pradesh
2) Tamil Nadu
3) Karnataka
4) UttaraKhand

141. Q. Which seeding and fertilizer application equipments is developed by CCSHAU, Hisar centre?

1) Ridge Seeder
2) Two-row bullock-drawn FESPO plough
3) Tractor drawn planter
4) Malviya seed-cum fertilizer drill

142. Q. The Shoot and fruit borers, Jassid, spider mites and leaf rollers are the major pests of which of the following vegetable crops?

1) Tomato
2) Okra or Bhindi
3) Cucumber
4) Peas

143. Q. The Larvae of which of the following Pests of Sorghum crop, cut growing points and cause dead heart of the plant?

1) Aphids
2) Termites
3) Cutworms
4) Stem-Borer

144. Q. Which is the most widely distributed and commercially reared honeybee species in the world?

1) Apis florea
2) Apis Dorsata
3) Apis Cerana
4) Apis Mellifera

145. Q. Share of the state in chillies production is about 29 to 28 % in India?

1) Andhra Pradesh 2) Maharashtra
3) Karnataka 4) Tamil Nadu

146. Q. Which one of the following states has the largest area under Kharif Maize?

1) Uttar Pradesh 2) Rajasthan
3) Madhya Pradesh 4) Bihar

147. Q. Presently, which of the following chemical fertilizers is not produced in India and is being imported?

1) Triple Superphosphate (TSP) 2) Potassium Sulphate
3) Ammonium Sulphate 4) All of these

148. Q. Which is the most widely used green manuring crop in Assam, West Bengal, Bihar, Haryana, Punjab, TN and Uttar Pradesh (This crop does well on Alkaline and Waterlogged soils?)

1) Sunnhemp 2) Dhaincha
3) Egyptian Clover 4) Senji (*Melilotus Parviflora*)

149. Q. Which of the following methods of surface irrigation is considered as water and fertilizer efficient and ideal for several crops?

1) Check basin and border strip irrigation 2) Furrow irrigation
3) Surge irrigation 4) Flood irrigation

150. Q. Dhaman, Karad and Anjan are the

1) Varieties of Sheep in Rajasthan 2) Varieties of caster seed of Gujarat
3) Varieties of Grass in Rajasthan 4) Three Heros of Gawari dance

151. Q. Which is not basic principle of Agronomy?

1) To select appropriate materials for seed and sowing
2) Management of soil and climate
3) Appropriate intercropping activities management for corp
4) Livestock management for Agriculture

152. Q. Which is not matched in relation to sugarcane?

1) Seed treatment-Aglol 3% 2) For seed-6-9 month old crop
3) Sowing-Upper portion is more used 4) After flowering-Used for sowing

153. Q. Which does not match in relation to Cotton?

1) C-520 - Diploid 2) G-29 - Diploid
3) Vikas - American 4) Ranivan - American

154. Q. Which is not true in relation to Gram?

1) Subfamily-Papilionaceae 2) Chromosome No.-22
3) Acid-Malic and Oxalic 4) Origin-North America

155. Q. Which variety of Barley is huskless?

1) Pragati (K 508) 2) Ritambhara (K 551)
3) Geetanjali (K 1149) 4) Karan -3

156. Q. Which disease occurs, when more sorghum is consumed?

1) Rickets | 2) Scurvy
3) Nightblindness | 4) Pellagra

157. Q. Which is not true in relation to Bajra?

1) Pennisetum Typhoides | 2) Graminae Family
3) Chromosome No. - 20 | 4) Origin Africa

158. Q. Which Sorghum variety is not multicut?

1) Pusa Chari-2 | 2) M. P. Chari-2
3) M. P Chari | 4) U. P. Chari-1

159. Q. Which is the highest digestible protein nonleguminous crop among the following?

1) Napier | 2) Maize Silage
3) Maize | 4) Jowar

160. Q. Which is not an inorganic matter in the following?

1) Magnesium | 2) Iron
3) Fat | 4) Iodine

161. Q. The crop with yarns of sunn-hemp is prepared in

1) 12-15 weeks | 2) 15-19 weeks
3) 10-12 weeks | 4) 8-10 weeks

162. Q. How much radiation energy percentage radiating on plant is used in photosynthesis?

1) 0.50% - 2.10% | 2) 0.42% - 1.66%
3) 0.25% - 0.30% | 4) 0.16% - 0.24%

163. Q. At the vegetative growth stage, flowering is stopped in food-grain crops, known as

1) Sigmoid growth curve | 2) Determinate growth
3) Indeterminate growth | 4) Grand growth period

164. Q. How does the moisture stress affect the cell?

1) Affect cell division | 2) Affect cell expansion
3) Cell mortality rate is affected | 4) No effect on cell

165. Q. How many factors are identified for influencing plant growth till now?

1) 55 | 2) 60
3) 52 | 4) 50

166. Q. The animals produced by mating of two different breeds of the same species are known as

1) Mixed breed | 2) Cross breed
3) Exotic breed | 4) Pure breed

167. Q. Recording of milk production in dairy farm is done mainly for

1) Selection of good producer | 2) Increase in production of milk
3) Ensuring quality of milk | 4) Quick sale of milk

168. Q. The average gestation period in buffalo is of how many days?

1) 310 2) 210

3) 400 4) 345

169. Q. Citrus tristeza virus is transmitted through

1) Aphid 2) Thrips

3) Nematode 4) Plant hopper

170. Q. Which one of the pathogens is monocylic?

1) Ustilago 2) Alternaria

3) Phytophthora 4) Puccinia

171. Q. Caenocytic mycellium is found in

1) Mastigomycotina 2) Deuteromycotina

3) Ascomycotina 4) None of these

172. Q. Penicillin acts on

1) Cell wall 2) RNA

3) Cell membrane 4) None of these

173. Q. Blue colour tag is issued for

1) Foundation seed 2) Certified seed

3) Nucleus seed 4) None of these

174. Q. Generally, cereals are deficient in

1) Protein 2) Tryptophan

3) Methionine 4) Lysine

175. Q. The book 'Mutation Research' is written by

1) Muller 2) Stadler

3) Nilsson Enle 4) Auerbach

176. Q. Each anther has how many pollen sacs?

1) Four 2) Two

3) One 4) Three

177. Q. Rice and wheat has how many stamens?

1) 3, 3 2) 6, 3

3) 3, 6 4) 6, 6

178. Q. The chemical, which attracts opposite sex insects of a species, is known as

1) Hormones 2) Allomones

3) Kairomones 4) Pheromones

179. Q. Damaging satge of potato tuber moth is

1) Adult 2) Pupa

3) Larva 4) All of these

180. Q. Piercing and sucking type mouth parts are present in the insect

1) Hemiptera 2) Orthoptera
3) Lepidoptera 4) Isoptera

181. Q. Classification of insects and rules of their nomenclature comes under the branch

1) Morphology 2) Taxonomy
3) Ecology 4) Physiology

182. Q. Beetles belong to order

1) Lepidoptera 2) Isoptera
3) Coleoptera 4) Diptera

183. Q. Bacteriophage virus is the

1) Bacterial virus 2) Fungal Virus
3) Algal virus 4) Protozoal virus

184. Q. Micro organism, which can grow at higher temperature, is called

1) Thermophils 2) Mesophils
3) Phycrophils 4) None of these

185. Q. Who has first time seen the microorganisms?

1) Robert Koch 2) John Tyndall
3) Antonie van Leeuwenhoek 4) Louis Pasteur

186. Q. White colour of soil is due to the presence of

1) Silica 2) Iron
3) Manganese oxide 4) All of these

187. Q. Which of the following is 'complex fertilizer'?

1) Ammonium sulphate nitrate 2) Single superphosphate
3) Ammonium phosphate 4) Calcium ammonium nitrate

188. Q. Drip irrigation is useful in which region?

1) Humid 2) Dry
3) High rainfall 4) None of these

189. Q. Among the following crop rotations, which is good for increasing soil Nutrient status?

1) Rice Wheat 2) Groundnut Wheat
3) Pearlmillet Wheat 4) Sorghum Wheat

190. Q. For waterlogged rice cultivation, the fertilizer that may be avoided is

1) Sodium nitrate 2) Urea
3) Ammonium chloride 4) None of these

191. Q. The ratio between marketable crop yield and water used in evapotranspiration is known as

1) Field water use efficiency 2) Economic irrigation efficiency
3) Consumptive use efficiency 4) Water use efficiency

192. Q. Sulphur, containing amino acid is

1) Valine
2) Isolucine
3) Cystine
4) None of these

193. Q. Glycolysis occurs only in the

1) Absence of O
2) Presence of O
3) Both (1) and (2)
4) None of these

194. Q. Photorespiration is inhibited by

1) 2, 4 Dinitrophenol
2) α hydroxy sulphonates
3) CMU and DCMU
4) None of these

195. Q. Biofertilizers are

1) Organic manures
2) Green manure
3) Culture of micro organism
4) None of these

196. Q. 'Chanchal' is a variety of

1) Brinjal
2) Tomato
3) Chilli
4) Capcicum

197. Q. Central Soil Salinity Research Institute is located at

1) Karnal
2) Bihar
3) Dehradun
4) Jodhpur

198. Q. Seed plant technique is followed in

1) Wheat
2) Bajra
3) Potato
4) Paddy

199. Q. For providing inputs like quality seeds, fertilizers and pesticides, the agency present at the Village Panchayat Samiti Level is

1) Nationalised Banks
2) Cooperative Society
3) Insurance Companies
4) NABARD

200. Q. Where do the female mango leaf hoppers lay their eggs?

1) Inside the tissue of leaf margin
2) On the dorsal surface of leaves
3) On the ventral surface of leaves
4) Inside the mid rib of leaves

201. Q. In H.T.S.T. pasteurization, which one of the following organisms is chosen as index organism for killing?

1) S.thermophilus
2) S.lactis
3) B.subtilis
4) M.tuberculosis

202. Q. Thermophilic micro organism grow well at temperature

1) 10°C-20°C
2) 20°C-40°C
3) 50°C-60°C
4) 5°C-9°C

203. Q. Pink bollworm is a pest of

1) Gram
2) Okra
3) Mustard
4) Cotton

204. Q. The cropping intensity of maize, potato and tobacco is

1) 200% 2) 300%
3) 100% 4) None of these

205. Q. National Sugar Institute (N.S.I.) is located at

1) Kanpur 2) New Delhi
3) Varanasi 4) Lucknow

206. Q. Khaira disease of rice can be controlled by spraying

1) Copper sulphate 2) Calcium sulphate
3) Zinc sulphate 4) Borax

207. Q. Which one of the following can be suitable for cropping as a wheat mixed crop?

1) Cabbage 2) Cotton
3) Mustard 4) Jowar

208. Q. The optimum cardinal temperature point for germination of rice seeds is

1) 20°C-25°C 2) 18°C-22°C
3) 30°C-32°C 4) 39°C-39°C

209. Q. What culture should be given priority in groundnut cultivation?

1) Mycorrhiza 2) Rhizobium
3) Phosphobacteria 4) Azospirillum

210. Q. Prabhat is an early short duration variety of

1) Black gram 2) Red gram
3) Green gram 4) Gram

211. Q. In maize plants

1) Silk appear first 2) Both of these appear at same time
3) Tassels appear first 4) None of these

212. Q. Blind hoeing is recommended for

1) Wheat 2) Maize
3) Groundnut 4) Sugarcane

213. Q. Kisan Mitra is an employee of

1) Central Govt. 2) Corporation
3) None of these 4) State Govt.

214. Q. Red Delicious is a variety of

1) Mango 2) Papaya
3) Apple 4) Guava

215. Q. The number of essential mineral elements of plant is

1) 16 2) 21
3) 13 4) 20

216. Q. Which of the following award is associated with Agriculture?

1) Bourlog Award 2) Shanti Swaroop Bhatnagar
3) Arjun Award 4) Vyasa Samman

217. Q. Which material should be higher in the ratio of the pregnant cow?

1) Fat 2) Protein
3) Carbohydrates 4) Dry matter

218. Q. As standard how much is the weight in gram of an egg?

1) 90 gm 2) 58 gm
3) 68 gm 4) 48 gm

219. Q. In how many years does a bull get ready for insemination?

1) 2-2 years 2) 3-3 years
3) 1-2 years 4) None of these

220. Q. How much percentage of income comes from animals, out of India's total income?

1) 20% 2) 25%
3) 15% 4) 10%

221. Q. Which is not a hybrid variety of Mango?

1) Mallika 2) Ratna
3) Arka Puneet 4) Dashehari

222. Q. What is place of India in the World in Tea production?

1) First 2) Second
3) Third 4) Fourth

223. Q. Which fruit crop has the largest area in India?

1) Banana 2) Citrus
3) Mango 4) Guava

224. Q. Which country is the Second highest producer of fruit and vegetables in the world?

1) Brazil 2) North America
3) China 4) India

225. Q. Which crop is affected by Tobacco caterpillar?

1) Jute 2) Sugarcane
3) Lucerne 4) Sugarbeet

226. Q. What optimum temperature is needed for the growth of Potato tuber?

1) 19°C to 19°C 2) 14°C to 16°C
3) 10°C to 12°C 4) 22°C to 25°C

227. Q. Which variety of Groundnut is grown in summer?

1) Avtar 2) Chitra
3) Chandra 4) Amber

228. Q. **Which is not fodder variety of Cowpea?**

1) Russian Giant
2) K 585
3) Sirsa 10
4) Azad 1

229. Q. **Which variety of Barley is not for Malt purpose?**

1) Pragati (K-508)
2) Geetanjali (K-1149)
3) Ritambhara (K-559)
4) D.L. 88

230. Q. **Which is not true in case of lentil?**

1) Chromosome 14
2) I.P.L. High yield
3) Seed rate 35 40 kg
4) Quantity of protein in lentil seed 18%

231. Q. **Which is not a variety of Vegetable Pea?**

1) Arkel
2) Azad Pea 3
3) Pant Matar 2
4) Aparna

232. Q. **How many days old paddy seedling is used for SRI technology?**

1) 8-12 days
2) 12-15 days
3) 25-30 days
4) 30-35 days

233. Q. **How much nursery area is required for transplanting one hectare of paddy crop?**

1) 1000 m
2) 950 m
3) 500 m
4) 250 400 m

234. Q. **Which variety is not susceptible to insects & disease?**

1) Pant Dhan 10
2) Govind
3) Narenda Dhan 2
4) Saket 4

235. Q. **Which paddy variety is not suitable for upland situation?**

1) Narendra Dhan I
2) Renu
3) Saraju 52
4) Narendra Dhan 118

236. Q. **Where is the Headquarters (HQ) of FAO?**

1) Rome
2) Washington
3) New York
4) Venezuela

237. Q. **Which is the highest digestible protein fodder from the following?**

1) Lucerne
2) Cowpea
3) Clusterbean
4) Berseem

238. Q. **How much biomass in quintal per hectare is obtained from green manure of the sunnhemp and dhaincha crops?**

1) 300-325 quintals
2) 225-295 quntals
3) 200-225 quintals
4) 325-350 quintals

239. Q. **Which is not an organic matter in the following?**

1) Crude protein
2) Carbohydrate
3) Vitamins
4) Hormones

240. Q. In how many days is the sunnhemp fibre rotten in normal conditions?

1) 10-12 days
2) 8-10 days
3) 6-8 days
4) 5-6 days

241. Q. Which herbicide resides for the longest period in the soil?

1) Chlorpropham
2) Linuron
3) Propachlor
4) Simazine

242. Q. Recognition site of t-RNA is?

1) Anticodon
2) 3 OH end
3) Loop -I
4) Loop -IV

243. Q. Mass flow mechanism was proposed by whom?

1) Munch
2) Darwin
3) Hugo de Vries
4) Banda

244. Q. Virus free plants can be obtained by which of the following?

1) Shoot tip culture
2) Pollen culture
3) Meristem culture
4) Ovary culture

245. Q. Which of the following is not a method of knowing seed life?

1) Respiration test
2) Embryo culture method
3) Seed dormancy method
4) Indigocarmine method

246. Q. Which of the following is not a variety of seeds?

1) Hybrid seed
2) Composite seed
3) Breeder seed
4) Mutant seed

247. Q. Opening and closing of stomata depends on

1) Sunlight
2) Water pressure
3) Transpiration
4) Temperature

248. Q. At what temperature does the wilt disease virus grow faster?

1) 40°C-45°C
2) 35°C-40°C
3) 24°C-28°C
4) 22°C-26°C

249. Q. Evaporation is measured by which instrument?

1) Barometer
2) Psychrometer
3) Lysimeter
4) Hygrometer

250. Q. At which height from soil level are the synoptic meteorological observations done?

1) 2.0 metre
2) 1.25 metre
3) 2.2 metre
4) 1.0 metre to 2.0 metre

251. Q. Success of rural projects depends upon

1) Agriculture Extension
2) Management
3) Soil Science
4) Regular training of staff

252. Q. 'Pheromone Trap' attracts

1) Male moths
2) Female moths
3) Caterpillar
4) Female bugs

253. Q. What is the average temperature of cow and buffalo?

1) 98.4°F
2) 100°F
3) 101.5°F
4) 102°F

254. Q. How many days can the Aonla be kept in salt solution?

1) 15 days
2) 30 days
3) 60 days
4) 95 days

255. Q. At the time of Apple fruit setting what is the minimum temperature required?

1) 10°C
2) 4.5°C-5.5°C
3) 8°C-10°C
4) 2°C-3°C

256. Q. Which variety of Papaya gives maximum Papain?

1) Pusa Delicious
2) Pusa Majesty
3) Pusa Gaint
4) Pusa Dwarf

257. Q. How much cloves of garlic is required for one hectare?

1) 400 kg
2) 500 kg
3) 600 kg
4) 300 kg

258. Q. In which state of India is the area of Coffee maximum?

1) Kerala
2) Andhra Pradesh
3) Karnataka
4) Tamil Nadu

259. Q. The yellow colour in onion is due to which pigment?

1) Carotene
2) Quercetin
3) Anthocyanin
4) Lycopene

260. Q. Potato tuber growth is stopped at what temperature?

1) 40°C - 42°C
2) 30°C - 32°C
3) 35°C - 39°C
4) 38° - 40°C

261. Q. Which is not prepared from patato?

1) Farina and Alcohol
2) Paper
3) Wine
4) Acetic acid

262. Q. Varieties Miscavi and Pusa Visal are of which crop?

1) Cotton
2) Jute
3) Oat
4) Berseem

263. Q. Seed treatment of which crop is done by Captan or Cerasan @ 5 gm/kg seed?

1) Cotton
2) Jute
3) Safflower
4) Mondua

264. Q. In which season is the highest yield of Maize obtained?

1) Zaid
2) Kharif
3) Rabi
4) All of these

265. Q. Soldier insect harms which crop more?

1) Urad
2) Arhar
3) Moong
4) Paddy

266. Q. How much paddy seed is needed for transplanting one hectare area by SRI technique?

1) 30-35 kg
2) 1-1.5 kg
3) 5-6 kg
4) 10-12 kg

267. Q. From where is Indian Journal of Agriculture Sciences published?

1) UPCAR
2) ICAR
3) CISR
4) NBRI

268. Q. Which is the hybrid of Pusa Giant Napier?

1) Napier × Jowar
2) Napier × Bajra
3) Jowar × Bajra
4) Bajra × Jowar

269. Q. What is Azofication?

1) It is also known as composite fixation of nitrogen
2) It is also known as free fixation of nitrogen
3) It is also known as free fixation of nitrogen fixed by *Rhizobium* bacteria
4) It is also known as nitrogen gain through rains or snow

270. Q. Plant which becomes dormant during summer is known as?

1) Decidous
2) Caducous
3) Evergreen
4) None of these

271. Q. The hybrid mango developed from the cross of Neelum and Alphonso is -

1) Amrapali
2) Dasheri
3) Ratna
4) Badami

272. Q. Mauritius, Poovan, Lal Velchi are varieties of -

1) Tomato
2) Banana
3) Litchi
4) Carrot

273. Q. White bud in maize is caused due to the deficiency of -

1) Zinc
2) Amonium
3) Iron
4) Sulphur

274. Q. COJ-64 and CO-7717 are early maturing varieties of -

1) Cotton
2) Sugarcane
3) Jule
4) Maize

275. Q. Biofertlizers can supply which of these nutrients?

1. Nitrogen
2. Phosphorous
3. Potassium

Select the correct answer using the codes given below:

1) 1 only
2) 1 and 2 only
3) 1 and 3 only
4) 1, 2 and 3

276. Q. Black soils is ideal for cultivation of cotton as -

1) its colour is black
2) it can retain moisture
3) it is made up of lava
4) it is found on plateau regions

277. Q. Name the first State of India which is fully dependent on organic farming.

1) Madhya Pradesh
2) Kerala
3) Sikkim
4) Arunachal Pradesh

278. Q. What is the ideal minimum temperature for the growth of sugarcane?

1) 10°C
2) 20°C
3) 30°C
4) 40°C

279. Q. In India Bihar ranks in terms of production of jute?

1) First
2) Second
3) Third
4) Fourth

280. Q. Which one of the following most appropriately describes the nature of Green Revolution of late sixties of 20th century?

1) Intensive cultivation of green vegetable
2) Intensive agriculture district programme
3) High-yielding varieties programme
4) Seed-Fertilizer-Water technology

281. Q. Which of the following States has very little alluvial soil?

1) Bihar
2) Madhya Pradesh
3) Tamil Nadu
4) Punjab

282. Q. The soils of the Plains have not been derived -

1) from the Himalayan rocks
2) from the Peninsular rocks
3) onlv from the rocks existing locally
4) from material brought by the rivers

283. Q. Match the following types of soil and regions where they are found in India -

List-I	**List-II**
Alluvial soils	1. Highland areas of the Plateau
Black soils	2. Periphery of the Plateau
Red soils	3. Deccan lava tracts
Laterite soils	4. River basins and coastal plains

1) 4, 3, 1, 2
2) 4, 2, 3, 1
3) 1, 2, 3, 4
4) 4, 3, 2, 1

284. Q. Cotton was produced first by the?

1) Egyptians
2) Harappans
3) Mesopotamians
4) Sumerians

285. Q. Nicotiana Rustica is a variety of -

1) Coffee
2) Tobacco
3) Sugarcane
4) Coconut

286. Q. Leaf Curl disease in Okra (Lady finger) is caused by -

1) White fly
2) Fungus
3) Bacteria
4) Virus

287. Q. Which one of the following is the most productive soil in India?

1) Red soil
2) Black soil
3) Alluvial soil
4) Calcareous soil

288. Q. Generally Orobanche weed is found in -

1) tobacco field
2) gram field
3) rice field
4) wheat field

289. Q. Which one of the following States of India is the largest producer of coconut?

1) Kerala
2) Karnataka
3) Tamil Nadu
4) Andhra Pradesh

290. Q. UP Council of Agricultural Reserach is located at -

1) Meerut
2) Bulandshahar
3) Lucknow
4) Gorakhpur

291. Q. Potato Research Institute in UP is located in the district -

1) Farrukhabad
2) Meerut
3) Kanpur
4) Allahbad

292. Q. The rotation intensity of Maize-Potato-Mung bean is -

1) 100%
2) 200%
3) 250%
4) 300%

293. Q. "White rust" is an important fungal disease of -

1) Wheat
2) Maize
3) Mustard
4) Cotton

294. Q. "Pusa Sindhu Ganga" is a variety of -

1) Maize
2) Wheat
3) Mustard
4) Cotton

295. Q. "Yellow Vein Mosaic" is a disease of -

1) Okra
2) Maize
3) Wheat
4) Rice

296. Q. "Sonalika" is an early maturing variety of -

1) Rice 2) Wheat

3) Maize 4) Millet

297. Q. "Ganga 101" and "Ranjit Decan" are the varieties of -

1) Wheat 2) Millet

3) Rice 4) Maize

298. Q. Minimum Support Price is determined by the Government of India on the recommendations of -

1) Commission for Agricultural Costs & Prices (CACP)

2) NITI Aayog

3) NABARD

4) NABARD & NAFED

299. Q. Concept of 'Climate smart agriculture' given by-

1) WHO 2) FAO

3) PFA 4) WTO

300.Q. Which one of following is not a breed of sheep?

1) Megra 2) Malpuri

3) Bagri 4) Nachna

301. Q. Which one of the following is the pathway to increase productivity in agriculture?

1) Efficient irrigation 2) Quality seeds

3) Use of pesticides 4) None of the above/More than one of the above

302. Q. Koter spot disease of turnip is caused due to the deficiency of -

1) Calcium (Ca) 2) Zinc (Zn)

3) Sulphar (S) 4) Iron (Fe)

303. Q. Little leaf disease of mango and brinjal is caused due to the deficiency of -

1) Calcium (Ca) 2) Iron (Fe)

3) Zinc (Zn) 4) Sulphar (S)

304. Q. Crinckle leaf of cotton is mainly caused by

1) Al toxicity 2) Mn toxicity

3) Mg toxicity 4) N toxicity

305. Q. The most popular fertilizer for foliar application is -

1) Potassium 2) Phospate

3) Urea 4) Ammonium

306. Q. Fertility gradient approach was given by

1) B. Maheshwari 2) C. D. Mayee

3) B. Ramashwamii 4) B. Ramamoorthy

307. Q. Which of the following is the primary mineral that occurs predominantly in igneous rocks

1) Qurazite
2) Feldspar
3) Micas
4) Pyroxenes

308. Q. With reference to agricultural soils, consider the following statements :

1. A high content of organic matter in soil drastically reduces its water holding capacity.
2. Soil does not play any role in the sulphur cycle.
3. Irrigation over a period of time can contribute to the salinization of some agricultural lands.

Which of the statements given above is/ are correct ?

1) 1 and 2 only
2) 3 only
3) 1 and 3 only
4) 1, 2 and 3

309. Q. Which of the following are the sexual spores of fungi

1) Zoospores
2) Chlamydospores
3) Zygospores
4) Sporangiospore?

310. Q. With reference to the 'Global Alliance for Climate-Smart Agriculture (GACSA)', which of the following statements is/ are correct?

1. GACSA is an outcome of the Climate Summit held in Paris in 2015.
2. Membership of GACSA does not create any building obligations.
3. India was instrumental in the creation of GACSA.

Select the correct answer using the code given below:

1) 1 and 3 only
2) 2 only
3) 2 and 3 only
4) 1, 2 and 3

311. Q. Which of the following is an ethylene absorbant?

1) $NaNO_3$
2) $CaCO_3$
3) $CaCl_2$
4) $KMnO_4$

312. Q. What is the correct chronological order of the following laws enacted for the conservation and protection of environment?

I. Environment (Protection) Act.
II. Water (Prevention & Control of Pollution) Act.
III. Air (Prevention & Control of pollution) Act.
IV. National Green Tribunal Act.

1) II-III-I-IV
2) I-II-III-IV
3) III-II-I-IV
4) IV-III-II-I

313. Q. If the tip of sugarcane plant is removed from the field, even then it keeps on growing in length. It is due to the presence of -

1) Cambium
2) Apical meristem
3) Lateral meristem
4) Intercalary meristem

314. Q. Seva Bhoj Yojana, launched by Ministry of Culture, GoI, in 2018-19 is related to

1) Free distribution of cooked food to destitutes
2) Goods and Services Tax
3) Establishment of subsidized kitchens in towns of cultural and religious importance
4) Establishment of community kitchen in scheduled castes and scheduled tribes localities

315. Q. Gir Sahiwal, Red Sindhi, and Deoni are the breeds of -

1) Buffaloes 2) Sheep
3) Cows 4) Goat

316. Q. Which of the following is a degenerative disease ?

1) Kwashiorkor 2) Arthritis
3) Paranoia 4) Sickle cell anaemia

317. Q. SAARC Agriculture Centre (SAC) is based in which city ?

1) Islamabad 2) Dhaka
3) Colombo 4) Kathmandu

318. Q. Where is the greatest variety of flowers found?

1) Kerala 2) Uttar Pradesh hills
3) Assam 4) Sikkim

319. Q. Nodal Agency for Promoting export-oriented production and development of the Scheduled products –

1) CRIDA 2) APEDA
3) NABARD 4) EXIM

320. Q. Which one of the following substances is a herbicide?

1) Chlorpyrifos 2) Carbendazim
3) Quinolphos 4) Butachlor

321. Q. Among Indian States, which state has the highest yield (per hectare) of rice?

1) West Bengal 2) Uttar Pradesh
3) Haryana 4) Punjab

322. Q. Which one of the following pairs is not correctly matched?

1) Cuscuta - stem parasite 2) Chandan - root parasite
3) Orchids - epiphyte 4) Nepenthes - hydrophyte

323. Q. Among the Indian States Uttar Pradesh is the largest producer of which of the following crops?

1) Wheat, Potato, Groundnut 2) Wheat, Potato, Sugarcane
3) Potato, Sugarcane, Cotton 4) Potato, Sugarcane, Paddy

324. Q. Which among the following statements is not true?

1) Rust is a disease found in wheat 2) Early blight is a disease found in Potato
3) False smut is a disease found in barley 4) Khaira is a disease found in paddy

325. Q. The water holding capacity of defferent types of soils decreases in the order -

1) Clay > Silt > Sand 2) Clay > Sand > Silt
3) Sand > Silt > Clay 4) Silt > Sand > Clay

326. Q. Groundwater mining in coastal areas can result into -

1) increase in the salinity of groundwater
2) decrease in the toxicity of groundwater
3) decrease in the salinity of groundwater
4) increase in the water table

327. Q. Which of the following is not an important characteristic of the Green Revolution?

1) Mechanized agriculture 2) Hybrid seeds
3) Slash and burn 4) Monoculture

328. Q. The three primary soil macronutrients are -

1) carbon, oxygen, and water 2) copper, cadmium and carbon
3) potassium, phosphorus and nitrogen 4) boron, zinc and manganese

329. Q. Which of the following are negative effects on the soil and water due to conventional, mechanized farming practices?

1) Reduction in soil organic matter
2) Soil erosion
3) Leaching of pesticides and fertilizers into the groundwater
4) All of the above

330. Q. Green revolution deals with

1) Fish and Aquaculture 2) Foodgrains production
3) Milk and milk production 4) Oil seed production

331. Q. Crop logging is a method of -

1) Soil fertility evaluation
2) Plant analysis for assessing the requirement of nutrients for crop production
3) Assessing crop damage
4) Testing suitability of fertilisers

332. Q. Seed that is changed every year is known as -

1) Breeder seed 2) Certified seed
3) Foundation seed 4) Hybrid seed

333. Q. The gas which emits for rice field is -

1) Ethane 2) Methane
3) Nitrogen 4) All of the above

334. Q. 'Dapog' method of rice nursery was developed in -

1) China 2) Indonesia
3) Japan 4) Philippines

335. Q. First dwarf rice variety developed in India was -

1) IR-8
2) Jaya
3) Padma
4) Ratna

336. Q. Which was the principal plant used in Green Revolution?

1) Japonica Rice
2) Indian Rice
3) Emmer Wheat
4) Mexican Wheat

337. Q. The first transgenic crop was -

1) Pea
2) Rice
3) Tobacco
4) Cotton

338. Q. Which of the following fruits is not a nut?

1) Coconut
2) Litchi
3) Betel nut
4) Groundnut

339. Q. The soils which have supported agriculture for centuries without much manuring or fallowing are -

1) Alluvial and laterite soils
2) Red and laterite soils
3) Black and alluvial soils
4) Laterite and black soils

340. Q. 'Small Farmers' are those whose landholdings are -

1) Above five hectare
2) Below one hectare
3) Betwen four to ten hectare
4) Between one to two hectare

341. Q. Depending on the area in the South Asian region, the Kharif crops are cultivated and harvested during the months of -

1) April and October
2) January and April
3) November and February
4) October and December

342. Q. The practice of raising grazing livestock such as cattle or sheep for meat or wool is known as -

1) Silviculture
2) Permaculture
3) Ranching
4) Breeding

343. Q. The practice of growing a series of dissimilar or different types of crops in the same area in sequential seasons is known as -

1) Mixed farming
2) Cover cropping
3) Mixed cropping
4) Crop rotation

344. Q. Which of the following crops may be treated as a plantation crop?

1) Cereals and Pulses
2) Fruits and Vegetables
3) Wheat, Rice, Maize, Millets
4) Tea, Coffee, Coconut, Rubber

345. Q. Generally standards in 'Organic Farming' are designed to encourage the use of -

1) Manmade substances
2) Artificial substances
3) Genetically modified substances
4) Natural substances

346. Q. Which of the following Institute has recently developed genetically-modified cotton varieties?

1) G. B. Pant University of Agriculture and Technology
2) Punjab Agricultural University
3) Tamil Nadu Agricultural University
4) Indian Agricultural Research Institute

347. Q. Which of the following green manure crops contains highest amount of nitrogen?

1) Dhaincha
2) Sunnhemp
3) Cowpea
4) Guar

348. Q. Sugarcane crops are examples of which type of croping?

1) Ratoon
2) Multiple
3) Mixed
4) Parallel

349. Q. India's first Agriculture University is established in which State?

1) Jharkhand
2) Haryana
3) Uttar Pradesh
4) Maharashtra

350. Q. The Blue Revolution is related with -

1) Fish production
2) Meat production
3) Grains production
4) Pulses production

351. Q. What is the scientific name of cotton plant?

1) *Ocimum sanctum*
2) *Coriandrum sativum*
3) *Curcuma longa*
4) *Gosspium herbaceum*

352. Q. 'Sabarmati' and 'Jamuna' are two new varieties of -

1) Wheat
2) Rice
3) Maize
4) Mustard

353. Q. What is the rank of India in the world as a fruit producer?

1) Third
2) Fourth
3) First
4) Second

354. Q. Which one of the following settlement pattern is likely to develop in plain fertile agricultural regions?

1) Star-shaped
2) Circular
3) Rectangular
4) Linear

355. Q. The hybrid mango developed from the cross of Neelum and Alphonso is -

1) Amrapali
2) Dasheri
3) Ratna
4) Badami

356. Q. In Artificial Insemination

1) Transfer of embryo is done
2) Ovum is harvested
3) Semen is collected
4) In vitro fertilization is done

357. Q. Rate of milk feeding to new born calves should be

1) 1/10th of body weight
3) 1/20th of body weight
3) 1/5th of body weight
4) equal to body weight

358. Q. Before the first calf birth animal is called

1) Calf
2) Heifer
3) Cow female
4) Adult/animal

359. Q. The minimum standards prescribed by the PFA (1976) rules for cow milk is

1) 3 to 4 per cent fat only
2) 8.5 to 9 per cent solids not fat only
3) Both 1 and 2
4) None of these

360. Q. The minimum standards prescribed by the PFA (1976) rules for buffalo milk is

1) 5 to 6 per cent fat only
2) 9 per cent solids not fat only
3) Both 1 and 2
4) None of these

361. Q. How many kg. each of 28% cream and 3% milk will be required to make 500 kg. of a mixture having at least 45% fat

1) 25 kg. Cream and 475 kg. Milk
2) 30 kg. Cream and 470 kg, Milk
3) 20 kg. Cream and 480 kg. Milk
4) 45 kg. Cream and 455 kg. Milk

362. Q. In HTST pasteurization the milk is heated to 72°C for

1) 15 Minutes
2) 15 Seconds
3) 30 Minutes
4) 30 Seconds

363. Q. Plastic cream contains

1) 65 to 85% milk fat
2) 55 to 60% milk fat
2) 43 to 53% milk fat
4) 90 to 95% milk fat

364. Q. The lactic acid percentage by weight maximum in sweet dahi should be

1) 0.90
2) 0.80
3) 0.70
4) 0.60

365. Q. The lactic acid percentage by weight maximum in sour dahi should be

1) 0.90
2) 1.00
3) 2.00
4) 3.00

366. Q. Inadequate homogenization of ice cream mix may result is a texture defect called as

1) Ley
2) Coarse
3) Buttery
4) Sandy

367. Q. Stomata are regulated by

1) N | 2) P
3) K | 4) Ca

368. Q. Maximum density of water exists at

1) 0°C | 2) 4°C
3) 40°C | 4) 100°C

369. Q. Plant lost water in transpiration upto the extent of

1) 80% | 2) 90%
3) 95% | 4) 99%

370. Q. The chemical nature of GA_3 is

1) Phenolic | 2) Terpene
3) Purine | 4) Indole

371. Q. Guttation is not favoured under

1) Low humidity | 2) High humidity
3) Low root pressure | 4) High humidity and low root pressure

372. Q. The xylem and phloem elements in the plant are surrounded by a layer of living cells called

1) Casparian strips | 2) Pericycle
3) Stele | 4) Endodermis

373. Q. A plant hormone, which is primary regulator of abscission process is

1) Ethylene | 2) Auxin
3) ABA | 4) Gibberellins

374. Q. Growing of plant in soilless nutrient solution is referred as

1) Aeroponics | 2) Hydroponics
3) Xeroponics | 4) Thaloponics

375. Q. Most commonly grown crop plants are included in

1) Halophytes | 2) Glycophytes
3) Sciophytes | 4) Xerophytes

376. Q. Optimum temperature for maximum crop development in wheat is

1) 10-15°C | 2) 20-25°C
3) 25-30°C | 4) 30-35°C

377. Q. 'Little leaf' and 'rosette' of apple, 'white bud' of maize are the deficiency symptoms of

1) Fe | 2) Zn
3) Cl | 4) Mo

378. Q. In citrus plant, die back diseases is the result of deficiency of

1) N | 2) P
3) Boron | 4) Copper

379. Q. Acid rains are due to which of the following gases?

1) CO_2 and CO
2) Ozone and CO_2
3) NO_2 and SO_2
4) NH_3 and CO_2

380. Q. Which one of the following is a most harmful pollutant by automobiles?

1) SO_2
2) CO
3) N_2O
4) CO_2

381. Q. Callus is induced to form roots in the medium of

1) Auxin
2) Cytokinins only
3) Morecytokinins than auxin
4) Moreauxin than cytokinins

382. Q. Blue light is always less efficient in photosynthesis than

1) White
2) Red
3) Orange
4) Violet

383. Q. Protein content in pulses ranges from

1) 10-15%
2) 20-25%
3) 25-30%
4) 40-45%

384. Q. Protein content of cereals ranges from

1) 8-12%
2) 12-15%
3) 15-20%
4) 20-25%

385. Q. Natural inhibitor of IAA oxidases is

1) Caffeic Acid
2) Coumaric acid
3) ABA
4) Lactic Acid

386. Q. How many ATP are required to produce 1 mole of hexose in photosynthesis?

1) 8
2) 18
3) 28
4) 38

387. Q. Which state has the largest acreage and highest production of sugarcane in country?

1) Tamil Nadu
2) Karnataka
3) U.P.
4) Bihar

388. Q. The best suited temperature for growth of sugarcane lies between

1) 15-20°C
2) 20-25°C
3) 26-32°C
4) 32-35°C

389. Q. Consider the following pairs of crops and varieties and select the pair which is not correctly matched.

1) Barley : Clipper
2) Cotton : Sujata
3) Cowpea : Pusa Phalguni
4) Green gram : UPAS 120

390. Q. Botanical name of Ragi is

1) *Elesine coracana* 2) *Echinochloa frumentacea*
3) *Panicum miliacium* 4) *Eleusine panica*

391. Q. Stomata closing can be induced by

1) Kaoline 2) Linseed oil
3) 2, 4 – D 4) PMA

392. Q. *Virachola isocrates* is a fruit pest of:

1) Mango 2) Citurs
3) Apple 4) Pomegranate

393. Q. *Callosobruchus chinesis* is storage pest of:

1) Wheat 2) Gram
3) Rice 4) Groundnut

394. Q. Certain secretions attract the opposite sex of the same species which are termed as:

1) Hormones 2) Kairomones
3) Synomones 4) Pheromones

395. Q. Following insecticide is safely recommended on vegetables

1) Carbaryl 2) Aldicarb
3) Endrin 4) Malathion

396. Q. Following insecticide belongs to organophophate group

1) Sulphur 2) Carbofuran
3) Malathion 4) Endosulfan

397. Q. Aphids and white flies are effectively controlled by

1) Fumigants 2) Stomach poisons
3) Contact insecticides 4) Systemic insecticide

398. Q. The spotted boll warm is

1) *Earias vittela* 2) *Earias insulana*
3) *Helicoverpa armigera* 4) *Pectinophora gossypiella*

399. Q. Sugarcane is recently infested by following wooly aphid

1) *Caratovacuno lanigera* 2) *Eriosoma lanigera*
3) *Aphis gossypii* 4) *Lipaphis spp*

400. Q. Nicotine cause failure of nervous system and commercially available as

1) Nicotine sulphate 2) Nicotine phosphate
3) Nicotine 4) Nicotine nitrate

401. Q. Growth regulators produce
   1) Stimulation of growth
   2) Retardation of growth
   3) Some cause stimulation while others bring about retardation
   4) Shedding of leaves

402. Q. Household pesticide sprays are
   1) Finit (Flit) 2) Finit and baygon
   3) Finit, baygon, mosquito coils and cakes 4) DDT

403. Q. The first organic pesticide to be used commercially was
   1) Bordeaux mixture 2) Burgandy mixture
   3) DDT 4) 2: 4 – D

404. Q. Bordeaux mixture is
   1) Organochlorine 2) Antibiotic
   3) Organophosphate 4) Inorganic fungicide

405. Q. The most famous pesticide of world is
   1) BHC 2) DDT
   3) Baygon 4) Flit

406. Q. In India, the most commonly used pesticide BHC is
   1) Carbamate 2) Triazine
   3) Organochlorine 4) Antibiotic

407. Q. The chemical present in flit (finit) is
   1) Malathion 2) DDT
   3) BHC 4) Aldicarb

408. Q. One of the earliest pesticides employed by human was
   1) Nicotine 2) Margosa (Neem) leaves
   3) Pyrethnum 4) DDT

409. Q. DDT is
   1) Carbamate 2) Organophosphate
   3) Organochlorine 4) Triagine

410. Q. Urea derivate pesticides belong to the category of
   1) Organochlorines 2) Organophosphates
   3) Carbamtes 4) Triazines

411. Q. Carbamates employed as insecticide are
   1) Phenylcarbamates 2) Thiocarbamates
   3) Propoxur 4) Dithiocarbamates

ANSWER SHEET

Q. No.	Ans.	Q. No.	Ans.	Q. No.	Ans.	Q. No.	Ans.	Q. No.	Ans.	Q. No.	Ans.	Q. No.	Ans.	Q. No.	Ans.
1.	4	36.	1	71.	3	106.	4	141.	3	176.	2	211.	3	246.	4
2.	4	37.	4	72.	1	107.	4	142.	2	177.	1	212.	4	247.	3
3.	3	38.	4	73.	1	108.	2	143.	4	178.	4	213.	4	248.	3
4.	1	39.	2	74.	3	109.	3	144.	4	179.	3	214.	3	249.	3
5.	3	40.	1	75.	2	110.	4	145.	1	180.	1	215.	1	250.	4
6.	2	41.	4	76.	4	111.	3	146.	1	181.	2	216.	1	251.	1
7.	1	42.	2	77.	3	112.	4	147.	2	182.	3	217.	2	252.	1
8.	2	43.	2	78.	1	113.	3	148.	2	183.	1	218.	2	253.	3
9.	4	44.	2	79.	2	114.	3	149.	3	184.	1	219.	1	254.	4
10.	3	45.	3	80.	4	115.	3	150.	3	185.	4	220.	3	255.	3
11.	3	46.	3	81.	1	116.	4	151.	4	186.	3	221.	4	256.	3
12.	2	47.	2	82.	1	117.	1	152.	4	187.	3	222.	1	257.	1
13.	2	48.	3	83.	2	118.	1	153.	4	188.	2	223.	3	258.	3
14.	4	49.	3	84.	3	119.	4	154.	4	189.	2	224.	4	259.	2
15.	1	50.	4	85.	2	120.	3	155.	4	190.	4	225.	1	260.	2
16.	4	51.	4	86.	2	121.	2	156.	4	191.	1	226.	1	261.	2
17.	4	52.	4	87.	3	122.	4	157.	4	192.	3	227.	1	262.	4
18.	1	53.	2	88.	2	123.	1	158.	4	193.	1	228.	4	263.	1
19.	1	54.	1	89.	1	124.	3	159.	4	194.	3	229.	2	264.	2
20.	4	55.	3	90.	4	125.	1	160.	3	195.	3	230.	2	265.	4
21.	4	56.	4	91.	3	126.	1	161.	1	196.	3	231.	4	266.	3
22.	2	57.	1	92.	1	127.	2	162.	2	197.	1	232.	1	267.	2
23.	3	58.	4	93.	1	128.	1	163.	2	198.	4	233.	1	268.	2
24.	1	59.	2	94.	4	129.	1	164.	1	199.	4	234.	4	269.	1
25.	4	60.	2	95.	4	130.	1	165.	3	200.	3	235.	1	270.	2
26.	2	61.	4	96.	3	131.	4	166.	2	201.	1	236.	1	271.	3
27.	4	62.	1	97.	1	132.	1	167.	1	202.	3	237.	4	272.	2
28.	3	63.	3	98.	1	133.	1	168.	1	203.	4	238.	1	273.	1
29.	1	64.	1	99.	4	134.	2	169.	4	204.	2	239.	4	274.	2
30.	1	65.	3	100.	3	135.	4	170.	1	205.	1	240.	1	275.	4
31.	4	66.	3	101.	2	136.	2	171.	3	206.	3	241.	2	276.	2
32.	2	67.	2	102.	3	137.	1	172.	1	207.	3	242.	1	277.	3
33.	4	68.	4	103.	4	138.	2	173.	2	208.	1	243.	1	278.	2
34.	3	69.	1	104.	3	139.	4	174.	1	209.	3	244.	3	279.	2
35.	4	70.	4	105.	4	140.	2	175.	1	210.	2	245.	4	280.	4

Q. No.	Ans.	Q. No.	Ans.	Q. No.	Ans.	Q. No.	Ans.	Q. No.	Ans.	Q. No.	Ans.	Q. No.	Ans.	Q. No.	Ans.
281.	2	298.	1	315.	3	332.	4	349.	3	366.	3	383.	2	400.	1
282.	3	299.	2	316.	2	333.	2	350.	1	367.	3	384.	1	401.	3
283.	4	300.	4	317.	2	334.	4	351.	4	368.	2	385.	2	402.	2
284.	1	301.	4	318.	2	335.	2	352.	2	369.	4	386.	2	403.	3
285.	2	302.	1	319.	2	336.	4	353.	4	370.	2	387.	3	404.	4
286.	1	303.	3	320.	4	337.	3	354.	4	371.	3	388.	3	405.	2
287.	3	304.	2	321.	4	338.	2	355.	3	372.	2	389.	4	406.	3
288.	1	305.	3	322.	4	339.	3	356.	3	373.	3	390.	1	407.	1
289.	1	306.	4	323.	2	340.	4	357.	1	374.	2	391.	4	408.	2
290.	3	307.	2	324.	3	341.	1	358.	2	375.	2	392.	4	409.	3
291.	2	308.	2	325.	1	342.	3	359.	2	376.	2	393.	2	410.	4
292.	4	309.	3	326.	1	343.	4	360.	2	377.	2	394.	4	411.	3
293.	3	310.	2	327.	3	344.	4	361.	2	378.	4	395.	4		
294.	2	311.	4	328.	3	345.	4	362.	2	379.	3	396.	3		
295.	1	312.	1	329.	4	346.	2	363.	1	380.	2	397.	4		
296.	2	313.	4	330.	2	347.	1	364.	3	381.	4	398.	1		
297.	4	314.	2	331.	2	348.	1	365.	2	382.	2	399.	1		

Bacteria and Yeast Associated with Food Fermentation Having Probiotic Value

Unprocessed material	Fermented product	Microorganism
Olives, tomatoes, cabbage, cucumbers	Fermented olives, pickles, sauerkraut	Lactic acid bacteria
Dough and pastes prepared from cereals	Sourdough, kisra, yeast dough	Lactic acid bacteria, yeasts
Malt, koji, prepared from cereals	Beer, spirits, sake	Lactic acid bacteria, yeasts, molds
Spirits, beer, and wines	Vinegar	Acetic acid bacteria
Grapes and other fruits and vegetable	Wine	Yeasts, lactic acid bacteria
	Fruit juice concentrated	Yeast
	Fruit and vegetables dressed	*Escherichia coli*, *Pseudomonas*
Carob, soya	Natto, dawadawa, soy sauce, tempeh	Lactic acid bacteria, Bacillus spp., yeasts, molds
Milk	Sour milk and cream, kumis, yogurt, kefir	Lactic acid bacteria, yeasts Acetic acid bacteria
	Raw milk refrigerated	*Lactobacillus* spp.
	Raw milk normal temperature	*Streptococcus* and *Lactobacillus*
	Sour cream, butter	Lactic, acid bacteria *Pseudomonas, Bacillus*
	Cheese Hard cheese	Lactic acid bacteria, propionic, acid bacteria, yeasts, molds *Clostridium Acetobacter*
Meat	Fermented sausages	Lactic acid bacteria, micrococci, *Streptomyces*, yeasts, molds, staphylococci
	Ham	Lactic acid bacteria, Staphylococci, yeasts, molds
Fish	fermented fish, fish sauce	Staphylococci, lactic acid bacteria, *Vibrio costicola*
	Fermented products during process	*Leuconostoc*, *Streptocacetrobactor,* *Zygosaccharomyces*
	Canned foods processed	*Clostridium*

REFERENCES

Afzal Ahmad, Mubarik Khan, Ramjee Lal Meena, *Capsule in General Agriculture*, Jain Brothers, New Delhi, 4th Ed., 2019.

Amerine MA, Pangborn RM & Rosslos EB. 1965. *Principles of Sensory Evaluation of Food.* Academic Press.

AOAC International. 2003. *Official methods of analysis of AOAC International.* 17th Ed.

Bender DA. 2006. Benders *Dictionary of Nutrition and Food Technology* 8th Edition, Woodhead publishing limited, Cambridge, England.

Brennan JG, Butter JR, Corell ND & Lilly AVE. 1990. *Food Engineering Operations.* Elsevier.

Charg C. 2015. History of Research on the Plant Hormone Ethylene, *Journal of Law Growth Regulation* 34 (4) : 1–19.

Charm SE, McCabe WL, Smith JC & Harriott P.1993. *Unit Operations of Chemical. Engineering* McGraw Hill Pub. Co.

Chandra: Short *Notes on Food Safety Officer Examination*, 7th Ed. 2024 ISBN: 978-81-8360-214-3

Dictionary of Food Science and Nutrition 2006, A & C Black Publishers Ltd, 38 Soho Square, London W1D 3HB, eISBN-13: 978-1-4081-0219-0.

Evans J A. 2008. *Frozen Food Science and Technology*, Edited, Blackwell Publishing Ltd, ISBN: 978-1-4051-5478-9.

FAO. 2007. *Handling and Preservation of Fruits and Vegetables by Combined Methods for Rural Areas- Technical Manual.* FAO Agr. Ser. Bull., 149.

Frazier J & Westhoff DC. 1988. *Food Microbiology.* 4th Ed. McGraw Hill.

George AB. 2004. *Fenaroli's Handbook of Flavor Ingredients.* 5th Ed. CRC Press.

Hardenburg, R.E., Watada, A.E. and Wang, C.Y. (1986). *The Commercial Storage of Fruits, Vegetables and Florist and Nursery Stocks.* USDA, Agric. Handbook, 66, pp. 130.

Hoseney RS. 1994. *Principles of Cereal Science and Technology.* 2nd Ed. AACC.

Hui etal. 2006. *Handbook of Fruits and Fruit Processing*, Blackwell Publishing Professional, USA, ISBN-13: 978-0-8138-1981-5.

Jay JM, Loessner MJ & Golden DA. 2005. *Modern Food Microbiology.* 7th Ed. Springer.

Kalia M and Sood S. 2008. *Food Preservation and Processing* second revised edition, Kalyani publishers, New Delhi.

Kantwa SR. 2012. *Objective Agriculture*, 11th edition, New Vishal Publication, New Delhi.

Katyayan A. 2011. *Fundamentals of Agriculture Vol. I and II*, Kushal publication and distributors, Varanasi, U.P.

Khader V. 2001. *Text book of food science and technology*, DIPA, ICAR, New Delhi.

Kothakota, A, etc. *Subjective and Objective Food Technology*, 2nd Ed., 2019, Jain Brothers, New Delhi.

Kulp K & Ponte GJ. 2000. *Handbook of Cereal Science and Technology*.2nd Ed. Marcel Dekker.

Macrae R, Roloson R & Sadlu MJ. 1994. *Encyclopedia of Food Science & Technology & Nutrition*. Vol. XVI. Academic Press.

Madhavi DL, Deshpande SS & Salunkhe DK. 1996. *Food Antioxidants:Technological, Toxicological and Health Perspective*. Marcel Dekker.

Mahadeviah M & Gowramma RV. 1996. *Food Packaging Materials*. McGraw Hill Pub. Co.

Maitry R. S. 2015. *Agriculture updates*, volume 01, ISBN: 9832342-XC-15.

Meyer LH. 1987. *Food Chemistry*. CBS Pub. Dist. (P) Ltd.

Morton ID & Macleod AJ .1990. *Food Flavours*. Part A, BC. Elsevier.

Nielsen S. (Eds.). 1994. *Introduction to Chemical Analysis of Foods*. Jones & Bartlett.

Painy FA. 1992. *A Handbook of Food Packaging*. Blacker & Sons Pub. London

Pomrenz Y & Meloan CE. 1996. *Food Analysis - Theory and Practice*. 3rd Ed. CBS. Pub and Dist. (P) Ltd.

Pomeranz Y. 1987. *Modern Cereal Science & Technology*. VCH Publ.

Potter NN & Hotchkiss 1997. *Food Science*. 5th Ed. CBS.

Press. Information Bureau, Government of India. Ministry of finance, 28 Feb. 2016.

Ramaswamy H & Marcotte M. 2006. *Food Processing: Principles and Applications*. Taylor & Francis.

Ranganna S. 2001. *Handbook of Analysis and Quality Control for Fruit and Vegetable Products*. 2nd Ed. Tata-McGraw-Hill.

Rathore M S. 2024. *General Agriculture for I.C.A.R. and other Agri Competitive Exam* (J.R.F, S.R.F, A.R.S, Ph.D, M.Sc, Agri, IBPS AFO, AO, IFS, NABARD) – 35th Ed, pp-1-650.

Ray B. 2004. *Fundamentals of Food Microbiology*.3rd Ed. CRC.

Sacharow S & Griffin RC. 1980. *Principles of Food Packaging*. AVI Publ.

Salunkhe DK, Bolia HR & Reddy NR. 1991. *Storage, Processing and Nutritional Quality of Fruits and Vegetables*. Vol. I. *Fruits and Vegetables*. CRC.

Sharma A. 2017 *Text Book of Food Science and Technology*, 3rd Edition, CBS. Pub and Dist. (P) Ltd.

Sharma SK and Kalwit HK. 2020. *Objective food science* 10th revised and enlarged edition, Jain Brothers, New Delhi.

Shrilakshmi B. 2015. *Food Science*, New Age International Publishers, New Delhi.

Singh RP & Heldman DR. 1993. *Introduction to Food Engineering*. Academic Press.

Srivastava RP & Kumar S. 2003. *Fruit and Vegetable Preservation - Principles and Practices*. CBS Publishers and Distributors, New Delhi.

Sunda N. 2014. *A Competitive Book of Agriculture* 5th edition. Surahee Publication. Jaipur, Rajasthan.

Swaminathan M. 1974. *Essentials of Foods and Nutrition*. Vol.-I & II. Ganesh & Co.

Vimla V. 2009. *Advances in diet therapy, practical manual*, New Age International (P) Ltd., Publishers, ISBN (13): 978-81-224-2855-1.